The Faithfulness of Jesus the Messiah

The Faithfulness of Jesus the Messiah

A Gospel Emphasis

Walter D. Zorn

WIPF & STOCK · Eugene, Oregon

THE FAITHFULNESS OF JESUS THE MESSIAH
A Gospel Emphasis

Copyright © 2020 Walter D. Zorn. All rights reserved. Except for brief quotations in critical publications or reviews, no part of this book may be reproduced in any manner without prior written permission from the publisher. Write: Permissions, Wipf and Stock Publishers, 199 W. 8th Ave., Suite 3, Eugene, OR 97401.

Wipf & Stock
An Imprint of Wipf and Stock Publishers
199 W. 8th Ave., Suite 3
Eugene, OR 97401

www.wipfandstock.com

PAPERBACK ISBN: 978-1-7252-8313-8
HARDCOVER ISBN: 978-1-7252-8314-5
EBOOK ISBN: 978-1-7252-8315-2

Manufactured in the U.S.A.   10/09/20

Unless otherwise indicated, all Scripture quotations are from the ESV Bible (The Holy Bible, English Standard Version), copyright © 2001 by Crossway, a publishing ministry of Good News Publishers. Used by permission. All rights reserved. ESV Text edition: 2007.

Scripture taken from the HOLY BIBLE, NEW INTERNATIONAL VERSION. Copyright © 1973, 1978, 1984 International Bible Society. Used by permission of Zondervan Bible Publishers. Copyright 1986 by Holman Bible Publishers.

Walter D. Zorn. "The Messianic Use of Habakkuk 2:4a [sic] in Romans," *Stone-Campbell Journal* Volume 1. No. 2 (Fall 1998) 213–30. Edited by William R. Baker. Used by permission as an *Excursus* in chapter 2, "The Romans Riddle," in the book *The Faithfulness of Jesus the Messiah*, published by Wipf & Stock.

Dedicated to my family:

My devoted wife: Carolyn

My wonderful children and their spouses:
Angela and husband, Darin Bennett
Scott Zorn and wife, Kerri

My beautiful grandchildren:
Morgan (Bennett) and husband, Charlie Roberts
Haleigh Zorn
Jessica (Bennett) and husband, Juan Vidal
McKayla Zorn
Kyler Bennett
Jayson Zorn

Contents

Preface | ix
Acknowledgments | xiii
List of Abbreviations | xv

1. Introduction | 1
2. The Romans Riddle | 18
3. The Galatian Crisis | 64
4. The Other Occurrences | 88
5. The General Epistles | 140
6. The Synoptic Gospels and Acts | 181
7. The Johannine Literature | 212
8. Conclusion | 256

Glossary | 287
Bibliography | 293

Preface

IN THE FALL OF 1970, an article appeared in *The Reformed Theological Review* that jarred my mind at the time. It was entitled "Faith of Jesus Christ—a New Testament Debate," by D. W. B. Robinson. I was serving the Catlin Church of Christ, Catlin, Illinois, at the time as their director of education. Later, I moved to Lansing, Michigan, to serve as a professor at Great Lakes Christian College. The same article was republished in the fall of 1979 in a Lutheran journal from California: *Verdict: A Journal of Theology*, a journal to which I had recently subscribed. The article really caught my attention again and it became the beginning of the "subjective/objective genitive" debate for me. I studied the issue for several years while teaching biblical languages and Bible at GLCC. I became convinced that the subjective genitive position was the correct interpretation of the Pauline *pistis Christou* phrase as "the faithfulness of Christ."

After almost thirteen years, I moved to Lincoln, Illinois, to serve in administration (five years) and in teaching for twenty-five years, retiring in 2013. All the while, I was researching and attempting to stay up with articles and books that dealt with the debate. I stood on the sidelines and watched the debate progress. In 1991 at the SBL meeting in Kansas City, I was eyewitness to the debate between Dunn (objective genitive) and Hays (subjective genitive). At that time, I thought the debate had shifted toward the subjective genitive, but those who supported the traditional view (objective genitive) began a barrage of arguments against the subjective genitive. That only spurred those on the other side, the subjective genitive interpretation, to write vigorous articles as well.

Jesse Paul Pollard wrote a doctoral dissertation on the subject in 1982 entitled "The Problem of the Faith of Christ." His good work was not widely circulated. However, Richard Hays' published dissertation, *The Faith of Jesus Christ* (on Galatians) in 1983, caught the imagination of many New Testament scholars across the country. Ian G. Wallis published a significant book supporting the subjective genitive in 1995 entitled *The Faith of Jesus Christ in Early Christian Traditions*. Since then, Oliver E. Rogers published in 2008 a book entitled *The Faith of Christ: The Relationship of Christ's Faith, Our Faith, and Salvation*. This book, while very readable, has not been given much attention. Others more so. In 2009 Douglas Campbell published his massive tome of 1218 pages entitled *The Deliverance of God: An Apocalyptic Rereading of Justification in Paul*. This book was the result of two previously published books by Campbell: *The Rhetoric of Righteousness in Romans 3:21–26* (1992, his doctoral dissertation) and *The Quest for Paul's Gospel* (2005). Campbell pushed the subjective genitive interpretation to its fullest extent. The last book on the subject to my knowledge is a collection of essays edited by Michael F. Bird and Preston M. Sprinkle entitled *The Faith of Jesus Christ*, published in 2009. Evenly distributed essays argued the subjective/objective genitive interpretations, an attempt at being "balanced."

In the winter of 1996, I had the privilege of a teaching sabbatical at Springdale College, Birmingham, England. With three companions from the college, we made an appointment with N. T. Wright and his lovely wife for tea and theological discussion. Each of us had specific questions to ask the dean of Lichfield (Anglican Church). I had devoured Wright's *Climax of the Covenant*. With the subjective genitive clearly set in my mind, I was anxious to hear Wright's view on the matter. My question was: "In your book of collected essays, you have one place where you support the subjective genitive, another where you support the objective genitive, and still another where you are neutral. Which is it for Romans and Galatians?" His response was unexpected, but he replied: "You know the book better than I! However, as I work through the Greek text of Romans 3, I am convinced that the *pistis Christou* phrase should be subjective genitive." Every year after that, I often met Tom Wright at the SBL meetings in the USA and we had brief talks about the growing consensus among young scholars concerning the subjective/objective genitive debate. Of course, since those years N. T. Wright has become a world-renowned biblical scholar who has published over eighty books and many articles on theological issues, mainly in Pauline studies. I marvel at his writing skills and intellectual power in service to both the academy and the church. No one among modern day theologians has been more prolific than he. Because of his great hospitality and kind reception, I have been a supporter of Wright's published books and articles, from which I have quoted perhaps too often.

I retired from Lincoln Christian University in 2013. I then spent a couple of years preaching and teaching for a small church in Auburn, Illinois. I retired again and moved to Knoxville, Tennessee, only to teach for two more years at Johnson University as adjunct professor in Old Testament. Finally, I retired for good in 2019. The pandemic in the spring of 2020 forced me to shelter in my basement office and complete the book I have been thinking about for over forty years. Not being a gifted writer, I hesitated even finishing the project.

My original design was to reveal all the arguments from the subjective/objective genitive debate, weaving my way from its modern beginnings to the present. That became a dull and discouraging approach as I was certain not many would read such a back and forth conversation of highly trained theologians. Paul Pollard's update on the issue is a good example of this approach: "The 'Faith of Christ' in Current Discussion," in *Concordia*, 1997. Instead, I decided to do two things at once: cover the *pistis Christou* passages in the traditional Pauline Epistles and do a study of the *pistis* word group (verb, noun, and adjective) throughout the New Testament. Ian Wallis had already done this work to some degree, but I was intent on doing more and less. In doing so, I give brief introductory remarks concerning authorship, date, recipients, relevant theological issues, and literary outlines for each New Testament book to give a context for the *pistis* word studies.

I was convinced that the subjective genitive interpretation, if a correct interpretation, would have relevance throughout the New Testament on the subject of Jesus the Messiah's faithfulness. I was surprised at how true that became for the survey of the New Testament. Another decision was not to give all the arguments for the objective genitive and then to skillfully debunk each one! Rather, I simply argue *for* the subjective genitive, giving as simple and commonsense arguments as possible, yet relying on my knowledge of the original text of Hebrew and Greek to solidify some aspects of the issue. My attempt was to be as positive for the subjective genitive as possible without being too negative about opposing views.

I need to say a word about the bibliography. Because of the nature of this book, surveying the New Testament for the *pistis* word group, including the Pauline phrase of *pistis Christou*, the bibliography expanded considerably. I have attempted to include every possible book and journal article that supported the subjective genitive, though I am certain I have left out sources yet to be discovered. I have also included the best resources that argue for the traditional objective genitive, but they are limited. Of course, all the footnoted materials are included in the bibliography. For these reasons the bibliography is much larger than it should be for the size of this book.

Having taught in college, seminary, and the local church for almost sixty years, I hope that the constituents of all these communities will benefit from this project and my approach. My peculiar interpretations of many texts, I trust, will cause many to rethink their common traditional understandings of these texts. With a little fear and trembling, I recount these words in James 3:1—"Not many of you should become teachers, my brothers, for you know that we who teach will be judged with greater strictness." May God be gracious to us all in the end.

Acknowledgments

THE PERSON WHO HAS been my "cheerleader" these many years is Nancy Olson, library director of Lincoln Christian University. Nancy was the library director at Great Lakes Christian College while I served there from 1976 to 1988. She was diligent in providing me with journal articles and a few books on the "subjective/objective genitive debate." Interestingly, she moved with my family to Lincoln, Illinois, in 1988— she to become assistant librarian and I to become the academic dean at Lincoln Christian College (now Lincoln Christian University). During my career at LCU (1988–2013), Nancy continued to help me with research and up-to-date information on the subject until my retirement. Nancy Olson has been the library director for many years now and continues her quality service to LCU.

The third library I need to acknowledge is at Johnson University, Knoxville, Tennessee. The library director is Carrie Beth Lowe, a very pleasant servant to all who need her services. She has gone out of her way to accommodate me. Carrie Beth has made the library resources available in every way, including all her associates. They include John Jaeger, assistant librarian, who not only helped with research on the internet, but was a reader of my rough drafts. Rick Bower, part-time reference librarian, has been a superior researcher for journal articles and helping me find all I needed plus surprising obscure articles discovered by serendipity. I consider Rick a genius at research. Heidi Sise, circulation clerk, always obtained resources for me from the stacks with cheerfulness and enthusiasm. Others who gladly helped were Denny Eaton, periodicals clerk, and Jan Christy, technical services clerk. The entire library staff receives from me special gratitude for their enthusiastic support of this project, their expertise in obtaining indispensable resources, and their servant attitude toward all who enter the library.

I must mention my brief two-year ministry with the Auburn Christian Church, Auburn, Illinois. The day I retired from LCU in 2013, I began serving this small and wonderful church. They wanted me to teach them an overview of the Bible. The ideas in this book were "tried out" on them over the two-year period. They were very receptive and encouraging. Over 90 percent of the adults participated in a Wednesday study, morning (for our retired and elderly) and evening (for our working members). I will ever be grateful to this congregation for listening, loving, and encouraging me to finish my dream of putting these ideas in a book. The computer I now use was a gift by them when I left.

My greatest debt belongs to the readers of my rough drafts. Early on Dr. Carl Bridges, now retired New Testament professor from Johnson University, gave excellent recommendations and suggestions for arrangement of material and critical issues that needed attention. John Jaeger, mentioned above, read later editions and greatly helped in detail corrections undiscovered by others. His perspective in theology was greatly appreciated. Ron Simkins, a longtime friend from seminary days, and I had a mutual "admiration society" going, for I read and critiqued a small book he was publishing and he in turn read several rough drafts of my book. Ron was very encouraging throughout the experience. Finally, I must mention Dr. Tom Ewald. Tom is a longtime friend who served Lincoln Christian University for over forty years. He was dean of students while I was dean of the college for a short period. Tom is one of the great preachers and teachers among our church brotherhood (independent Christian churches and churches of Christ). He is a superior wordsmith and I have greatly benefited from his reading of a "final" rough draft.

I would be remiss if I did not mention my wife, Carolyn. She has been more than patient with this long-drawn-out project. I value her articulate ability over against my limited abilities to express myself properly. Because of her, we have a Christian family to be proud of and to whom I have dedicated this book.

List of Abbreviations

Hebrew Bible / Old Testament

Gen	Judg	Neh	Song	Hos	Nah
Exod	Ruth	Esth	Isa	Joel	Hab
Lev	1–2 Sam	Job	Jer	Amos	Zeph
Num	1–2 Kgs	Ps (*pl.* Pss)	Lam	Obad	Hag
Deut	1–2 Chr	Prov	Ezek	Jonah	Zech
Josh	Ezra	Eccl (or Qoh)	Dan	Mic	Mal

New Testament

Matt	Acts	Eph	1–2 Tim	Jas	Rev
Mark	Rom	Phil	Titus	1–2 Pet	
Luke	1–2 Cor	Col	Phlm	1–2–3 John	
John	Gal	1–2 Thess	Heb	Jude	

Apocryphal / Deuterocanonical Books

Tob	Tobit	Ep Jer	Epistle of Jeremiah
Jdt	Judith	Sg Three	Song of the Three Young Men
Add Esth	Additions to Esther	Bel	Bel and the Dragon
Ws	Widom of Solomon	Sus	Susanna
Sir	Sirach (Ecclesiasticus)	1–2 Macc	1–2 Maccabees
Bar	Baruch	3–4 Macc	3–4 Maccabees
1–3 Esd	1–3 Esdras	Pr Man	Prayer of Manasseh

Reference Works

ABD   *The Anchor Bible Dictionary*. Edited by David Noel Freedman. 6 vols. New York: Doubleday, 1992.

BDAG   Walter Bauer, Frederick W. Danker, W. F. Arndt, and F. W. Gingrich. *Greek-English Lexicon of the New Testament and Other Early Christian Literature*. 3rd ed. Chicago: University of Chicago Press, 2000.

BDB   Francis Brown, S. R. Driver, and Charles A. Briggs. *Hebrew and English Lexicon of the Old Testament*. Oxford: Clarendon, 1907.

DJG   *Dictionary of Jesus and the Gospels*. Edited by J. B. Green and S. McKnight. Downers Grove: InterVarsity, 1992.

DPL   *Dictionary of Paul and His Letters*. Edited by G. F. Hawthorne, R. P. Martin, and D. G. Reid. Downers Grove: InterVarsity, 1993.

L&N	Louw, J. P., and E. A. Nida, eds. *Greek-English Lexicon of the New Testament: Based on Semantic Domains*. 2nd ed. New York: United Bible Societies, 1989.
NIDNTT	*New International Dictionary of New Testament Theology*. Edited by C. Brown. 4 vols. Grand Rapids: Zondervan, 1975–85.
NIB	*The New Interpreter's Bible: A Commentary in Twelve Volumes*. Edited by Leander E. Keck. Nashville: Abingdon, 2015.
TDNT	*Theological Dictionary of the New Testament*. Edited by Gerhard Kittel and Gerhard Friedrich, translated by Geoffrey W. Bromiley. 10 vols. Grand Rapids: Eerdmans, 1964–76.
TDOT	*Theological Dictionary of the Old Testament*. Edited by G. Johannes Botterweck and Helmer Ringgren, translated by Geoffrey W. Bromiley et al. 14 vols. Grand Rapids: Eerdmans, 1974–2004.

Bible Translations

CEB	Common English Bible
ESV	English Standard Version
JB	Jerusalem Bible
KJV	King James Version
NET	New English Translation, NET Bible
NIV	New International Version
NJB	New Jerusalem Bible
NRSV	New Revised Standard Version
RSV	Revised Standard Version

Technical Abbreviations

AD	*anno Domini*, year of the Lord
BC	before Christ
ca./c.	*circa*, about, approximately
cf.	*confer* (see, by way of comparison)
cp.	compare
ed(s).	editor(s), edited by
e.g.	*exampli gratia* (for example)
esp.	especially
etc.	*et cetera* (and the rest)
f(f).	and the following one(s)
gen.	genitive
i.e.	*id est* (that is)
inter alios	among other persons
MS(S)	manuscript(s)
Mt.	Mount
lit.	literally
mng.	meaning
n.	note, footnote
no. (*pl.* nos.)	number
NT	New Testament
OT	Old Testament
p(p).	page(s)
pace	with all due respect, against
par(r).	parallel(s)
plur./pl.	plural
pt.	part
sic	*sic erat scriptum* (thus it is written)

v(v).	verse(s)
viz	*videlicet* (namely)
w.	with

Ancient Manuscripts

A	Codex Alexandrinus (fifth century AD). Witness to "my righteous one."
B	Codex Vaticanus (fourth century AD). Witness to "my fidelity."
C	Codex Ephraemi (fifth century AD). Witness to "my righteous one."
LXX	Septuagint (a Greek translation of the Hebrew text)
MS (*pl.* MSS)	manuscript(s)
MS 763	LXX manuscript, witness to harmonization with Pauline reading
MT	Masoretic Text (standard Hebrew text of the Old Testament)
OG	Old Greek (version of the LXX)
S	Codex Sinaiticus (fourth/fifth century AD). Witness to "my fidelity."
TDan	Theodotion's text of Daniel
P^{46}	Chester Beatty II (usually dated c. 200 AD or earlier) consists of the Pauline letters, beginning with Romans 5 and continuing to 1 Thessalonians, with Hebrews after Romans and Ephesians before Galatians.
Q	Codex Marchalianus (sixth century AD). Witness to "my fidelity."
V	Codex Venetus (eighth century AD). Witness to "my fidelity."
W (prophets)	Freer (third century AD). Witness to "my fidelity."

Dead Sea Scrolls and Related Texts

1QM   *War Scroll* from Cave 1.

1QS   *Rule of the Community*, (*Manual of Discipline*) from Cave 1.

1

Introduction

"For my many sins, the Pauline Theology Group has given me a foretaste of purgatorial fire by asking me to revisit the question of how to interpret Paul's notoriously enigmatic expression πίστος Ιησοῦ Χριστοῦ ('faith of/in Jesus Christ')."

—RICHARD B. HAYS[1]

The Subjective/Objective Genitive Debate

FOR MANY YEARS SCHOLARS have debated the translation of a phrase that appears in four of the Pauline letters: Romans, Galatians, Philippians, and Ephesians.[2] Almost all modern English versions translate the Pauline phrase as "faith in Jesus Christ" (see Rom 3:22). This translation is called by scholars of the Greek text the "objective genitive," because the word "faith" has as its object "Jesus Christ," which is in the genitive case in Greek. The Greek genitive case can be understood in various ways but is distinguished from a subject (of a verb), object (of a verb), and dative

---

1. Hays, "ΠΙΣΤΙΣ and Pauline Christology," 35.
2. Some scholars question Paul's authorship of Ephesians, but that opinion does not affect my approach to the issues of the debate. The whole New Testament will be considered in light of this debate. Thus, authorship of any of the New Testament letters, gospels, history (Acts), or apocalypse (Revelation) will not be considered as an issue with this study, though I will comment about such issues. I take traditional authorship or lack of it for granted.

(indirect object of a verb). The debate focuses on the following texts; note how the ESV (and most other English versions) translate the phrase using the word "faith" and the proper name of Jesus/Jesus Christ/Christ/Son of God or the pronoun (his/him) in reference to Jesus:

- Romans 3:22—"faith in Jesus Christ"
- Romans 3:26—"the one who has faith in Jesus"
- Galatians 2:16—"faith in Jesus Christ"
- Galatians 2:16—"faith in Christ"
- Galatians 2:20—"faith in the Son of God"
- Galatians 3:22—"faith in Jesus Christ"
- Philippians 3:9—"faith in Christ"
- Ephesians 3:12—"our faith in him"

While the above translations are possible, the same form can also be translated as a "subjective genitive," meaning the word "faith" is followed by its "subject" in the genitive case in Greek. In other words, the proper noun or pronoun is expressing the subject of the verbal idea of "faith," that is "believing." Thus, one would translate the Rom 3:22 phrase as "faith *of* Jesus Christ" instead of "faith *in* Jesus Christ." "Faith" can have other nuanced meanings such as "faithfulness." Thus, the best understanding, of which I would argue, would be "the faithfulness of Jesus Christ," the subjective genitive interpretation. Each of the above references can be translated in this way without misusing the grammar of the Greek New Testament. The translator has a choice. If the translator should choose the "subjective genitive" interpretation and interpret *pistis* as "faithfulness," then the references would refer to Jesus' faithfulness rather than human faith or faithfulness. Notice the differences in the following chart: (I am adding the preceding prepositions if any and a variant reading at Gal 3:26): [my translation]

	Objective Genitive	**Subjective Genitive**
Rom 3:22	"through faith in Jesus Christ"	"through the faithfulness of Jesus Christ"
Rom 3:26	"the one who has faith in Jesus"	"the one *who lives* from Jesus' faithfulness"
Gal 2:16	"through faith in Jesus Christ"	"through the faithfulness of Jesus Christ"
Gal 2:16	"from faith in Christ"	"from the faithfulness of Christ"
Gal 2:20	"by faith in the Son of God"	"by the faithfulness of the Son of God"
Gal 3:22	"from faith in Jesus Christ"	"from the faithfulness of Jesus Christ"
Gal 3:26 (P^{46})	"through faith in Christ"	"through the faithfulness of Christ"
Phil 3:9	"through faith in Christ"	"through the faithfulness of Christ"
Eph 3:12	"through faith in him [Christ]"	"through his [Christ's] faithfulness"

The choice of translating the Greek genitive case as a subjective genitive or objective genitive can make a huge difference in its meaning in context. Even more, the choice of this translation can also have an effect on how one approaches similar phrases and ideas throughout the New Testament. I will call these passages above the *pistis Christou* passages (the Greek words involved making a good shorthand for all such passages). *Pistis* is the Greek word that has a wide range of meanings according to context: faith or faithfulness, reliability, trust, confidence, fidelity, proof, pledge, solemn promise, oath, Christian virtue, or Christian doctrine. So, again, one must ask: what difference does it make? My answer is: it makes a huge difference! That is the reason for writing this book. Accordingly, Richard N. Longenecker has written: "There is, of course, much more that could be said—and, indeed, that needs to be said further—about Paul's understanding of 'divine faithfulness' and 'human faith' in Romans and his other letters."[3] Before one even begins the task of arguing for the subjective genitive interpretation instead of the objective genitive or other genitive ideas, here is a beginning list of what is at stake:[4]

1. It is a matter of arguing for more accuracy in English translations or at the minimum, allowing readers to know there is a viable alternative translation (example: footnote on Rom 3:22 in the NRSV). The subjective genitive translation would take away several redundancies found in Romans and Galatians (Rom 3:22; Gal 2:16; 3:22; and Phil 3:9). At present only the NET Bible and the Common English Bible interpret these passages as subjective genitives consistently. I know of only two one-person translations that support the "subjective genitive" interpretation: N. T. Wright and David Stern.

2. The subjective genitive does not take away the necessity for the human response of faith, overtly expressed in Rom 3:22, Gal 2:16, 3:22, and possibly Phil 3:9. This is usually the argument against the subjective genitive, but it lacks the preponderance of evidence.

3. The emphasis in each of the *pistis Christou* passages is christological, not the human response, meaning that what Jesus the Messiah has done on behalf of humanity is the main point of the text or context of these passages.

4. If interpreted properly, one has a broader understanding of *pistis*; i.e., "faithfulness" rather than simply "faith." This will be shown in the following chapters.

5. Centering of our salvation around the concept of "participation in Christ" as emphasized in Rom 5–8 does not contradict the idea of "justification by faith" in Rom 1–4. The idea of "participation" and "justification" by means of the Holy Spirit is only the beginning

---

3. Longenecker, *Epistle to the Romans*, 180.

4. Richard B. Hays has written an article entitled: "ΠΙΣΤΙΣ and Pauline Christology: What Is at Stake?" 35–60. In that article he lists six areas of his own work that he would revise and at the end five "serious theological issues at stake." I will touch upon these throughout this book and in my conclusion.

of the process of salvation. One must not read these two ideas as mutually exclusive as a few scholars have done.

6. Jesus' faithfulness (broadly speaking his whole life but specifically his death on the cross) has fulfilled God's promises to Abraham and brought gentiles into the family of God (Paul's "Israel of God," Gal 6:16).

7. By reading Rom 3:21–26 in this way, the revelation of God's righteousness is not accomplished by our faith or belief but by the faithfulness of Jesus to the cross. The resurrection vindicated Jesus as Son of God and exalted him to God's right hand (Rom 1:3–4).

8. With the subjective genitive understanding, the "works of law" do not contrast deeds with faith, rather the contrast is with the human deeds/works of the law over against the divine action of Jesus' faithfulness. Perhaps one should call this the faithfulness of "complete humanity."[5]

9. Human faith should reflect more of Jesus' faithfulness. Indeed, all of the book of Hebrews emphasizes this point—the faithfulness of Jesus encourages our responding faithfulness (Heb 12:1–2).

10. The "righteousness of God" is God's covenant faithfulness to His promises given to his people as well as God's saving action for his entire creation. The Old Testament background for God's righteousness can be found in the Psalms and particularly Isaiah 40–55. When there is the human response of faith to the gospel, one is declared or reckoned righteous based on Jesus' faithfulness to the cross. Jesus' resurrection is, thus, his vindication as Son of God. This idea will impact how one speaks of becoming righteous before God. Righteousness in this light gives life to God's people.

11. Paul's use of Hab 2:4b as a messianic passage will be argued and be the basis for understanding *pistis* as "faithfulness," based on the Hebrew word אֱמוּנָה (*'emûnāh*) which means "faithfulness/fidelity." Paul's rich Hebrew background should encourage all students of Paul's letters to look to the Hebrew Scriptures and vocabulary for understanding his use of "faith/faithfulness" (*pistis*), particularly in its Greek translation (the Septuagint, the Old Testament in Greek).

---

5. I am calling Jesus "complete humanity," rather than "perfect humanity." The reason is that it is difficult to relate to Jesus in terms of "perfection," but in terms of "completeness" the original language would allow such a thought. God's will is for all people to be "complete" in Jesus—the image of God (Rom 8:29).

12. Finally, commentaries on Romans and Galatians and Greek grammars should acknowledge the subjective genitive interpretation, but few do at present. R. N. Longenecker (Romans) and Wallace (Greek grammar) are exceptions. Galatians has more subjective genitive supporters than Romans, and that is ironic, for interpreters ought to interpret the *pistis Christou* passages the same in both letters.

Consequently, how one translates the *pistis Christou* passages will make a real difference in how one interprets the context of each passage as well as the theological emphasis in each.

I should say something about how to translate and interpret the simple Greek word *pistis*. The Greek word, πίστις (*pistis*), in the New Testament Greek period of the first century AD could refer to different but related ideas of "belief/believing" or "trust/trusting." The latter term can refer to trusting someone or something that is worthy of trust. As Campbell expressed it, "Trusting involves believing certain things—but 'trusting' is by no means *reducible* to 'believing.' *They are not simply the same.*"[6] In other words, "trust/trusting" is a broad designation that covers the idea of "belief/believing." To "believe something" is potentially at least different from saying "to trust something." Belief is one aspect of trusting. It has a relational depth to it (mind, emotion, behavior). Campbell gave Abraham as an example of the difference between belief and trust:

> Like all who trust, he believes certain things to be true about the person trusted, but he is also involved in a direct personal relationship with that person (here divine) and views him as reliable. Genesis 15:6 is therefore best translated in the broader setting of Romans 4:1–25 as 'Abraham trusted in God . . .' (and this is the connotation that it also carries in its original context).[7]

Another distinction in the use of this idea is that if one should "believe," or more particularly, "trust" over a long period of time, especially under duress, then one thinks of that person's "faithfulness" or "fidelity," "reliability," "commitment." The ideas of "steadfastness" and "endurance" are attached to this word *pistis*. Knowing the semantic range of this little Greek word, *pistis*, will help one interpret specific passages in the New Testament more accurately, if the assessment of the context is correct.

---

6. Campbell, *Deliverance*, 385.
7. Campbell, *Deliverance*, 387.

Hence, a possible translation of the subjective genitive could be "the faithfulness of Jesus Christ." There are, of course, other semantic meanings to *pistis* such as "solemn promise, oath," and "proof, pledge."[8]

If the above phrases turn out to be better translated as subjective genitives, then several other New Testament texts need examination as well: Rom 3:25; Mark 11:22; Acts 3:16; Eph 4:13; 2 Tim 3:15; Heb 12:2; Jas 2:1; 1 Pet 1:2; Rev 2:13; and 14:12, just to list a few. I contend that the use of *pistis* should be reexamined for the possible interpretation of "faithfulness" over against simply "faith." If this seems trivial, it is not. Scholars stumble over the concept "the faith of Christ," perhaps thinking that the incarnate Son should not have faith as we mortal and sinful humans have faith. But if *pistis* is understood as "faithfulness," then Jesus' faithfulness to the cross by the will of God makes excellent sense. Jesus' faithfulness is the result of Jesus' true humanity, true man, as man was meant to be. At the same time there should be no problem with seeing Jesus the Nazarene as a true human being having faith.

My strategy is to examine carefully Paul's use of this *pistis Christou* phrase, their various contexts, and how it affects other texts throughout the New Testament. This will mean a review of the New Testament for the contextual meaning of the noun *pistis* (trust/trusting; faith/faithfulness), the adjective *pistos* (trustful, trustworthy, faithful), and the verb *pisteuō* (to trust/to believe). I refer to these three words as the *pistis* word group. One must acknowledge that the use of the verb ("to believe") is almost always referring to human believing. I will note perhaps one exception. Thus, my purpose with this book is to argue for the subjective genitive interpretation of the *pistis Christou* passages in Paul's traditional letters and to survey the New Testament for the *pistis* word group. A few negative words with the *alpha privative* will be noted, such as *apistia*, (unbelief, unfaithfulness), *apistos* (faithless, unbelieving), and *apisteō* (disbelieve, be unfaithful). A fresh look at these words and their contexts is in order.

In the Epistle to the Romans one is forced to look at the whole book in this light because without question Rom 1:16–17 and Rom 3:21–26 are at the heart of Paul's presentation of his gospel. It will cause one to rethink Paul's use of Hab 2:4b as part of his theme statement in Rom 1:16–17. Romans 3:25 will take on a whole new meaning in contrast to the traditional readings. The way Paul uses Abraham in Rom 4 will need to be

---

8. See BDAG, 816–21. The "subjective genitive" possibility is mentioned from early German works and updated to the present (2000), but it is hardly encouraged in the article, 819.

reevaluated. Romans 5 becomes a pivotal passage in Paul's arguments. Even Rom 10 will read differently if the subjective genitive is considered.

In Galatians, chapters 2 and 3, especially, take on a very different emphasis and argument with the subjective genitive in mind. The emphasis is on the faithfulness of Jesus Christ over against works of law. The contrast is not between what a person may do (believing in Jesus Christ) and what another person may do (works of law, usually interpreted, inaccurately, as "doing good works in order to be saved"). Rather, the contrast becomes what God has done in Christ (Christ's faithfulness to the cross) in contrast to what Jews and some gentiles do with the law, whether seeking to obey its commands or using it as what it was, an identity marker for God's people Israel—i.e., circumcision, diet, and sabbath-keeping.

While Paul addresses two slightly different issues in Romans and Galatians, the same genitive phrases are found in both and should be interpreted similarly in spite of the differences in time and circumstances. In Galatians Paul speaks of both "the seed" (Messiah) and "faith" as *coming*, and somehow these are related to "promise" which has been fulfilled in Messiah's coming. The subjective genitive reading makes better sense of this phenomenon. Thus, Romans and Galatians should receive a thorough review and examination for understanding the *pistis Christou* phrase in its context.

The rest of the possible subjective genitive references will have similar effects upon their contexts. My main concern is this: the subjective genitive interpretation allows one to see Paul's emphasis in his gospel—*the faithfulness of Jesus the Messiah*—and how that truth is involved with the Christian's justification and sanctification. It should also give one a clearer view of Jesus as true humanity, the one Israelite who was truly obedient and faithful to God's will and plan for the salvation of the world. Without the faithful Jesus no one would have hope in a future life. Indeed, one's view of salvation (individual and/or corporate) and the concept of justification by faith will be greatly affected and enhanced by a review of all the uses of *pistis* in the New Testament, regardless of its use with the name of Jesus or the title "Messiah" or "Lord." I prefer to refer to the name of "Jesus Christ" as "Jesus the Messiah" in order to avoid the idea that "Christ" is just another *name* for Jesus (his last name?)! A brief history of the subjective/objective genitive debate is now given in order to understand where this interpretation is headed.

History of the Debate

When Douglas Campbell published his doctoral dissertation early in his career, he referenced at least three phases in the debate.[9] In the modern era, at least the first phase began by the 1891 publication of a monograph by Johannes Haussleiter entitled *Der Glaube Jesu Christi und der christliche Glaube* (translated: *The Faith of Jesus Christ and the Christian Faith*).[10] Gerhard Kittel and Adolf Deissmann supported Haussleiter's arguments for a subjective genitive reading of Rom 3:22, 26. However, German scholarship reacted strongly against such an interpretation and squelched subsequent studies to the point that the debate seemed dead for over sixty years!

A second phase began, however, in the English-speaking world in the 1950s by the publication of articles by A. G. Hebert and T. F. Torrance. The strength of the latter scholar was his study of Old Testament vocabulary that supported his idea that the Greek word *pistis* should be understood as faithfulness rather than faith. These scholars met instant rejection from a number of fellow English scholars such as C. F. D. Moule, John Murray, and James Barr (although Barr never rejected the new approach, he simply argued for better methodology). Unlike the German experience, the English debate created a rash of young scholars who saw the possibilities with the subjective genitive interpretation. They did not remain silent as their German counterparts had done.

This response moved the debate into its third phase by a number of scholars who began to see the positive results of the subjective genitive view (such as Karl Barth, G. M. Taylor, George Howard, Markus Barth, D. W. B. Robinson, J. J. O'Rourke, R. N. Longenecker, Luke Timothy Johnson, Sam K. Williams, Morna Hooker, Lloyd Gaston, Stanley K. Stowers, Leander E. Keck, N. T. Wright, and Richard B. Hays). Phase three came to a head in the 1991 Society of Biblical Literature meeting in Kansas City. James Dunn (objective genitive) debated Richard Hays (subjective genitive) with prominent scholars on the panel responding to their papers (Keck, Williams, and Wright).

---

9. Campbell, *Rhetoric*, 59–60.

10. Benjamin Schliesser has given scholars a more accurate picture of older German and Dutch teachers of the New Testament who proposed the subjective genitive reading. See Schliesser's "'EXEGETICAL AMNESIA,'" 61–89. The earliest document was dated 1656 AD.

A fourth phase began with the initial publication of Douglas Campbell's dissertation, *The Rhetoric of Righteousness in Romans 3.21–26* (1992). Campbell has taken the "bull by the horns" and pushed for a thoroughly christological reading of Paul's Epistles in the light of the subjective genitive. Campbell himself has put his stamp upon this phase by his latest book (a tome of 1218 pages!)—*The Deliverance of God: An Apocalyptic Rereading of Justification in Paul*. The fourth phase has even seen an advanced Greek grammar (mentioned above) endorse the subjective genitive as the better interpretation of the *pistis Christou* phrases.[11] In spite of a number of scholars who have opted for the subjective genitive in the 1980s and 1990s, the majority of the major commentaries on Romans still support the traditional objective genitive (see commentaries by Fitzmyer, Cranfield, Dunn, Schreiner, Moo, and Jewett, among others). Only a few recent commentaries on Romans have supported the subjective genitive (see Johnson, Stowers, Keck, Wright, and R. N. Longenecker).

On the other hand, most of the major new commentaries on Galatians have supported the subjective genitive (see Martyn, R. N. Longenecker, Matera, and Williams). This is ironic (as said above) because Romans and Galatians should be understood alike as far as the *pistis Christou* phrases are concerned. The *pistis Christou* phrases in both have similar contexts so that they should be viewed alike. Whatever view one holds for Galatians should be held for Romans and vice versa. Perhaps the subjective genitive has caught hold for the smaller letter of Galatians. The objective genitive does not seem to fare well in the tight arguments and ideas especially found in chapters 2–3 of Galatians, though many scholars would disagree. (This will be seen in chapter 3 below.) The commentaries reflect that assessment. On the other hand, Romans has always been the citadel of study for "faith only" advocates beginning with the Reformation and Luther's famous *dictum* on Romans—that is, justification *sola fide* (by faith alone).

There may or may not be a fifth phase to this debate. If so, it has started at the turn of the century and has been going on for the last twenty years. It is my hope that the leaders among the churches will seriously give the subjective genitive a fair hearing and hopefully accept the interpretation and its implications. I firmly think that the original hearers and readers of these biblical texts understood the phrases in this way. If so, the emphasis in Paul's presentation of the gospel is based upon Jesus'

---

11. Wallace, *Greek Grammar Beyond the Basics*, 114–16.

faithfulness in carrying out the will of God in terms of the crucifixion. Jesus' resurrection by "the Spirit of holiness" (Rom 1:4) is God's vindication of him as "the Son of God." On the basis of grace Paul received his apostleship, and the purpose of his apostleship was to bring about the "obedience of faith" (Rom 1:5) among the gentiles. The fifth phase will occur when there is a winner in this debate. One side or the other must prevail. If not, then we are suspended in phase four with significant commentaries divided on the issue.

Morna Hooker has recently (2016) assessed this phase four, updating the progress of the debate. She has suggested that "four changing emphases" have occurred that are helping to advance the subjective genitive interpretation: 1) the stress on "righteousness" as belonging to God; 2) the realization that Paul, especially in Romans, is concerned more about the Jew/gentile issues rather than individual salvation; 3) the recognition of Paul's emphasis on "participation in Christ" (Rom 5–8) over against "justification by faith" (Rom 1–4); and 4) the emphasis upon "the humanity of Christ is essential both to his Christology and to his soteriology."[12]

If the subjective genitive interpretation can prevail over Romans as it has received more acceptance over Galatians, then we will have begun a final fifth phase. This will result in English translations of the New Testament reflecting the subjective genitive interpretation rather than the present objective genitive. As mentioned above, only a few English translations reflect the subjective genitive such as the NET Bible and the Common English Bible (CEB). N. T. Wright's (one-man) translation, *The Kingdom New Testament (A Contemporary Translation)*, reflects the subjective genitive interpretation.[13] Until revised English versions (by committee) reflect the subjective genitive interpretation in the text and not just in footnotes (see NRSV at Rom 3:22), the English-speaking world will not understand these phrases as "Christ's faithfulness" and the often used *pistis* as "faithfulness" in the New Testament.

Why has there been such resistance to the subjective genitive interpretation? It seems to stem from the Protestant Reformation and the concept of salvation and justification by faith as taught by the various

---

12. Hooker, "Another look at Πίστις Χριστοῦ," 53.

13. Perhaps we should include David Stern's *Jewish New Testament*. Major English translations still reflect the objective genitive interpretation of Paul's *pistis Christou* phrases. The New Revised Standard Version has the subjective genitive interpretation in footnotes to recognize that possibility but translates in the text as objective genitive.

churches arising from that Reformation. Favorite phrases on "justification by faith" disappear with the subjective genitive interpretation.[14]

Protestant Concept of Salvation

Protestant scholars have their roots in the Lutheran concept of *sola fide*, "faith alone," the manner by which *most* Protestants say an individual is *saved*. Luther was fighting a corrupt church and difficult doctrines of the Roman Catholics. Rightly Luther stood his ground against the selling of indulgences (a lucrative doctrine) and all the other so-called righteous deeds required by the Roman Catholic Church of his day. He contrasted works of law and faith, emphasizing faith by the word "alone." Salvation was grasped by a two-tiered experience.

The first is the requirements of the law—perfect obedience. The individual person is required to perfectly obey God's law in order to be in God's good graces or considered righteous. However, the law only exaggerated sin, and the inability to obey the law led to despair. Human beings are seriously flawed by "original sin." The only way out is by "faith alone"! By this Luther meant that a person is justified by faith in Jesus Christ and not by works of law (a kind of self-righteousness).[15] This is how he interpreted the Pauline statements mostly in Romans and Galatians.

The second experience is faith in Christ. Jesus paid the penalty for all sin on the cross. The retributive justice of God is now satisfied by Jesus' death on the cross. God considers the believer to be righteous while Jesus has taken upon himself the sins of the whole world and Jesus' merit now becomes the believer's (2 Cor 5:21).

There are two primary views of "faith"—the Arminian and the Calvinist. The former sees faith as a choice and voluntary while the latter considers faith as revelation and by election. Both consider faith as a gift (usually supported by Eph 2:8). It is the Spirit that gives the individual the ability to have faith, either voluntarily (Arminian) or by election (Calvinist).

---

14. The statement "justification by faith" is not false entirely, just misleading. If we were to restate the formula it would be: "justification by Jesus' faithfulness for all who believe." That is my point.

15. The only use of "faith alone" or its equivalent in the New Testament is found in Jas 2:17: "So also faith *by itself*, if it does not have works, is dead" (NIV, my emphasis). No wonder Luther called James "a straw epistle"! However, recent scholarship has easily shown how Romans and James are compatible on the notion of faith and so-called works. See recent commentaries on both New Testament books.

Introduction

I can still hear the late Dr. Beauford Bryant (New Testament professor of formerly Emmanuel School of Religion [now Emmanuel Christian Seminary], Johnson City, Tennessee) say that in most Protestant approaches to salvation, two miracles have to occur before a person becomes a Christian: 1) the first deals with the concept of "original sin" where God must somehow bring to life a person "dead in [their] transgressions" (Eph 2:1–3) in order for that person to even respond to the gospel; 2) the second is also a miracle in the sense that no one has the capacity to believe unless God gives it to the person (Eph 2:4–10, particularly v. 8). The Arminian approach views "saving faith" as a gift, even though it is by choice and voluntary. The Calvinist views "saving faith" as a gift in the sense that God chooses who will be saved and who will not. All are predestined! However, the Calvinist would say people who are predestined for election also have freedom in making the decision to do so. It is two different definitions of believer's conversion as being by choice. Obviously, I am ambivalent about this latter view.

On a more extreme view, Douglas Campbell dismissed the concept of "justification by faith" entirely for salvation by claiming that the "false teachers" (Rom 16:17–20) and their teachings are found in Rom 1:18—3:20 as a "speech-in-character," the voice of the "False Teacher."[16] Campbell has not been followed on this unique idea by most scholars. It is necessary to mention this about Campbell because he supports the subjective genitive interpretation vigorously.

Before I proceed with the biblical texts, the subjective genitive interpretation of the *pistis Christou* phrases and the *pistis* word group (*pisteuō, pistis,* and *pistos*) found in the New Testament, I must give my own experience of personal salvation in order to give the reader an understanding of my theological background and perhaps biases. This will help explain why I am challenging the usual objective genitive interpretation of Paul's phrases (*faith in Jesus Christ*) and other texts in the New Testament and arguing vigorously as Campbell does for a thorough christological understanding as well as the Old Testament background to these texts.

---

16. Campbell, *Deliverance*, 495. Thus, Campbell includes almost all of Romans 1–3 as the words of the "False Teachers" in order to dismiss the "justification by faith" theory of salvation over against his advocating "participation in Christ" in Romans 5–8. Campbell has not been successful in this proposal. See the rebuke by Matlock, "Zeal for Paul," 115–49.

Personal Salvation Experience

As a young person of fourteen years, I accepted Jesus as my Lord and Savior and upon my repentance from sin and confession of faith (that "Jesus is the Christ, Son of the Living God") was baptized (immersed in water) in the name of the Father, Son, and Holy Spirit (Matt 28:19) for the "forgiveness of sins" and to "receive the gift of the Holy Spirit" (Acts 2:38). In many ways my experience was that of most Protestants. I knew that I was not perfect, a sinner, and thus "bound for hell" if I did not repent and turn to God. Somehow, through Bible school lessons, I learned that Jesus lived the perfect life that I could not; therefore, my imperfect life was replaced by his perfect obedience. Thus, I could be declared "righteous" in God's sight. Now, by baptism I was raised to "walk in newness of life" (Rom 6:4) and was "bound for heaven," a place where God resided with his Son at his side. Somehow all this made sense to me, although I understood very little of all the details. Basically, I was more motivated by escaping hell than by "going to heaven when I die." Also, I understood that obedience (to the law or the word of God in general) was frustrating and being perfect was an impossibility. It was comforting to think that Jesus had obeyed for me! Further, my concept of heaven at the time was simply escaping this earth and going "up there" where God was. Plucking a harp or guitar and sitting on a cloud was as far as my young mind would go and I didn't think about it very much. My culture and limited Bible knowledge controlled my understanding at this young age.

Although my church, the independent Christian churches and churches of Christ, part of the Restoration Movement (begun in the early nineteenth century), did not teach that one could be saved by "faith alone," we were still in line with the "justification by faith" doctrine. Our church emphasized that baptism was essential to the act of becoming a Christian and not separated from what it meant to be saved. The curious fact in all of this is that the Old Testament had nothing to say to my experience, other than the law could not be obeyed perfectly. Of course, God's wrath was upon all who did not obey perfectly. Thus, accepting Jesus as Lord allowed his obedience to be "given" to me, a gift undeserved, a "justification by faith," an escape from the wrath of God! At least, in my young mind's thinking, my "soul" was saved and I was promised "heaven" when I die. Passing through an earthly temporal home to an eternal spiritual home was my idea of salvation at the time.

Lest I be too negative on my early experience, I need to say that my early teachers were not consciously steering me wrong about salvation. It was all biblical and true. Yet, with maturity and a career of teaching the biblical languages and the Bible, there were "holes" in my thinking at that time and a very limited view of salvation in my own cultural experience. I suspect that is true for most of us when we were young.

First, the Old Testament story of Israel was almost completely neglected. Fearing that I could not obey God perfectly and that his wrath would send me to hell was in line with the "justification by faith" doctrine. Second, my concept of "soul" was purely Greek in every way. To me, the "soul," that immaterial part of a person that resides inside a body, was immortal and would be sent at death either to hell or to heaven. Thus, my purpose in life as a Christian was to "save souls," as many as would listen to the gospel. The clinching question would be: "If you died tonight, would you go to heaven?" The whole purpose of salvation was to escape this earth and "go to heaven when you die." Third, while I knew there was promised a resurrection of the body at the second coming of Christ, I did not know the full implications of this for the life to come, and especially for this present life. My young mind was only concerned about personal salvation and not about the cosmos (as stated in Romans 8). Fourth, my view of Christ was quite limited. It was like a last name: Jesus Christ (like Walt Zorn). Of course, I was taught correctly about Jesus, but it never registered with me the true meaning of Christ as Messiah (Anointed One), the King of the kingdom. In fact, all "kingdom talk" was foreign to me at the time. Only much later in life would the biblical concept of kingdom have genuine meaning. Fifth, the ascension of Jesus to God's right hand was not even in my mind! The idea that we reign with Christ now in the present (Eph 2:6) was never mentioned. This profound thought was not even a thought in my early experience. Jesus' Second Coming (better *Parousia*) was profoundly inaccurate and culturally oriented by thinking the "resurrection" meant we would meet the Lord in the "air" and so be with him forever (sitting on clouds? 1 Thess 4:16–17).[17]

All of these ideas have to do with the way one approaches Scripture, particularly the Pauline letters of the New Testament. By reading the objective genitive of Paul's *pistis Christou* phrases, one has emphasized

---

17. See Wright, *Surprised by Hope*, 128–34. Wright attempts to correct Christian thinking about the "intermediate stage," he calls "life after life," the meaning of "soul," the resurrection, and the full meaning of "cosmic salvation," thus the "the new heavens and the new earth." This book needs to be read by every young-in-the-faith Christian.

individual faith as most important and has lost the true emphasis of the gospel: the faithfulness of Jesus the Messiah. The so-called "corrections" to my early and young faith in understanding the gospel must be done, lest I continue to pass on to the next generation my false and limited understanding of the gospel. N. T. Wright was right (pun intended!) when he wrote:

> In other words, in much popular modern Christian thought we have made a three-layered mistake. We have *Platonized* our eschatology (substituting "souls going to heaven" for the promised new creation) and have therefore *moralized* our anthropology (substituting a qualifying examination of moral performance for the biblical notion of the human vocation), with the result that we have *paganized* our soteriology, our understanding of "salvation" (substituting the idea of "God killing Jesus to satisfy his wrath" for the genuinely Biblical notions we are about to explore).[18]

The Goal of This Study

While these theological ideas may seem tangential to the subjective/objective genitive debate, the goal of this study is to rediscover the emphasis in the gospel which is "the faithfulness of Jesus the Messiah," an emphasis that has been in the text of the New Testament from the beginning. The subjective genitive interpretation is not unrelated to the biblical concept of a new creation, our vocation as human beings, and our genuine salvation. This will become evident as one proceeds through the New Testament texts.

While I may speak of the subjective/objective genitive debate, actually the issue is broader than a simple grammatical interpretation. Hays has suggested that one should think in terms of making "a distinction between the *christological* and *anthropological* interpretations of πίστις Χριστοῦ. The christological reading highlights the salvific efficacy of Jesus Christ's faith(fulness) for God's people; the anthropological reading stresses the salvific efficacy of the human act of faith directed toward Christ."[19] One will discover that the "faithfulness of Jesus" goes beyond

---

18. Wright, *The Day the Revolution Began*, 147. Wright addresses the third point especially in chapters 11–13 where he uses the Letter to the Romans as his point of reference.

19. Hays, "ΠΙΣΤΙΣ and Pauline Christology," 39–40.

the cross. He is certainly faithful in the present as the risen and exalted Son of God at God's right hand serving as our High Priest (see Hebrews).

My objective is to look at every use of the *pistis*-word group (verb, noun, and adjective, and sometimes their negative forms) in each of the New Testament books to see how their usage is related to the subjective genitive interpretation and the broader christological readings of the *pistis Christou* texts. Special attention is given to Romans (chapter 2) and Galatians (chapter 3), since these two letters of Paul include the majority of the *pistis Christou* phrases. They deserve a chapter each. The rest of the New Testament will be divided in this way: the rest of the traditional Pauline letters (chapter 4); then the general letters of Hebrews, James, 1–2 Peter, and Jude (chapter 5); the Synoptic Gospels of Matthew, Mark, Luke, and Acts (chapter 6) and finally the Johannine literature: the Gospel of John, 1–3 John, and Revelation (chapter 7).

Each approach to the New Testament books will include brief introductory statements as to authorship, date, recipients, structural outline, and theological purposes just to give the reader a sense of the context for speaking about the *pistis* word group in a particular book and to give the reader a sense of how modern scholarship views each New Testament book. It is hoped that a fresh look at how the New Testament uses the *pistis* (noun), *pistos* (adjective), and *pisteuō* (verb) word group will give the reader a greater appreciation for the emphasis of the gospel—*the faithfulness of Jesus the Messiah.*

I begin with Romans even though it was written after the letter to the Galatians. If one can solve the "Romans riddle," it will make the study of Galatians easier to assess in terms of interpreting the *pistis Christou* phrases as subjective genitives.

All Scripture quotations will be from the ESV unless otherwise noted.

2

The Romans Riddle

> "The 'righteousness' of God which was called into question by the failure of Israel to be 'faithful' to the divine commission (3.2–3) has been put into effect through the faithfulness of the Messiah."
>
> —N. T. WRIGHT[1]

The Occasion for Romans

THE EPISTLE TO THE Romans is one of the few New Testament books where there is strong scholarly consensus as to its date, occasion, and background. Its purpose is considerably debated, but despite that, it becomes merely a matter of emphasis. Paul was on his third missionary journey and amid a three-month stay in Corinth c. AD 57. During the winter months (see Acts 20:2–3), he wrote the letter to the Romans. Having completed his missionary work in the East, he had plans for three journeys: 1) the apostle Paul needed to finish his collection for the poor saints in Jerusalem and Judea and deliver it personally, at great personal and theological risk (see Rom 15:19–32; also Acts 19:21; 1 Cor 16:1–4; 2 Cor 8–9); 2) Paul did not establish the churches in Rome but wanted to visit with them for the first time in order to involve them in his proposed Spanish mission (see Rom 1:11–15; 15:23–25); 3) Paul considered his calling to be primarily to gentiles and he wanted to preach to gentiles

---

1. Wright, *Paul and the Faithfulness of God*, 2:1000.

where no one else had gone (see Rom 15:20–22; Acts 9:15–16; 22:15, 21; 26:17–23; Gal 2:7), hence, his plan to preach in Spain.

Phoebe, a deaconess at the church in Cenchrea, apparently was a patroness to Paul and she bore the letter to Rome (Rom 16:1–2). Paul may have written the letter in Cenchrea, which served as a port town for Corinth, a short distance away, although Gaius was Paul's host (Rom 16:23) and lived in Corinth (1 Cor 1:14). It is obvious that Paul knew a number of people living in Rome and greeted them warmly, perhaps with the view toward their better accepting his letter and preparing the way for his Spanish mission (Rom 16:1–16). The Roman Christians are also greeted by Corinthian brethren (Rom 16:21–23). Tertius served as Paul's secretary who penned the letter at Paul's dictation (Rom 16:22). Some have suggested that Paul wrote Rom 16:17–20 in his own hand (large letters? See Gal 6:11–18).

The above information, however, does not give us the reason or reasons for the letter's body, which is clearly focused on Jew-gentile issues, even though Paul presents the gospel for which he is not ashamed (Rom 1:15–16). That "gospel" in Romans does not include detailed doctrines about Christ, the church, Lord's Supper, or of last things such as found in other letters of Paul. Instead, it is focused on matters of interest relating to both Jewish and gentile Christians at Rome. Paul addresses especially gentile Christians in Rome and how they should relate to their fellow Jewish Christian brothers and sisters, but also how to relate to their nonbelieving Jewish "brothers and sisters."

There is a historical occasion close at hand that can explain this tension between Jews and gentiles. In AD 49 Claudius expelled the Jews from Rome because, according to Suetonius, "Since the Jews constantly made disturbances at the instigation of Chrestus, he expelled them from Rome."[2] The term "Chrestus" is probably a spelling mistake for the Latin "Christos." The best explanation is there were disturbances between Jews and Christian Jews to the point that the emperor Claudius (ruled AD 41–54) became involved. Usually such rule was with a sledgehammer and thus "all Jews" were expelled. (Perhaps only those involved in the disturbance were expelled.) This scenario is confirmed by 1 Cor 18:2 when Paul met Aquila and Priscilla at Corinth. The church at Rome was started by the Jews, perhaps by those converted at Pentecost (Acts 2:10). Gentiles would be added later. When the Jews were expelled, the gentile converts

---

2. Suetonius, *Suetonius II*, 53 (xxv.4).

developed apart from the influence of their Jewish brethren. When Nero came to power in AD 54, he rescinded the edict of Claudius and allowed the Jews to return.

As the Jews and Jewish Christians returned, one can only imagine the difficulties and tensions that developed between Jewish and gentile Christians over those who observed portions of the Jewish laws and those who lived free of their restrictions (see Rom 14:1—15:13, Paul's discussion concerning the "weak" and the "strong"). It seems that Paul addressed primarily gentile converts and encouraged them to have the right attitude toward their Jewish brethren (see Rom 1:5–6, 13; 11:13; 15:15–16).[3] Thus, two situations prevailed as Paul addressed them in the body of his letter: Christian gentiles who are faced with non-Christian Jews (Rom 11:11–32) and Christian gentiles and Christian Jews in conflict over Jewish legal practices (Rom 15:7–13). N. T. Wright expressed it this way: "This historical sequence produces a situation into which Romans fits like a glove."[4]

But there is more to say about the occasion for Paul's epistle to the Romans. Hardly anyone deals extensively with Rom 16:17–20 (Paul's warning against false teachers) and how it relates to the argument of the letter. Campbell comments that this warning about the "false teachers" (he calls "the Teacher") is strategically located at the end of the letter for emphasis and that it is the key to understanding the rhetorical nature of Paul's thoughts. Campbell wrote:

> Fundamentally, Romans was written for the same reasons that Galatians was written—to defend Paul's gospel against the depredations of certain hostile countermissionaries.... But Romans is best understood as an attempt by letter to forestall an attack on Paul's gospel in Rome, so it is a full-fledged engagement with "another gospel that is really no gospel at all" (see Gal. 1:6b–7a).[5]

> So the argument in Romans 1–3 goes on to show, in three further steps from 2:1 through 3:20, how the implicit theological commitments of this first definition of "the problem" by the

---

3. Recently, a few young scholars are advocating that Romans is written for gentile Christians exclusively and that the "interlocuter" in Romans is throughout a gentile who "calls himself a Jew." See Rafael Rodríguez, *If You Call Yourself a Jew* and Rafael Rodríguez and Matthew Thiessen, eds., *The So-Called Jew in Paul's Letter to the Romans*. This approach is given below in my overview of Romans.

4. Wright, "Letter to the Romans," 406.

5. Campbell, *Deliverance*, 495.

Teacher lead to the complete futility of his consequent "solution," or gospel! The result of the entire maneuver by Paul is to suggest that the Teacher's opening proclamation can be shown ultimately to save no one—*not even its proclaimer!*[6]

While Campbell's interpretative offer is ingenious, it is hardly proven, though he attempts to answer major objections.[7] While I agree with Campbell's christological readings of Paul's letters to the Romans and Galatians, I have difficulties with his approach to Rom 1:18—3:20. Campbell's inspiration for this approach seems to have come from Thomas H. Tobin's rhetorical analysis of the argument of Romans.[8] Tobin shows the subversive nature of Rom 1:18-32, and his analysis of Romans is an interesting and unique structural outline.

The Literary Structure of Romans

While Tobin supports the objective genitive interpretation for Romans (and Galatians) with which I disagree, his analysis of the literary structure of Romans is interesting. His approach is based on the setting for the Roman arguments. The apostle Paul is being attacked from all sides, from his enemies as well as his friends. The main issue was Paul's rejection of the Jewish law for any value in salvation for either Jews or gentiles. Many thought Paul rejected the law even for ethical living. This seemed scandalous to the Jewish world and even gentiles who bought into Torah observance. To these people Paul had called into question the future of the Jewish people. Thus, Paul was falsely accused of great heresy by the Jewish community as well as the growing Christian community, both with which Paul was greatly concerned. Thus, the structure of Romans was shaped by Paul's desire to answer his critics. Tobin comments:

> As Paul began to dictate his letter to the Roman Christians during his stay in Corinth during the winter of 56-57, how was he going to deal with this situation? He not only risked losing their support for his mission to Spain; he also risked alienating himself and his communities from the important community in Rome in addition to the communities in Jerusalem and Antioch. Paul obviously needed and wanted to persuade the

---

6. Campbell, *Deliverance*, 529.
7. Campbell, *Quest for Paul's Gospel*, 257–61.
8. See Tobin, *Paul's Rhetoric*, 108–10.

Roman Christians of the correctness of the gospel he preached. To do this, he needed to persuade them that his gospel was indeed based on convictions they held in common and that it flowed from these same common convictions.[9]

There are certain parts of the Roman letter that all agree on. Romans 1:1–15 is the beginning of the letter which includes an address and greeting (1:1–7) followed by a thanksgiving (1:8–10). Romans 1:11–15 is Paul's explanation for his long delay in visiting Rome. Paul is here attempting a warm hearing by mutual encouragement. At the end of the letter some disagree as to the Pauline authorship of Rom 16:25–27 (and sometimes 16:17–20, which I think are authentic). Aside from this, Rom 15:14—16:24 continues the letter framework which includes his further reasons for delay in visiting Rome (Rom 15:14–19), his desire to go to Spain where no one has gone (Rom 15:20–22), and thus to see the Romans on his way—to enlist their assistance and support (Rom 15:23–24). In the meantime, Paul must deliver his collection for the poor saints in Jerusalem, and thus he asks for Roman prayers that he will be successful as he anticipates his trip to Jerusalem and then to Rome (Rom 15:25–33). The final greetings are like all of Paul's greetings except that they are more elaborate here than in other letters, perhaps to help smooth the way for his planned trip to Rome (Rom 16:1–16, 21–23). Verse 24 may have been the end of the letter if vv. 25–27 were added later. However, with vv. 25–27 part of the authentic letter, v. 24 is extraneous and left out as superfluous.[10] The one section (Rom 16:17–20) about false teachers, mostly neglected or passed off as of little consequence, I have already commented as to its importance.

Thus, the letter body includes Rom 1:16—15:13 and should be taken as a whole, evidenced by the *inclusion* of 1:16–17 with 15:7–13. In Tobin's words: "In 1:16–17 Paul states the basic proposition or thesis of 1:16—15:13 by claiming that the gospel is the power of God to everyone who has faith, to the Jew first and also to the Greek, i.e., Gentiles. In 15:7–13 he restates this proposition about the centrality of Christ for both Jews and Gentiles and concludes the arguments he has made in the letter."[11]

All agree that Romans 12:1—15:6 is a distinct hortatory section, much like Paul's other letters. That leaves Rom 1:16—11:36 to figure out. Tobin has convincingly argued that the genre of Rom 1:16—11:36 is a

---

9. Tobin, *Paul's Rhetoric*, 77.
10. See Gamble, *Textual History*.
11. Tobin, *Paul's Rhetoric*, 80.

diatribe, which alternates between exposition and argumentation. His structural outline of the body of the letter is as follows:

1:16–17 (proposition)

1. 1:18—3:20
    a. 1:18–32 (expository)
    b. 2:1—3:20 (argumentative)
2. 3:21—4:25
    a. 3:21–26 (expository)
    b. 3:27—4:25 (argumentative)
3. 5:1—7:25
    a. 5:1–21 (expository)
    b. 6:1—7:25 (argumentative)
4. 8:1—11:36
    a. 8:1–30 (expository)
    b. 8:31—11:36 (argumentative)
5. 12:1—15:7 (hortatory)

15:8–13 (conclusion)[12]

While I agree to some extent with this structural outline for Romans, I disagree with Tobin's objective genitive interpretation of the relevant texts.[13] My subjective genitive approach does not change the structural (diatribal) outline of Romans as presented by Tobin. He gives us this insight: "In Rom 1:16—11:36, however, Paul is not dealing with issues and problems of the Roman Christians themselves but with issues and problems they have with him and his understanding of the gospel. . . . Romans, then, is noticeably more general in that it is an explanation and defense of his understanding of the gospel."[14] In the expository sections Paul is appealing to the beliefs and commitments the Romans have in common with him. On this basis Paul then argues in diatribe form to

---

12. Tobin, *Paul's Rhetoric*, 87–88.
13. Tobin, *Paul's Rhetoric*, 133 for an example.
14. Tobin, *Paul's Rhetoric*, 97–98. However, Paul is dealing with some internal problems of the Roman Christians (Jews and gentiles) by addressing the "strong" and "weak" in faith (Rom 14:1—15:7).

show how their misgivings about him and his teaching are wrong and that, indeed, the Hebrew Scriptures authoritatively support his stance.[15]

Most scholars on Romans divide the letter into four main sections: Rom 1–4, 5–8, 9–11, and 12–16. There are good reasons to follow this more general outline which cuts across Tobin's "expository" and "argumentative" outline.

Romans 1–4 has to do with how both gentiles and Jews are in danger of experiencing the wrath of God, both in the present and on Judgment Day (Rom 1:18—3:20), but with the revelation of the righteousness of God both Jews and gentiles are able to experience salvation by trusting in the God who raised Jesus from the dead (Rom 3:21–31). As a result, Paul explains how God has fulfilled his promise to Abraham in that Abraham has become the paradigm of those who believe; that is, how he has become "the father of us all" (both Jew and gentile believers belonging to the same family—Rom 4:1–25).

Romans 5–8 is held together by the *inclusio* of the idea of "hope" (compare Rom 5:2–5 with Rom 8:20–25). With this section Paul draws out the implications of our salvation in Christ[16] as described in Rom 3:21–26 and belonging to Abraham's family of faith (Rom 4:1–25). Romans 5 contrasts our "death" in Adam to "life" in Christ. Christ's obedience has brought righteousness to all who believe, whether Jew or gentile (Rom 5:19). Paul shows how this grace enables the baptized to live the "resurrection life," being dead to sin and alive to God in Christ Jesus (Rom 6:1–14). We have become slaves to righteousness, which leads to our sanctification (Rom 6:15–23). Not only have we died to sin, but we have died to the law (Rom 7). We have married another (Rom 7:1–6). The law of Moses only worked death in us all because of the weakness of the flesh (Rom 7:7–25). Those who seek to live by law are condemned to this "body of death." But there is hope for those who are "in Christ" (Rom 8:1–17). Jesus has become our sin offering and condemned sin in the flesh (Rom 8:3). Therefore, all who are baptized (Rom 6:1–4) have received not only the forgiveness of sin but also the gift of the Holy Spirit

---

15. The diatribe form has certain features which include the following questions and answers: "What then?"—Rom 3:9; 6:15; 11:7. "What then shall we say?"—Rom 3:5; 4:1; 6:1; 7:7; 8:31; 9:14, 30. "Certainly not!—3:4, 6, 31; 6:2, 15; 7:7, 13; 9:14, 30 (implied). "O, man!"—2:1, 3; 9:20. I have not included all of these features in the content outline, but they certainly belong as part of the diatribe form.

16. I prefer to translate all "Christ" references to "Messiah," but our English Bibles do not do that. I will do both for variety's sake.

(see Acts 2:38). We now have God's Holy Spirit dwelling in us and so we must live by the Spirit who will give life to our mortal bodies one day (Rom 8:11)! One day we will recover the glory from which we all fall short (Rom 3:23) in a new creation of the heavens and the earth and the resurrection of our bodies (Rom 8:18–30). Nothing can separate us from the love of God in Messiah Jesus because the faithfulness of Jesus has brought about his lordship over all creation and his kingdom to which we belong (Rom 8:31–39).

Romans 9–11 are Paul's climactic arguments for the one family of God made up of both Jews and gentiles. God created a "people" in the past (Rom 9:1–29) but had always planned to include gentiles in that family (Rom 9:24). Since the Messiah is the goal of the law "for righteousness to everyone who believes" (Rom 10:4), the Jews missed it by not submitting to God's righteousness as revealed in the Messiah (Rom 10:1–21), and many gentiles have obtained this righteousness by believing Jesus is Lord and that God raised him from the dead (Rom 10:8–13). But gentiles must not take God's grace for granted! If gentiles can be grafted into the family of God (even a remnant), God can truly graft back in Jews who believe (Rom 11:1–24). By so doing "all Israel" (meaning both Jews and gentiles who belong to God's one family) will be saved (Rom 11:25–36).[17] With Paul's main theological purposes accomplished, he now exhorts his readers to live out in practice what they believe.

Romans 12–15 are chapters that exhort God's people to be a "living sacrifice," not conformed to the world's values, but transformed by the renewal of the mind, thus doing the will of God (Rom 12:1–21). Humility and love become the major characteristics of believers. Even subjection to governing authorities and paying proper taxes are part of this "sacrifice" (Rom 13:1–7). Again, love and "put[ting] on the Lord Jesus Christ" as a garment enables the Christian to live the ethical life (Rom 13:8–14). Finally, and I think what Paul was driving at all along, he encourages the "strong" in faith to put up with the "weak" in faith. Brothers and sisters, whoever they are (Jew or gentile?) and whatever opinions they may have ("strong" or "weak") must not cause us to pass judgment against one another (Rom 14:1—15:7). How difficult it is to bring Christians together who are quarreling over minor things! Paul

---

17. See Staples, "Gentiles," 371–90. Staples wrote: "Since 'all Israel' includes both houses of Israel and the northern house is indistinct from the nations, 'all Israel' must include both Jews and Gentiles" (388). I think Staples is correct in his stance and arguments throughout his article.

concludes his letter with a paean of praise from the Hebrew Scriptures that shows how gentiles are to glorify God for his mercy (Rom 15:8–13). Paul's plans to evangelize in Spain are now hanging on the critical acceptance of the offering in Jerusalem and the Roman Christians' acceptance of Paul's visit to follow (Rom 15:14–33).

Romans 16 concludes the letter with Paul's very personal greetings, a final warning, and doxology.

Cohesiveness of Romans

One must remember that ancient letters for important purposes may not be in any particular outline that we moderns may approve. There was no such thing as chapters or verses laid over the text (even though that is convenient for us today for reference). Ancient letter writing did use several devices to indicate what we would call paragraphs or units of thought such as inclusions and the use of different types of conjunctions and transition words. Paul used these and more. If one takes for granted Paul's purposes for writing as considered above, one can observe the cohesiveness of Romans quite well.

Perhaps the main topic of Paul is Jesus the Messiah himself, for he is at the center of the gospel (see Rom 1:2–4; cp. 15:1–13). The incarnation and resurrection of the Son of God are essential ingredients to understanding who Jesus really is.[18] Paul is not ashamed of this gospel because it is God's power to save all (Jews and gentiles) who believe (Rom 1:16). This gospel reveals God's righteousness, that is, God's covenant loyalty and fidelity to the promises he has made to Israel. God in an impartial way wants to vindicate his people in the end. He wants to put Israel and the world right with himself, restoring mankind to a relationship as at the beginning before "the fall." The call of Israel was the means by which God would save the world and it was Israel's Messiah who was at the heart of that redemptive process. What Israel had been looking for over the centuries was now being revealed once and for all. How? "Out of faith[fulness] unto faith[fulness]" (Rom 1:17b).

It is my opinion that when Paul quotes Hab 2:4b at this point, he is using the text first and foremost as a *messianic* passage. "But the righteous

---

18. The importance of *the resurrection* of the Messiah Jesus is highlighted and given much weight for the proper interpretation and understanding of Paul's letter to the Romans by J. R. Daniel Kirk. See his *Unlocking Romans*.

[One] shall live out of faithfulness" (Rom 1:17c). The "righteous One" is Jesus. The fact that Paul insists after much argument that there is no one righteous (see Rom 3:10; cp. Ps 14:1–3; Eccl 7:20) the question is: "Who, then, is the righteous one?" We get the answer fairly quickly at Rom 3:21–26 when Paul writes in terms of the revelation of God's righteousness through the faithfulness of Jesus the Messiah. He must be the righteous one! God will justify (put to the right) the one who [shares] in Jesus' faithfulness (Rom 3:26). God will even *reckon* righteousness—"It will be counted to us who believe in him who raised from the dead Jesus our Lord" (Rom 4:24b). It is not until Rom 5:19, however, that we can truly comprehend Paul's use of Hab 2:4b: "so by the one man's obedience the many will be made righteous." Thus, I view Paul's commentary on Hab 2:4b as "out of [Messiah's] faithfulness unto [our] faithfulness." By virtue of being "in Christ" we too can live by faith[fulness] and be considered "a righteous one." Jesus the Messiah will be at the heart of the rest of Paul's letter to the Romans.

Paul begins and ends his letter with the same phrase, "obedience of faith" (see Rom 1:5 and 16:26; also 15:18). Almost half of the words in Rom 16:25–27 are used early in the letter. When Paul begins to explain his theme statement in Rom 1:16, 17, he starts with the revelation of the "wrath of God" (Rom 1:18). This will not be an isolated idea but one scattered throughout the letter (see Rom 2:5, 8; 3:5; 4:15; 5:9; 9:22 [twice]; 12:19; 13:4, 5), used in exposition, diatribe, and exhortation.

In Rom 1:28 Paul writes: "And since they did not *see fit* to acknowledge God, God gave them up to an *unfit* mind to do what ought not to be done" (my translation). This statement makes the later statement in Paul's exhortation more powerful: "Do not be conformed to this world, but be transformed by the renewal of your mind" (Rom 12:2a). In the same way the word *to dikaiōma*, "God's righteous verdict of condemnation," in Rom 1:32, where in spite of it sinful people still approve of sinning, is contrasted with *to dikaiōma* in Rom 8:4: "in order that the righteous verdict of the law may be fulfilled in us who walk not according to flesh but according to Spirit" (my translation; see also Rom 2:26; 5:16, 18).

When Paul discusses the advantage of being a Jew (occasioned by the fact that Paul seemed to be saying there was no advantage whatever to being a Jew [Rom 2:28–29]), he begins a list by saying: "First of all, they have been entrusted with the oracles of God" (Rom 3:2, my translation). This list will not be picked up again until Rom 9:4–5, where a list of

Jewish privileges is given. God has truly worked through Israel to bring forth the Messiah and the possibility for salvation for the world.

It is clear that the theme statement of Rom 1:16–17 is unfolded in more detail in Rom 3–4. Because of this, three statements in this part of Romans make more sense if understood as subjective genitives: Rom 3:3—God's faithfulness; Rom 3:22, 25, 26—Jesus' faithfulness; and Rom 4:16—Abraham's faithfulness. When we understand the meaning of *pistis* from Hab 2:4b, then the translation "faithfulness" is best (taken from the Hebrew word אֱמוּנָה (*'emûnā*ʰ), which is usually understood as "faithfulness/fidelity."

Paul connects the beginning of chapter 5 with the end of chapter 8 with the term "hope" (ἐλπίς, *elpis*). The noun is found in Rom 4:18; 5:2, 4, 5; 8:20, 24; 12:12; 15:4, 13, while the verb form is in Rom 8:24, 25; 15:12, 24. In spite of this, Tobin (see his unique outline of expository and argumentative sections above) argues that "Paul consistently moves beyond the previous argumentative section to a new stage in his argument. . . . He moves his whole argument in the direction of a universalizing eschatology, which is explicitly the subject of 8:18–30 and 8:31—11:36."[19] The exposition and diatribe sections are also linear in that Paul places them in temporal sequence. Tobin summarized it this way:

> Romans 1:18—3:20 deals with the previous equally sinful situation of both Jews and Gentiles. Romans 3:21—4:25 deals with the new situation of righteousness through faith made possible by the death of Christ. This new righteousness is apart from the law and intended for Jews and Gentiles alike. Romans 5:1—7:25 deals with the ethical consequences for both Jews and Gentiles that follow on this new righteousness. Finally, 8:1—11:36 deals with the future eschatological fate of Jews and Gentiles. The framework of Paul's arguments in Romans, then, is intentionally and essentially temporal or historical in character.[20]

Tobin's analysis works especially well with the subjective genitive interpretation of the relevant passages even though Tobin, himself, holds to the objective genitive, as evidenced to some degree in the quotation above.

Just to mention a last point, though the above discussion on the cohesiveness of Romans is far from complete, the "law" is interestingly discussed throughout the epistle. The law is discussed early (Rom

---

19. Tobin, *Paul's Rhetoric*, 86.
20. Tobin, *Paul's Rhetoric*, 87.

2:12—3:20). Law only increased the sin (Rom 5:20). But the law is not the culprit, for the law is "holy and righteous and good" (Rom 7:12). Messiah Jesus did what the law could not do—he allowed the "righteous verdict" of the law to be placed upon himself and thus the cross (Rom 8:4); and as a consequence, gave us life in the Spirit (Rom 8:9–11). Therefore, Paul can say: "For the Messiah is the goal/climax of the law for righteousness to everyone who believes" (Rom 10:4, my translation). Earlier in the letter Paul had written: "And hope does not put us to shame, because God's love has been poured into our hearts through the Holy Spirit who has been given to us" (Rom 5:5). Now, in his exhortations Paul can show that Christians indeed fulfill the law through loving others: "Therefore love is the fulfilling of the law" (Rom 13:10b; see vv. 8–14).

The Theme Statement of Romans 1:16–17

The NIV translates Rom 1:16–17 in the following manner:

> I am not ashamed of the gospel, because it is the power of God for the salvation of everyone who believes: first for the Jew, then for the Gentile. For in the gospel a righteousness from God is revealed, a righteousness that is by faith from first to last, just as it is written: "The righteous will live by faith."

An observation needs to be made with this translation. It is clearly emphasizing human faith, and somehow humans receive a righteousness *from* God by that faith. It is a gift given to the believer, an *imputed* righteousness. Faith begins the Christian life and faith is essential throughout and at the end of the Christian's life, "faith from first to last." Habakkuk 2:4b is then understood as referring primarily to the believer who is righteous by faith or at least is a righteous person living by faith. Thus, the key text for this debate in Rom 3:21–26 is understood to be referring to the Christian's faith *in Christ* following an objective genitive interpretation.

The Greek text can be translated in a different way. Verse 16 is clearly connected to what goes before by use of the γάρ, *gar*, "for," a connecting word (left out in the NIV!) that Paul uses often for both major and minor references to what he has said previously. Paul has expressed his obligation to preach to all peoples regardless of ethnic or educational backgrounds (v. 14) and thus he is eager to preach the gospel to those in

Rome. Based on this conviction Paul states his theological theme for the entire letter (vv. 16–17) and says "for" (*gar*, see ESV).[21]

Cranfield considers Rom 1:16–17 to be a "statement of the theological theme which is going to be worked out in the main body of the epistle."[22] Byrne writes: "Every element in the long thematic statement that concludes the introduction to the letter bears great theological and rhetorical weight. Many of the terms and ideas that are to be of central significance in the argument of the letter as a whole appear here for the first time."[23]

Romans 1:16 has been translated by the NIV accurately with the one exception of leaving out the *gar*, "for." But verse 17 has some major concerns for those who would support the subjective genitive interpretation. First of all, it is *God's* righteousness that is being revealed, not a "righteousness *from* God." Paul is not here talking about an *imputed* righteousness. If so, it makes Rom 3:21 very problematic as well as the discussion in Rom 9–11.[24] "Righteousness" is a characteristic of God. Isaiah 40–55 and Psalms are the Old Testament background for this characteristic of God. I would suggest, too, that the allusion in Rom 3:20 to Ps 143:2, 11 refers to this characteristic of God. God's righteousness is a righteousness that keeps covenant, the covenant promise to Abraham to bless the world, until that world is recreated and renewed (Gen 12:1–3).[25] Denny Burk has written an insightful article about how to view this genitive phrase: "the righteousness of God." He argues that the word for God, θεοῦ, *theou*, in the genitive should not be considered objective ("from God") or subjective ("of God"), but rather "as the nominalization of an attribute."[26] He suggests that the original hearers of Paul's letter would

---

21. My friend Ron Simkins observed that Paul uses four *gar*s ("for") in this text: 1) "For I am not ashamed"; 2) "For it is God's power"; 3) "For God's righteousness is revealed"; and 4) "For the wrath of God is revealed." Each item is then addressed in the body of the letter in reverse order: 1) God's wrath (1:18—3:20); 2) God's righteousness (3:21—5:21); 3) God's power to save (6:1—8:39); and 4) Paul not being ashamed of the gospel (9:1—11:36). Ron Simkins is writing a book entitled: *Jesus Is One of Us: Recovering God's Firstborn, Glorified, and Completed Human*, soon to be published by Wipf and Stock.

22. Cranfield, *Romans*, 87.

23. Byrne, *Romans*, 51. See also Morris, *Romans*, 66; Käsemann, *Romans*, 21; Dunn, *Romans 1–8*, 37, 38, 46; Fitzmyer, *Romans*, 253.

24. Wright, "Letter to the Romans," 425. See also his introductory remarks, 403.

25. Wright, *Justification*, 164. See also, 178–80.

26. Burk, "The Righteousness of God," 347. "Righteousness" is derived from an

have heard the phrase "as the nominalization of an attribute or quality, not of verbal action."[27]

Now attention must be given to the quotation of Habakkuk in order to discern its context. The following *excursus* is more technical in content and can be skipped over by the reader. The main point made here is that Paul is using Hab 2:4b as a messianic text first and foremost and only then in application to all believers. One will discover that "the righteous (One)" is a term used for the Messiah throughout the New Testament. This fact, plus the emphasis in Rom 3:10 that "none is righteous, no, not one," implies that a person should look beyond Jewish and gentile sinners for "the righteous (One)." Romans 3:21–26 reveals that fact. But the application to "every believer" as being "righteous" will not be revealed by Paul until he compares and contrasts "Adam" with "Christ" in chapter 5 (see Rom 5:19).

Excursus[28]

The Messianic Use of Habakkuk 2:4b

Habakkuk is a unique prophecy because it is primarily a complaint to God about the way things are (Hab 1:2–4). God's response is a prophecy about the coming Babylonians who will destroy the land and take the people into exile (Hab 1:5–11). Habakkuk is overwhelmed by this because he perceives the Babylonians to be a more wicked nation than Judah (Hab 1:12—2:1). God's second response is a prophecy of judgment against the Babylonians themselves (Hab 2:2–20). This judgment will occur in 539 BC, about sixty-six years after Habakkuk's prophecy. Even though the revelation or vision may linger, the people and prophet are to wait for it. At this point (Hab 2:4), the "arrogant" (the Babylonians) are contrasted

---

adjective, not a verb.

27. Burk, "The Righteousness of God," 352. Burk continues: "*God's righteousness* is somehow revealed in Christ's redemptive work in behalf of his people. Thus *God's righteousness* is at its root an attribute of the divine nature, but it is also that which grounds and motivates the saving events that are narrated in the gospel of Jesus Christ. His righteousness is a metonym for his saving activity through Jesus" (357).

28. This excursus is used by permission by the editor of the *Stone-Campbell Journal*, Dr. Bill Baker. The original article, "The Messianic Use of Habakkuk 2:4a [*sic*] in Romans," can be found in Volume 1. No. 2 (1998) 213–30. Minor changes to the text have been made to update the article, including additions to the bibliography supporting the excursus.

with "the righteous" (the prophet? or prophet and people?). As a fitting conclusion, Habakkuk offers a prayerful hymn (Hab 3:1–19) with the twin themes of a sovereign and faithful God (Hab 3:19) to his revelation/vision and the faithful waiting (Hab 3:16) of the prophet (and people) for the terrible (Hab 3:17) unfolding of the revelation/vision. It is interesting that at the beginning of this prayer hymn Habakkuk asks of God: "In wrath remember mercy" (Hab 3:2d; however, "wrath" and "mercy" used in this verse are not the usual words for these ideas). Habakkuk is a *theodicy*, wrestling with the justice of God and questioning it. (The same can be said of Romans.) The entire message of Habakkuk probably influenced Paul as he wrote Romans. "In wrath remember mercy" suggests Rom 1:18—3:20 on "wrath" and Romans 3:21—5:21 on "mercy." The fact that God has to be "vindicated" in Habakkuk is Paul's approach in Romans which also vindicates God's way of putting things right.

The Hebrew text of Hab 2:2–4 is difficult to translate. Where most English translations have seen verbs, the study by J. Gerald Janzen has convinced me that we should see nouns (see words in italics below). Without going into detailed study of the Hebrew text, I offer Janzen's reconstructed translation as a possible clarification of what "the vision" is:

> Write the vision,
> make it plain upon tablets,
> so that he may run who reads it.
> For the vision is a *witness* to a rendezvous,
> a *testifier* to the end—it does not lie:
>
> > "If he tarries, wait for him;
> > he will surely come, he will not delay!"
>
> As for the sluggard, he does not go straight on in it;
> But the righteous through its reliability shall live.[29]

The "it" for Hab 2:4b in NIV and ESV refers to the "revelation" or "vision," while Janzen's "he" refers to "God" or "something" close to God (his messenger?). Janzen's commentary is worth quoting at length:

> The two lines beginning, "If he tarries . . . ," contain the content of the vision. Grammatically, of course, the antecedent to the third person pronoun elements in the couplet is unclear: it may be the vision, it may be the *mōed/qetz*, or it may be God. In any case, if it is the end, that end will be marked by God's

---

29. Janzen, "Habakkuk 2:2–4," 76. Also, see Janzen, "Eschatological Symbol," 404.

coming (compare 3:3!); if it is God's coming, that coming will bring about the end; and if it is the vision, that vision concerns an end marked by God's coming. I do not rest a great deal on my preference; but I am inclined toward it for reasons given in the previous study, and because it dovetails nicely with 3:3 and may be interpretively reflected in Isa 40:10 (in which case Isa 40:10 and 40:31 jointly carry forward the language of these two lines in Habakkuk).[30]

With this vision the prophet is boxed into a corner with his complaints. While the prophet Habakkuk thought of himself as "the righteous one," God forces the possibility that he, the prophet, may be cast in the role of the *sluggard* (the "puffed up soul" ESV). "The righteous one" will live by the reliability of the vision. One must trust that the vision will come to pass and rest or wait in that assurance. "The coming" of God and his judgment/salvation will not delay. That is exactly what one expects from Rom 1:17 which is stated in Rom 3:21–26, deliberately *interrupted* by Rom 1:18—3:20, the revelation of God's wrath.

The Hebrew and Greek Text (LXX) of Habakkuk 2:4b

Janzen has set Hab 2:2–4 in its proper context, even though his translation of *beĕmûnātô*, "through its reliability," is troubling, both for the Hebrew text and the Septuagint (LXX). While his translation has merit, the LXX did not understand the suffix as referring to the vision's reliability. But even Janzen moderates his translation with an appropriate comment in a footnote:

> One could construe the pronoun suffix on *beĕmûnātô* as referring to God, especially if one takes God as subject of the verb *bō*. In any case, since the vision is from God, God's reliability is bound up with that of the vision. But in view of the six proverbs cited in n.2 above, it seems clear the the [sic] suffix in 2:4b refers back to the vision as a reliable witness.[31]

The Hebrew text reads *wetsaddiq beĕmunātô yichyeh*, "but [the] righteous one shall live by his (its) faithfulness/fidelity." In other words, if Habakkuk considers himself a "righteous one," then he must be "faithful" to God and his vision. That is the only way he will "live." Or as Fitzmyer

---

30. Janzen, "Eschatological Symbol," 404.
31. Janzen, "Eschatological Symbol," 406.

expressed it: "Chaldean invaders, who are expected and whose god is their might, are contrasted with Judah, whose deliverance lies in fidelity to Yahweh. God tells Habakkuk that at the coming invasion the upright Judahite will find life through his fidelity."[32]

The LXX offers three versions of Hab 2:4b:

> In MSS S, B, Q, V, W* one reads *ho de dikaios ek pisteōs mou zēsetai*, "but the upright one shall live by my fidelity," i.e., by YHWH's fidelity to his people. In this instance, the translator read the final *waw* on Hebrew *beʾĕmûnātô* as *yodh*, the suffix of the first sg. pers. pron. (*beʾĕmûnātî*). This reading of the LXX is regarded by D. A. Koch ("Der Text") as the oldest and original form of the Greek version. In MSS A and C, however, one finds rather *ho de dikaios mou ek pisteōs zēsetai*, "my upright one shall live by fidelity," i.e., the one righteous in my [God's] sight. It is not easy to explain how the first pers. pron. came to be shifted to "upright one." Finally, in MS 763* one finds simply, *ho de dikaios ek pisteōs zēsetai*, as it appears in Paul's text. This last reading, however, may be owing to a copyist's harmonization of the LXX with the Pauline reading and is to be regarded as secondary in the LXX tradition.[33]

The second reading in MSS A and C can be found in the New Testament at Heb 10:38. Fitzmyer is right that the third reading is no doubt an attempt by the copyist to harmonize Paul's reading with his copy of the LXX. The first reading of the LXX and the Hebrew text (Masoretic Text) was not followed by Paul. Paul probably knew both versions of the LXX and the MT readings. He very skillfully avoided the "error" of the LXX, mistaking a *yodh* for a *waw*, and so using the Greek μου (*mou*), "my." At first the *mou* would have been with *pistis*, "faithfulness," but perhaps a later copyist realized this to be in error but was reluctant to do away with the *mou*, thus transposing it to go with *dikaios*. Regardless of what theory one can give for the LXX versions, Paul either leaves the *mou* out deliberately or he used a Septuagint (LXX) version that reflects his quote, a less likely scenario.

Why would Paul leave out the *mou*? Perhaps he wanted to avoid the clear differences of the LXX versions with the MT reading. As we have suggested earlier, the suffix in the MT is a *waw* and can be translated as "his" or "its." And the antecedents could be "God," the "vision," "witness,"

---

32. Fitzmyer, *Romans*, 264.
33. Fitzmyer, *Romans*, 264-65.

or the "end."³⁴ If Janzen is correct in his "re-translation" of Hab 2:2–4, then the *waw* refers more to the "vision," and should be translated "its reliability." While "reliability" would fit in terms of Paul's discussion in Romans 1–3 concerning God—especially at 3:3 where he writes: "Does their faithlessness nullify the faithfulness of God?"—it is best to see Paul avoiding such an antecedent altogether. Fitzmyer writes: "He [Paul] not only drops the poss. pron. altogether, but understands *pistis* in his own sense of 'faith,' and 'life' not as deliverance from invasion and death, but as a share in the risen life of Christ (see 6:4, 8). In this way Paul cites the prophet Habakkuk to support the theme of his letter."³⁵ Fitzmyer's statement sounds plausible, especially if one has already decided that the genitives at Rom 3:22, 26 (and others related) are understood to be objective genitives.

But suppose that is not Paul's thinking about the Habakkuk passage precisely. It is very possible that Paul understood Hab 2:4b to be "messianic," referring to Christ himself and that he is "the righteous One" who shall live (resurrection) by (*ek*, literally "out of") *pistis*, "faithfulness." Thus, Paul could avoid the well-known "error" of the *mou*, highlight the "messianic" use by effectively using the "catchphrase" *ek pisteōs* throughout his letter, and allow the *pistis* its nuances of "faith/trust" or "faithfulness/fidelity," depending on the initial use at Rom 1:17 for Christ and its later understanding for Christians incorporated "into Christ," i.e., "the one who is *ek pisteōs Iesou*," "the one who shares the faith[fulness] of Jesus" (Rom 3:26, my translation). Campbell's thinking on this matter supports the subjective genitive framework:

> The absence of the pronoun specifically liberates the meaning of *pistis* from precise reference either to God's faithfulness (as in the LXX according to B and S), or to humanity's (as in the MT). Two conclusions are possible: (1) Paul intended the phrase to include all three possible objects (God, Christ, and a human being), or at least two of these three; or (2) Paul intended the phrase to refer specially to Christ, in which case the pronouns would also have had to be omitted. . . . Paul's choice of textual variants is best explained if he intended the text to refer primarily to the faithfulness of the messiah.³⁶

---

34. Janzen, "Eschatological Symbol," 404.
35. Fitzmyer, *Romans*, 265.
36. Campbell, *Rhetoric*, 211–12.

The Catchphrase: *ek pisteōs*

Campbell argues that *ek pisteōs* in the Pauline letters of Romans and Galatians constitutes a "catchphrase" that refers to Christ's and not to God's or the believer's "faith."[37] Campbell notes that Corsani was one of the first to point out Paul's unique use of *ek pisteōs* in Romans and Galatians, as a "catchphrase" taken from Hab 2:4b, but "failed to delineate its implications."[38] Corsani notes:

> A close scrutiny of the texts shows that ἐκ πίστεως is found only in Galatians (9 times) and in Romans (12 times). At the same time it may be recalled that in these two letters Paul employs the Habakkuk quotation "He who through faith [ἐκ πίστεως] is righteous shall live" (Hab 2:4; Rom 1:17; Gal 3:11). In the LXX there is only one occurrence of the words ἐκ πίστεως and that is precisely in Hab 2:4.[39]

Campbell not only delineates the implication for Corsani's observation, but he has presented his arguments in a most convincing fashion. "Paul's use of ἐκ πίστεως in 17a is also a clear stylistic anticipation of his quotation of Hab. 2.4 in 17b. So any explanation of the section must interpret the two phrases in parallel, in a manner that also makes sense of the later quotation from Scripture."[40] Additionally, several references in Romans and Galatians to *pistis* with or without other prepositions such as *dia* may refer to "the faithfulness of the Messiah."

While the phrase could refer to God's faithfulness, especially in light of the statement ("the faithfulness of God") in Rom 3:3 and the theocentric perspective of the letter as a whole, it would be saying the obvious.[41] Also, it would not work with the full explanation of Rom 3:21-26. Paul could have made this obvious by leaving in the personal pronoun of the LXX where *mou* modified *pistis*. On the other hand, the "anthropological" approach, i.e., the faith of the believer, presents several problems: 1) it shifts the focus from an emphasis on the gospel itself in Rom 1:1-16

---

37. Campbell, *Rhetoric*, 212, n.2.
38. Campbell, "Meaning of ΠΙΣΤΙΣ," 100, n. 27.
39. Corsani, "ΕΚ ΠΙΣΤΕΩΣ," 87 (see 87-93).
40. Campbell, *Rhetoric*, 205.
41. This is the interpretation by N. T. Wright in his "Letter to the Romans," 425—"But in the light of 3:21-22 and other passages, its most natural meaning is 'from God's faithfulness to human faithfulness.'" He is following James D. G. Dunn here. See Dunn, *Romans 1-8*, 44.

to its appropriation, a minor theme at 1:5, 12; 2) the phrase is "disjointed," functioning as a means and a goal; as Campbell asks: "This seems unusual, and even contradictory, for if faith is the goal, how can it be a means?—can it function before it is created? But if faith is the means, why then is it also the goal?";[42] 3) finally, Campbell argues that, considering the verb ἀποκαλύπτω (*apocalyptō*, "to reveal") as revealing the "eschatological saving righteousness of God," how can the believer's faith "have anything to do with this sovereign and cosmic process. Mankind's faith receives the gospel, but it does not pour God's eschatological salvation into it in the first place!"[43] The anthropological reading simply does not work. How can my faith in Christ be a "revelation" of God's righteousness? Surely "my faith" is expressed in the Rom 1:17a phrase but only in the latter prepositional phrase (*eis pistin*—"unto/toward faith").

To conclude this long discussion concerning the theme statement of Rom 1:16–17, there are a growing number of scholars who see Paul using Hab 2:4b as a messianic passage.[44] If this is so, then the cryptic phrase *ek pisteōs eis pistin* can be seen as a "teaser" by Paul by his not stating precisely what the phrase meant at first. If the first listeners understood the quotation of Hab 2:4b as messianic, then the *ek pisteōs* would retrospectively be understood as "out of [Messiah's] faithfulness unto [our] faithfulness." In other words, from Messiah's faithfulness demonstrated by his obedient and bloody death on the cross comes the possibility of my responding faithfulness as I live "in Christ." Therefore, I would translate Rom 1:16–17 in the following way (while giving my interpretation behind the cryptic phrases):

> For I am not ashamed of the gospel, for it is God's power unto salvation to everyone who believes: first for the Jew, then equally [also] to the Greek (gentile). For God's righteousness is revealed in it [the gospel] out of/from [Messiah's] faithfulness unto [our] faithfulness, just as it is written: "But the righteous [One] shall live [the resurrection] out of faithfulness [to God's will]."

---

42. Campbell, *Rhetoric*, 205.
43. Campbell, *Rhetoric*, 207.
44. See the following references: Manson, "Argument from Prophecy," 134; Dodd, *According to the Scriptures*, 51; Brownlee, "Messianic Motifs," 209; Sanders, "Habakkuk in Qumran," 233; Lindars, *New Testament Apologetics*, 231; Hanson, *Studies in Paul's Technique*, 39–45; Hays, *Faith of Jesus Christ*, 154; Hays, "'The Righteous One,'" 191–215; Campbell, *Rhetoric*, 212–13; Wallis, *Faith of Jesus Christ*, 81–82, 111–12; Watson, *Paul and the Hermeneutics of Faith*, 42–77; and Campbell, *Deliverance*, 613–16.

For Paul, *ho dikaios*, "the righteous One," was a messianic title used (*arthrous* or *anarthrous*, with or without the article) by the church-at-large (see Acts 3:14; 7:52; 22:14; Jas 5:6; 1 Pet 3:18; 1 John 1:9; 2:1, 29; 3:7; 2 Tim 4:8; see also Matt 27:19 and Luke 23:47). *Dikaios* is used seventeen times in the Pauline epistles and seven times in Romans. Twice it is used of the "good" person (2:13; 5:7); once to the "good" law (7:12); once to God as "just" (3:26); once where no one is "righteous" (3:10); and once where the "many" are made *dikaioi*, "righteous ones" (5:19). Used in an absolute sense, then, *ho dikaios* never refers to humanity, but only to God, to Christ, or to the Torah (law). Campbell summarizes:

> For ὁ δίκαιος to refer to a just person in Rom 1:17 would be to cut across Paul's use of δίκαιος everywhere. In addition to this, it would contradict his explicit statements in Romans that humanity is not righteous, but ἀδίκαιος and guilty of ἀδικία. Given Paul's usual deployment of δίκαιος, therefore, Hab 2:4 should be read as a reference to Christ.[45]

So ends the excursus on Hab 2:4b as a messianic text. The next issue is the key paragraph in Romans concerning the subjective genitive debate—Rom 3:21–26. This *pericope* (paragraph) picks up the theme statement of Rom 1:16–17 after the exposition and diatribe of Rom 1:18—3:20.

The Revelation of God's Righteousness: Romans 3:21–26

The NIV translates Romans 3:21–26 in the following manner:

> But now a righteousness from God, apart from law, has been made known, to which the Law and the Prophets testify. This righteousness from God comes through faith in Jesus Christ to all who believe. There is no difference, for all have sinned and fall short of the glory of God, and are justified freely by his grace through the redemption that came by Christ Jesus. God presented him as a sacrifice of atonement, through faith in his blood. He did this to demonstrate his justice, because in his forbearance he had left the sins committed beforehand unpunished—he did it to demonstrate his justice at the present time, so as to be just and the one who justifies those who have faith in Jesus.

---

45. Campbell, *Rhetoric*, 210.

Much has already been said about this important paragraph as it relates to Rom 1:16, 17, the theme statement, but the repetition will help clarify the issue. Paul has compressed his thoughts in stating his theme in Rom 1:16, 17, and at 3:21 he picks it up again, only in more detail. Compare Rom 1:17 with 3:22:

Romans 1:17	Romans 3:22
righteousness of God	righteousness of God
is revealed (present tense)	has been manifested [understood] (perfect tense)
out of (*ek*) faith[fulness]	through (*dia*) faith[fulness] of Jesus Christ
unto (*eis*) faith[fulness]	unto (*eis*) all who believe (present participle)

Thus, if Hab 2:4b is read messianically, then *ek pisteōs eis pistin*, "from faithfulness to faithfulness" in Rom 1:17, in anticipation of the LXX quote, should be understood as "from the Messiah's faithfulness unto the Christian's faithfulness." The first phrase is instrumental for the gospel and the second is the goal. The flow of thought beginning with Romans 3 and going through Romans 4 would be understood in this way: 3:3—"the faithfulness of God" vs. the unfaithfulness of Israel and all humanity, 1:18—3:20; 3:21-26—"the faithfulness of Jesus," the means by which God has revealed his righteousness (salvation/deliverance) and evidenced by Jesus' obedience unto death on the cross (3:25); and finally 3:22—"the faithfulness of the believer" ("unto all who believe," also 3:26, "those who live out of the faithfulness of Jesus") which has its prototype in Abraham in 4:16—"the faithfulness of Abraham," hence, the "father of us all."

Several modifications, then, need to be made to the NIV translation. First of all, we must understand *dikaiosune theou* as God's righteousness, not "a righteousness from God," in spite of the statement in Phil 3:9—"the righteousness that comes from God." N. T. Wright has argued persuasively for the proper meaning of *dikaiosune theou*:

> When the latter phrase occurs in biblical and post-biblical Jewish texts, it always refers to God's own righteousness, not to the status people have from God; and Jewish discussions of "God's righteousness" in this sense show close parallels with Paul's

arguments in Romans (obvious passages include Deut 33:21; Judg 5:11; 1 Sam 12:7; Neh 9:8; Pss 45:4; 72:1–4; 103:6; Isaiah 40–55 [e.g., 41:10; 45:13; 46:12–13]; Dan 9:7–9, 14, 16; Mic 6:5; Wis 6:18; *Ps Sol*. 1:10–15; 2 Bar 44:4; 78:5; 4 Ezra 7:17–25; 8:36; 10:16; 14:32; *TDan* 6:10; 1 QS 10:25–26; 11:12; 1 QM 4:6). I believe the detailed exegesis will bear out this interpretation.[46]

In Rom 3:20 Paul has certainly alluded to Ps 143:2—"for no one living is righteous before you." In a later verse the psalmist cries out, "For your name's sake, O LORD, preserve my life! In your righteousness bring my soul out of trouble" (v. 11). What the psalmist was crying out for, Paul is now saying God has fulfilled or has made known. Wright observes that "God's righteousness" has three "interlocking spheres of reference in mind": lawcourt, covenant, and eschatology.[47] In other words, in the final cosmic lawcourt God has fulfilled his covenant promises to Israel (and the world) by making the cosmos right in the Messiah, condemning sin in him and exalting him to Lordship. Jesus is the firstfruit of all who will one day be resurrected bodily to a new earth and new heavens.

Paul says this "righteousness of God" has been manifested (πεφανέρωται, *pephanerōtai*), a perfect tense, meaning it occurred in the past and the results continue up to the present and on into the future. The Hebrew Scriptures testified to this "righteousness," as explained above in the lengthy quote from Wright, but this righteousness is manifested apart from the Hebrew Scriptures. Romans 3:22 is verbless and therefore the verb in v. 21 ("has been manifested") should be used for v. 22. So, I would translate the Greek of Rom 3:21–22 in the following manner: "But now apart from Torah God's righteousness has been manifested, being witnessed to by the Torah and prophets [Hebrew Scriptures], indeed, God's righteousness [has been manifested] through Jesus [the] Messiah's faithfulness for all who believe for there is no distinction." It is very improbable that Paul is saying that my "faith in Christ" is a manifestation of God's righteousness. How could that be? Much more probable is the fact that Jesus' faithfulness to the cross, which includes his death and resurrection of necessity, is that manifestation.

One more thought must be presented at this point. Shuji Ota has written an insightful article that proposes that Jesus' faithfulness is not just faithfulness to God's will by going to the cross but also "the faithfulness

---

46. Wright, "Letter to the Romans," 403.
47. Wright, "Letter to the Romans," 459.

of *Jesus Christ toward humanity* in the sense of his being steadfast, truthful, and trustworthy as God's Christ."[48] He has a good point and I would argue Jesus' faithfulness does go both ways—to God and to humanity! Jesus is the perfect mediator!

Verses 23–24 are translated well in the NIV as far as the English can express it. However, the English language often cannot communicate the tenses of the verbs. Another point to be made is that there probably is a parenthetical statement in this text beginning with "There is no distinction" and ending with "justified freely by his grace." So picking up the Greek tenses and using the parenthesis I would translate: "(for there is no distinction, for all sin [aorist—looking at the entire act of sinning] and they [continually] fall short of the glory of God, being justified freely by his grace) through the redemption which [is] in Messiah Jesus."[49] Paul is here looking back to Rom 1:18—3:20 to show that both Jews and gentiles "fall short of the glory of God." But he is now in the midst of showing how the "faithfulness of Jesus" operates for the benefit of Jews and gentiles in terms of God's grace and the manifestation of his righteousness. Humankind has continually fallen short of God's glory ever since Gen 3, but now Jesus the Messiah through his faithfulness is restoring humankind's glory. This coordinates with Ota's statement above.

Verse 25 has been an enigma for many commentaries on Romans. Many do not think Paul wrote these words; rather they were a cryptic theological formula or early hymn that Paul used. No speculation is needed for verse 25 other than the fact that Paul wrote it. The problem is that Paul used minimal words to express his ideas. Commentaries and translations have assumed that the verse expresses the "objective genitive" viewpoint. That is why the NIV has a comma after the word "atonement," implying that the next phrase is saying something about our faith in the blood of Christ. If so, it is the only place in the Bible where we are told to have "faith in the blood of Jesus." One can certainly have trust in the efficacy of Christ's blood, but Paul is not saying that here or anywhere else. Even the ESV (a more literal English translation for the most part) places a comma after "blood" and then translates "to be received by faith," a rather inaccurate translation of what is in the Greek text.

If in Greek words can be implied from a previous use just as in verses 21–22, then the short phrases can make perfect sense. Paul has

---

48. Ota, "Holistic *Pistis* and Abraham's Faith," 1. I will elaborate on this thought more thoroughly when I review Galatians in the next chapter.

49. See Campbell, *Rhetoric*, 182–83 for commentary on this translation.

already used the phrase "through [the] faithfulness of Jesus [the] Messiah" in v. 22 and repeats the name in reverse order in v. 24—"Messiah Jesus." Therefore, he need only use the essential phrase with the name implied. Thus, v. 25 would read this way with the implied words in brackets: "whom God presented as a place/means of atonement through [Jesus'] faithfulness by [at the cost of] his blood [death on the cross] for a demonstration of his [God's] righteousness [reference to v. 21] because of the 'passing over' of the sins happened beforehand." Whether or not the term "passing over" (πάρεσιν, *paresin*) means "forgiveness" or literally "passing over" in the sense of delaying any forgiveness until the coming of Messiah is immaterial to the discussion. Indeed, either situation would be "by the forbearance of God" (v. 26a).[50]

Verse 26 is another critical phrase related to discussion on the subjective genitive. The NIV translates the last phrase: "those who have faith in Jesus," an objective genitive interpretation. The exact same Greek construction can be found in chapter 4 in relationship to Abraham. Only the case is different. Note: *ton ek pisteōs Iesou* (3:26d) compared to *to ek pisteōs Abraam* (4:16c). Certainly, one would not say "faith in Abraham," rather "faith[fulness] of Abraham." Thus, Rom 3:26 should be translated: "by the forbearance of God, toward the demonstration of his righteousness in the present time, in order that he might be righteous and the one who makes righteous the one [who lives] out of Jesus' faithfulness." Recently, Scot McKnight has written on this subject and I like his interpretation of this phrase: "it was to prove at the present time that he himself is righteous and that he justifies the one *who is rooted* in the faithfulness of Jesus" (my emphasis).[51]

A brief word needs to be said about the concentration of the *dik*-words in this verse: "righteousness," "righteous," and "making righteous." Unfortunately, the English translations offer another set of words corresponding to the above: "justification," or "justice," "just," and "one who justifies." Which is right? Both are right! God is in the business of putting things right that have been wrong for a long time. As mentioned above, N. T. Wright interprets "righteousness" in the Jewish context of covenant, lawcourt, and apocalyptic. God is faithful to his covenant promises to the

---

50. The Greek word *paresin* could very well be translated "incapacitated, paralyzed." This would be in reference to how God dealt with sin and rebellion in Rom 1:24, 26, and 28 in terms of "giving them over" to the consequences of sin. See Holmes, "'Utterly Incapacitated,'" 349–66.

51. McKnight, *Reading Romans Backwards*, 123.

patriarchs. The world is to be put to rights through Israel's representative, the Messiah. All of this is suddenly "revealed" through Messiah's faithfulness to the mission of God—his death on the cross. Wright expressed it this way:

> All this brings into view a final dimension of the phrase "God's righteousness." Precisely because the term evoked covenant loyalty, on the one hand, and commitment to putting the whole world to rights, on the other, it was perhaps inevitable that Jews who longed for all this to happen would come to describe it in what we now call "apocalyptic" language.[52]

Scot McKnight gives a good summary of this section of Romans (3:21–26): "God alone has now put a complete end to sins in the faithful obedient death of Christ. The faithful covenant God is demonstrated faithful in the covenant faithfulness of Jesus."[53]

The Law of Faithfulness: Romans 3:27–31

In light of all the above, Rom 3:27–31 will be heard differently than it is normally. Instead of the word "faith" in this paragraph referring to human faith, it should be understood as "faithfulness," that is, of Jesus and perhaps of God's faithfulness as well. The following is my translation of Rom 3:27–31:

> Therefore, where is the boasting? It is closed off! Through doing of Torah? Of the works [of Torah]? No! But through [the] Torah of faithfulness. For we consider a person to be put right by [Jesus' and/or God's] faithfulness apart from works of Torah. Or is God of Jews only? No! Also, of gentiles; yes, also of gentiles! If indeed God [is] one, who shall justify [the] circumcision out of [Jesus'] faithfulness, [then also he shall justify] [the] uncircumcision through the [same] faithfulness. Therefore, do we nullify Torah through [this] faithfulness? By no means! Rather, we uphold Torah.[54]

---

52. Wright, "Letter to the Romans," 400–401.
53. McKnight, *Reading Romans Backwards*, 123.
54. My translation is not far from R. N. Longenecker's translation in his *Epistle to the Romans*, 388. His translation of "by faith" at v. 28 probably should be "faithfulness" as I have expressed above.

Romans 3:21–22 reveals that Torah bears testimony to Messiah's faithfulness. By preaching the faithfulness of the Messiah, Paul is claiming to uphold the Torah (Hebrew Scriptures). The revelation of God's righteousness through the faithfulness of Jesus is for *all who believe*, both Jews and gentiles alike! This is the premise for Paul's argument in chapter 4, concluding that Abraham is the father of both Jews and gentiles who trust in the God who raised Jesus from the dead (see Rom 4:16–25).

Abraham—The Father of Us All: Romans 4

Romans 4 is not about using Abraham as an example of "justification by faith alone." Rather, it is about "the scope and nature of Abraham's family."[55] It begins with a difficult verse in Rom 4:1 which Richard Hays has made clearer: "What, then, shall we say? [Have we] found [on the basis of Scripture] Abraham [to be] our forefather according to flesh?"[56] The implied answer is "No!" Abraham's family is to be defined by "faith[fulness]." When Abraham believed the promises of God it was reckoned to him as "righteousness," that is, the status of being a member of the covenant that God was making with Abraham. Paul argues that Abraham was considered "righteous" before he was circumcised (Gen 17) and long before the Torah was given (Exod 20). Thus, Rom 4:1–16 reveals how Jews and gentiles belong to the one family of Abraham by sharing in his faithfulness (v. 16). Paul applies this to his present-day by emphasizing that we, too, must trust in the God who raised Jesus from the dead (4:24). On this point Wright makes a relevant statement:

> Paul is careful, therefore, to speak of Christian faith as "believing in the God who raised Jesus our Lord from the dead." God, not Jesus, is the primary object of Christian faith (one of many reasons why πίστις Χριστοῦ [*pistis Christou*], "the faith of

---

55. Wright, "Letter to the Romans," 489.

56. Hays, "'Have We Found Abraham,'" 76–98. Wright modified Hays' new translation with Hays' approval: "What shall we say, then? Have we found Abraham to be our ancestor in a human, fleshly sense?" See Wright, "Paul and the Patriarch," 226–27. This entire article argues against using Abraham as only an "example" of "justification by faith." Rather, Rom 4 is showing "the contrast of (a) a human family κατὰ σάρκα, marked out by the 'works' which give them their distinctive ethnic identity, and (b) the worldwide family promised by God as Abraham's 'reward', the family created by God's gracious act in 'justifying the ungodly,'" 234. Paul's "overuse" of the noun *pistis* and the verb *pisteuō* (sixteen times) is found in this chapter 4.

Christ," is more likely to mean the faithfulness of Jesus himself than the faith people put in Jesus).[57]

Romans 4:25 has been an enigma to many as to how to understand the two parallel prepositional phrases in that verse: "*because* of our trespasses" and "*because* of our justification." The first phrase is fairly clear. Jesus was given over to death on the cross because of our trespasses. The second phrase, however, is literally: "and he [Jesus] was raised because of our justification." How do we understand this second use of the Greek διὰ, *dia* (with the accusative case following it)? Michael Bird has addressed this conundrum in an early article:

> Granted that the resurrection vindicates Christ's sin-bearing death (cf. Acts 2:24, 32–33; 3:15; 5:30; Rom 1:3–4; Phil 2:5–11), but it seems strange to think of justification as causing Christ's resurrection. Rather, the second διὰ-clause should be understood as being prospective, i.e. "he was raised for (the purpose of) our justification." What stands behind this passage is Isa 53:11. There, the Servant of the Lord suffers and is justified in the heavenly courtroom upon seeing "the light of life." The result of the Servant's own resurrection-justification is that he will "justify many." Hence, justification is primarily a function of Christ's resurrection.[58]

Bird clarified this thought by noting: "The death of Christ constitutes the divine verdict against sin, whereas the resurrection transforms that verdict into vindication."[59] Bird's article is about a critique of the idea of "imputed righteousness," which is not stated as such in the New Testament. He also critiqued Wright's view of "a new status" and "a new people" as the meaning of justification. He makes an attempt to correct both sides with this evaluation of Rom 4:

> In sum, Romans 4 does not assert that one is justified because of the imputed righteousness of Christ or that God reckons faith as covenantal conformity. Instead, God regards faith as the condition of justification (reckons faith as righteousness) and justifies believers (credits righteousness) because of their union with Christ (raised for our justification).[60]

---

57. Wright, "Letter to the Romans," 502.
58. Bird, "Incorporated Righteousness," 266–67.
59. Bird, "Incorporated Righteousness," 267.
60. Bird, "Incorporated Righteousness," 267.

In more recent days, Michael Gorman has attempted to bring some "correction" to Wright's analysis of Rom 4. Gorman is arguing for a more robust concept of transformation in the process of "justification by faith" over against Wright's insistence on a "divine status" proclaimed by God. A lengthy quote is necessary here to get his point:

> However, if God declares those who have πίστις to be in the family, and if participation in the death and resurrection are the "basis" of this reality, then πίστις and participation, it seems to me, are fundamentally synonymous. Tom, in fact, also sees πίστις as sharing, or participation: "in other words, one is reckoned to be within the justified people, those whom this God has declared 'righteous', 'forgiven', 'members of the covenant', on the basis of πίστις and that alone. That—the Messiah's faithfulness, *in which his people share* through their own πίστις as in (my reading of) [Rom] 3.26, and also in 4.24-25—is the basic sign of membership" (p. 847, emphasis added). And if this is true, then justification must be participatory.[61]

The key to understanding all of these so-called "corrections" is Paul's phrase "in Christ." Gorman emphasizes "participation in Christ." Bird uses the phrase "union with Christ": "Justification cannot be played off against union with Christ, since justification transpires in Christ. . . . Rather, union with Christ comprises Paul's prime way of talking about the reception of the believer's new status through incorporation into the risen Christ by faith."[62] Although some scholars have attempted to separate Rom 1–4 from 5–8, the two sections of Romans are really a unity of thought. The concept of "justification by faith" (Rom 1–4) is further described by Paul as "participation in Christ" (Rom 5–8). This "participation" begins at baptism (Rom 6:1-4). The believer's identification with the death, burial, and resurrection of the Messiah is the beginning of what Bird calls "incorporated righteousness." We turn now to that discussion in Rom 5–8.

---

61. Gorman, "Wright about Much," 35–36. The reference in the quote to Tom Wright's thoughts are on p. 847 in his *Paul and the Faithfulness of God*. Gorman concluded: "Justification is about participation and transformation. If the mode of justification has radically changed (faith as sharing in the Messiah's faithfulness), so also has its substance" (36).

62. Bird, "Incorporated Righteousness," 275.

Justified by Faithfulness: Romans 5:1–11

Romans 5:1–11 is a summary of what Paul had written up to this point and the beginning of what will unfold through Rom 8:18–25, these two sections acting as an inclusion. It is precisely in Rom 5:1–11 where Paul will use the catchphrase *ek pisteōs* to summarize briefly what he has said in Rom 1–4, which is based on the messianic use of Hab 2:4b.[63] A unique inclusion can be found in this paragraph that helps establish the interpretation of the catchphrase.

Paul wrote: "Therefore, having been justified out of faithfulness we have peace with God through our Lord Jesus Christ" (Rom 5:1, my translation). The very same participle is found in v. 9 where it says: "Therefore, much more rather having been justified now by his blood we shall be saved through him from the wrath" (my translation). Notice the two phrases: "out of faithfulness" (v. 1) and "by his blood" (v. 9). These two phrases can be found together at Rom 3:25: "through faith[fulness] by/in his blood." The first phrase is referring to Jesus' faithfulness which cost him his blood (life). It is probable that Paul has *split* these two synonymous phrases to form an inclusion for this section or paragraph.[64] We have been justified (made right before God) by Jesus' faithfulness. This approach would not make redundant the next phrase in v. 2: "through whom we have gained access by [our] faith into this grace in which we now stand." On the other hand, it is possible that the second use of *pistis* (v. 2) refers to the "faithfulness of Christ" as well. Campbell translates these verses: "Being delivered 'through faithfulness' [i.e., the faithfulness of the righteous one], we will have peace with God through our Lord Jesus Christ, through whom we *also* have access [now] by means of that fidelity into this favor, by means of which we stand."[65] Either way, Rom 1:17 makes sense: "out of [Jesus'] faithfulness unto [our] faithfulness." The inclusion for Rom 5:1–11, therefore, includes the following words: "having been justified" (vv. 1, 9); "out of faithfulness" (v. 1) with "by his

---

63. This phrase, *ek pisteōs*, is used twelve times in Romans: 1:17 (twice); 3:26, 30; 4:16 (twice); 5:1; 9:30, 32; 10:6; 14:23 (twice).

64. Campbell, *Deliverance*, 824–25. I made this point with Campbell at an SBL meeting before he had matured his thoughts on this paragraph. I am gratified that he confirmed the idea. Interestingly, a young (pun!) scholar, Stephen L. Young, thought that Campbell was the only one he found to take 5:1 as referring to "Christ's faithfulness." Now, at least, there are two! See Young, "Paul's Ethnic Discourse," p. 12 of 13, nn. 48–49.

65. Campbell, *Deliverance*, 823.

blood" (v. 9); "we have peace" (v. 1) with "we received the reconciliation" (v. 11); "rejoice" (vv. 2, 11); "toward God through our Lord Jesus Christ" (v. 1) with "in God through our Lord Jesus Christ" (v. 11). Not many see the above for Rom 5:1–11 but with variation some do.[66]

One Man's Obedience: Romans 5:19

After the Rom 5:1–11 passage which concludes Rom 1–4 and introduces chapters 5–8, Paul begins a section comparing and contrasting Adam and Christ (Rom 5:12–21). In this section Paul shows how Christ, the implied Second Adam, has undone all the evil brought into the world through the First Adam. Verse 19 is key to the concerns about the "faithfulness of Messiah": "For just as through the disobedience of the one man [Adam] the many were made sinners, in like manner also through the obedience of the one [man, Jesus] the many will be made righteous" (my translation). Ever since Rom 1:17 the reader/listener has perhaps puzzled over who the "righteous one" is if Hab 2:4b was not immediately grasped as messianic. Romans 3:10 pronounced through Scripture: "There is no one righteous, not even one." It implied the question: "Who is the righteous one, then?" Certainly, Rom 3:21–26 gave some answers to this question, but the emphasis was on God's righteousness and rightness (Rom 3:26). Romans 5:1, 9 gave more hints, but now in Rom 5:19 the answer is plain: Jesus is the one obedient human being who is righteous; and because of his faithfulness to the Father's mission of keeping promises, he will make many to be made righteous—that is, put in a right covenant relationship with God.

How do sinful human beings do this? By a responding "faith" or "trust" in the God who raised Jesus from the dead: "Out of faithfulness unto faithfulness." At this point Paul is ready for his argumentative section (Rom 6:1—7:25) against those who slander his law-free and grace-filled gospel. He will, in a sense, exegete in chapter 6 his sentence in Rom 5:21—"so that, as sin reigned in death, grace also might reign through righteousness leading to eternal life through Jesus Christ our Lord." In chapter 7 Paul will exegete v. 20—"Now the law came in to increase the trespass, but where sin increased, grace abounded all the more."

---

66. Campbell, *Deliverance*, 822–25.

Free from Sin and the Law: Romans 6–7

The faithfulness of Jesus is found precisely in his death on a cross. God vindicated him by raising him from the dead by his sanctifying Spirit (Rom 1:4). Subsequent exaltation to God's right hand (Rom 8:34) is not discussed here but it is certainly implied, and the implications will be addressed at the end of chapter 8. At this point in Paul's arguments he has fully discussed the revelation of God's righteousness through Jesus' faithfulness. Now he shows how this is effective for "all who believe." Throughout chapters 6–8, Paul is explaining how God's power is at work in the gospel. By baptism into Christ, an immersion into the death of Christ, Christians are raised to new life. "Therefore, we were buried with him through baptism into death, in order that just as Messiah was raised from dead ones through the glory of the Father, in like manner also we should walk (live) in newness of life" (my translation). So, then, the person who is incorporated into Messiah Jesus by baptism has completely left the old life of sin (Rom 6:8–14).

Christians are living the resurrected life, which means a life characterized by righteousness (see Rom 6:13, 18–20; refer to 3:21–26; 5:21). Paul puts it in a strange way: *all of life is slavery!* (Rom 6:16). We are either slaves to sin which leads to death or slaves to obedience which leads to righteousness. Both terms have a reference to the Messiah—"obedience" (Rom 5:19) and "righteousness" (Rom 3:21). Wright summarized: "In particular, chap. 6 has explored the meaning of 5:12–21 in terms of the human renewal that results from the 'new exodus' of baptism."[67] It is a clean cut with the past and a renewed life for the present and future.[68]

Paul also shows how the law is no longer binding upon the Christian. We have died in the Messiah's death to the law and are free to marry another (the Messiah! 7:1–3). As a consequence, we can "bear fruit for God" (7:4). The law plus flesh exaggerated sin and thus the Israelite (Paul = "I") said: "I am . . . sold under sin" (7:14c). In spite of

---

67. Wright, "Letter to the Romans," 546.

68. David I. Starling has written an article in defense of the use of the term "imputed righteousness" for the believer, over against N. T. Wright's insistence that our "righteousness" is simply a "status." The argument is over the interpretation of 2 Cor 5:21. Does it refer only to the apostles and their ministry (Wright) or can it refer also to all believers in terms of an "imputed righteousness" (Starling)? See Starling's article: "Covenants and Courtrooms," esp. 43–46. I am not comfortable with either "status" or "imputed," but prefer the former. These are words we are imposing on the text. The text itself uses the word "reckon."

the law's role in pointing out sin, Paul declared "the law is holy, and the commandment is holy and righteous and good" (7:12). Sin used the law and the weakness of the flesh to ensure every human being was condemned before God's law court (Judgment Day). So how could the Israelite be delivered from this "body of death" (7:24b)? Answer? *The faithfulness of Jesus the Messiah!*

Cosmic Salvation: Romans 8

Romans 8 is Paul's greatest writing, perhaps due to the subject matter: cosmic salvation. For Christians no greater words could have been written: "There is therefore now no condemnation for those who are in Christ Jesus" (Rom 8:1). This is the result of having been baptized into Christ (Rom 6:3–4) and having received the forgiveness of sins as well as the gift of the Holy Spirit (see Acts 2:38). The whole theme of the "faithfulness of Jesus" (Rom 3:21–26) is found in Paul's next thought. The Torah was unable to give life to God's people because of the weakness of the flesh. However, God sent his Son, Jesus, into this world, a genuine human being ("in likeness of sinful flesh"), as "a sin offering" (*peri hamartias*, ESV only has "for sin"). By so doing, the "righteous requirements" (NIV) or "righteous requirement" (ESV) or better "righteous verdict"[69] of the Torah was fulfilled by those "in Christ" who walk not according to flesh but according to Spirit. Not only is this a summary and commentary on Rom 3:21–26 (the revelation of God's righteousness through the faithfulness of Jesus Christ for all who believe) but Paul now begins to give the implications of what it means to be "in Christ," i.e., we must now "live" (the Greek is literally "walk around") in the Spirit (Holy Spirit). We have moved from an "unfit mind" (Rom 1:28) to a mind led by the Spirit. Paul makes the comparison stark: "For the mind of flesh is death, but the mind of the Spirit is life and peace" (Rom 8:6, my translation).

In a remarkable flow of thought in a brief span of one verse Paul will refer to the "Spirit" as "Spirit of God" and "Spirit of Christ" (v. 9). Just as we must be "in Christ" (v. 1), so too, Christ must be "in us" (v. 10). As Paul expressed it: "But if Christ is in you, although the body is

---

69. Wright, *Justification*, 236. This is Wright's translation of *to dikaiōma* in Rom 8:4 instead of the usual "requirement." Note that it is singular. The NIV translates it plural: "righteous requirements." ESV keeps it singular as is the Greek text. I agree with Wright's assessment. He has also translated it "just decree" at Rom 1:32, stated in his commentary on Romans.

dead because of sin, the Spirit is life because of righteousness" (v. 10). The mention of "righteousness" in this context indicates that Paul is still "fleshing out" the revelation of "God's righteousness" at Rom 3:21–26. Or as Wright notes: "'Righteousness' here serves as a catch-all term for the entire sequence of covenantal and lawcourt thinking developed in the earlier parts of the letter."[70] Ultimately our personal salvation has to do with bodily resurrection: "If the Spirit of him who raised Jesus from the dead dwells in you, he who raised Christ Jesus from the dead will also give life to your mortal bodies through his Spirit who dwells in you" (Rom 8:11). Those who experience the bodily resurrection will also experience the wonder of a whole new creation of the cosmos (Rom 8:18–25). Daniel Kirk summarized his thoughts at this point for Rom 8:

> Moreover, the idea that the resurrection of Jesus provides the appropriate lens for making sense of Paul's citation of Hab 2:4 also finds warrant here:
> God's action in the faithful death of Jesus results in resurrection life both for the Righteous One and for those who are in him. God pours out his Spirit's power leading to salvation in the resurrection life of Jesus.[71]

As Paul finishes this great chapter, he clearly connects the "God who justifies" (v. 33b—*theos ho dikaiōn*) with the death of the Messiah which puts us right with God, a new status[72] (see Rom 3:25). But Paul does not stop there. He gives the full implications of the death of Christ by emphasizing his resurrection ("was raised") and exaltation at God's right hand, thus "interceding for us" (Rom 8:34b). The reign of Christ is a priestly reign, and therefore nothing shall separate us from the love of Christ (Rom 8:35–39). These are Paul's climactic thoughts concerning the power of the gospel (Rom 1:16) and the manifestation of God's righteousness through Jesus' faithfulness to the cross. But how does this square with the fact that most of Israel has rejected the Messiah, has not experienced the power of the gospel by means of the Spirit, and continues to be "hardened in part" (NIV) or "a partial hardening" (ESV)?

---

70. Wright, *Justification*, 237.
71. Kirk, *Unlocking Romans*, 130.
72. While I questioned the use of "status" and "imputed," some word must be used to express the idea of "being reckoned" righteous. "Imputed" implies more than the text declares, "status" perhaps less! I will use the word "status" for want of a better expression. We are declared "righteous" by virtue of being "in Christ."

Paul must address the most difficult issues at hand in terms of Jew-gentile relationships (Rom 9–11). He must answer such questions as: "Has God's word failed?" (Rom 9:6); "Is God unjust in all this?" (Rom 9:14); "Why does God still blame us?" (Rom 9:19); "Did God reject his people?" (Rom 11:1); "Did [Israel] stumble so as to fall beyond recovery?" (Rom 11:11); and in a benediction, "Who has known the mind of the Lord?" (Rom 11:34).

All Israel Will Be Saved: Romans 9–11

Paul agonized over the recalcitrance of most of Israel in rejecting Jesus as their Messiah (Rom 9:1–5), especially in the face of all their privileges as enumerated in vv. 4–5 (started at 3:2!). Now he must answer the question: "Has the word of God failed?" (literally, "fallen"). Paul, then, makes a proposition that will overshadow all his discussion through the three chapters (see Rom 11:26): "For not all who are descended from Israel are Israel" (Rom 9:6b). The average Israelite would agree, nod the head, and approve of Paul's unfolding the "story of Israel" as found in Rom 9:7–24a. At that point Paul takes a turn in the road. Gentiles have been added to God's people and God's people have been reduced to a "remnant" (Rom 9:24b–29). Nonbelieving Jews would have reacted strongly against Paul's last statement, but one must remember that he is addressing primarily gentile Christians and probably a much smaller number of Jewish Christians, if he has them in mind. They, the gentile Christians, are the ones who must understand their stance toward the Jewish people as a whole. Paul is "not ashamed" of this stance (see 1:16).

Romans 9:30—10:6 includes a cluster of the catchphrase *ek pisteōs* (Rom 9:30, 32; 10:6), which I have suggested harks back to Hab 2:4b as quoted in Rom 1:17. This is Paul's condensed thoughts on Israel's response to the coming of Messiah and the preaching of the gospel. Paul writes: "What then shall we say? That gentiles who were not pursuing righteousness have obtained righteousness, indeed, the righteousness *ek pisteōs* ('out of faithfulness')? But Israel pursuing the Torah of righteousness did not obtain unto the Torah [of righteousness]. Why not? Because [it was] not *ek pisteōs* ('out of faithfulness') but as out of works [of the Torah]. They stumbled upon the stone of stumbling" (Rom 9:30–32; my translation). By now one should recognize that the phrase "out of faithfulness" is referring to the exposition of the gospel found in Rom 3:21–26 (a resumption of Rom 1:16–17). The manifestation of God's righteousness is through the faithfulness of Jesus to the cross. This death is a *hilastērion* (Rom 3:25), the means/place of atonement for all who believe or trust the God who raised Jesus from the dead. The "stumbling stone" was Jesus!

Israel made two missteps: First, she rejected the Messiah, thus stumbling upon him as a stumbling stone. The word of God has not stumbled (Rom 9:6), Israel has (see Rom 9:33, a combination of Isa 28:16 and 8:14). Secondly, she pursued life based on the Torah, whether by righteous activity based on the Torah or holding on to the Torah markers of identity as God's people (circumcision, diet, and sabbath-keeping). "For being ignorant of God's righteousness and seeking [their] own [righteousness], they did not submit to God's righteousness" (Rom 10:3, my translation). The NIV translates the first part of this verse in such a way as to keep "righteousness" something *imputed* to the believer. But the NIV translates the very same phrase as "God's righteousness" at the end, which is inconsistent with the Greek but consistent with the NIV presupposition about Rom 3:21–26 and the objective genitive ("faith in Christ").

Romans 10:4 is the *climactic* text in our discussions. The Greek text literally reads: "For end/goal/climax of Torah Messiah unto righteousness to all who believe." There is no verb and so one must decide where to provide the "is." The obvious choice is "Messiah" as the subject and "end/goal/climax" (τέλος, *telos*) as the predicate complement. It would read: "For Messiah [is] the end/goal/climax of the Torah for righteousness to everyone who believes." But what is the meaning of *telos*—end, goal, or climax?

The word could be translated in all three ways. Those who support the objective genitive readings usually translate *telos* "end" as with the Jerusalem Bible translation: "But now the Law has come to an end with Christ, and everyone who has faith may be justified." The NIV is similar, perhaps more literal: "Christ is the end of the law so that there may be righteousness for everyone who believes." The ESV does the same: "For Christ is the end of the law." These translations make the second half of the sentence a separate thought from the first. But the Greek would have us understand that there is a connection, a purpose fulfilled or accomplished, a "goal" if you will. That "goal" is "righteousness for all who believe." What makes the status of believers "righteousness"? Christ! Christ is the "goal" of the Torah so that there may be "righteousness" (a new status) for believers. Wright articulates clearly his preference for "goal" as against most Protestant views:

Thus, 10:4, one of the most controversial verses in Paul (because telos can mean "end" and "goal," and because Paul seems to mean some combination of the two with the weight on the latter), gives off its full resonances not within the Lutheran scheme whereby the law is a bad thing abolished in Christ, nor within the Calvinist scheme whereby the law is a good thing which Christ obeyed and thus procured "righteousness" (works-righteousness, we note) to be then "imputed" to those who believe, but within Paul's own Jewish framework of thought, the narrative of God and his faithfulness to Israel which has reached its destination in the Messiah.[73]

Interestingly, Douglas Campbell observes the metaphor of a "race" throughout these texts (Rom 9–10), and thus he opts for both meanings to be held in *telos*. He writes: "If the Christ event is the end of the race for the law, in the sense almost of being the finish line, then the key point is that the race is over (see Phil. 3:2–16). Any subsequent racing on the part of Jews is therefore misdirected if not ludicrous. The advantage of this reading is that it can integrate the strong contextual signals that τέλος in 10:4 suggests some sort of goal."[74] While Campbell makes a compelling argument, I favor Wright's stance on *telos* meaning "goal": "Israel has not 'attained Torah', because the mode of 'works' is not the way whereby one can attain it. Torah, Israel's covenant charter, leads the eye forward along the story line from Abraham all the way to the Messiah, who is the goal of Torah. That is how the story works. It is the narrative logic of the entire section."[75]

Most scholars play v. 5 off against v. 6 of chapter 10. "For Moses writes [about] the righteousness out of Torah, 'The one doing [the Torah] a man shall live in it'" (Rom 10:5, my translation). This is understood as simply doing the "works of Torah" over against "faith." Verse 6, then, speaks of the "righteousness by faith," understood as our "faith in Christ" and the subsequent imputation of God's righteousness upon the believer. However, Wright takes a complete reversal to that idea. He suggests that Paul is really showing that the Torah all along led the person who "did it" to the "righteousness" that is found in the Messiah, the goal of Torah. This thought is a continuation of Rom 2:25–29 and such passages as 1 Cor 7:19—"Circumcision is nothing and uncircumcision is nothing. Keeping God's commands

---

73. Wright, *Justification*, 244.
74. Campbell, *Deliverance*, 791.
75. Wright, "Letter to the Romans," 657.

is what counts." Thus, v. 6 is a continuation of this thought. "This 'doing of the law,' Paul declares, is announced by 'the righteousness of faith,' that is, by the message of the faith-based covenant renewal."[76]

Just as Moses offered to Israel a covenant renewal as recounted in Deut 30, so now Paul uses that same text to show that God has made a covenant renewal with his people through the Messiah. Paul does this by personifying the phrase "the righteousness by faith[fulness]" (Rom 10:6a). It speaks a great message about Messiah—you don't have to go to heaven to bring him down nor must you go to the abyss to bring him up—He has already come to earth (incarnation) and he has been raised from the dead (resurrection)! All one needs to do is believe it ("the obedience of faith," Rom 1:5; 16:26). *"When people believe the gospel of Jesus and his resurrection, and confess him as Lord, they are in fact doing what Torah wanted all along, and are therefore displaying the necessary marks of covenant renewal."*[77]

What marks God's people now, whether Jew or gentile, is "faith," and specifically "righteousness by [Messiah's] faithfulness." This kind of faith is found in Abraham even while he was "ungodly" (Rom 4:13, 16, 24–25; 5:6). No longer are God's people marked out by "works of the Torah" (whether understood as "obedience to the whole Torah" or "circumcision, diet, and sabbath-keeping" as marks of the Jew). Paul's quotation of Joel 2:32 at v. 13—"For everyone who calls on the name of the Lord will be saved,"—implies that God's Spirit has been poured out upon all who believe and have been baptized into Christ. Indeed, there is no difference between Jew and gentile (v. 12), and both must come into the Abrahamic family the same way—through the "faithfulness of Messiah," trusting that God has raised him from the dead and one day will raise our mortal bodies from the dead. This is why I interpret "all Israel" in Rom 11:26 to mean "all believing Jews and gentiles, the renewed covenantal family of God." This is a minority view when comparing the major Roman commentaries, but it seems the best interpretation in light of the previous statement in Rom 9:6.[78]

---

76. Wright, *Justification*, 245.

77. Wright, *Justification*, 245, emphasis is Wright's.

78. Staples, "Gentiles," 371–90. I agree with Staples' arguments that "all Israel" includes believing Jews and gentiles. See also Wright, "Letter to the Romans," 690, who says "Israel" includes Jews and gentiles.

Living By Faithfulness: Romans 14:23

The last two instances of the catchphrase *ek pisteōs* are found in Rom 14:23. Verses 22–23 are Paul's concluding thoughts to his discussion concerning the "weak" and the "strong" in Rom 14:1–23. The discussion will continue in Rom 15:1–13. Verse 23 reads: "But the one disputing with himself (wavering), he is condemned if he eats, because [he has eaten] not *out of faithfulness*; indeed, all which is not *out of faithfulness* is sin (missing the mark)" (my literal translation). One should note that this is precisely what Abraham did not do—"waver" in his faith. He trusted God for his promises. In that same background is the double use of *ek pisteōs* in Rom 4:16. The first use would suggest the "faithfulness of Messiah" which gave us all "grace" (v. 16a). The second use refers to gentiles who participate "out of the faith[fulness] of Abraham" (v. 16c). Paul is trying to locate the "strong" and the "weak" in direct relationship to God and his kingdom, his emphasis (Rom 14:5–18). "For the kingdom of God is not a matter of eating and drinking, but of righteousness and peace and joy in the Holy Spirit" (Rom 14:17).

To live *ek pisteōs* ("out of faithfulness") is to live like Jesus lived. Jesus is the paradigm as well as Abraham in terms of *ek pisteōs*. Paul's concluding statements on this matter (Rom 15:1–13) clearly demand that we understand the catchphrase in this way: "We who are strong have an obligation to bear with the failings of the weak, and not to please ourselves. Let each of us please his neighbor for his good, to build him up. For Christ did not please himself" (Rom 15:1–3a) and "therefore welcome one another as Christ has welcomed you, for the glory of God" (Rom 15:7). As Campbell expressed it: "The life of the kingdom, imparted by the Spirit, and beyond matters of food and drink, is a participation in the thinking of the self-sacrificing Christ (as Rom. 12:1–2 also suggests), who did not please himself but others."[79] It seems to me the catchphrase is saying to the Christian that "everything that is not *of Christ and his faithfulness* is sin." Otherwise, we are "of Adam" and continue to sin against one another according to the flesh. To live *ek pisteōs* is to live by the Spirit of Christ, the Holy Spirit.

Wright related Romans 14:23b more toward Abraham but I like his thought: "In other words, you are either with Abraham or with Adam. You are either living, like Abraham, in unwavering trust in God

---

79. Campbell, *Deliverance*, 831.

and God's promises; or you are turning away from God and living by some other means."[80]

In this exhortation section (Rom 12–15) Paul has concluded his practical application to the Jew-gentile issues by using the catchphrase *ek pisteōs* twice in a compact and powerful thought (Rom 14:23). I suggested above that Paul is appealing to Jesus as well as Abraham as paradigms of the kind of life one must live—that is, "out of faithfulness," in order to solve the Jew-gentile relationships of the "strong" and the "weak." The Messiah was destined to rule over all nations (Rom 15:8–12). Therefore, whether a person is Jew or gentile, "strong" or "weak," he or she must pay attention to the Messiah, whose faithfulness saved us. Paul concluded: "May the God of endurance and encouragement grant you to live in such harmony with one another, in accord with Christ Jesus, that together you may with one voice glorify the God and Father of our Lord Jesus Christ" (Rom 15:5–6).

Conclusion

Romans, no doubt, is a complex letter of Paul. He clearly had several purposes for writing, but the most important was his desire to evangelize among gentiles (pagans) in Spain where no one had preached. Without the Roman Christians' support and encouragement, Paul knew the mission would be vastly more difficult to accomplish. Yet, he was well aware of the Roman situation with many friends and companions who had lived there (Rom 16). Many were accusing Paul of denigrating the Torah, the Jewish Holy Scriptures. They were asking how one could live ethically without obeying the Torah. Paul's grace-filled gospel was too much for them. Roman Christians (both Jews and gentiles) were having difficulties with how to relate to one another when they had such different opinions concerning eating meat or only vegetables, esteeming one day over another or all days alike (Rom 14). The edict of Claudius in AD 49 had certainly created a problem when some of the Jewish community (including Christian Jews) had been expelled. Their return after AD 54 surely led to many difficulties reestablishing former property and homes and fellowship with either the synagogues or the Christian house churches. Surely Paul knew he had to address the relationship between

---

80. Wright, "Letter to the Romans," 742.

Jews and gentiles, particularly Christian gentiles with their fellow Jewish brothers and sisters, Christian or not.

Ultimately, Romans is a theodicy—showing how God's righteousness is revealed and how that revelation has upheld all God's promises to his people, the Jews. God's plan from the beginning was to redeem all people through his chosen people, the Jews, and that plan has now reached its goal in Jesus the Messiah, their representative. God's covenant faithfulness is assured. Paul could exclaim: "Oh, the depth of the riches and wisdom and knowledge of God! How unsearchable are his judgments and how inscrutable his ways!" (Rom 11:33). So how does Paul vindicate God's righteousness through his letter? He basically presents his gospel, actually the "gospel of God, which he promised beforehand through his prophets in the holy Scriptures, concerning his Son" (Rom 1:1b–3a). The following presentation is how one would see Paul's gospel if the subjective genitive interpretation is vigorously applied throughout. This is a general review of all exposition above for a conclusion to the study of Romans.

Paul began with the very human Jesus, a descendant from David, but also his glorification as the resurrected Son of God by the power of the Spirit (Rom 1:3–4). He continued with his theme statement: "For I am not ashamed of the gospel, for it is the power of God for salvation to everyone who believes, to the Jew first and also to the Greek. For in it the righteousness of God is revealed from faith for faith, as it is written, 'The righteous shall live by faith'" (Rom 1:16–17). While this theme at this stage in Paul's letter may be puzzling, later it will reveal that Hab 2:4b is being used messianically—"the righteous (One) shall live (resurrection) by faithfulness." Therefore, the enigmatic phrase earlier will take on a precise meaning: "from Messiah's faithfulness unto our faithfulness" (my translation). The fact that Habakkuk's message is a theodicy, asking about God's justice, lends weight to Paul's use of this text for his own wrestling with the justice of God with regard to his people and how gentiles relate to them.

The revelation of God's righteousness has two sides: the dark side is God's wrath upon human sin (Rom 1:18—3:20), and so Paul elaborates this reality showing how both Jews and gentiles are in the same position: "None is righteous, no, not one" (Rom 3:10). In spite of the sinfulness of gentiles and the unfaithfulness of some of the Jews, God remains faithful, righteous, and true (Rom 3:3, 5, 7). The bright side of God's righteousness is the heart of the gospel of God. God's righteousness has been manifested through the faithfulness of Jesus the Messiah (Rom 3:21–22). God had presented Jesus as a means of atonement (propitiation) by his faithfulness at the cost of his blood (Rom 3:25). This one act of crucifixion demonstrated God's righteousness in terms of his divine forebearance, having "passed over" former sins. No longer! Not only is God righteous but he makes righteous all who share in the faithfulness of Jesus, i.e., "for all who believe" (Rom 3:25b–26).

Romans 3:27–31 is greatly changed when one interprets *pistis* as faithfulness rather than simply human faith. A person is justified by Jesus' faithfulness as testified by the Torah of faithfulness (the Torah bears witness to God's righteousness). Since God is one, Jews and gentiles are justified on the same basis—the faithfulness of Jesus, the goal of which is the responding faithfulness of those who trust the God who raised Jesus from the dead. The Torah is not overthrown by this faithfulness, rather Paul says: "We uphold the Torah!"

Romans 4, then, is not about using Abraham as an example of a "sinner" who believed and thus it was counted to him as righteousness. Rather, it is about Abraham's trust in God's promise that he would have a son who in turn would become a great nation and a blessing to all other nations. Abraham's trust in God to fulfill his covenant promises came before he was circumcised and long before the law was given. Thus, Abraham, under these circumstances, could become "the father of us all" (Rom 4:16). Such trust in a God who can raise the dead (his own body) and the dead womb of Sarah to bear a child of promise was what counted as righteousness (Rom 4:19–22). When Jews and gentiles trust in God the way Abraham did, trusting that he raised Jesus our Lord from the dead, then they know that Jesus "was delivered up for our trespasses and raised for our justification" (Rom 4:25). Romans 4 is pointing toward how God created his one family made up of Jews and gentiles. This will be explained fully in Rom 9–11.

"Therefore, since we have been justified by [Messiah's] faithfulness, we have peace with God through our Lord Jesus the Messiah" (Rom 5:1, my translation). As an inclusion for Rom 5:1–11, Paul wrote: "Since, therefore, we have now been justified by his blood, much more shall we be saved by him from the wrath of God" (Rom 5:9). Being justified "by his faithfulness" and "by his blood" is saying the same thing—a parallelism. When Paul compared and contrasted Adam with Jesus (Rom 5:12–21), he pinpointed the faithfulness of Jesus by this contrast: "For as by the one man's disobedience the many were made sinners, so by the one man's obedience the many will be made righteous" (Rom 5:19). Who is the righteous One of Rom 1:17? The one obedient Israelite, the Messiah, who accomplished God's will by redeeming the world through the cross.

On the basis of what the Messiah has done on the cross and the resurrection, all nations can now participate in Messiah's death, burial, and resurrection by means of baptism. Christians have been buried with Christ and raised with him to "walk in newness of life" (Rom 6:4). Therefore, by participation in Christ, we are "dead to sin and alive to God in Christ Jesus" (Rom 6:11). Paul says we are no longer slaves to sin but slaves to righteousness which leads to sanctification—and its end, eternal life (Rom 6:15–23).

The faithfulness of Jesus to the cross not only freed us from sin but also freed us from the law (Rom 7). In a strange twist of an analogy Paul proclaims that our "old self" is like a husband that has died, and thus our "new self" is like a wife who is free to marry another—namely Jesus who has been raised from the dead (Rom 7:1–4). Being free from the law means that a person can now be fruitful as that person participates in Christ by the indwelling of the Holy Spirit (Rom 7:5–6).

Skipping over Paul's great discussion on the law and the flesh which produces sin (Rom 7:7–25), he reaches a climax about what God's righteousness has done: "God having sent his own Son in likeness of flesh of sin and as a sin-offering (concerning sin), he condemned sin in the flesh, in order that the just verdict of the law may be fulfilled in us to the ones who walk not according to flesh but according to Spirit" (Rom 8:3b–4, my translation). In a subtle way, Paul changes his imagery of being "slaves to righteousness" to something much better. Christians "received the Spirit of adoption as sons, by whom we cry, 'Abba! Father!' The Spirit himself bears witness with our spirit that we are children of God, and if children, then heirs—heirs of God and fellow heirs with Christ, provided we suffer with him in order that we may also be glorified with him" (Rom 8:15b–17).

This future glory is cosmic in scope: we will be glorified by our resurrected bodies (Rom 8:23), but more than that, the creation itself will be restored, renewed, and glorified (Rom 8:19–22). This is where the faithfulness of Jesus becomes a reality for the believer, for all who accept Jesus as Lord are "predestined to be conformed to the image of [his] Son" (Rom 8:29b). Being like Jesus is to be justified and one day to be glorified just as he is glorified (Rom 8:30b). Having reached such a high theological point of how God's righteousness has saved both Jews and gentiles on the same basis—the faithfulness of Jesus—conforming us to his image, Paul can now tackle the sticky situation of the relationship of Jews and gentiles in the Roman community.

In the next section (Rom 9–11) Paul reaches his objective to address the issue of Jewish and gentile relationships in light of God's promises to the patriarchs. After expressing his agony over Israel's rejection of the Messiah in unbelief, Paul gives a key to understanding his entire argument: "But it is not as though the word of God has failed. For not all who are descended from Israel belong to Israel, and not all are children of Abraham because they are his offspring, but 'Through Isaac shall your offspring be named'" (Rom 9:6-7). Thus, Paul shows how God reduced the seed of Abraham to one—Jacob who fathered the twelve sons who became the new nation of Israel. But from that point God promised that the family of God would be greatly expanded into a multitude like sand on the shores and stars in the heavens. How could this be, for Israel had been reduced to a remnant by two exiles (Israel of the north by Assyrians and Judah of the south by the Babylonians)? It was God's plan from the beginning to call gentiles to join his chosen family (Rom 9:24b). Paul expresses how this was done in Rom 9:30-33 in his use of the catchphrase *ek pisteōs*. He basically says that gentiles, though not pursuing righteousness, have attained such righteousness from [Messiah's] faithfulness. Israel, though pursuing the law of righteousness, did not attain it because they sought it on the basis of "works," not "out of [Messiah's] faithfulness." The majority of Israel stumbled on the stumbling stone, Jesus! Jesus became a scandal to them.

God's righteousness which is revealed through Jesus' faithfulness is clarified by Paul when he declares: "For Messiah is the goal of the Torah for righteousness to everyone who believes" (Rom 10:4, my translation). This is essentially the same thought as found in Rom 3:21-22. At that point Paul launches into an exposition of how a person believes or trusts in the Messiah. First of all, a person confesses that Jesus is Lord. Secondly, that person must believe that God raised Jesus from the dead. Both Jews and gentiles must call on God on the same basis: the resurrected Lord! (Rom 10:8-12). "For everyone who calls on the name of the Lord will be saved" (Rom 10:13). Then a series of logical "steps" in obtaining salvation: calling on the Lord requires one to believe, believing requires one to hear with acceptance the message of the gospel, the message requires one to preach it, and preachers must be sent. Paul's conclusion is: "So faith comes from the message (ἀκοῆς, *akoēs*), indeed the message through the word about the Messiah" (Rom 10:17, my translation). I have translated the Greek word for "hearing" as "that which is heard, that is, the message."

Then Paul argues that Israel's stumbling has brought salvation to gentiles: "through their trespasses salvation has come to the gentiles, so as to make Israel jealous" (Rom 11:11b). However, Paul will not allow gentiles to have an arrogant attitude toward the Jews, for it is "the root that supports you" (Rom 11:18b, see vv. 11–27). Even though only a remnant of Israel, Paul included, accepted the Lord, gentiles are continually being added to believing Israelites (as God had promised from the beginning, Rom 9:24b). So when Paul says "And in this way all Israel will be saved" (Rom 11:26a), he means to say that gentiles have now been added to Israel—"all Israel" includes Jews and gentiles. Gentiles must love their fellow Jews, whether they become Christian (believe in Messiah) or not!

Having finished his main climactic theological issue of Jewish/gentile relationships, Paul applies the gospel of God to the everyday lives of his gentile audience (obviously Jewish Christians can be included). Paul exhorts his listeners to die to selfishness by presenting their bodies as "living sacrifice(s)" and "to be transformed by the renewal of [their] minds" (Rom 12:1–2). After addressing the divisive issues between the "weak" and the "strong" (Rom 14:1—15:7), Paul concludes his exposition of the gospel with a series of quotes from the Hebrew Scriptures with gentiles praising the Lord alongside God's people (Rom 15:8–13). Paul's introductory statement to these texts confirms the faithful Jesus as the heart of the gospel: "For I tell you that Messiah became a servant to the circumcised to show God's truthfulness, in order to confirm the promises given to the patriarchs, and in order that the gentiles might glorify God for his mercy" (Rom 15:8–9a, my change of "Christ" to "Messiah").

A Summary of the Pistis Word Group in Romans

Πιστεύω, *pisteuō*, (verb: "to believe/to trust") is used twenty-one times in Romans. All refer to human believing or trusting. About eight times no object is expressed. When objects are expressed it is to God (4:3, 5, 17, 24), Jesus (9:33; 10:11, 14), a message (6:8; 10:16), and what is believed ("to eat anything" 14:2). Once, the verb clearly means "entrusted" (3:2). The Jews were "entrusted" with the oracles of God. Three times the verb is part of a quote from the prophecy of Isaiah (9:33, Isa 28:16; 10:11, Isa 28:16, and 16, Isa 53:1). It may be instructive to note that the verb is clustered in two chapters: chapter 4 with Abraham's believing or trusting God and chapter 10 where Paul is referring to the proper response to God's salvation—believe it!

Πίστις, *pistis*, (noun: "faith/faithfulness") is used forty times. The so-called "catchphrase" taken from Hab 2:4b, ἐκ πίστεως, *ek pisteōs*, is used twelve times and I have chosen to translate it "faithfulness" each time (1:17 twice; 3:26, 30; 4:16 twice; 5:1; 9:30, 32; 10:6; and 14:23 twice. "Faithfulness" is never far removed from "faith" itself, so it is difficult to determine which is meant; and perhaps one should not try. However, I see "faithfulness" as a better translation in many of the other references: (1:8, 12, 17; 3:3, 22, 25, 27, 28, 31; 5:1; 10:8; and 11:20). Twice, Paul refers to the "obedience of faith" (1:5; 16:26) which basically is the idea of "faithfulness." Once, it is clearly God's faithfulness (3:3) but see also 3:28. I have argued vigorously that many references are to Jesus' faithfulness (1:17 twice; 3:22, 25, 26, maybe 28, 30, 31; 4:16; 5:1, maybe 2; 9:30, 32; and maybe 14:23 twice as earlier explained. Once it could be translated as "firmness" or "conviction" at 14:22. Of course, the rest of the references are referring to "human" faith(fulness): (see 1:8, 12; 4:5, 9, 11, 12, 13, 14, 16, 19, 20; 5:2; 10:17; 11:20; 14:1). Once, it is used with "word of faith," and I take it to mean the "word of faithfulness that we proclaim" (10:8, my translation). Twice, it is used as referring to "faith" as a measure of a spiritual gift (12:3, 6). Most English translations use only the word "faith" in these references.

Πιστός, *pistos*, the adjective ("faithful") is not used in Romans.

Ἀπιστέω, *apisteō*, (verb: "to be unfaithful") is used once at Rom 3:3 where "some Jews" were unfaithful.

Ἀπιστία, *apistia*, (noun: "faithlessness") is used four times: Rom 3:3 "faithlessness," 4:20 "distrust," 11:20 "unbelief," and 11:23 "unbelief."

We now move to Galatians, where all that has been discovered about Romans can now be applied to a much smaller letter with a narrower concern. Galatians will prove very productive for the subjective genitive interpretation. David Stubbs wrote an insightful article that highlighted three facets in Paul's epistles that will be addressed throughout this book: "The overall theological vision which includes three facets—a christologically centred understanding of the *pistis Christou* passages, a broader understanding of *pistis*, and the centring of soteriology around the concept of 'participation in Christ'—provides the most convincing interpretational matrix for reading Paul."[81] All of these facets and more will be addressed in the following chapters.

---

81. Stubbs, "Shape of Soteriology," 139.

3

The Galatian Crisis

> "In effect, then, Paul uses πίστις Ἰησοῦ in his writings to signal the basis for the Christian gospel: that its objective basis is the perfect response of obedience that Jesus rendered to God the Father, both actively in his life and passively in his death."
>
> —RICHARD N. LONGENECKER[1]

The Occasion for Galatians

ALL ARE AGREED THAT Paul is the author of the letter to the Galatians (Gal 1:1). Everything else is debated among scholars for various and good reasons. In addition, all are agreed that the letter is addressed to "Galatians," wherever they may be (northern or southern Galatians? See Gal 1:2 and 3:1.). Most everything else, i.e., date, occasion, purpose, and background hinges on which Galatians Paul is addressing—those in the northern or the southern part of the province.

The more popular view is that Paul addressed the southern province of Galatia in this letter. This fits well with Luke's account of Paul's so-called first missionary journey in the southern Galatian province as recorded in Acts 13–14. Paul and Barnabas made a brief visit through Cyprus, moving from Salamis to Paphos and preaching along the way. From there they sailed up to Perga where John Mark left the group (Acts

---

1. R. N. Longenecker, *Galatians*, 87.

13:13). Then they trekked to Pisidian Antioch where Luke records a "lengthy" message by Paul to the local synagogue (Acts 13:14-41). While some gentiles honored God's word through Paul, the Jews stirred up the city to expel them from the region (Acts 13:48-52). They moved on to Iconium where they were more effective in converting some Jews as well as gentiles. But the unconverted Jews persisted in persecuting the evangelistic group to the degree that they had to flee to Lystra and Derbe. The healing of a man lame from birth, perhaps at the city gate of Lystra, brought about an embarrassing attempt by the pagan inhabitants to worship Paul and Barnabas as gods—Zeus (for Barnabas) and Hermes (for Paul, Acts 14:8-13). Paul and Barnabas were barely able to keep the city of Lystra from sacrificing to them (Acts 14:14-18). The Jews from Antioch and Iconium came down to Lystra and convinced them that Paul deserved the death penalty by stoning, and so they proceeded to impose it (Acts 14:19). Apparently, Barnabas and the rest of the group along with a few new disciples gathered around Paul and "healed" him, though the text is silent as to how Paul was able to get up and return into the city (Acts 14:20). Paul and Barnabas immediately go to Derbe and there they have great success with "a large number of disciples" (Acts 14:21a).

The boldness of the evangelistic group was evidenced by their return through the very cities where they had been persecuted. They retraced their steps in order to establish leadership among the new churches made up of a few Jews and mostly gentile believers (Acts 14:21b-25). From Attalia they sailed back to Antioch and gave a report of what God had done through them to open the "door of faith to the gentiles" in the southern Galatian region (Acts 14:26-28). The volatile circumstances under which these new disciples were converted, both Jews and gentiles, would certainly provide opportunity for unscrupulous but conscientious "agitators" to come in among them in order to impose circumcision as a requirement toward being *true Christians*! Just as the Lystrian pagans had so quickly turned against Paul and his group by the influence of Jews from Antioch and Iconium, so the new disciples of Christ were turning away from the faith by listening to the false teaching of the "agitators" (see Gal 1:7; 3:1; 4:17; 5:7-12; and 6:12-13).[2]

---

2. See Frank J. Matera's discussion of Paul's opponents in his commentary: *Galatians*, 7-11. He prefers the term "agitators" throughout the letter of Galatians. These "agitators," probably gentile proselytes to Judaism, having been circumcised, wanted other gentiles to be circumcised as well.

Such a shift in thinking among the new churches in the southern Galatian province (Antioch, Iconium, Lystra, and Derbe) is the occasion for the Galatian letter from Paul, possibly written from Syrian Antioch c. AD 48–49 (his home base). The thinking is that Paul surely wrote Galatians before the Jerusalem Council of AD 49 (Acts 15). Otherwise, he would have referred to this important decision of the Jerusalem leaders. This is an argument from silence, to be sure, but it is a puzzle of omission if the letter were written later, as suggested by the "northern Galatian theory."

The northern Galatian theory is given without reference to Acts where there is no record of Paul in this area of north-central Asia Minor. This theory suggests that Paul traveled into this area on his second missionary journey, visiting cities such as Pessinus, Ancyra, and possibly Tavium. Gauls had invaded and settled this area in the third century BC. Thus, it would have been to these people Paul addressed his letter sometime between AD 53 and 57 from either Ephesus or Macedonia (Philippi?).

J. Louis Martyn refines the above summary to say that Paul visited the north-central area after the conference in Jerusalem and his painful breakup with Barnabas (see Acts 15:36–40; Gal 2:11–14). Luke only records a revisit through the southern portion of Galatia (Acts 15:41—16:1–8). On the basis of Paul's references to the "collection" for the poor in Jerusalem, Martyn dates Galatians c. AD 50, after 1 Thessalonians and before Philippians, certainly before the Corinthian correspondences and the Roman epistle.[3] This is not much different from the AD 48–49 date for the "southern Galatian theory." Martyn argues strongly that there were no Jews among the Galatian Christians as may have been suggested by the "southern Galatian theory." He writes: "On the contrary, Paul speaks throughout the letter to former Gentiles, uncircumcised persons with some degree of Hellenistic culture, who previously worshiped pagan gods (4:8–9). There were no Jews in Paul's Galatian churches."[4] References to Acts 16:6 and 18:23 are considered allusions to Paul's ministry in this area in support of the "northern Galatian theory."

Richard N. Longenecker lays out the arguments for the "northern Galatian theory" by both J. B. Lightfoot and James Moffatt and also the counter arguments for a "southern Galatian theory" by W. M. Ramsey and E. DeWitt Burton (two versions!). After weighing all the arguments

---

3. Martyn, *Galatians*, 19–20, see n. 20.
4. Martyn, *Galatians*, 16.

on both sides, both old and contemporary, Longenecker decides for the "southern Galatian theory" for both addresses and a date c. AD 48 before the Jerusalem Council in AD 49.[5]

In spite of the fact that Martyn supports the "northern Galatian theory" over against Matera and Longenecker who support the "southern Galatian theory," all three interpret the significant *pistis Christou* phrases as subjective genitives rather than the usual objective genitives of most English translations. Apparently, one's view of the occasion of Galatians does not determine how one interprets a significant type of phrase in the letter to the Galatians.

Structure of Galatians

These three commentaries offer good analyses concerning the structure and outline of Galatians. It should be noted beforehand that the three commentaries used here are all different to some extent in purpose. Longenecker (Word Biblical Commentary) is more scholarly and detailed while Martyn (Anchor Bible) and Matera (Sacra Pagina) are more general and focused for the general public.

Longenecker sees the structure of Galatians as follows:

1:1–5	*Salutation*;
1:6—4:11	*Rebuke Section*, with the inclusion of autobiographical details and theological arguments;
4:12—6:10	*Request Section*, with the inclusion of personal, scriptural, and ethical appeals;
6:11–18	*Subscription*.[6]

Martyn gives a similar structural outline that in its detail matches Longenecker:

1:1–5	Prescript
1:6–9	Theme
1:10—6:10	A Series of Explicating Theses and Supporting Arguments
6:11–18	Subscript[7]

---

5. R. N. Longenecker, *Galatians*, lxiii–lxxxviii.
6. R. N. Longenecker, *Galatians*, cix.
7. Martyn, *Galatians*, 24. Martyn is following R. G. Hall. See note 34.

Matera offers both a structural and content outline that is very beneficial in terms of following the content and argument of the letter:

The Greeting 1:1–5

A STATEMENT OF ASTONISHMENT 1:6–10

I. *The Truth of the Gospel 1:11—2:21*

1:11–12	Paul's gospel is not of human origin.
1:13–17	Paul received his gospel through a revelation of Jesus Christ.
1:18–20	The Jerusalem Church did not commission Paul.
1:21–24	Those in Judea glorified God because of Paul.
2:1–10	Paul defended the truth of the gospel at Jerusalem.
2:11–14	Peter betrayed the truth of the gospel at Antioch.
2:15–21	We are justified by the faith of Jesus Christ.

II. *The Children of the Promise 3:1—5:12*

A. ABRAHAM'S TRUE DESCENDANTS 3:1–29

3:1–6	The Spirit did not come through legal works.
3:7–14	The people of faith are Abraham's descendants.
	3:7–9 The blessing of Abraham.
	3:10–14 The curse of the Law.
3:15–20	The Law does not annul the promise.
3:21–25	The Law is not opposed to the promise.
3:26–29	Those in Christ are Abraham's descendants.

B. REBUKE AND APPEAL 4:1—5:12

4:1–11	Do not return to the period of your religious infancy.
4:12–20	Become as I am!
4:21–31	Expel the children of the slave woman.
5:1–12	Avoid circumcision!

III. Living by the Spirit 5:13—6:1-10

5:13–15	Love fulfills the Law.
5:16–26	Walk by the Spirit.
6:1–10	Fulfill the Law of Christ.

The Conclusion 6:11–18[8]

Paul's Defense of His Gospel—Galatians 1

Paul's introduction (1:1-5) and "statement of astonishment" (1:6-10) emphasize the *revelatory nature of the gospel* as coming from God alone and not from man, and thus should not be tampered with by humans: "not from men nor through man" (1:1); all of v. 4 as the divine work of God; emphasis on the "grace of Messiah" (1:6); statement of condemnation to the preaching of any other gospel than the one revealed (vv. 8-9); and Paul's sole desire for the approval of God not men (v. 10).

Paul says it plainly: "For I did not receive it [the gospel] from any man, nor was I taught it, but I received it through a revelation of Jesus Christ" (v. 12). Paul appeals to his own life experience to emphasize this *revelation of the gospel* (vv. 13-17). God had set Paul apart for this gospel even at birth, in spite of the fact he was an early persecutor of the church. Paul says that God "was pleased to reveal his Son to me, in order that I might preach him among the Gentiles" (v. 16). At this point he says: "I did not immediately consult *anyone* (literally, *flesh and blood*), again, emphasizing the revelatory nature of the gospel. From Damascus Paul went *immediately* into Arabia and only then returned to Damascus. After three years (some ambiguity here) Paul went up to Jerusalem to *meet* Peter and stay with him only fifteen days. Of the other apostles, Paul only saw James, the Lord's brother, not of the original twelve! With an oath Paul declares this to be true and then he adds: "Then I went into the regions of Syria and Cilicia [specifically Tarsus, Acts 9:30]. And I was still unknown in person to the churches of Judea that are in Christ" (vv. 21-22). Paul's opponents accused him of having a "second-hand gospel, being dependent on and subordinate to the apostles at Jerusalem."[9] So Paul has established

---

8. Matera, *Galatians*, 12-13.
9. R. N. Longenecker, *Galatians*, 39.

two truths: 1) his gospel came by revelation in his conversion/commission process, and 2) his gospel was not dependent upon the original apostles or Jerusalem leadership. It was from the Messiah himself!

The Visit—Galatians 2:1–14

The "after fourteen years" probably is concurrent with the three years in Galatians 1:18, to be counted from Paul's conversion. Paul recounted his second Jerusalem visit to help with the famine as predicted by Agabus and other prophets (Acts 11:27–30).[10] He made this trip to Jerusalem with Barnabas. Titus, a subordinate, is mentioned perhaps to emphasize Paul's ability to associate fully with both Jews (Barnabas) and gentiles (Titus) in preaching the law-free gospel. Additionally, Paul mentioned that his trip was the result of a revelation given to him. Perhaps this revelation is related to the presence of prophets having come down from Jerusalem to Antioch. The point Paul is making in Galatians is that he went to Jerusalem by divine revelation, not by human request. This theme is developed from the beginning of the epistle.

False brothers tested Paul with regard to circumcising gentiles before they could be considered "true Christians." Yet, Titus was not compelled to be circumcised and nothing was to be added to Paul's gospel as he preached it according to the Jerusalem leaders' estimation. Recognition that God had called Paul to evangelize the gentiles and Peter the Jews, the "right hand of fellowship" was extended to Paul and Barnabas by the "pillars" of the church at Jerusalem: James, Peter, and John. Remembrance of the poor was all that was asked of Paul—a project Paul took seriously during his missionary work (see Rom 15:25–26; 1 Cor 16:1–3; and 2 Cor 8–9). So far, all that Paul has argued for during this letter is that he has acted upon divine revelation not human impulse. But, now, Paul considered an incident that seemed to clinch his approach to the Galatians for their consideration—his dispute with Peter (Gal 2:11–14).

"But when Cephas came to Antioch" cannot be confidently placed, some arguing that these events occurred earlier than the Jerusalem famine visit (Gal 2:1–10) and some afterward. Perhaps Acts 15:1–2 alludes to this encounter and aftermath. This is Longenecker's assessment:

---

10. Some see Gal 2:1–10 as referring to Acts 15, the Jerusalem Council, but this is not my conclusion.

The Antioch episode most likely took place *after* Paul and Barnabas returned to Syrian Antioch from their mission to Cyprus and southern Galatia as recorded by Luke in Acts 13:4—14:25, *during* the time when "they stayed there [at Antioch] a long time with the disciples" as told us in Acts 14:26-28, and *before* the Jerusalem Council of Acts 15:1-29.[11]

Peter was the apostle to open the door to the gentiles when he witnessed the Holy Spirit come upon Cornelius and his household. Consequently, they were immersed in water in the name of Jesus (Acts 10:47). For that reason, Peter was in the habit of eating with gentiles, especially in Antioch where such table fellowship was shared between Christian Jews and Christian gentiles. But "certain men came from James" who apparently influenced Peter to begin to withdraw from such association with gentiles due to "the circumcision party." At that time, there was great pressure from zealous nationalistic Jews on the Christian Jews of Jerusalem led by James, the Lord's brother, to not associate with the heathen gentiles. (Verse 12 indicated that Peter had further compromised himself by having eaten a gentile diet!) Even Barnabas was led astray by "their hypocrisy."

Because of these events, Paul publicly confronted Peter because he stood condemned (before God).[12] Paul's rebuke (2:14) confronted the integrity of the gospel preached by both Paul and Peter. His rhetorical question has a bite to it: "If you, though a Jew, live like a gentile and not like a Jew, how can you force the gentiles to live like Jews?" (Gal 2:14c). The issue was the identifying marks of being a son of God, the most important being circumcision. Related to circumcision were the dietary rules that had characterized Jewish eating habits for centuries. Thus, it was very difficult for Jews to have any table fellowship with gentiles. For Christian Jews it was very difficult to overcome these customs of only eating certain foods and then only with the circumcised. Peter, Barnabas, and others knew better, but they did not do better, and so Paul calls them to account for their hypocrisy. This is the context of the first text dealing with the subjective/objective genitive debate.

---

11. R. N. Longenecker, *Galatians*, 71. This is a better scenario.

12. R. N. Longenecker, *Galatians*, 72. This word is stronger than just being "in the wrong" (NIV) or "not in step with" (ESV). See Longenecker's commentary. The pressure to cave in to the culture of the Jews must have been tremendous since some of the great leaders of the faith were led astray by their actions.

The Proposition—Galatians 2:15–21

Galatians 2:15–21 is compact and difficult to interpret. Yet, if one understands the Galatian letter to be a typical apologetic letter, then it makes sense to see this brief text to be the *propositio* (proposition) of the letter. Longenecker quotes Betz's analysis when he wrote: "In particular, 2:15–21 should be seen as Paul's *propositio* that 'sums up the *narratio*'s material content' and 'sets up the arguments to be discussed later in the *probatio*' (so Betz, *Galatians*, 114)."[13] In such a *propositio* there are points of agreement (vv. 15–16), points of disagreement (vv. 17–20), and a concluding statement drawing the brief statements together as a whole (v. 21). The following *probatio* (Gal 3:1—4:11) will argue in detail the brief statements of 2:15–21. In other words, the *probatio* is an exposition and argument for the *propositio* (proposition).

There are actually three possible subjective genitives in Gal 2:15–21, two with the phrase *pisteōs Christou* (v. 16 twice) and one with *pistei . . . te tou huiou tou theou* (v. 20). While almost all English translations of this text use the objective genitive interpretation (see NIV, NRSV, and ESV, among others), all three can be understood as subjective genitives. N. T. Wright translated this paragraph in his series of brief commentaries, *Paul for Everyone: Galatians and Thessalonians*, using the subjective genitive interpretation:

> We are Jews by birth, not "Gentile sinners." But we know that a person is not declared "righteous" by works of the Jewish law, but *through the faithfulness of Jesus the Messiah*.
>
> That is why we too believed in the Messiah, Jesus: so that we might be declared "righteous" *on the basis of the Messiah's faithfulness*, and not on the basis of works of the Jewish law. On that basis, you see, no creature will be declared "righteous."
>
> Well, then, if, in seeking to be declared "righteous" in the Messiah, we ourselves are found to be "sinners," does that make the Messiah an agent of "sin"? Certainly not! If I build up once more the things which I tore down, I demonstrate that I am a lawbreaker.
>
> Let me explain it like this. Through the law I died to the law, so that I might live to God. I have been crucified with the Messiah. I am, however, alive—but it isn't me, it's the Messiah who lives in me. And the life I do live in the flesh, I live *within the faithfulness of the son of God*, who loved me and gave himself for me.

---

13. R. N. Longenecker, *Galatians*, 82.

I don't set aside God's grace. If "righteousness" comes through the law, then the Messiah died for nothing.[14] (Italics mine.)

These three genitives (italicized) are very similar to what has already been seen in Romans, Philippians, Ephesians, and the rest of Galatians as the following list confirms:

Paul's Use of *Pistis Iesou Christou*
(subjective genitive interpretation)

- Rom 3:22 *dia pisteōs Iesou Christou* ("through the faithfulness of Jesus the Messiah")
- Rom 3:26 *ek pisteōs Iesou* ("the one *who lives* from Jesus' faithfulness")
- Gal 2:16 *dia pisteōs Iesou Christou* ("through the faithfulness of Jesus the Messiah")
- Gal 2:16 *ek pisteōs Christou* ("from the faithfulness of Messiah")
- Gal 2:20 *en pistei zō tē tou huiou tou theou* ("by the faithfulness of the Son of God")
- Gal 3:22 *ek pisteōs Iesou Christou* ("from the faithfulness of Jesus the Messiah")
- Gal 3:26 (P[46]) *dia pisteōs Christou* ("through the faithfulness of Messiah")
- Phil 3:9 *dia pisteōs Christou* ("through the faithfulness of Messiah")
- Eph 3:12 *dia tes pisteōs autou* ("through his [Messiah's] faithfulness")[15]

There are at least four possible kinds of genitives these phrases may be, two of which are unlikely. One unlikely is the genitive of possession (*pistis* belonging to Christ) which merges with the subjective genitive meaning. Another unlikely genitive is the *adjectival* (Christ-faith; or Christic-faith).[16] The two possibilities remain: either subjective or objective genitive. Grammatically either is possible.

---

14. Wright, *Galatians and Thessalonians*, 23–24.

15. While many scholars today question Pauline authorship of Ephesians, I prefer to see Paul as the author. Authorship is not critical to my arguments here for the subjective genitive, except to say that the Ephesians passage *sounds* Pauline.

16. See Cosgrove, *The Cross and the Spirit*, 56, and Williams, "Again *Pistis Christou*," 446.

However, before I argue for the theological meaning of the subjective genitive, let me review the semantic range of *pistis*. In the Introduction chapter, I suggested that *pistis* should be understood as "faithfulness," taking its passive sense. The semantic range can move from passive to active: faithfulness/fidelity, constancy, firmness, confidence, reliance, trust, and belief. The objective genitive requires the active sense of trust or belief. The subjective genitive can be either active or passive. Only the context can determine the decision. The active meaning of "faith of Christ" creates many problems for scholars and the ambiguity is difficult to untangle. "However, if one understands πίστις Χριστοῦ in the *passive* sense as 'the faithfulness of Christ,' it may readily be linked with Paul's 'obedience' theme in Romans 5:19 and Philippians 3:8."[17] While there is much resistance to this interpretation of *pistis*, Caneday has spoken to the underlying fear of those mostly from Protestantism:

> How one reads πίστις Ἰησοῦ Χριστοῦ depends on its significance or function within one's thought world, within a frame of reference. This may be illustrated by the fact that a primary reason for resistance against reading the phrase as "Jesus Christ's faith/faithfulness" is concern lest the Reformation emphasis on faith be undermined. However, to read the expression as a reference to Christ's faithfulness need not detract from the believer's faith, for everywhere Paul uses the phrase he juxtaposes another expression which unambiguously denotes the human response. Instead, it may be that to interpret it as the Christian's *belief in* Christ neglects important Pauline instruction concerning Christ's redemptive work.[18]

Most exegetes see Gal 2:16 as contrasting two modes of seeking justification: one by "doing" (works of the law) and the other by "believing" (in Jesus Christ). But if the subjective genitive is accurate, the contrast is between that which marks the true people of God and that which no longer does. "Works of the law" (meaning circumcision, dietary laws, and sabbath-keeping) or simply "doing what the law requires" no longer marks God's true people.[19] Only a faith response to the faithfulness of Jesus (meaning Jesus' obedience to the Father's will by going to the cross)

---

17. Caneday, "Galatians 3:22ff.," 11. Peter Enns also supports the reading "the faithfulness of Jesus Christ." See his unique contribution to these thoughts in *The Sin of Certainty*, 101, 221, 222.

18. Caneday, "Galatians 3:22ff.," 11, 12.

19. Dunn, "Yet Once More," 100.

now marks the true people of God. Thus, when Jews and/or gentiles respond to the latter by faith in Messiah, *pistis* becomes the mark of the new people of God, whether one understands it as Jesus' faithfulness or the Christian's responding faith. In fact, Paul interjected the statement in the middle of the two subjective genitives by saying: "So we [Jews] also have believed in Christ Jesus" (Gal 2:16b). Why? Because justification does not come by "works of the law" (Gal 2:16a, d). The last phrase of Gal 2:16 ("because by works of the law no one will be justified") is an echo of Ps 143:2, found also in Rom 3:20 (see chapter 2, "The Romans Riddle").

Reading these statements in Gal 2:16 as objective genitives is to read three statements in a row referring to "faith in Christ." To make sense of this possible repetition is much more difficult than to see them differently, that is, as two subjective genitives with the clear verbal statement in the middle expressing the fact of Jewish belief in Messiah (Paul being the foremost example). This fits well with Paul's arguments in Galatians as a whole. Determining one's identity as God's people is no longer based on circumcision (Titus a test case!), or food laws (Peter and Barnabas with others withdrawing from table fellowship with gentile Christians), or keeping special days. Justification for God's people is based on Christ's faithfulness to the cross (see Rom 5:1–11).

Paul wrote: "I died to the law" (Gal 2:19). How is this? He says: "I have been crucified with Christ, yet I no longer live but Messiah lives in me; but what now I live in flesh, I live by [the] faithfulness of the Son of God who loved me and gave himself on my behalf" (Gal 2:19b–20, my translation). The latter two participle phrases express the content of the Son's faithfulness—sacrificial love which went to the cross on behalf of all others. Shuji Ota has made this observation about Gal 2:20: "The phrase πίστις τοῦ υἱοῦ τοῦ θεοῦ does not mean "[my] faith in the Son of God" nor "the faith(fulness) of the Son of God to the Father," but "the faithfulness of the Son of God *toward humanity*" in the sense of Christ's being steadfast, truthful, and trustworthy as God's Christ."[20]

With this I can agree. When one reads Rom 3:21–23, it is evident Jesus was faithful, not only to the Father, but also to sinful humanity who needed forgiveness. Verse 21 clinches the idea: "I do not nullify the grace of God, for if righteousness (justification) were through law, then Messiah died without reason" (my translation). In other words, the contrast is between "the law" and "the Messiah's faithfulness," not between a person's

---

20. Ota, "Holistic *Pistis* and Abraham's Faith," 3.

"doing the law" or "believing in Christ." When both Jews and gentiles realize that the basis of justification is Messiah's death on a cross, the proper response is *pistis* ("trust/faith"). The human response is clearly stated in three, and possibly four, of the subjective genitive passages: Rom 3:22; Gal 2:16; 3:22; and perhaps Phil 3:9.[21]

Exposition—Galatians 3:1-14

Galatians 3:1—4:11 will unpack the dense statements of Gal 2:15-21, especially chapter 3. If the understanding of Gal 2:15-21 is correct with the subjective genitive reading, then one should expect chapter 3 to be consistent with that interpretation as well as to clarify much of what has already been said. Admittedly, my presupposition about the subjective genitive will have a bearing on how I interpret certain phrases, but this is done for consistency's sake and not for undermining any other view. If one can't be consistent throughout the epistle with the subjective genitive interpretation, then the argument may be in danger of being weakened or even defeated.

Immediately in v. 2, Paul confronts with a question: "Did you receive the Spirit by observing the law, or by believing what you heard?" (NIV, the same in v. 5; the ESV has "hearing with faith"). Those who accept the objective genitive interpretation have no problem with the NIV or other major English translations of the phrase *ex akoēs pisteōs* ("by believing what you heard" or "hearing with faith"). Even a Greek lexicon cannot express it any other way when it accurately suggests "preaching" for *akoēs* but explains the genitive of *pisteōs* as follows: "as the result of preaching which demanded (only) faith Gal 3:2, 5."[22]

However, a different understanding is obtained in Gal 2:15-21 if you read *pistis* as "faithfulness," according to a subjective genitive understanding. Thus, Paul is speaking about the "preaching of faithfulness" and all that entails as he explains in the remainder of chapter 3. Also, the juxtaposition is with "works of law" (ESV), not necessarily the NIV's "observing the law" in terms of some kind of obedience that brings merit. The contrast is the same as in Gal 2:16 where "works of law" is contrasted with

---

21. Although I have not quoted him, Chad Harrington from Asbury Theological Seminary has written an excellent journal article on Gal 2:15-21 entitled "Justification by the Faithfulness of Jesus Christ," 7-25.

22. "*akoēs*," in *BDAG* 30.

"the faithfulness of Jesus Christ." The context indicates this. In Gal 2:21 Paul wrote: "I do not nullify the grace of God, for if righteousness [justification] were through the law, then Christ died for no purpose." Now Paul reports on how he has portrayed the Messiah before the Galatians: "Before your very eyes Jesus Christ was clearly portrayed as crucified" (3:1b, NIV). In the context of the crucifixion of Jesus, Paul forces his question upon the Galatians. They know that they received the Spirit not by the marks of Jewishness (circumcision, foods, or days) or simply works or deeds of the law, but rather by the preaching of [Jesus'] faithfulness, that is, to the cross. Yes, we had to receive the message by faith and baptism, but that is not Paul's point here (see Gal 3:27). After arguing against all the possible renderings of this phrase, Douglas Campbell remarks:

> Ἀκοὴ πίστεως can speak directly of Paul's depiction of Christ if it is construed as "the proclamation of the faithful one" (that is, a genitive of content, and this particular content for the gospel is well attested elsewhere in Galatians and in Paul; a more literal translation would be "proclamation of fidelity," with an implicit reference to the text, "the righteous one through fidelity will live"). There is nothing objectionable about such a construal, while, as we have just seen, all the other more conventional suggestions are problematic in certain respects.[23]

I would object to Campbell's translation of *pisteōs* as "faithful one"; rather I would stay with the simple understanding of *pisteōs* as "faithfulness," which will prove valuable in chapter 3, for it is a "coming" faithfulness. However, Campbell's point is well taken. To refer to "faithfulness" is to refer to "the faithful one." Richard Hays put the contrast in this way: "The contrast is not between two modes of human activity (works/ believing) but between human activity (works) and God's activity (the proclaimed message)."[24] In Gal 3:3 the NIV perpetuates the idea of "observing the law" (i.e., "works-righteousness") by the use of the phrase "by human effort." But the Greek text literally reads "in/by flesh" (a dative). The markers of being Jewish (circumcision and diet) certainly could be referred to as "in flesh." Indeed, the marker of Jewishness is "in flesh" (keeping Torah), while the marker for the Spirit-filled Christian is *pistis*, understood first as Messiah's faithfulness (*pistis*) and then as our responding *pistis*, trust/faith in the Almighty God. Paul has completed a

---

23. Campbell, *Deliverance*, 855.
24. Hays, "Jesus' Faith and Ours," 5.

brief inclusion with the phrase "preaching of faithfulness" at the end of v. 5 (see end of v. 2).

In the next section or paragraph (vv. 6–14) Abraham is the paradigm of "faithfulness" in the sense that he "trusted in God and it was reckoned to him unto righteousness" (v. 6, my translation, quoting Gen 15:6). The catchphrase *ek pisteōs* is used no less than five times in this section. Twice the plural article is used with the phrase to indicate a *kind of people*. The phrase *ek pisteōs* comes from the Old Testament text (LXX) used in the paragraph (see v. 11): Hab 2:4b—"The righteous (One) shall live by/from faithfulness." My translation reflects the original Hebrew that uses the word "faithfulness" (אֱמוּנָה, *'emûnā*ʰ).

A sixth use of *pistis* ends the paragraph and it is accompanied by the article, probably referring to all the other uses of *pistis* in the paragraph. Once, the adjective *pistos*, "faithful," is used of Abraham (v. 9).

Campbell has already argued that Paul's use of Hab 2:4b controls the meaning of the phrase *ek pisteōs* and that the phrase is messianic in the sense that it is used to refer to the promised Messiah. Thus, the "righteous one" would suggest the Messiah, while "lives by faithfulness" would suggest his resurrection from death on a cross. Jesus' obedience to the Father's will meant a death on a tree (under a curse according to the law), but by being faithful he also experienced resurrection—he lives!

Campbell has also suggested that vv. 6–14 has a chiastic arrangement which helps one further in understanding Paul's emphases: "I concur that some such pattern seems unavoidable, with discussions revolving around Abraham (vv. 6–9 and 14) flanking statements about curse (vv. 10 and 13), that flank in turn contrasting, symmetrical quotations concerning life (vv. 11–12)."[25]

> A. Abraham trusted God . . . all nations blessed in you (vv. 6–9).
> B. Under the curse of the Law in disobedience (v. 10).
> C. "The righteous shall live by faith."—Hab 2:4b (v. 11).
> C¹. "The one who does them shall live by them."—Lev 18:5 (v. 12).
> B¹. Christ redeemed us from the curse of the Law (v. 13).
> A¹. The blessing of Abraham comes to gentiles by Christ's faith (v. 14).[26]

---

25. Campbell, *Deliverance*, 856.

26. Note should be made here that N. T. Wright sees these two Old Testament references as parallel, not contrasting. In other words, if one "does the Torah," that person will live by Messiah's faithfulness by trusting God's promises as Abraham did. See Wright, *Justification*, 125.

From the above, a new reading to vv. 7–14 is offered which is informed by the proposition of Gal 2:15–21 and the arguments of Gal 3:1–5.

> Just as [it has been written] "Abraham trusted in God, and it was reckoned to him unto righteousness"; note then that the ones from [Messiah's] faithfulness, these are sons of Abraham. But the Scripture having foreseen that God justifies the gentiles by [Messiah's] faithfulness announced beforehand to Abraham, "All gentiles shall be blessed in you," so that the ones out of [Messiah's] faithfulness shall be blessed with the faithful Abraham. For whoever are out of works of law are under a curse; for it has been written: "Cursed are all who do not abide in everything having been written in the book of the law to do them." But that by [works of] law no one is being justified from God; [it is] clear—"The righteous [One] shall live out of faithfulness." But the [works of] law is not out of faithfulness, but "the one who does them shall live in them." Messiah redeemed us from the curse of the law having become on behalf of us a curse, for it has been written: "Cursed every man who is hung upon a tree," in order that unto the gentiles the blessing of Abraham may be in Messiah Jesus, in order that the promise, [which is] the Spirit, we might receive through the [Messiah's] faithfulness. (My literal translation)

More Exposition—Galatians 3:15–29

This section of Galatians has peculiar vocabulary and grammar that lends itself to a strong christological reading of the text. First of all, the singular use of *pistis* in vv. 22–26[27] is controlled by its use in v. 22. The NIV and ESV translate the phrase as an "objective genitive" and it should read awkwardly to anyone who pays careful attention to the text: "But the Scripture declares that the whole world is a prisoner of sin, so that what was promised, being given through faith in Jesus Christ, might be given to those who believe" (NIV). It is difficult to comprehend how that came to be. "What was promised" is given through my faith in Christ and yet so that "idea" might be given to those who believe (a participial phrase). How can the "means" also become the "goal" at the same time? (This same problem was found in Rom 3:22!) The subjective genitive interpretation insists that these are two separate entities. I translate v. 22 in the following

---

27. I am following Campbell's five arguments presented in his *Deliverance*, 867–70.

manner: "But the Scripture has imprisoned all things under sin in order that the promise out of Jesus [the] Messiah's faithfulness might be given to those who believe." Hays translates similarly: "But Scripture locked everything up under sin in order that what was promised might be given through Jesus Christ's faithfulness to those who believe."[28] Hence, Jesus' obedience to the Father's will in terms of the cross (see Gal 2:19–20) is the "means" by which the promise has now come and been fulfilled. Those who believe can participate in Messiah's life and faithfulness. The participial phrase is very similar to the reading in Rom 3:22: "Indeed, God's righteousness [has been manifested] through Jesus [the] Messiah's faithfulness for all who believe" (my translation).

Secondly, in the next five uses of *pistis*, three of them are used with the repeated term "coming" (using two different Greek words for the same idea):

> v. 23a—"before the faith[fulness] came (*elthein*) . . ."
>
> v. 23b—"unto the coming (*mellousan*) faith[fulness] to be revealed . . ."
>
> v. 25—"but the faith[fulness] having come (*elthouses*) we are no longer under a tutor."

The Greek lexicon translates v. 23b with reference to *pistis* accordingly: *"that is destined to be revealed."*[29] It would be a strange statement to this *pistis* as my faith or believing somehow "destined to be revealed," but it would not be if the *pistis* involved was about the "coming Messiah." With Messiah's faithfulness comes salvation for the whole world, for both Jews and gentiles. Ota is right, Messiah's faithfulness is for all humanity!

The third observation is Paul's use of the word "seed," already used earlier in Paul's deliberations (see Gal 3:16 [three times], 19, and 29). In Gal 3:16 Paul identified the singular "seed" promised to Abraham as the coming Messiah. It is a strange argument to Western ears, but nevertheless, a good one where the Messiah is the representative Israel—the "seed" of Abraham—finally faithful to the Father's will. Paul has taken the term "seed" (see LXX Gen 12:7; 13:15; 17:7; 24:7) which in Hebrew is singular but can be collective for the plural idea (example is "fish" in English). In v. 19 Paul emphasized the "coming" of this "seed": "until when the seed should come (*elthē*) to whom it was promised." Campbell observed: "The

---

28. Hays, "Jesus' Faith and Ours," 4.

29. "*méllō*," in *BDAG* 627.

seed and the *pistis* both come and so both seem to be the same thing."[30] Note how the "seed" and "faith[fulness]" (italics) are interchangeable in the following passages:

> v. 16—"and to Abraham was spoken the promises and to his *seed*. It does not say,
>
> 'and to the *seeds*', as upon many but as upon one, 'and to your *seed*', who is Messiah."
>
> v. 19—"until when the *seed* should come to whom it was promised."
>
> v. 22—"the promise out of Jesus [the] Messiah's *faithfulness* may be given to those who believe."
>
> v. 23a—"before *faithfulness* came . . ."
>
> v. 23b—"unto the coming *faithfulness* to be revealed . . ."
>
> v. 24—"in order that out of *faithfulness* we might be justified"
>
> v. 25—"but the *faithfulness* having come . . ."
>
> v. 26—"through the *faithfulness* [in Messiah Jesus]."
>
> v. 29—"but if you [are] of Messiah, then you are of Abraham's *seed*, heirs according to promise."

Fourthly, the use of the word "promise" in Gal 3:16, 19, 22, and 29 shares in the use of *pistis* and *seed*. Campbell comments: "So the seed and the πίστις share the motif of coming *and* the motif of promise."[31] "Seed" and "faithfulness" are related to the "promise" and these are somehow "coming." All these ideas are integrated.

Fifth and finally, there is the fact that both the "seed" and "faithfulness" are single entities. They are spoken of as having already come as a single event. Once again, quoting Campbell: "Paul seems to be speaking here of a singular entity making a single arrival."[32] This would suggest a narrow meaning for *pistis*, Messiah's faithfulness to the Father's will takes him to the cross to shed his blood for the sins of the world (see Rom 3:25 and my interpretation in chapter 2).

---

30. Campbell, *Deliverance*, 869. This quote was in a Greek font even though it should have been in an English font. However, it was readable and I simply quoted what it should have been.

31. Campbell, *Deliverance*, 869.

32. Campbell, *Deliverance*, 870.

These single entities strung out throughout Gal 3:16–29 suggest that Paul interpreted them all as not-so-veiled references to the Messiah.[33] Yes, this chain exists! "If this chain exists—and there seem to be numerous good reasons for thinking it does—then 'the seed,' 'the coming one,' 'the promised one,' and 'the πίστις' are all merely different references by Paul to Jesus Christ."[34] Jesus, indeed, is the "seed" of Abraham through whom the "promise" is fulfilled that through the Messiah all the families of the earth would be blessed (Gen 12:1–3). It is precisely Jesus' *faithfulness* that has made the promise effective. The Holy Spirit has come upon all who have been baptized, having clothed themselves with Messiah (his resurrected life—Gal 3:27).

Galatians 3:24 now makes more sense in this light: "Therefore, the Torah became our tutor (*paidagōgon*) unto [the] Messiah, in order that out of [his] faithfulness we might be justified" (my translation). This verse should be compared to my commentary on Rom 5:1, 9 above. There, the text stated that we are justified *ek pisteōs* (Rom 5:1) and "by his blood" (Rom 5:9), an inclusion that echoes Rom 3:25 where God presents Jesus as a *hilastērion* (propitiation, or mercy-seat) "through [his] faithfulness by his blood." All these texts make good sense reading them as subjective genitives instead of the traditional objective genitives.

A Variant Reading—Galatians 3:26

Special attention to Gal 3:26 must be given because of its use by Barry Matlock to argue for the "objective genitive."[35] Matlock has challenged those who support the subjective genitive with various arguments in other articles.[36] On the surface this text seems to support the objective genitive contention in that here there is a *clear statement* of "faith in Christ" with the text translated: "You are all sons of God through faith in Christ Jesus" (NIV). The Greek text reads: *Pantes gar huioi theou este dia tes pisteōs en Christō Iesou*. There is an article before *pistis* and *Christō*

---

33. Ron Simkins suggested, via personal e-mail: "Or, perhaps not so much originally veiled references to the coming Messiah as promises and patterns filled to the fullest in the Messiah? Now looking back, it is easily seen as God working in patterns and promises toward a good God always intended to bring to fruition."

34. Campbell, *Deliverance*, 871.

35. See Matlock, "ΠΙΣΤΙΣ in Galatians 3.26," 433–39.

36. See Matlock, "Detheologizing the ΠΙΣΤΙΣ ΧΡΙΣΤΟΥ Debate"; also, "'Even the Demons Believe'" and "Rhetoric of πίστις in Paul."

is in the dative case following the preposition *en* ("in"). Matlock uses a variant reading from P⁴⁶, an early manuscript, which lacks the article, omits the preposition *en*, and changes the ending of *Christō* to a genitive *Christou*, to argue this is evidence that the copyist understood the phrase to be an objective genitive in conformity with the others, especially conforming this phrase to Gal 3:22. While this is an ingenious suggestion, it is not likely the case. Campbell has shown the difficulty of this argument with regard to the variant reading.³⁷ One could argue that the copyist was conforming a text that looked as though it were objective genitive to a subjective reading in line with all the others in context. But Campbell is right that the copyist is not that skillful of a reader of Greek to lean upon anything "he" has done one way or the other.

A parallel is close at hand with Gal 3:28b where it is translated: "for you are all one in Christ Jesus." The Greek text parallels 3:26: *pantes gar humeis heis este en Christō Iesou*. Thus, the phrase "in Christ Jesus" is understood to be used adjectivally, modifying the subject: "For all of you [who are] in Messiah Jesus are one [and the same]." If Gal 3:26 is read in the same way, the phrase *dia tes pisteōs* can function adverbially and thus instrumentally: "For all of you [who are] in Messiah Jesus are sons of God through the [perhaps translating this article as a possessive "his"] faithfulness." The use of the article is found in Gal 3:23 (twice) and 25, all interpreted above as referring to the Messiah's faithfulness.³⁸ There is no good reason to deny that Gal 3:26 is referring to Messiah's faithfulness as well. Caneday, in an early article, makes this conclusion: "It is *in Christ* that Gentiles are made to be God's sons, and this is accomplished *through the faithfulness* that God has revealed in Abraham's seed, who is Christ. So understood, Gal 3:26 informs Paul's earlier use of the same expressions in 3:14 (ἐν Χριστῷ Ἰησοῦ; διὰ τῆς πίστεως) and in turn the entire theological development throughout Gal 2:15—4:10."³⁹

---

37. Campbell, *Deliverance*, 877–78.

38. Campbell, *Deliverance*, 878. Campbell translates *dia tes pisteōs* "by means of that faithful one," but I prefer the term "faithfulness" throughout to help smooth the reading of the Greek text in Gal 3:15–29. I think Paul is thinking in terms of "the faithfulness" found "in Messiah Jesus" which has *come in a point in time (history)*.

39. Caneday, "Galatians 3:22ff.," 20.

A New Interpretation—Galatians 5:5, 6

One last text in Galatians needs some attention, especially since the astute observations of Hung-Sik Choi.[40] Campbell has also commented on this verse in relationship to the subjective genitive interpretation.[41] The NIV reads for Gal 5:5, 6: "But by faith we eagerly await through the Spirit the righteousness for which we hope. For in Christ Jesus neither circumcision nor uncircumcision has any value. The only thing that counts is faith expressing itself through love." It is clear that the NIV is interpreting the use of "faith" in these two verses as referring to human faith. The ESV does the same.

A look at the Greek text and context will help one to see better the "subjective genitive" interpretation. Translated literally, the Greek reads: "For we by Spirit out of faith[fulness] a hope of righteousness we eagerly await; for in Messiah Jesus neither circumcision nor uncircumcision is capable of something but faith[fulness] working itself through love." I am using the passive sense of *pistis* according to the Greek lexicon (*BDAG*). The phrase "out of faithfulness" (Greek: *ek pisteōs*) is the catchphrase from Hab 2:4b and is used seven times in Galatians (Gal 3:7, 8, 9, 11, 12, 24; 5:5). One must keep in mind that the Hebrew word in Hab 2:4b is אֱמוּנָה, *'emûnā*[h] ("faithfulness"). The context of three passages will help one to see clearly the "subjective genitive" reading: Gal 3:8; 3:23–26; and 5:2–6.

Galatians 3:8 uses the catchphrase *ek pisteōs* and quotes the LXX in a conflated form from possibly Gen 12:3; 18:18; 22:18; 26:4; 28:14. Paul wrote that the Scripture (Hebrew Scriptures) foresaw that the gentiles would be justified *out of faithfulness* by God and that God announced good news beforehand to Abraham: "All the gentiles shall be blessed in you." The phrase *en soi* ("in you") refers to Abraham's descendant(s) which Paul says is the Messiah (cf. 3:14, 16). Gentiles receive the blessing of Abraham by being "in Christ" (see Gal 3:26, 29). In Gal 3:14 "promise of the Spirit" is the Spirit himself, used epexegetically, "the promise, that is, the Spirit." Thus, the gospel as God's blessing of the gentiles through Christ, the one offspring of Abraham (Gal 3:16), is "good news of Christ" (Gal 1:7).

Galatians 3:23–26 has several unqualified uses of *pistis* with the article which seem to be in turn referring to its qualified use in Gal 3:22 ("in order that the promise out of [from] Jesus [the] Messiah's faithfulness

---

40. Choi, "Galatians 5:5–6," 467–90.
41. Campbell, *Deliverance*, 886–92.

might be given to those who believe"). There is no good reason to deny this use of the articles. The catchphrase is found in this context: "in order that we might be justified *out of faithfulness*" (Gal 3:24). Also, there is "justification" in common with Gal 5:5. Therefore, it would seem that the *ek pisteōs* of Gal 5:5 recapitulates the *ek pisteōs Christou* of Gal 2:16; 3:22; and 3:24.

Having observed above that *pistis* is the subject of "coming" (Gal 3:23a, 25a), it is a redemptive historical event. Paul is referring to the divine action of sending his Son—an Old Testament theme! Indeed, this is an eschatological event—the "coming" of a "Son," "Seed" and "Faithfulness" (see Gal 1:16; 3:19, 23, 25; 4:4). Another important observation to make is that when Paul talks about the "goal/climax" of law, it is Christ himself that is left (see Gal 3:13, 23; 4:5; 5:1, 13). Jesus has freed us from the law (Gal 1:4; 3:13; 4:5). Jesus' death changes our status (see Rom 5:6, 8, 10; 2 Cor 5:17–19). Thus, it is clear that Paul is describing the coming and revelation of Christ's faithfulness, an event, rather than the Christian's act of believing in Christ. Since in Gal 3:24 the phrase *ek pisteōs* means we are justified by Jesus' faithfulness, Gal 5:5 must mean the same.

Galatians 5:2–6 has a context that encourages the subjective genitive interpretation. The contrast is between two exclusive systems of justification: either the law or Christ. Paul even says that if one seeks to be justified by the *Torah* that person has been "alienated from Christ; you have fallen away from grace" (Gal 5:4b). Galatians 5:5 is about how people are justified: "For we by [Holy] Spirit out of [from Jesus'] faithfulness eagerly await hope of righteousness." One can see here how the mission of the Spirit works with the mission of the Messiah (see Gal 3:1–5; 4:4–6; and 4:28—5:1). The objective condition of justification is found in the "faithfulness of Christ." Of course, one must receive it by a responding faith (see Rom 3:22; Gal 3:22; Phil 3:9), but even in that context Paul talks in terms of an "obedient faith" (see Rom 1:5; 16:26). Galatians 5:5 is not describing the Christian's ethical life in the Spirit, rather "Christ's faithfulness as the cause and guarantee of the fulfillment of final righteousness (cf. Rom 8:23; 2 Cor 1:22; 5:5)."[42]

Of all Galatian commentaries, Matera is the only one to my knowledge which supports the subjective genitive reading for Gal 5:5. He writes: "*Ek pisteōs* (2:16; 3:8, 9, 11, 12, 22, 24) also has an instrumental

---

42. Choi, "Galatians 5:5–6," 480.

sense. The phrase should be read in light of 2:16, *ek pisteōs Christou*."[43] Or as Choi expressed it: "They fail to see that the phrase ἐκ πίστεως is an abbreviation of ἐκ πίστεως Χριστοῦ and that the two phrases have the same meaning when both appear in the context of justification."[44]

Galatians 5:6, then, "refers to Christ's faithfulness working powerfully through his self-giving love to humanity on the cross."[45] This idea is reminiscent of Gal 2:20—"I live by the faithfulness of the Son of God who loved me and gave himself on my behalf" (my translation). A strong point for this reading is that Paul never uses "human faith" as the subject of "working" (Greek: *energeō*). Paul is using the language of *power* in this verse with the use of *ischuō* and *energeō* in relationship to Christ (see Gal 1:4; 3:13; 4:4–5; 5:1; cf. 1 Cor 1:18, 24). Christ's death somehow is the key to the power of salvation (see Gal 1:4; 3:13). Campbell's comment about the word *pistis* in Gal 5:6 summarizes this verse: "Such 'faith', which is really to say 'Christ', should put itself into effect 'through love', just as Christ's act of fidelity in relation to the cross was a supreme expression of his love for humanity (see Galatians 2:20)."[46] The contrasts being made by Paul in these contexts indicate that the opposing, positive term is "faithfulness of Christ," not something human in terms of sinful human's faith.

Summary of the *Pistis* Word Group in Galatians

If the subjective genitive readings are accurate above, then a study of *pistis* in Galatians reveals the following: There are twenty-two nouns (*pistis*), one adjective (*pistos*), and four verbals (three indicative verbs and one participle). The four verbals have as their objects the following: 1) "the gospel" (2:7), 2) "in/into Messiah Jesus" (2:16), 3) "in God" (3:6), and 4) no object stated for the participle "to the ones believing" (3:22, presumably those trusting in God or Jesus the Messiah). The subjects for the four verbals include: 1) Paul (2:7), 2) Paul along with other Jews, 3) "we" (2:16), and 4) Abraham [Genesis 15:6] (3:6). What may be given "to those believing" (3:22) is the "promise out of Jesus Christ's faithfulness." That promise, of course, is the gift of the Holy Spirit. The one adjective is describing "faithful" Abraham (3:9).

---

43. Matera, *Galatians*, 182.
44. Choi, "Galatians 5:5–6," 482.
45. Choi, "Galatians 5:5–6," 482.
46. Campbell, *Deliverance*, 888.

It is now possible to say that of the twenty-two nouns, twenty may be translated "faithfulness," understood primarily as "the faithfulness of Jesus." The two left are possible references to "human faith" (6:10) or "a body of doctrines, i.e., the faith" (1:23). No commentaries, including Matera, offered any other suggestion. However, Campbell thinks that "such creedal formation postdates Paul by a considerable margin," and suggests that both Gal 1:23 and 6:10 should be understood as "the faithful one," referring to Christ.[47] The only "human believing" in Galatians are the four verbals, but one of those has to do with God "entrusting" the gospel to Paul for the gentiles. One has Abraham *trusting* God. One has Paul as part of a remnant of Jews *trusting* in Messiah Jesus. Finally, one has no object, but it is clear it is either God or Christ, i.e., *the ones believing* [in God/Christ].

From this summary of the *pistis* word group in Galatians, we can say that human faith in itself does not make one righteous or just. However, when there is complete trust in the obedience and faithfulness of Jesus, then that commitment places one by means of repentance and baptism "in Christ," or as Galatians states it: "For as many of you as were baptized into Christ have put on Christ" (Gal 3:27). That is how one becomes part of the family of Abraham—"heirs according to promise" (Gal 3:29c). Putting on Christ like a garment is saying that we must live the life of Christ (Spirit-filled, Gal 3:2, 5; "faithfulness" a fruit of the Spirit, Gal 5:22), having been justified by his faithfulness (Gal 3:24). As Tom Ewald commented: "We ride on the back of Jesus' faithful obedience into the kingdom."[48]

Romans and Galatians have taken a chapter each to explain the *pistis Christou* passages as well as the usages of the *pistis* word group. But there are two *pistis Christou* passages yet to be discussed, one in Philippians (3:9) and one in Ephesians (3:12). Examining the *pistis* word group in these two letters and the rest of the "traditional" Pauline letters in chapter 4 will reveal some new and fresh interpretations of several passages throughout these New Testament letters. The subjective genitive interpretation affects many more passages than previously thought.

47. Campbell, *Deliverance*, 893, 894. See especially his footnote on 1165, n. 148 and 150 where he says: "I push the christological envelope in Galatians as far as it will go, but see no reasons for not doing this, and suggest further that the resulting interpretation is actually stronger, because it involves no concessions to competing alternatives. Paul is both more consistent and more christocentric—surely good things."

48. Dr. Tom Ewald, longtime administrator and professor at Lincoln Christian University, was a reader for my final rough draft. His comments and critique are greatly appreciated.

4

The Other Occurrences

> "If the 'faith of Christ' is taken to mean Christ's obedient faithfulness to God, even to the point of death on a cross, then many substantial passages in Romans, Galatians, Philippians, and 1 and 2 Corinthians specifically refer to it and Paul's 'theology of the cross' is linked to it."
>
> —DAVID L. STUBBS[1]

Philippians

HAVING CONSIDERED SEVEN OCCURRENCES of the genitive of Jesus' name (or pronoun) and/or title with the word πίστις, *pistis* ("faith/faithfulness") in Romans and Galatians (Rom 3:22, 26; Gal 2:16a, 16b, 20; 3:22, and 26 [P[46]]), the idea of the subjective genitive, "the faithfulness of Jesus [Christ]," permeated the letters, and the contexts of each fit the subjective genitive readings very well. The more vigorously one interpreted *pistis* as "faithfulness," a concept of exercising faith over a period of time, the more it makes sense in various contexts, whether referring to the Christian or to the Christ ("Messiah"). To state it another way: "*Pistis Christou* usually takes on a subjective genitive meaning, which has implications for theology. The other uses of *pistis* are consistent with the first thesis."[2]

---

1. Stubbs, "Shape of Soteriology," 156, n. 44.
2. A suggested clarification offered by Dr. Carl Bridges, reader of my rough drafts.

Only two more occurrences of the genitive of Jesus' name (or pronoun) and/or title used with *pistis* can be found in Paul's letters: Phil 3:9 and Eph 3:12. While many scholars deny Pauline authorship to Ephesians, that argument does not affect this study of the subjective/objective genitive debate. In spite of authorship, I am surveying the entire New Testament for this idea of "the faithfulness of Jesus" as the basis for our own faith and salvation. The letter of Philippians will be examined first since it uses the title of Jesus, Χριστοῦ, *Christou*, after *pistis*. Ephesians will use a pronoun, αὐτοῦ, *autou* ("his, of him"), which refers to Jesus.

Philippians is one of Paul's most personal letters to a church he greatly loved and appreciated for its involvement and support of his ministry (Phil 4:10-20). Paul wrote from prison (whether in Rome or elsewhere such as Ephesus) and he was concerned about a potentially divisive issue between two women leaders in the church who had worked earlier with Paul (Phil 4:2-3). Paul asked a "true companion" to help these women work out their differences. This accounts for the major theme of a "joyful unity" running through the letter (see Phil 1:4, 18, 25; 2:2, 17, 18, 28, 29; 3:1; 4:1, 4, 10 for "joy" and "rejoice"). Paul began and ended the main theme of his letter with these verses: Phil 1:27—"Only behave as citizens worthy of the gospel of Christ" (taking the footnote of ESV) and Phil 3:20-21—"But our citizenship is in heaven, and from it we await a Savior, the Lord Jesus Christ, who will transform our lowly body to be like his glorious body, by the power that enables him even to subject all things to himself." Such behavior demands a humble spirit and a mind like Christ. Thus, Jesus Christ is our paradigm (Phil 2:5-11), Timothy and Epaphroditus are good examples (Phil 2:19-30), and Paul himself serves as such an example (Phil 3:1-17). Many do not live in "joyful unity" (Phil 3:18-19).

In Phil 3:9 Paul describes what behavior will qualify him as a citizen worthy of the gospel. Paul repudiated all confidence in the "flesh" (Phil 3:2-7). Now he shows what he values the most, that which gives life—Phil 3:8-11: "What is more, I consider everything a loss compared to the surpassing greatness of knowing Christ Jesus my Lord, for whose sake I have lost all things. I consider them rubbish[3] that I may gain Christ and be found in him, not having a righteousness of my own that comes from the law, but that which is through faith in Christ—the righteousness that comes from God and is by faith. I want to know Christ and the power of

---

3. Wright in *Justification*, 149, notes: "(*skybala*: students usually enjoy being told, which is the truth, that the best translation of this is 'shit' or 'crap', though the word can simply mean 'kitchen scraps' or 'garbage')."

his resurrection and the fellowship of sharing in his sufferings, becoming like him in his death, and so, somehow, to attain to the resurrection from the dead" (NIV).

As in most English translations, the objective genitive is taken for granted—"through faith in Christ" (NIV above). However, the subjective genitive reading does more justice to the entire context. Paul repudiates all human accomplishments (his whole past life as a *blameless Pharisee*), which were thought to attain a righteousness based on the Torah. Instead, Paul now is found to be in Messiah, not having a righteousness of his own that comes from the law, but that which comes through Christ's faithfulness, the righteousness from God that depends *upon that very faithfulness*.

I emphasize this last phrase which is a reflection of the Greek phrase *epi te pistei*. Foster writes: "There is virtually uniform agreement among all commentators that the last three words—a preposition and a dative construction—designate an act of human response."[4] Even those who support the subjective genitive in this phrase think that the last prepositional phrase is about human response. In spite of these interpretations, the article before *pistis* is pointing out its immediate antecedent as the "faithfulness of Christ." In other words, Paul is not commenting about the human response to such faithfulness; rather, he is emphasizing that he now has a "righteousness" through Christ's faithfulness, indeed, the "righteousness from God" *upon the faithfulness* or as paraphrased above: *upon that very faithfulness*. Paul is emphasizing the contrast between his own human efforts at a "righteousness" by adherence to the law, relying on the "flesh," and a "righteousness" that is from God based upon Messiah's faithfulness.[5]

"Righteousness" is not manifested by our faith in Christ (see Rom 3:21–22) as argued in chapter 2 on Romans. Paul's human effort is expressed differently in that he wants to "gain" Christ and to "know" him and the power of his resurrection, sharing in his sufferings, becoming like him in his death. It is possible that this last prepositional phrase is referring to

---

4. Foster, "Πίστις Χριστοῦ Terminology," 97. N. T. Wright also sees the last phrase and use of *pistis* as referring to our responding faith—*Justification*, 151 ("bestowed on faith").

5. Koperski, "Meaning of *Pistis Christou*." Koperski has a good analysis of most arguments for and against up to 1993 but ultimately argues for the objective genitive interpretation. In my opinion her arguments at the end are not convincing. I stand by my approach emphasizing the subjective genitive which puts the emphasis on Jesus' faithfulness.

the human response of faith in the Messiah, but it is best to see it as referring back to the kind of "faith" just mentioned: Messiah's faithfulness, the basis of the righteousness from God. The two uses of *pistis* in Phil 3:9 refer to the "faithfulness" of the Messiah. O'Brien's commentary on Philippians admits as much when he writes that the last phrase "could then designate either the ground on which God's righteousness has come to Paul, that is, Christ's πίστις" or, as O'Brien prefers, man's answering response.[6]

Besides the argument of the contrast between human effort and God's work on our behalf, George Howard makes this grammatical observation:

> The construction of πίστις followed by the genitive of a person or of a personal pronoun occurs 24 times in the Pauline Corpus not counting the places where πίστις Χριστοῦ and its equivalent appear. Twenty times this construction refers to the faith of Christians, individually or collectively, one time to the faith(fulness) of God (Rom. 3:3), two times to the faith of Abraham (Rom. 4:12, 16), and one time to anyone who has his faith reckoned to him for righteousness (Rom. 4:5). In all cases the phrase refers to the faith *of* the individual, never faith *in* the individual.[7]

Outside the Pauline corpus there are at least four references where the genitive of the person of Christ or of God is used: Mark 11:22; Jas 2:1; Rev 2:13; and 14:12. These, too, are to be interpreted as subjective genitives, as will be argued later. In terms of translating *pistis* as "faithfulness," one should always remember Paul is using the quotation from Hab 2:4b from the Septuagint and this is a translation of the Hebrew word אֱמוּנָה (*'emûnā*ʰ) which means "faithfulness/fidelity." Scholars have not made this point often enough. The use of *pistis* in the literature of the Hellenistic era plus the Septuagint includes ideas of fidelity, firmness, or faithfulness.[8]

In spite of my view that both uses of *pistis* in Phil 3:9 refer to Christ's faithfulness, there is the necessary human response to God's grace that is termed "trust/faith" (see Rom 3:22 and Gal 2:16; 3:22, as argued above). God's righteousness, that is, his salvation, is available on the basis of the Messiah's faithfulness to the cross (his obedience to the Father for humanity). People obtain a right status with God by an "obedient faith" that

---

6. O'Brien, *Philippians*, 400.

7. Howard, "Notes and Observations," 459–60. See this reference in O'Brien, *Philippians*, 398.

8. Bird and Sprinkle, *Faith of Jesus Christ*, 96, 99.

identifies with the Messiah (Rom 5:19; 6:1–4; also Acts 2:38). In other words, Christ's faithfulness is the means by which God is able to make righteous all who trust that Jesus is the Messiah and that God has raised him from the dead.

The verb *pisteuō* ("to believe") is used only once in Philippians: Phil 1:29–30—"For it has been granted to you that for the sake of Christ you should not only believe in him but also suffer for his sake, engaged in the same conflict that you saw I had and now hear that I still have." Paul equates "believing/trusting in him" with "knowing Christ" (Phil 3:10). Suffering is a necessary experience once one believes, for the Philippians (Phil 1:29–30) and for Paul (Phil 3:10). Trusting God is a major idea for this verb throughout the New Testament.

The noun *pistis* is used three other times in Philippians (1:25, 27, and 2:17), the first two perhaps meaning the "truth believed, the object of one's trust,"[9] which is O'Brien's preference. Philippians 2:17 has a slightly different nuanced meaning, "the life of faith," which is equal to the Christian's "sacrificial service." It is possible to translate this phrase as: "of your faithfulness." I translate it as follows: "But even if I am being poured out [as a drink offering] upon the altar [of sacrifice] and ministry [worship] of your faithfulness, I rejoice, indeed, I rejoice with all of you" (Phil 2:17).

At the heart of this letter is Paul's presentation (whether a quote from another source or Paul's original thoughts) of the humility of Christ, the model for all Christians (Phil 2:5–11). Paul bases his entire exhortation of humble service toward others (Phil 2:3–4) upon the action of Jesus—"becoming obedient to the point of death," that is, how Jesus "humbled himself"—"even death on a cross"! Paul is encouraging the Philippians to obey once again, using Jesus as their model. He wrote: "Work out your own salvation with fear and trembling" (Phil 2:12b). As suggested above, Jesus' humility became the model for Timothy, Epaphroditus, Paul, and then for the Philippians. All are to look "to the interests of others" (Phil 2:4b).

Jesus' *obedience* is another way of speaking of his "faithfulness" (apparently to God in going to the cross on behalf of humanity), and this "faithfulness" is how "the righteousness from God" is manifested (see Rom 3:21–22; 5:19; Phil 3:9). The exaltation of Jesus (Phil 2:9–11) is the means by which God's righteousness can be revealed. Paul seeks to "gain Christ" (Phil 3:8c) and "be found in him, not having my righteousness

---

9. O'Brien, *Philippians*, 140.

the one from the law, but the [righteousness] through Messiah's faithfulness, the righteousness from God [that is based] upon the [that very] faithfulness!" (my translation).

Thus, Paul's use of *pistis* in Philippians can have a couple of nuanced meanings: primarily "faithfulness" in Phil 2:17; 3:9 (twice) and "truth believed" (Phil 1:25, 27).[10] The verb *pisteuō* is used only once (Phil 1:29) and its object is the prepositional phrase "in him," where one learned that when one "believes/trusts in him" one should also expect to "suffer for his sake." Not many preachers today say such a thing to new converts!

Ephesians

Ephesians 3:12 is the one verse where a pronoun is used in the place of the proper name of "Jesus" and/or his title "Messiah." Most English translations, of course, translate the phrase as "through our faith in him," an objective genitive reading. The "our" must be understood from a Greek article before *pisteōs*. The KJV and Rhiems New Testament translate it "by the faith of him." The NET Bible and Common English Bible, more modern versions, translate it as a subjective genitive, as also Wright's New Testament translation: "his faithfulness." The NRSV has the subjective genitive reading in a note, not in the text. The Greek text is as follows using the subjective genitive: "in whom we have [the] boldness and access with confidence through his [Jesus'] faithfulness." In other words, the faithfulness of Jesus to the cross (Eph 2:13) brought about the possibility for all believers, whether Jews or gentiles, to have "boldness and access" to the Father's presence through the indwelling of the Holy Spirit (see a parallel in Eph 2:18). Closer in context to verse 12 are the appropriate comments by Foster:

> Ephesians 3:8–12 stresses what Christ has achieved on behalf of Gentiles, and it is this "mystery" which Paul makes known. Therefore, the key theme is the revelation of the divine plan which is linked implicitly to Christ's own obedience to the Father's will through faithfully accepting death on the cross. Such obedience results in the bestowal of riches, which in turn believers share and through which they obtain boldness and access by participating in this divinely inaugurated order.[11]

---

10. Of course, this interpretation goes against the references in *BDAG*, 819.
11. Foster, "Πίστις Χριστοῦ Terminology," 104.

But this is not the only place in Ephesians where the idea of "the faithfulness of Jesus" can be found. The verb form, *pisteuō* ("to believe"), is found only twice in Ephesians: 1:13 and 19. Both verses are referencing Christians believing in the Messiah. Verse 13 specifically is referring to the moment (aorist participle) when the believer obeys the gospel ("word of truth") in repentance and baptism (see Acts 2:38) and thus receives the gift of the Holy Spirit ("sealed with the promised Holy Spirit," Eph 1:13) as well as the forgiveness of sin. Verse 19 is a present participle, probably referring to the ongoing faithfulness of the believer by means of the power of the Holy Spirit, the same power that raised Jesus from the dead (see vv. 19–21).

The noun, *pistis* ("faith/faithfulness"), is used eight times: Eph 1:15; 2:8; 3:12, 17; 4:5, 13; 6:16, 23. It is clear that Eph 1:15 is referring to the Christian's faith, but even here, I would argue that Paul is speaking about the "faithfulness" Christians manifest in the Lord. Just as "love toward all the saints" is an ongoing experience, so is "faith in the Lord Jesus." It is not an action that occurs one time. As such, "faithfulness" would be the nuance of *pistis* in this context. The other uses of *pistis* can be argued for a more nuanced reading.

Ephesians 2:8 reads in the ESV: "For by grace you have been saved through faith. And this is not your own doing; it is the gift of God, not a result of works, so that no one may boast." My proposal is that this "faith" is referring to Messiah's faithfulness: "For by grace you have been saved through [Messiah's] faithfulness." That is why Paul wrote: "And *this* (neuter in Greek) is not from you." What is "not from you"? The whole salvation process whereby Jesus was raised from the dead and then was enthroned at the right hand of God to reign as Lord of lords and King of kings (vv. 5–7). Note the same phrase at the end of v. 5—"by grace you have been saved." What Paul means by "through faith" has been already stated in vv. 6–7, Jesus' death, burial, resurrection, and exaltation to the Father's right hand; in other words, his faithfulness!

This same thought was proposed by Markus Barth in his two-volume commentary on Ephesians when he suggested that "through faith" may refer to three possibilities: "God's faithfulness," "Christ's faithfulness," or "the faith of the saints." Barth's footnote (n. 85) on the first two interpretations fully supports the "subjective genitive" reading. Barth, himself, does not want to exclude any of the three possibilities, but he leans toward the subjective genitive reading when he concludes: "The 'faith' by which 'you are saved' would be no good if it were not first shown by God himself and then begun and completed on earth by Jesus Christ (cf. Heb 12:2)."[12] So when one places Eph 2:8 with 2:18 (a parallel to 3:12), there is strong evidence that Eph 3:12 should be understood as "subjective genitive," i.e., "through his [Jesus'] faithfulness."

In Eph 3:17 Paul is making an emphatic statement about the permanent dwelling of Christ in the believer (see also Col 1:19; 2:9). I propose that this "faith" is that of the believer, who invites the Messiah to dwell permanently within his/her heart ("the inner person" v. 16). This is most likely the meaning here. Yet, Markus Barth has an interesting, if not insightful, comment about this verse:

> The instrumentality ascribed to faith excludes the idea that the indwelling Christ and the person in whom he dwells might ultimately melt into one and lose all distinctive traits. Each of them has and retains his personality. Faith—whether God's, the Messiah's, or the saints'—presupposes a covenant relationship between at least two persons in which one partner trusts and is faithful to the other without trying to absorb him and remain alone on the field. The parallel words "through the Spirit" (3:16) show that faith is understood as a gift of the Spirit (cf. 2:8–9; Gal 5:22–23).[13]

Harold Hoehner wrote that we should not see this indwelling of Christ as occurring at a person's conversion: "Instead, it denotes the contemplated result, namely, that Christ may 'be at home in,' that is, at the very center of or deeply rooted in believers' lives."[14]

Ephesians 4:5 lists "one faith" along with one body, one Spirit, one hope, one Lord, one baptism, one God and Father (Eph 4:4–6). Since "baptism" comes immediately after "one faith," this *pistis* is probably referring to the personal faith exercised by Christians in the Lord Jesus the Messiah and God the Father of all (compare Rom 10:9, 10).

Ephesians 4:13 suggests possibilities of understanding differently from most commentaries. Hoehner argues for "an objective genitive" reading of *pistis* (the content of faith).[15] The ESV translates Eph 4:13 as follows: "until we all attain to the unity of the faith and of the knowledge

---

12. Barth, *Ephesians 1–3*, 225. See also 224 and n. 85.

13. Barth, *Ephesians 1–3*, 370. "Saving faith" is not necessarily a gift of the Spirit, but "faithfulness" as explained above could be. The so-called "gift" is simply God's gospel proclaimed!

14. Hoehner, *Ephesians*, 481.

15. Hoehner, *Ephesians*, 553.

of the Son of God, to mature manhood, to the measure of the stature of the fullness of Christ." Hoehner ties this statement about "the unity of the faith" to the "one faith" mentioned in v. 5. This is a reasonable analysis. However, Markus Barth thought Paul had inserted part of a hymn at this point, found nowhere else in his letters.

Barth pointed out that there are three references to a person in this verse: God's "Son," the "Man," the "Messiah." All three terms referred to Jesus. Each term is accompanied by qualifications: "oneness of faith and knowledge" (Son of God); "perfect/mature/complete" (man, *andra*); and "the stature of fullness" (Messiah).[16] The key to understanding this verse is understanding the verb: *katantesomen* ("we come to meet," "arriving at a certain place"). Barth argued in this context that the verb can have both political (1 Thess 4:15–17) and marital (Matt 25:1–13) imagery. The use of Ps 68 earlier (Eph 4:8) suggested the political usage, but the references to "husband and wife" (Eph 5:22–33) and garment imagery (Eph 4:22–24) suggested the marriage imagery. While Barth is tentative about this interpretation, his concluding statements are interesting:

> In conclusion, just as a king or bridegroom, by his advent and through his meeting with those expecting him, fulfills the hope and changes the status of many, so according to Eph 4:13 does the Son of God, the Perfect Man, the Messiah. He makes his people participants in his perfection and riches. All that is his become theirs. The transformation of the many, effected by the meeting with the Man, is in this case distinct from a gradual improvement. It resembles a sudden change comparable to the effect of forgiveness and sanctification.[17]

The Greek text suggests strongly that "the faith and the knowledge of the Son of God" is something that belongs to the Son. That means when we "meet" this One, Jesus, the "Son of God," his faithfulness and knowledge will become ours! Or as Barth expressed it: "To be specific, 4:13 appears to describe Christ's 'faithfulness' to God and his 'knowledge' of the bride."[18] As the church, the Bride of Christ, continues on her journey to meet the Lord, we are dependent upon his "faithfulness" and his "knowledge" of God the Father. Two texts outside Ephesians come to mind for this thought: John 14:10a—"Do you not believe that I am

---

16. Barth, *Ephesians 4–6*, 485.
17. Barth, *Ephesians 4–6*, 487.
18. Barth, *Ephesians 4–6*, 489.

in the Father and the Father is in me?"—and 1 John 3:2—"Beloved, we are God's children now, and what we will be has not yet appeared; but we know that when he appears we shall be like him because we shall see him as he is." Jesus' faithfulness and knowledge of God will be ours. His perfection or completeness as a man, perfect man, man as man was meant to be, will be ours. The standard of perfect (mature or complete)[19] manhood is found in the Messiah and it will become ours! "Jesus Christ is in person the perfection of the saints."[20] This will all take place at Jesus' *Parousia* (his Second Coming), if the interpretation of the verb *katantaō*, "come to, arrive at," is correct as stated above.

Ephesians 6:16, on the "shield of faith" that the Christian warrior is to take up and use as a defensive weapon against the "evil one," is another reference that can go either way: human faith or divine faithfulness. Hoehner, as most other commentators, see this "faith" as "the subjective faith of believers."[21] If so, it refers to human "faithfulness," not just the idea of "faith." But once again, Markus Barth, argues for a more nuanced concept of "faith" here, especially as it relates to the idea of a "shield," which in the Psalms is related to God. The Messiah (anointed one) may be called a "shield" in Ps 84:9. Barth wrote: "The same 'shield' which Yahweh is asked to take up in Ps 35:2 is to be seized by all the saints, according to Eph 6:16."[22] In a rather lengthy footnote Barth explains:

> The congruence of the terms "putting on the armor of God," "putting on the new man," "putting on Christ" in the Pauline exhortation (1 Thess 5:8; Gal 3:28; Rom 13:12, 14; Eph 4:24; 6:11–17, etc.), suggests that Christ and *his* faith can be meant by the "shield of faith." The allusion to Isa 11:4–5 in Eph 6:14 has clearly shown that a weapon of the Messiah is given to the saints; the allusions to Isa 59:17 and Wisd Sol 5:17–20 reveal that divine attributes are in mind.[23]

The "armor of God" is that which the Messiah Jesus has already "put on" to defeat the devil at his own game (see Heb 2:14). That armor is available to the Christian for his/her defense against the "schemes of

---

19. Ron Simkins opines in an e-mail to the author that to be like Jesus is "to be fully matured as a completed human."
20. Barth, *Ephesians 4–6*, 491.
21. Hoehner, *Ephesians*, 846.
22. Barth, *Ephesians 4–6*, 773.
23. Barth, *Ephesians 4–6*, 773, n. 91.

the devil" (Eph 6:11). Barth's comments are still relevant and possible for this interpretation.

Ephesians 6:23 is a peculiar text to end this letter: "Peace to the brothers [and sisters] and love with faith from God [the] Father and Lord Jesus Christ" (my translation). What is the meaning of "love with faith"? Barth suggested that "faith" is given priority over "love" by translating the phrase: "and above all, faith."[24] Hoehner acknowledged Barth's suggestions but dismissed them, and perhaps rightly so. Hoehner points out the theme of "love" in Ephesians and how at various places the author of Ephesians speaks of "love" and "faith" in the same context (Eph 1:15; 3:17; and 6:23). Hence, this "faith" is referring to human faith or faithfulness. Hoehner does state for v. 23: "In the present verse this prepositional phrase ['from God (the) Father and Lord Jesus Christ'] indicates that the attributes of peace and love with faith have their origin in God the Father and the Lord Jesus Christ."[25] This comes close to what was inferred about Eph 4:13; i.e., that Jesus' faithfulness becomes ours.

The adjective *pistos*, "faithful," is used twice in Ephesians: 1:1—referring to the saints who are "faithful in Christ Jesus"—and 6:21—referring to Tychicus as a "faithful minister in the Lord." The use of this little word at the beginning and end of the letter functions very much like an inclusion, deliberately used by the author. Tychicus could also be described as a "trustworthy minister" as well as "faithful."

The verb *pisteuō*, "to believe, trust," is used twice. Once, it is an aorist participle, "having believed" (1:13), referring to the act of conversion which includes obedience in terms of repentance and baptism, an "obedient faith." The phrase "you were sealed with the promised Holy Spirit" suggests this approach. The second use is a present participle, "ones who believe" (1:19), simply referring to "believers." God's resurrection power is available to believers who *trust* that God raised Jesus from the dead!

The noun *pistis*, "faith/faithfulness," is used eight times, three instances of which I would translate as "faithfulness" of the Christian (Eph 1:15; 3:17; and 6:23). Once, it is used as the Christian's initial confession of "faith" (4:5). Four times the word *pistis*, as "faithfulness," referred to Messiah's faithfulness (Eph 2:8; 3:12; 4:13; and 6:16), applying the subjective genitive interpretation.

---

24. Barth, *Ephesians 4–6*, 811.
25. Hoehner, *Ephesians*, 874.

Conclusion of the *Pistis Christou* Passages

Nine *pistis Christou* passages in the Pauline letters have been examined, expanded by use of a pronoun (Eph 3:12), the noun "Son of God" (Gal 2:20), and a variant (Gal 3:26 P[46]). The other references had "Jesus Christ" (Rom 3:22; Gal 2:16; 3:22), "Jesus" (Rom 3:26), or "Christ" (Gal 2:16c; 3:26 P[46]; Phil 3:9) in the genitive case after the noun *pistis* ("faithfulness"). All of these references were determined to be "the faithfulness of Jesus the Messiah," a subjective genitive interpretation. But it did not stop with these nine references. This interpretation affected the context of several other texts, which were related to the subjective genitive idea.

In Romans, Paul's reference to Jesus as God's Son, descended from David, and "declared to be the Son of God" by his resurrection (Rom 1:3–4), an early emphasis on "the gospel of God" (Rom 1:1), set the stage for the reading of the *pistis Christou* passages. Paul's goal for his calling as an apostle was to bring about "the obedience of faith" among all the nations (Rom 1:5; 16:26). These early statements helped reach a deeper understanding of Paul's theme statements at Rom 1:16–17.

In the gospel the righteousness of God is revealed "from faith for faith." This enigmatic phrase was interpreted as "from Messiah's faithfulness unto our faithfulness." This was established by the messianic use of Hab 2:4b—"The righteous [One] shall live by faithfulness." This means Jesus' faithfulness to the Father's will by going to the cross and giving his life for the sins of the world. God the Father vindicated his Son by raising him from the dead by means of the power of God's Holy Spirit. The argument for this helped to see that Rom 3:21–31 was a continuation and explanation of this theme. Not only were vv. 22 and 26 seen as subjective genitives (the faithfulness of Jesus Christ) but also v. 25 was seen to be the same without twisting the original Greek text to make it the Christian's responsive faith (as in most English translations). Paul's thought then flows accordingly: the faithfulness of God (Rom 3:3); the faithfulness of Jesus the Messiah (Rom 3:22, 25, 26); and the faithfulness of Abraham (Rom 4:16).

Even though the human response of faith was essential to receive the gift of justification (Rom 3:22, 24—"for all who trust/believe"), a radical reinterpretation of Rom 3:27–31 for "faith" being not human faith, but rather either God's or Jesus' faithfulness was offered. In Rom 4 Abraham "trusted" God's promise of a son and that trust was counted as "righteousness." Those who share in the faithfulness of Abraham (Rom

4:16), both Jews and gentiles, are now part of God's world-wide family, a family promised to Abraham in a covenant relationship (Gen 12, 15).

All the above allows us to interpret Rom 5:1 as "Therefore, since we have been justified by [Messiah's] faithfulness, we have peace with God through our Lord Jesus Christ." This makes sense with the parallel phrase at v. 9—"Since, therefore, we have now been justified by his blood." Paul created an *inclusio* in Rom 5:1–11 by using the phrases in Rom 3:25! In Rom 3:10, "None is righteous, no, not one" raised the question: "Who is the righteous one, then?" That question was partly answered by Rom 3:21—4:25, but ultimately it was revealed at Rom 5:19 in terms of "one man's obedience," meaning Jesus' obedience to the cross, already clearly expressed in Rom 3:25. The "righteous One" was Jesus, and by his obedience to the Father's will by going to the cross, his death was a justifying death for all who believe, thus making the believers right with God ("many will be made righteous").

Another key text in Romans was Rom 10:4—"For Christ is the goal/climax of the law for righteousness to everyone who believes" (my translation). Paul revealed the marvelous plan and purpose of God in bringing gentiles into the family of God (Rom 9:24), but he warned Christian gentiles not to boast and neglect the Jews as God's people (Rom 11:11–24). This is the "mystery" revealed regarding gentile inclusion (Eph 3:6) and the breaking down of the wall of hostility between Jews and gentiles (Eph 2:14–15), accomplished by Jesus' death on the cross.

When Paul finished his discussion of the gentile/Jewish relationship, it is clear that his statement "And in this way all Israel will be saved" included both Jews and gentiles (see Rom 9:6—"For not all who are descended from Israel belong to Israel"). God's family as originally promised to Abraham always included the "blessing" of gentiles (Gen 12:3; see Gal 3:14). That "goal" has now been fulfilled in Christ's faithfulness and those who respond in faithfulness, both Jews and gentiles.

Finally, the catchphrase *ek pisteōs* ("out of faithfulness"), which was the first prepositional phrase in the "out of faithfulness unto faithfulness" (my translation) of Rom 1:17a, helped to interpret the statement in Rom 14:23b—"For whatever does not proceed from/out of faith[fulness] is sin" (see chapter 2).

In Galatians the *pistis Christou* passages were concentrated in chapters 2–3. The key text for Galatians was found to be Gal 2:15–21, a *propositio* for the entire letter. It contained three parts: the points of agreement (vv. 15–16), disagreement (vv. 17–20), and a conclusion (v. 21). Thus, all that followed in the letter is an explanation in detail of this proposition. It is "the central affirmation of the letter."[26] Rather than have a triple phrase ("through faith in Jesus Christ") meaning the same thing (Gal 2:16), as most English translations do, the *pistis Christou* phrases should be understood as subjective genitives: "the faithfulness of Jesus Christ." Gal 2:16: "But knowing that a person is not justified by works of law except (lit., "if not") through the faithfulness of Jesus Christ, even we [Jewish believers] believed/trusted in Messiah Jesus, in order that we might be justified by Messiah's faithfulness and not by works of law, because by works of law all flesh will not be justified" (my translation). This made more sense than having triple statements saying the same thing—"faith in Jesus Christ."

Galatians 2:20 was best understood as a subjective genitive: "I live by the Son of God's faithfulness who loved me and gave himself on my behalf" (my translation). The latter two phrases explain the faithfulness of the Son of God; i.e., Jesus gave himself in death on a cross for the sins of the whole world (John 3:16). This approach allowed a closer look at the contents of Galatians 3, understanding the phrase "hearing with faith" (ESV) as "preaching of faithfulness" instead. Such preaching, of course, led the Galatians to an obedient faith in order for them to receive the gift of the Holy Spirit. It was not "by works of the law," whether that be obedience to the commands of the Torah or simply the covenant marks of the Jewish people (circumcision, diet, and sabbath-keeping). As in Romans, the catchphrase *ek pisteōs* is found in these chapters only, coming from the quotation of Hab 2:4b (Gal 3:11), a messianic passage as argued for Romans.[27]

The remaining *pistis Christou* passages (Gal 3:22 and 3:26 P[46]) were best understood as subjective genitives, especially Gal 3:22, since the human response of faith/faithfulness was expressed: "But the Scripture shut up/imprisoned all things under sin in order that the promise from/out of the faithfulness of Jesus Christ might be given *to those who believe/trust*" (my translation and emphasis). Because of this, Gal 3:24 was translated: "So then, the law was our guardian unto/until Messiah came, in order that we might be justified by/out of the faithfulness [of the Messiah]" (my translation). Then, v. 25 proclaimed that *pistis*, "faith," has come! That would make the variant at v. 26 make good sense as a subjective genitive: "For you all are sons of God through the faithfulness of Messiah [Jesus]"

---

26. R. N. Longenecker, *Galatians*, 83.
27. See Hays, *Faith of Jesus Christ*, 150–54.

(my translation). Thus, vv. 27–29 concluded Paul's argument by saying that all (whether Jew or gentile; slave or free; male *and* female) who are baptized (immersed) into Messiah have been clothed with the Messiah. All are one in Messiah Jesus—Abraham's "seed" (children of God) and "heirs according to promise."

In light of all the above, it was discovered that Gal 5:5–6 revealed not human faith working through love, rather Messiah's faithfulness working through love. Galatians 5:5–6 can be read with the subjective genitive in mind, noting the catchphrase *ek pisteōs* in v. 5: "For we by/through the Spirit from [Messiah's] faithfulness await the hope of righteousness, for in Messiah Jesus neither circumcision nor uncircumcision has any validity/meaning, but only [Jesus'] faithfulness working through love" (my translation).[28] Choi's arguments have convinced many that this translation and interpretation are correct, but all English Bible translations reflect only the human response of "faith working through love."

Beyond Romans and Galatians, only Ephesians and Philippians have a *pistis Christou* passage. Having translated Eph 3:12 as a subjective genitive, "his [Jesus'] faithfulness," it is possible to see Jesus' or God's faithfulness in other passages in Ephesians that are ordinarily viewed as the Christian's faith: Eph 2:8; 4:13; 6:16, and possibly 6:23. When the word *pistis* is used of humans (Christians), it can be understood as "faithfulness" or "trust" (Eph 1:15; 3:17). Twice, the adjective *pistos*, "faithful," is used: of the Ephesians (1:1) and Tychicus (6:21).

Philippians 3:9 was considered a subjective genitive, even twice, against most English translations. The latter use of *pistis* in Phil 3:9, *epi tei pistei*, "based on faith," may possibly be the human response of faith, but the subjective genitive was also a possibility. However, Peter O'Brien had a good argument summary: "In sharp and decisive contrast (ἀλλά) a different kind of righteousness is what Paul will have as one who is perfectly found in Christ when he stands before God's tribunal. This righteousness is different as to its origin (ἐκ θεοῦ), its basis or ground (διὰ πίστεως Χριστοῦ), and the means by which it is received (ἐπὶ τῇ πίστει)."[29] The question is whether Paul is emphasizing Christ's faithfulness ("based upon [that very] faithfulness") or giving the means by

---

28. Thanks to the work of Hung-Sik Choi, "Πιστις in Galatians 5:5–6," esp. 482–83. Choi's main argument is that only "God" is the subject of the verbal "working" and that the context would indicate that the Messiah is the content to "faith/faithfulness," thus, my translation as expressed above.

29. O'Brien, *Philippians*, 396.

which righteousness is received ("based upon faith, belief"). I preferred the former interpretation.

Beyond these two uses of *pistis*, Philippians only had three other uses of *pistis* (1:25, 27; 2:17) and one of the verb, *pisteuō* (1:29). Philippians 1:25 was the "object of one's trust," while 1:27 is a singular use of *pistis*, "faith of the gospel." O'Brien calls this a dative of interest or advantage.[30] The last reference of Phil 2:17 and its context suggested that *pistis* is "faithfulness" of the Philippians. "The sacrificial offering of your faithfulness" makes good sense in this context. Of course, at the heart of the Philippian letter is the great hymn-like presentation of Jesus as the obedient Son, Jesus Messiah and Lord (Phil 2:5–11). This text directed and controlled all the arguments and purposes of Paul for the Philippians as noted above.

Having completed the discussion of the *pistis Christou* phrases in Romans, Galatians, Ephesians, and Philippians, the rest of the traditional Pauline letters will now be examined in the following order for the *pistis* word group: Colossians, Philemon (to finish the so-called "prison epistles"), 1–2 Thessalonians, 1–2 Corinthians, 1 Timothy and Titus, and 2 Timothy (supposedly Paul's last letter).

Are there any other texts in the New Testament that may be interpreted differently as a result of this approach to the *pistis Christou* passages in Paul? Can this idea of "the faithfulness of Jesus the Messiah" be found in other letters in the New Testament, perhaps using different vocabulary or with different genres (such as gospel storytelling)? Is human faith more "faithfulness" than the idea of "faith" in today's English language and culture? These are questions to ask of the following traditional letters of Paul.

Colossians

The so-called "prison epistles" include Colossians, Philemon, Ephesians, and Philippians. Recent scholarship on the prison epistles has suggested an earlier date and different place from the traditional Roman imprisonment and the date of c. AD 60–62.[31] Now many are advocating an

---

30. O'Brien, *Philippians*, 152.

31. See Dunn, *Colossians and Philemon*, 39–41 and many others for the traditional place and dating.

Ephesian imprisonment sometime c. AD 52–55.[32] These are the two best possibilities for the prison epistles but not much is riding on these problems of place of writing and dating, as almost all commentators agree. Personally, I hold tentatively the Ephesian imprisonment with the dates as suggested, AD 52–55. This position best presents the scenario for Paul, the prisoner, meeting Onesimus, the run-away slave from Colossae and Philemon's household. Also, Ephesians, as a companion to the letter to the Colossians, was a general circular letter beginning at Ephesus. The traditional view of the prison epistles would place the Ephesian letter sometime late AD 62.[33] This goes for Philippians as well.[34] The strongest argument against an Ephesian imprisonment is that there is no direct evidence of Paul having been imprisoned in Ephesus. None of the above dates or places effects the *pistis* statements found in Colossians and in the specific letter to Philemon.

While Colossians is similar in many ways to Ephesians, they are not similar in the use of the *pistis* word group. The verb, *pisteuō*, "to believe," is not found in Colossians. The adjective, *pistos*, "faithful," is found four times in reference to people. In Paul's greeting he refers to the Christians at Colossae as "saints and faithful brothers (and sisters) in Christ." Immediately following in his thanksgiving and prayer, Paul praises Epaphras who served as a minister of the gospel to the Colossian community and certainly brought many to believe "the word of truth" and then to bear fruit and continue growing in Christ. Paul calls him "a faithful minister of Christ on your behalf." The word *pistos*, "faithful," describing Epaphras probably should be translated as "trustworthy," for he was not only a preaching, teaching minister, he reported to Paul how things were at Colossae, the good ("your love in the Spirit," 1:8) and the bad (deluded by "human precepts and teachings," 2:22). The latter is perhaps only a possibility if the Colossians do not remain faithful to what they already know and have attained.

---

32. See Wright, *Colossians and Philemon*, 37–42 and more recent commentaries supporting the Ephesian imprisonment and earlier dating. However, critical scholarship repudiates Paul's authorship of Ephesians and dates it quite late.

33. See Hoehner, *Ephesians*, 92–97. Hoehner supports the traditional view of a Roman imprisonment c. AD 62. He gives the arguments for all other alternatives. Of course, these dates have the presupposition of Pauline authorship.

34. O'Brien, *Philippians*, 19–26. O'Brien presents all possible views on date and place of writing and still supports the traditional view.

Paul's exhortations are wide-ranging and general in nature (Col 2:6—4:6), for he had not visited personally this community of believers. In Paul's final greetings he referred to Tychicus as "a beloved brother and faithful minister and fellow servant in the Lord" (4:7) and Onesimus as "our faithful and beloved brother, who is one of you" (4:9). As in Epaphras' case, so also for Onesimus and Tychicus, the idea of trustworthiness can be applied to these two. Tychicus was Paul's letter writer and trusted coworker (Acts 20:4), who will carry this letter as well as Ephesians and Philemon (Eph 6:21–22).

The noun, *pistis*, "faith/faithfulness," is used five times in Colossians. Two are used similarly: "your faith in Christ Jesus" (1:4) and "your faith in Christ" (2:5). Both of these references should be understood as "faithfulness" due to the circumstances in which their faith is exercised. Colossians 2:5: "For though I am absent in body, yet I am with you in spirit, rejoicing to see your *good order* and *the firmness* of your faith in Christ" (my italics). N. T. Wright has suggested that Paul uses military terms in this context to highlight this type of faith or faithfulness: "'Orderly' and 'firm' are most probably military metaphors: the church is drawn up in proper battle array with a solid wall of defence, namely, its faith in Christ. Paul is there in spirit, like a general inspecting the troops before a battle."[35]

Colossians 1:23 may be a reference to *pistis* as being "faithfulness": "if indeed you continue in the faith, stable and steadfast, not shifting from the hope of the gospel that you heard." On the other hand, this use of *pistis* may be similar to its use at 2:7: "rooted and built up in him and established in the faith, just as you were taught, abounding in thanksgiving." This would suggest the teachings about Christianity as a whole, i.e., what it means to be a Christian in both doctrine and practical living (the content of the letter to the Colossians itself!). However, it is a "faith" that must be held on to against possible attacks by true enemies of that faith. This will result in "faithfulness" of the believers to their faith!

One last reference, Col 2:12, is a different usage from the above. While it is in the same context as Col 2:5, the word is used in a different way: "having been buried with him in baptism, in which you were also raised with him through faith in the powerful working of God, who raised him from the dead." The Greek text has: "through the faith of the working of God the one having raised him from dead (ones)." Most commentaries interpret the phrase "the faith" as "your faith," and that is

---

35. Wright, *Colossians and Philemon*, 100.

possible. This would correspond with Rom 4:24: "It will be counted to us who believe in him [God] who raised from the dead Jesus our Lord." In other words, our faith is to be directed to God, the Father, just as Abraham's faith was directed. Our "faith" is to trust a God who can raise the dead, particularly, Jesus. So, somehow "faith in Christ" and "faith in God who raises the dead" merge and that is what happens when one becomes a baptized believer. Wright's comment is: "As in Romans 4:16–25, this faith is characterized not simply as 'faith in Jesus Christ', but as *faith in the power of God, who raised him from the dead*. To believe that God raised Jesus from the dead is to believe in the God who raises the dead. Such faith not merely assents to a fact about Jesus, it recognizes a truth about God" (Wright's italics).[36]

A possible interpretation makes "the faith" refer to God's faithfulness in terms of his raising Jesus from the dead. Hence, Col 2:12 could be translated: "having been buried with him in baptism, in which also you were raised with [him] through the [his, i.e., God's] faithfulness in the working of God who raised him out of the midst of dead (ones)" (my translation). The phrase, "the faithfulness in the working of God" may sound awkward but it is possible. This would not be a problem with either.

Philemon

Pistis, "faith," is used only twice in Philemon (vv. 5–6). It is peculiar in the Greek text of v. 5. The ESV reflects that peculiarity by translating it literally: "because I hear of your love and of the faith that you have toward the Lord Jesus and for all the saints." Read literally, it is saying that "love" and "faith" are directed toward Jesus and the saints. Taken this way, "faith" would have to be understood as "trust" toward the Lord and "faithfulness" unto all the saints. "Love" would not be a problem with both. Most English versions interpret the phrase to place "love" for the saints and "faith" toward the Lord Jesus. Wright suggested this solution: "Better to read it as a literary pattern in which the first and fourth elements, and the second and third, are matched up (AB: BA); i.e. taking A with A (love . . . to the other Christians) and B with B (faith towards Jesus Christ)."[37] This seems reasonable and adds clarity.

---

36. Wright, *Colossians and Philemon*, 112–13.
37. Wright, *Colossians and Philemon*, 180.

Philemon 6 reads: "and I pray that the sharing of your faith may become effective for the full knowledge of every good thing that is in us for the sake of Christ." Dunn revealed the many different interpretations offered by several English versions of this phrase.[38] Ultimately he concluded similarly to Wright: "The thought is of the shared experience of faith as a dynamic relation with the Lord Jesus which constantly fed their understanding and consciousness, making them aware of how much they were benefiting as a result."[39] The issue is how to understand the Greek word *koinōnia*, "fellowship." Wright wrote: "The key idea is 'mutual participation'. The whole phrase then means 'the mutual participation which is proper to your faith.'"[40] Both references are similar to what was found in Col 1:4 and 2:5: "faith in Messiah Jesus."

This concludes the discussion of Ephesians and Philippians on the meaning of *pistis Christou* phrases and the *pistis* word group in the remaining prison epistles of Colossians and Philemon. The rest of Paul's traditional letters include 1–2 Thessalonians, 1–2 Corinthians, and the Pastorals (1–2 Timothy, Titus).

First Thessalonians

Acts records how the church in Thessalonica started (Acts 17:1–9). For three weeks, at least, Paul, Silvanus, and Timothy argued in the Jewish synagogue for understanding that Jesus was the Jewish Messiah and that it was necessary that he suffer (by crucifixion) but consequently was raised from the dead. Luke reports that some Jews were persuaded. Many gentiles ("God-fearers") as well as several "leading women" were also persuaded and thus apparently believed and were baptized. This preaching infuriated the unpersuaded Jews of the synagogue and they attacked Paul's host, Jason and some of his companions, forcing him to pay security money that no more "disturbances" by the Pauline group be allowed. They had said: "These men who have turned the world upside down have come here also, and Jason has received them, and they are all acting against the decrees of Caesar, saying that there is another king, Jesus" (Acts 17:6b–7). Ironically, they got it right! But they refused to believe.

---

38. Dunn, *Colossians and Philemon*, 318.
39. Dunn, *Colossians and Philemon*, 319.
40. Wright, *Colossians and Philemon*, 181.

No one knows exactly how long Paul and his companions stayed with the new believers, mostly gentiles, in Thessalonica. It was at least three weeks, but more likely much longer, but not long enough to be assured of their complete understanding of the faith in terms of doctrine and their faith in terms of conviction and perseverance. The letters of Paul to the Thessalonians manifested his anxiety for them and his hope for their continuing faithfulness. After Paul, Silas, and Timothy left Thessalonica, they entered Berea where they were welcomed by the synagogue in contrast to the Jews in Thessalonica. Being chased by the Thessalonian Jews, Paul left his companions in Berea and traveled to Athens. Later, he settled in Corinth for a long stay (Acts 18:1–17). Having received reports from Timothy and Silas (Acts 18:5), Paul probably wrote two letters to the Thessalonian Christians from Corinth during his eighteen months' evangelistic efforts c. AD 51 (Acts 18:11).

Traditionally the second letter to the Thessalonians was a follow-up to some misunderstanding about the Second Coming of the Messiah and a few other issues. Recent scholarship has tried to reverse the order of these letters.[41] This critical issue will not affect my look at the *pistis* word group as used in these two letters.

The noun, *pistis* ("faith"), is used eight times in 1 Thessalonians, the adjective, *pistos* ("faithful") only once, and the verb, *pisteuō* ("to believe, trust") five times. I will comment on this usage in reverse order.

The verb is used three times in participial form to simply mean "believers" (1 Thess 1:7; 2:10; and 2:13), that is, "the ones believing." What one believes is partly revealed at 1 Thess 4:14: "For since we believe that Jesus died and rose again, even so, through Jesus, God will bring with him those who have fallen asleep." The object of believing is the death, burial, and resurrection of Jesus, thus his exaltation as Lord and King! The Thessalonian Jews understood what Paul was saying: Jesus was another king, the only true king (Acts 17:7). The fifth use of the verb is properly translated "entrust": "but just as we have been approved by God to be entrusted with the gospel, so we speak, not to please man, but to please God who tests our hearts" (1 Thess 2:4). The same idea can be found in Gal 2:7 (see also Gal 1:16).

The adjective, *pistos* ("faithful"), is used only once. First Thessalonians 5:24: "He who calls you is faithful; he will surely do it." This is a reference to the benediction that the "God of peace" will sanctify them

---

41. See Wanamaker, *1 and 2 Thessalonians*, 37–45. Wanamaker supports the "priority of 2 Thessalonians."

completely. Paul assures the Thessalonians that God is faithful and he will indeed make them holy and blameless (in "spirit and soul and body") at Jesus' Second Coming (1 Thess 5:23).

The noun, *pistis* ("faith"), is used in a variety of nuanced ways. In an opening prayer Paul uses a popular trinity of words: faith, love, and hope (1 Thess 1:3): "remembering before our God and Father your work of faith and labor of love and steadfastness of hope in our Lord Jesus Christ."[42] The idea of "work of faith" includes the idea of "faithfulness" in terms of its endurance in the face of tribulation. The Thessalonians believed in spite of "much affliction" (1:6) and thus became examples to all believers in Macedonia and Achaia (1:7). The word "work" includes the idea of the "results" of that work. As Wright expressed it: "It means thinking the gospel through, and bringing our minds and wills into line with it."[43] In the same context Paul commended their "faith in God" (1 Thess 1:8) which has been "talked about" everywhere.

Many of these Thessalonian gentiles had been idol worshipers and had "turned to God from idols to serve the living and true God" (1:9). "Faith in God" probably includes "trust," because the object of their faith is the expected coming of the resurrected Jesus who will deliver them from the wrath (1:10). They trust that God will do what he has promised in Jesus the Messiah.

First Thessalonians 3:2 reports how Timothy was sent by Paul from Athens to "establish and exhort" them in their faith. Exercising faith in the midst of affliction includes the idea of "faithfulness" (3:3–4). Paul writes: "For this reason, when I could bear it no longer, I sent to learn about your faith, for fear that somehow the tempter had tempted you and our labor would be in vain" (1 Thess 3:5). If they proved to be unfaithful, Paul would have considered his labor to be in vain. Paul was seeking to learn that the Thessalonians' faithfulness and love were true (1 Thess 3:6–7). Paul explained their "faithfulness" as "standing fast in the Lord" (v. 8b).

The next use of *pistis* is interesting. Paul ended his long introduction and prayer for the Thessalonians as he wrote: "as we pray most earnestly night and day that we may see you face to face and supply what is lacking in your faith" (3:10). Paul knew they were not through with the afflictions

---

42. The most popular use of this trinity is found at 1 Cor 13:13. But see also 1 Thess 5:8; Rom 5:1–5; Gal 5:5–6 (see my interpretation!); Col 1:4–5; Eph 4:2–5; Heb 6:10–12; 10:22–24; 1 Pet 1:3–8, 21–22.

43. Wright, *Galatians and Thessalonians*, 90.

that had come their way in the face of believing and trusting in Jesus. Therefore, he was anxious to come to them and "supply anything that may be needed to make their faith (in all senses: belief, trust, faithfulness and loyalty) grow yet stronger and stand firm for the future."[44] They have much to learn about "the Christian way of life" and that is the content of 1 Thess 4:1—5:22.[45]

The last use of *pistis* in 1 Thessalonians has an Old Testament background. "But since we belong to the day, let us be sober, having put on the breastplate of faith and love, and for a helmet the hope of salvation" (1 Thess 5:8). Paul used the ideas from Isaiah 59:17, except that the "breastplate of righteousness" (see Eph 6:14) is changed to "faith and love." By this means Paul is able to close his letter by another use of the triad of the words faith, love, and hope (see 1:3 for the same order!). "Faith" should be understood as "faithfulness," as argued for the use of *pistis* in 1 Thess 1:3 (above). In terms of referencing Isaiah 59:17, Wanamaker comments:

> This is probably why Paul does not add a third item of armor to his formulation even though he uses the triad of faith, love, and hope, which would have fit more neatly with three items of armor (cf. Eph. 6:14–17, which develops the theme of Is. 59:17 more explicitly as other items of equipment are added to the original two; each item is then correlated with a particular Christian virtue or concept). Paul has only used Is. 59:17 as a point of departure, applying an image used exclusively of God in that text to himself and his readers. He does so by modifying the characteristics associated with the two pieces of armor to conform to the Christian triad of faith, love, and hope. The original connection of salvation with the helmet of God in Is. 59:17 may have suggested to Paul the possibility of using the imagery of armor in this context in the first place.[46]

If Galatians is Paul's first letter c. AD 48 (in terms of the canon, see our discussion above on Galatians), then 1–2 Thessalonians would have been among Paul's earliest letters (c. AD 51) to a mainly gentile audience. First Thessalonians certainly includes the idea of "faithfulness" for most of its use of *pistis* (1 Thess 1:3; 3:2, 5, 6, 7, 10; 5:8).

---

44. Wright, *Galatians and Thessalonians*, 112–13.
45. Wanamaker, *1 and 2 Thessalonians*, 139.
46. Wanamaker, *1 and 2 Thessalonians*, 186.

Second Thessalonians

One expects that Paul's use of the *pistis* word group would be similar if not the same in 2 Thessalonians—and that proves true. The verb *pisteuō* ("to believe") is used four times, the adjective *pistos* ("faithful") once, and the noun, *pistis* ("faith"), five times.

The adjective *pistos* ("faithful") describes the Lord (2 Thess 3:3), rather than God as in 1 Thessalonians (1 Thess 5:24). Note the verse: "But the Lord is faithful. He will establish you and guard you against the evil one" (2 Thess 3:3). The context indicates that "the Lord" is Jesus himself, perhaps to be understood as "the Spirit of the Lord" (see 2 Thess 3:1–5). He is the one who will establish [them in their faithfulness] and guard the Thessalonians against the evil one (3:3b).

The verb *pisteuō* ("to believe") is found twice in 2 Thess 1:10: "when he comes on that day to be glorified in his saints, and to be marveled at among all who have believed, because our testimony to you was believed." The first use is equivalent to the term "believers" (see 1 Thess 1:7; 2:10, 13 in the use of the participle). The second use is simply a past tense but has the idea of "trust" in regard to the apostle's testimony. They trusted the word of the apostle Paul and his companions, Silas and Timothy, and accepted it as "the word of the Lord" (3:1; also 1 Thess 2:13). Second Thessalonians 2:11–12 is referring to unbelievers who have "pleasure in unrighteousness." Paul wrote: "Therefore God sends them a strong delusion, so that they may believe what is false, in order that all may be condemned who did not believe the truth but had pleasure in unrighteousness." Thus, two verb references are to faithful Christians (2 Thess 1:10) and two to those deceived by the lawless one (2 Thess 2:8–12).

The noun *pistis* ("faith") is used similarly as in 1 Thessalonians. The idea of "faithfulness" is clearly included in the word *pistis* in 2 Thess 1:3–4. Paul commended them because their "faith" was "growing abundantly" (2 Thess 1:3). Perhaps "faith" here included the whole of the Christian life, including faithfulness. Clearly the second use includes the idea of faithfulness: "Therefore we ourselves boast about you in the churches of God for your steadfastness and faith in all your persecutions and in the afflictions that you are enduring" (2 Thess 1:4). Steadfastness or endurance accompanies this faith, including persecutions and afflictions. Enduring these things, this faith is to be understood as "faithfulness," faith exercised over a long period of time under duress. This is exactly what the Thessalonians experienced. The use of faith at 2 Thess 1:11 is similar if not the same as at 1 Thess 1:3: "work of faith by his power." God's power enabled the Thessalonians to persevere in faithfulness, a faithfulness Paul called "every work of faith."

By contrast Paul used *pistis* in 2 Thess 2:13 to refer to "belief in the truth." This is what Greek scholars would call the "objective genitive" use. The object of "believing" is the truth of the gospel. Finally, the use of *pistis* at 2 Thess 3:2 indicates "faithfulness" in spite of English translations: "and that we may be delivered from wicked and evil men. For not all have faith." I contend that the meaning of *pistis* in this context is "faithfulness." The Greek text does not have the word "have." It does have the article before it, but this would not preclude the phrase being translated as follows: "Faithfulness is not [the response] of all to the word of God. But the Lord is faithful. He will establish you and guard you against the evil one" (ESV with my change in v. 2b).[47] In a sense, to "have faith" is to "have faithfulness" as well as to "be faithful." In 2 Thessalonians four of the uses of *pistis* should include the idea of "faithfulness" (1:3, 4, 11; 3:2), while only one has the idea of "believing/trusting in the truth" (2:13).

First Corinthians

Paul wrote 1 Corinthians toward the end of his three-year ministry in Ephesus (1 Cor 16:5–9), probably in the spring of AD 54/55, just before Pentecost (1 Cor 16:8). Paul had a vigorous and a riotous ministry in Ephesus at the time (Acts 19:21–22 and context). He had sent Timothy and Erastus into Macedonia before he himself would follow, probably in Philippi when he wrote 2 Corinthians.[48] Paul had invested himself in Corinth for a year and a half because the Lord had revealed to him the fact that many would respond to the gospel in that city (Acts 18:9–11). Paul had the help of Aquila and Priscilla and later the great apologist Apollos

---

47. Wanamaker, *1 and 2 Thessalonians*, 275. Wanamaker's "faith" should be translated "faithfulness." Wanamaker goes on to say: "ἡ πίστις probably does not mean 'the faith' in the sense of the peculiarly Christian set of beliefs. Rather, it refers to the act of believing or trusting in the gospel of salvation. As Best (326) points out, this interpretation of the word leads more naturally to v. 3, where πίστος is used in the sense of 'faithfulness,'" *1 and 2 Thessalonians*, 275, 276. I would say that *pistin* in v. 2 should be "faithfulness" and *pistos* in v. 3 should be as is, "faithful," in describing the Lord.

48. Most interpreters understand that Paul had written a letter before the 1 Corinthians correspondence (1 Cor 5:9) and then wrote a "harsh letter" before the 2 Corinthians letter (2 Cor 2:3–4), hence four letters of which we have two in the canon of the New Testament.

(Acts 18:24—19:1; 1 Cor 1:12; 3:4–6, 22; 4:6; 16:12). In the latter part of Paul's three-year ministry in Corinth (Acts 20:31), Paul had written his first letter to Corinth about sexual immorality (1 Cor 5:9; also 5:1–13; 6:12–20). Later, he received an oral report from Chloe's household (1 Cor 1:11) that there were divisions among the house churches in Corinth (1 Cor 1–4). The arrogance of some even tolerated sexual immorality and engaged in public lawsuits against fellow Christians (1 Cor 5–6). At the same time a "letter" was received by Paul about some questions the Corinthians had concerning marriage, divorce, eating meat that had been sacrificed to pagan idols, idolatry itself, order within public worship, and use and misuse of spiritual gifts. This letter's concerns can be discerned by Paul's use of *peri de*, "now concerning" (see 1 Cor 7:1, 25; 8:1; 12:1; 16:1, 12; also see 11:3, 17).

Finally, Paul will address the fact that some in Corinth were denying the resurrection from the dead, a long and informative argument for the resurrection of Jesus as well as for Christians at his Second Coming (1 Cor 15). In this pastoral and occasional letter Paul addressed a people whom he loved, and he wanted them to overcome all problems (as recounted above) by exercising true love toward one another and toward God (1 Cor 13). In light of the context above one would expect the *pistis* word group to be manifested greatly. This is partly true. The noun, *pistis*, "faith," is found first at 1 Cor 2:5 but not used again until 12:9 and following for five more times. The use of this word is not uniform in 1 Corinthians.[49]

Paul emphasized that his preaching to the Corinthians did not come from human wisdom or lofty speech, such as abounded in Corinth at the time, but rather he came "in weakness and in fear and much trembling, and my speech and my message were not in plausible words of wisdom, but in demonstration of the Spirit and of power, that your faith might not rest in the wisdom of men but in the power of God" (1 Cor 2:3–5). This "faith" has the strong sense of trust and fidelity toward a divine message. As Thiselton commented: "It means a mind-set which includes both an

---

49. Thiselton, *First Epistle to the Corinthians*, 223. He wrote: "It would be a mistake to define πίστις, faith, apart from a given context in which this term functions. Elsewhere I have described it as 'a polymorphous concept' . . . since any attempt at an abstract definition encounters contexts which will not match some *single* meaning or 'essence' of the term."

intellectual conviction of truth ... and a stance of heart and will which exhibits trust in God's salvific act in Christ as the basis of life."[50]

Previously to this use of *pistis*, Paul had written that God had chosen what is "foolish," "weak," and "low and despised" so that no one can boast in "the presence of God" (see 1 Cor 1:26–31). Rather, by being in Christ Jesus, he has become to us "wisdom from God, righteousness and sanctification and redemption" (1 Cor 1:30). Jesus is the very incarnation of true "wisdom," what the Jews in the first century understood as "a quasi-independent power, as in Proverbs 1–9, Ben-Sira 24 and the Wisdom of Solomon, going out to create a beautiful world, to enable humans to be genuinely and gloriously human, and to live, in particular, in Israel, in the temple, in and through the Torah."[51]

Jesus has become "wisdom" to the Christian and abundantly more. "Righteousness" is the status every Christian has by virtue of being "in Christ." "Sanctification" is the ongoing work of God upon his people by means of the Holy Spirit to be holy, both individually and corporately. "Redemption" is the great "exodus event" for every believer, both in the present and in the future return of the Messiah. N. T. Wright is instructive at this point: "The fact that the three nouns not only carry different meanings but are also different sorts of things—broadly, a status, a process and an event—indicates that Paul is not here trying to make a precise theological statement about what exactly it means that the Messiah has 'become for them' any of these things, or how each of them relates to the primary attribute, 'wisdom.'"[52] Thus, Paul's use of *pistis* in 2:5 included at least the idea of trust and fidelity to the gospel ("Jesus Christ and him crucified," 1:2b), since this "faith" rests "in the power of God." Since the gospel has a divine source, Christians must show *faithfulness* to it! After 1 Cor 2:5 Paul did not use the noun, *pistis*, again until 1 Cor 12:9, and then in a very different context.

In 1 Cor 12 Paul wrote about the issue of spiritual gifts—"Now concerning spiritual gifts" (1 Cor 12:1a). Paul listed various gifts of the Spirit that enhanced the growth of the body of Christ such as wisdom, knowledge, faith, healing power, miracles, prophecy, ability to distinguish between spirits, various kinds of tongues, and the interpretation of tongues. Third on this list Paul included "faith"—"to another faith by

---

50. Thiselton, *First Epistle to the Corinthians*, 223.
51. Wright, *Justification*, 155.
52. Wright, *Justification*, 156.

the same Spirit." This cannot be referring to the "faith" that all believers have toward God and the gospel of Jesus Christ. Rather, it is a spiritual gift given to an individual who exercises it for the benefit of the whole church, the body of Christ. This kind of gift of faith leads to "prodigious acts of faith, such as 'faith to move mountains,' whatever the metaphorical status of this image (Matt 17:20; 1 Cor 13:2)."[53] Paul seemed to be using this same idea for "faith" as a spiritual gift at 1 Cor 13:2—"And if I have prophetic powers, and understand all mysteries and all knowledge, and if I have all faith, so as to remove mountains, but have not love, I am nothing." In this context Paul concluded: "So now faith, hope, and love abide, these three; but the greatest of these is love" (1 Cor 13:13). How does "faith" abide? Thiselton attempts to help us here by quoting Barrett and adding his own commentary:

> Our question is, rather, Paul's meaning *in this present context.* Barrett assists us here. Faith ceases, he argues, if the context is that of what he calls "miracle-working faith" in 13:2. But in the sense used when Paul asserts "whatever is not of faith is sin" (Rom 14:23), "the life of the age to come will rest on faith as completely as does the Christian life now." Similarly, unless we conceive of heaven as a "closed" or static state, the openness of the heavenly life towards the future maintains the relevance of hope.[54]

Thus, Thiselton argues that "faith" and "hope" will be exercised in the so-called "heavenly life" (I would say on "the new heavens and the new earth") as much as love will be. While Thiselton and Barrett's arguments are possible, it seems best to say that faith and hope are realized in the life to come. We no longer see through a glass darkly. What has been hoped and believed are there realized! Love can continue since it has eternal qualities, but this does not seem to be the same for the future of faith and hope.

In 1 Cor 15:14, 17, Paul used "faith" in its normal understanding of "believing" that God had raised Jesus from the dead and that Jesus appeared to many for forty days until his ascension to the right hand of God. Paul provoked the Corinthians by proposing the opposite: "If Christ has not been raised" (v. 14). If Christ has not been raised from the dead, then "your faith is in vain," and "your faith is futile" (vv. 14, 17). "In vain" basically means "empty." There is nothing to our faith if

---

53. Thiselton, *First Epistle to the Corinthians*, 946.
54. Thiselton, *First Epistle to the Corinthians*, 1073.

Jesus has not been raised. "Futile" suggests "lack of content."⁵⁵ Whenever Paul mentions his gospel to be "Jesus Christ and him crucified" (1 Cor 2:2b), he actually never preaches this gospel without mentioning the resurrection of Jesus. "Christ's death alone has no atoning, redemptive, or liberating effect in relation to human sin."⁵⁶ The resurrection of Jesus is the foundational teaching of Christianity. Without it there is no "faith" and no Christianity.

Finally, in Paul's final instructions to the Corinthians, he wrote: "stand firm in the faith" (1 Cor 16:13). In other words, be faithful! While Paul emphasized "love" in these final words (vv. 14, 22, 24), he wanted them above all to be faithful to the gospel and to exhibit faithfulness to the God who raised Jesus from the dead.

The adjective, *pistos*, "faithful," was used throughout the letter in a similar fashion to mean "trustworthy." Twice, Paul wrote that "God is faithful" (1:9; 10:13). Paul considered himself and other apostles as stewards and then wrote: "Moreover, it is required of stewards that they be found trustworthy" (1 Cor 4:2). In the same context the ESV translates *pistos* as "faithful" when Paul referred to his beloved servant, Timothy: "That is why I sent you Timothy, my beloved and faithful child in the Lord" (1 Cor 4:17). Surely this word included the idea of "trustworthiness." In 1 Cor 7:25 Paul referred to himself in a similar manner: "Now concerning the betrothed, I have no command from the Lord, but I give my judgment as one who by the Lord's mercy is trustworthy." Paul considered his opinion on this topic to be "trustworthy." All uses of *pistos* in 1 Corinthians are used similarly so that one can translate it as "faithful" (1 Cor 1:9; 4:17; 10:13) but must include at least the idea of "trustworthiness" (1 Cor 4:2 and 7:25).

The verb, *pisteuō*, "to believe," was used in 1 Corinthians in at least four or five different ways. The first is the use of the simple present participle to refer to "believers," i.e. "those who believe" (1 Cor 1:21; 14:22 [twice]). A recent article by Schellenberg has made a strange argument that the present participle, "those who believe," as found in Romans (1:16; 3:22; 4:11, 24; 9:33; 10:4, 11) and Galatians (3:22) should be understood as "believers," and thus all the *pistis Christou* phrases are to be understood as objective genitives, "faith in Christ." He wrote: "It is unlikely that the

---

55. Thiselton, *First Epistle to the Corinthians*, 1220.
56. Thiselton, *First Epistle to the Corinthians*, 1220.

latter phrase [*pistis Iesou Christou*] designates Christ's own faithfulness."[57] On the contrary, translating the present participle as "believers" or "the one(s) believing" does not change the arguments for the subjective genitive ("the faithfulness of Jesus Christ"). Schellenberg is following Dunn, Matlock, and Schliesser in his arguments for the objective genitive. Schellenberg's concluding statement revealed his true argument: "that human faith is the grounds of righteousness."[58] That sounds right but is fundamentally not what Paul said about the revelation of God's righteousness (Rom 3:21–22). God's revelation of his own righteousness is precisely the faithfulness of Jesus to the cross (Rom 3:22, 25). Once that truth is understood, Paul says it is "for all who believe" or "for all believers." The latter translation does not appear to support the objective genitive. In fact, Jesus' faithfulness is the ground of righteousness, not the believers' faithfulness! The goal of Jesus' faithfulness is for the believers.

A second use is when the verb is used in the aorist active indicative (past tense) form to indicate the inception of an event (1 Cor 3:5; 15:2, 11). Thus, the translation of "came to believe" or "came to belief" would be accurate for all three in contrast to the ESV and other versions as simply "believed."

A third use is in 1 Cor 9:17: "For if I do this of my own will, I have a reward, but if not of my own will, I am still entrusted with a stewardship." This use of the verb is the same as with the adjective at 1 Cor 4:2 (see above). This use of the verb is with the form of the perfect passive (*pepisteumai*, "I have been entrusted (with an abiding result)." The ESV communicates this idea by adding the word "still": "I am still entrusted with a stewardship."

A fourth use is found at 1 Cor 13:7: "Love . . . believes all things." Commentaries for many years have debated the meaning of this phrase. In 1991, Elizabeth Stuart debated with C. J. Walters concerning this phrase and as a result Thiselton concluded: "Meyer's exegesis and our proposed translation lend weight to the assumption which lies behind the debate between Elizabeth Stuart and C. J. Walters that here 'Love is Paul,' i.e., Paul perceives himself as so manifesting his love and concern for Corinth as the Other that his love never tires of support, never loses faith, never exhausts hope, never gives up."[59] "Love never loses faith."

---

57. Schellenberg, "οἱ πιστεύοντες," 33.
58. Schellenberg, "οἱ πιστεύοντες," 42.
59. Thiselton, *First Epistle to the Corinthians*, 1058.

Perhaps one could say that "love trusts all things," i.e., "never loses trust." In other words, Paul never loses the trust he has in the Corinthians coming around to his way of living the Christian life in the context of a pagan society. This makes best sense in its context.

A possible fifth use is found at 1 Cor 11:18: "For, in the first place, when you come together as a church, I hear that there are divisions among you. And I believe it in part." This has nothing to do with any kind of "religious" faith, but of a trusting in someone's testimony about a certain issue such as the problems surrounding the Corinthians' misuse of the Lord's Supper (1 Cor 11). Thiselton translated the phrase *kai meros ti pisteuō* as "and to some extent I believe it." Hays interpreted it in an opposite way as an expression of outrage: "*I can hardly credit it; I can't believe it.*"[60] The ESV translated it literally without any interpretative nuances ("I believe it in part") except for a footnote: "I believe a certain report." Thiselton's translation is not much different from the ESV's literal approach. Regardless, Paul believed the report! Readers certainly have free choice in this "human" form of the practice of believing.

Second Corinthians

Second Corinthians was the fourth letter Paul sent to the Corinthians (see above). Paul probably wrote this letter while he was in Philippi (Macedonia, Acts 20:1) c. AD 55/56, a year after writing 1 Corinthians and a year before writing to the Romans during the winter of AD 57 (Acts 20:2–3). Second Corinthians was a very different letter from 1 Corinthians. For one thing, it came after a painful visit and after a subsequent "harsh letter" had been sent (2 Cor 2:4; 7:8–16). For another, Paul had to defend his apostleship and ministry among the Corinthians against his opponents, whom he called "super-apostles" (2 Cor 11:5). Paul minced no words against these agitators: "For such men are false apostles, deceitful workmen, disguising themselves as apostles of Christ. And no wonder, for even Satan disguises himself as an angel of light. It is no surprise if his servants, also, disguise themselves as servants of righteousness. Their end will correspond to their deeds" (2 Cor 11:13–15). Paul anticipated a third visit with the Corinthians before he proceeded to Jerusalem with the special offering for the Jewish Christians in Jerusalem (2 Cor 12:14; 13:1).

---

60. Hays, *First Corinthians*, 195.

Thus, Paul's "fourth" letter can be divided into three parts: 2 Cor 1–7 (defense of Paul's apostleship); 2 Cor 8–9 (exhortation to participate in and complete an offering for the Jewish Christians suffering in Judea); and finally, 2 Cor 10–13 (Paul's appeal to the remaining rebellious minority in Corinth to repent). In this context a different use of the *pistis* word group than what was found in 1 Corinthians could be expected. But what was discovered was less use of the terms. The verb, *pisteuō*, "to believe," is used only twice in one verse! These will be considered at the end of the study on 2 Corinthians. The adjective, *pistos*, "faithful," is used only twice as well. The noun, *pistis*, "faith," is used seven times and will be considered first.

After Paul's painful visit and "harsh" letter, he wrote what might seem contradictory to the Corinthians: "Not that we lord it over your faith, but we work with you for your joy, for you stand firm in your faith" (2 Cor 1:24). Barnett commented:

> But what is here meant by "faith"? This word (*pistis*) and its cognates, so important elsewhere in Paul's letters, is used infrequently in 2 Corinthians and, with one exception, not in contexts that clearly determine the meaning. That exception is: "Examine yourself to see whether you are in *the* faith" (13:5), that is, the gospel of the Son of God, toward whom their faith is directed. But in v. 24 "the faith by which you stand" appears to be their activity of faith, their personally held faith in the Son of God (cf. 1:19), as implied in the first part of the sentence ("*your* faith").[61]

Barnett's statement proved true. Leaving aside 2 Cor 1:24 and 13:5, as explained above, Paul's use of *pistis* in the next four references is now considered. Second Corinthians 4:13 makes a difficult statement that will be discussed with the verb *pisteuō*: "Since we have the same spirit of faith according to what has been written" (4:13a). Second Corinthians 5:7—"for we walk by faith, not by sight." The context indicated that "faith" here referred to those things (or persons?) that can't be seen in the present time; i.e., the Lord in his exalted position. Living by faith is to live with the reality of the Lord's place and position in heaven and with the fact that beyond this life every person will be faced with the "judgment seat of Christ" (5:10).

While people can't see the Lord or the coming judgment, faith structures people's lives on earth; that is, living on the basis of what is

---

61. Barnett, *Second Epistle to the Corinthians*, 116.

unseen. In 2 Cor 8:7 Paul exhorts the Corinthians to excel in the grace of giving. They excelled in other graces, such as faith, speech, and knowledge (see 1 Cor 12:9–10). Barnett suggested that this faith is the gift of "'faith' (to work miracles of healing)."[62] The assessment of 1 Cor 12:9, 10 above is the same: "faith" is a spiritual gift, but a broader application rather than simply to "work miracles of healing" was suggested. Finally, Paul, in defending his ministry among the Corinthians, wrote: "We do not boast beyond limit in the labors of others. But our hope is that as your faith increases, our area of influence among you may be greatly enlarged" (2 Cor 10:15).

What does Paul mean by "as your faith increases (or grows)"? The context indicated that Paul wished for the Corinthians to help Paul evangelize regions beyond Corinth. For this to happen they must increase in faith or better in their "faithfulness." Without their faithfulness to Paul's exhortations, the Corinthians will not be able to participate in Paul's expansive plans to evangelize where no one had preached before, and before that, to gather a gentile offering for the poor Christian Jews in Jerusalem (2 Cor 8–9).

The adjective, *pistos*, "faithful," is used twice in this letter. Once it is used in a familiar phrase expressed before: "God is faithful" (2 Cor 1:18; cf. 1 Cor 1:9; 10:13; 1 Thess 5:24; 2 Thess 3:3). Paul implied that God is faithful in three ways: 1) the eternal "Yes" that is found in the Son of God, Jesus the Messiah; 2) the fulfillment of all the promises of God; and 3) the gifting of the Holy Spirit to the believers in Corinth.[63] As God is faithful, so Paul assured his readers in Corinth that he was faithful in his words to them (1:18–24). There appears to be a play on words in this section by Paul's use of "yes" and "amen" (vv. 18–20). The Hebrew root, אמן, *amn*, "to be firm, trustworthy, safe"[64] for the words "faith," "faithfulness," "yes," and "amen" seems to give Paul the opportunity for this bit of literary play, even if written in Greek.

The second use of *pistos*, "faithful," is a well-attested use of the adjective as a substantive or noun (see Acts 16:1; 1 Tim 4:10). The Greek text literally translated is: "or what part believer with unbeliever" (2 Cor 6:15b). It is the only place in the New Testament where these two words

62. Barnett, *Second Epistle to the Corinthians*, 403.
63. Barnett, *Second Epistle to the Corinthians*, 103.
64. Koehler and Baumgartner, *Hebrew and Aramaic Lexicon*, 63–64. See also Paul's play on words with the Hebrew concept of "glory" (Hebrew כבד), which can also mean "weight," 2 Cor 4:17—"weight of glory" (see 2:455–58).

are juxtaposed. It is instructive to see how *pistos*, which does mean "faithful," can also stand for the noun "believer."

Second Corinthians 4:13, as stated above, used the verb, *pisteuō*, "to believe." One of the arguments that opponents to the subjective genitive interpretation use is that Jesus was never the subject of the verb *pisteuō*, "to believe." Moisés Silva summarized his thoughts on the subject: "In summary, one must openly acknowledge that both Paul and all early Christian writers repeatedly use the verb πιστεύω with reference to our faith in God or Christ, but never once of Christ's own faith."[65] In the same sentence he even denies that the noun πίστις, *pistis*, is ever used for the "faithfulness of Jesus." That is his opinion and totally unsubstantiated. He ignores the present manifold articles and arguments to the contrary. He also ignores the following history and development of the argument.

In 1927, a very minority opinion was offered by H. L. Goudge in his commentary on 2 Corinthians.[66] He is one of the first to suggest that the words of Ps 116 (Hebrew) are placed on the lips of Jesus by Paul. Paul, of course, used the Septuagint version (Psalm 115:1 LXX). Much later, Anthony T. Hanson concurred with his opinion; and after observing the context of the Psalm passage,[67] wrote: "Just as Christ still believed in God despite the deep humiliation of his days on earth, so do the apostles believe despite their humiliating situation. They too know the value of the death of Christ and therefore of the death of all his faithful."[68] Thus, Hanson attempted to understand why Paul would use such a psalm to apply not only to Jesus' trust in God, but to himself and his fellow disciples. Hanson concluded: "In Paul's hermeneutic the psalm is a prophetic utterance inspired by the Holy Spirit expressing the sentiments of the Messiah when he should appear on earth. We may therefore safely assume that Paul thought of the historical Jesus as having expressed faith in God."[69]

Others have offered their opinions. Morna Hooker approached the subject, acknowledged Hanson's interpretation (as a messianic psalm), but denied it because she can't seem to accept that Jesus "believed" and "spoke." She seemed to limit this idea to Paul. However, after examining

---

65. Carson et al., *Justification and Variegated Nomism*, 2:233.

66. Goudge, *Second Epistle to the Corinthians*, 41–42.

67. The LXX has split what was one psalm in the Hebrew (Ps 116) into two psalms: LXX Ps 114 = 116:1–9 and LXX Ps 115 = 116:10–19. Thus, the Hebrew text of Paul's quoted words is found in MT Ps 116:10 or in Greek LXX Ps 115:1.

68. Hanson, *Paradox of the Cross*, 53.

69. Hanson, *Paradox of the Cross*, 53.

two passages (2 Cor 1:17–22 and 3:14), she noted: "Paul sees Christian faith/faithfulness as a sharing in the faith/faithfulness of Christ, even though neither of them uses the phrase πίστις Χριστοῦ. . . . But faith in 4.13 is certainly parallel to the faith of believers, for it is faith in God who brings life out of death (cf. Rom. 4.17, 24)."[70]

Collins and Kendall were not reticent about attributing "faith" to Jesus. In examining the Gospels concerning faith in relationship to Jesus and his disciples, they wrote: "He [Jesus] speaks about faith as an insider, one who knows personally what the life of faith is and wants to share it with others (see 2 Cor 4:13)."[71] A footnote on this quotation is most instructive: "Paul may be applying to Christ the words of the psalm 'I believed and so I spoke' and imagining that he (Christ) speaks here. If this interpretation is correct, 'Paul in all probability takes the verse from Ps. 116 as an utterance of the Messiah, an utterance of faith in God's salvation'" (quoting from Hanson).[72] Soon after, Veronica Koperski made the same suggestion in a brief statement.[73] But the scholar who made this interpretation more feasible and encouraged others to look more closely at it was Richard Hays.[74] However, he failed to give a detailed analysis of the text of 2 Cor 4:13. Two scholars since have given much analysis to 2 Cor 4:13: Thomas D. Stegman[75] and Douglas A. Campbell.[76]

Stegman referred to Hays' work which argued that New Testament authors used certain psalms as utterances of Jesus.[77] Before Stegman's arguments are given for his christological reading, the text of 2 Cor 4:13–14 needs observation: "Since we have the same spirit of faith according to what has been written, 'I believed, and so I spoke,' we also believe, and so we also speak, knowing that he who raised the Lord Jesus will raise

---

70. Hooker, "ΠΙΣΤΙΣ ΧΡΙΣΤΟΥ," 335.

71. O'Collins and Kendall, "The Faith of Jesus," 417.

72. O'Collins and Kendall, "The Faith of Jesus," 417. See n. 57.

73. Koperski, "Meaning of *Pistis Christou*," 209. But she continued to support the objective genitive for the *pistis Christou* phrases. She calls it "a possible case" and "ambiguous."

74. Hays, "Christ Prays the Psalms."

75. Stegman, "(2 Corinthians 4:13)," 725–45.

76. Campbell, "2 Corinthians 4:13," 337–56. Essentially the same information can be found in Campbell's book, *The Deliverance of God*, 913–24.

77. Stegman, "(2 Corinthians 4:13)," 725. In n. 2 Stegman gave examples: Rom 15:3 (quoting Ps 68:10b LXX); Matt 13:35. (Ps 77:2a LXX); Mark 15:34 (Ps 21:2a LXX); Luke 23:46 (Ps 30:6a LXX); John 2:17 (Ps 68:10a LXX); Heb 2:12 (Ps 21:23 LXX); and Heb 10:5–7 (Ps 39:7–9a LXX).

us also with Jesus and bring us with you into his presence." Even this English translation (ESV) raises a few questions about the interpretation of the text. Stegman worked through the entire context of 2 Corinthians concerning Paul's *apologia* for his apostolic ministry among the Corinthians (2:14—7:4). He noted that "Jesus" is the name used five times in 2 Cor 4:10-14. Also, in 4:10a "Paul aligns his own experience of suffering and endurance of hardships with the *story* of Jesus."[78] Stegman showed how Jesus "gave himself over" in love for the sake of others (2 Cor 4:11a), connecting this to Gal 2:20 (as was interpreted above!). At v. 13, Stegman interpreted "having the same spirit of faith" as the "Holy Spirit of faithfulness." He argued: "Indeed, in the verses immediately preceding 4:7–15, the apostle has identified the Spirit as the source of transformation of Christians 'into the same image' (3:18), that is, into the likeness of Christ, who is named in 4:4, as 'the image of God.'"[79]

He concluded: "First, 'the *same Spirit* of faithfulness' refers to the transforming Spirit named in 3:18—the 'Spirit of the Lord.' Second, 'the *same* Spirit of *faithfulness*' refers to what the Spirit empowers, namely, the loving, self-giving mode of existence manifested by Jesus."[80] Given these arguments and many more, Stegman gave his own translation of 2 Cor 4:13: "That is, because we have the same Spirit of faithfulness according to what has been written—'I have been faithful, therefore I have spoken'—so also are we faithful, and therefore we also speak."[81] Stegman has shown the emphasis in Paul's letter to the Corinthians is "Jesus' faithfulness." Therefore, he reevaluated the usual interpretation of 2 Corinthians 13:5: "I propose that the apostle challenges the Corinthians to look in the mirror to ascertain whether or not they are participating in Jesus' faithfulness by embodying the latter's loving, self-giving mode of existence."[82]

While Stegman argued with the broader context of 2 Corinthians in mind, Douglas Campbell argued in the opposite direction focusing on the localized data.[83] He concentrated on 2 Cor 4:13, then v. 14, then

---

78. Stegman, "(2 Corinthians 4:13)," 728.
79. Stegman, "(2 Corinthians 4:13)," 735.
80. Stegman, "(2 Corinthians 4:13)," 735.
81. Stegman, "(2 Corinthians 4:13)," 736.
82. Stegman, "(2 Corinthians 4:13)," 745. Since I agree with Stegman's analysis and translation, one needs to reevaluate Barnett's quotation as used above for 2 Cor 13:5. "The faith" should be understood as "the faithfulness [of Messiah and His Spirit]." See n. 58.
83. Campbell, "2 Corinthians 4:13," 338, note 1.

chapter 4, and finally chapter 5. With these "localized texts," Campbell cogently wrote: "Because Christ has spoken and has been resurrected and glorified, those who participate in his steadfast believing and speaking now are guaranteed that resurrection in the future, and this should fill them with hope. The one who resurrected Christ will resurrect both Paul and his auditors (and this is of course God)."[84] As Stegman offered a translation of 2 Cor 4:13, so did Campbell: "Having the same Spirit of belief [as Christ] in accordance with what was written [that he spoke], 'I believed, therefore I spoke,' so also we believed, therefore we also spoke [to you], knowing that the one who raised the Lord Jesus will also raise us with Jesus and will present us together with you."[85]

One can see that Stegman emphasized the idea of "faithfulness" for the verb "to believe," whereas, Campbell stayed with the verbal idea of "believing." Again, when one believes under duress or persecution, even the threat of death, it can be called "faithfulness" as the end result. "Trusting" may be another way of saying the same thing. However one expresses it, I like Stegman's presentation among all the contributors to this text of 2 Cor 4:13. But I also must agree with Campbell's last word in his article: "Many considerations seem to suggest that this Christocentric, and ultimately participatory, reading of 2 Cor 4:13 is the correct one."[86]

One more scholar has weighed in on this text of 2 Cor 4:13: Kenneth Schenck.[87] Schenck was more vigorous in his exegesis, using the context of the entire Psalms of the LXX (Pss 114 and 115), which in Hebrew consists of only one psalm, Ps 116. The theme, of course, is how the righteous sufferer is vindicated by God by deliverance from trial. But Schenck noticed Paul was thinking in terms of Jesus' future resurrection and the resurrection of all the dead in Christ. Concluding this thought, he wrote: "Paul has the human, earthly, suffering Jesus *and his faith* primarily in view throughout the passage. It is this faith of Jesus that Paul aspires to emulate as he participates in Jesus' sufferings and anticipates Jesus' resurrection (cf. Phil 3:10)."[88]

---

84. Campbell, "2 Corinthians 4:13," 349.

85. Campbell, "2 Corinthians 4:13," 356.

86. Campbell, "2 Corinthians 4:13," 356.

87. Schenck, "2 Corinthians," 524–37. Schenck thinks the apostle Paul considers the context of both psalms (Ps 114 LXX and Ps 115 LXX = Heb Ps 116) in his letter to 2 Corinthians.

88. Schenck, "2 Corinthians," 528.

All three scholars, Douglas, Stegman, and Schenck, have contributed greatly to this interpretation of 2 Cor 4:13. Douglas used only the "localized" context, while Stegman included almost all of 2 Corinthians, but the best presentation is by Schenck, who studied the contexts of LXX Psalm 114 and 115. His remarks serve an appropriate conclusion to my thoughts on this text:

> Paul's train of thought in 2 Corinthians 4, however, is much tighter, more coherent, and full of meaning if we suppose that he was reading Psalms 114 and 115 LXX christologically. The words of Ps 115:1 become prophetic words to be read as the words of Jesus and, thus, as a statement of Jesus' faith. Paul sees that Jesus had faith that God would raise him from the dead. Paul and his co-workers also have this faith, for the same God who raised Jesus from the dead would raise them as well.[89]

The Pastoral Letters

The so-called "Pastoral Letters" have been a source of higher critical controversy for over two hundred years. Even though all three letters, 1–2 Timothy and Titus, claim the apostle Paul as their author, most critics of the Pauline letters reject this claim and essentially consider the three letters as pseudonymous (as some scholars do with Ephesians). The problems that scholars have with the Pastorals have been addressed by Knight's commentary: method of communication, the manner of addressing and instructing Timothy and Titus, warnings against false teaching, ecclesiastical organization, theological differences, vocabulary and style, pseudonymity, and even Luke's possible involvement.[90]

The dating of the Pastorals is significantly affected by one's position on authorship. Most who argue pseudonymity for these letters also assign a very late date into the second century AD. Knight, who takes a conservative stance in regard to both authorship and dating, holds on to Paul's authorship and dates the letters accordingly: 1 Timothy and Titus, c. AD 61–63 and 2 Timothy c. AD 64–67 (supposedly Paul's last letter just before his execution in Rome). Knight's arguments against the critical views that deny Pauline authorship and late date the letters seem to be

---

89. Schenck, "2 Corinthians," 537.

90. See Knight, *The Pastoral Epistles*, 21–52. Possible dates, if Paul is the author, are discussed on pp. 53–54.

strong. Either view will not affect the review of the *pistis* word group in these epistles, but I will refer to the author as "Paul."

There is a strong use of the *pistis* word group and a rich diversity of contexts that affect the meaning and/or the nuances of these words:

First Timothy—*pisteuō*: 1:11, 16, 3:16; *pistis*: 1:2, 4, 5, 14, 19²; 2:7, 15; 3:9, 13; 4:1, 6, 12; 5:8, 12; 6:10, 11, 12, 21; *pistos*: 1:12, 15; 3:1, 11; 4:3, 9, 10, 12; 5:16; 6:2²; additionally the negative words of *apistia*: 1:13 and *apistos*: 5:8.

Second Timothy—*pisteuō*: 1:12; *pistoomai*: 3:14; *pistis*: 1:5, 13; 2:18, 22; 3:8, 10, 15; 4:7; *pistos*: 2:2, 11, 13; additionally the negative verb of *apisteō*: 2:13.

Titus—*pisteuō*: 1:3; 3:8; *pistis*: 1:1, 4, 13; 2:2, 10; 3:15; *pistos*: 1:6, 9; 3:8; additionally the negative adjective *apistos*: 1:15.

Counting the negative words, 1 Timothy has a total of thirty-five words of the *pistis* word group; 2 Timothy a total of fourteen words; and Titus a total of twelve words. Discussion of these letters will be in presumably chronological order: 1 Timothy, Titus, and 2 Timothy.

First Timothy

First, a peculiar construction in both 1 and 2 Timothy (parallel occurrences) was noted by Ian Wallis:

> An anarthrous occurrence of πίστις is qualified by an attributive prepositional phrase including Χριστῷ Ἰησοῦ:
>
> 1 Tim. 1.14 ἡ χάρις τοῦ κυρίου ἡμῶν μετὰ πίστεως καὶ ἀγάπης τῆς ἐν Χριστῷ Ἰησοῦ
>
> 1 Tim. 3.13 καὶ πολλὴν παρρησίαν ἐν πίστει τῇ ἐν Χριστῷ Ἰησοῦ
>
> 2 Tim. 1.13 ὧν παρ'ἐμοῦ ἤκουσας ἐν πίστει καὶ ἀγάπῃ τῇ ἐν Χριστῷ Ἰησοῦ
>
> 2 Tim. 3.15 εἰς σωτηρίαν διὰ πίστεως τῆς ἐν Χριστῷ Ἰησοῦ
>
> The placement of the article after πίστις and not before underlines the qualificatory nature of what follows and cautions against an interpretation along the lines of "faith in Christ Jesus."[91]

Wallis also noted 2 Tim 1:1 and 2:10 in this same light where the "promise of life" and "salvation" are associated with being "in Christ."

---

91. Wallis, *Faith of Jesus Christ*, 135.

First Timothy 1:14—"And the grace of our Lord overflowed for me with the faith and love that are in Christ Jesus." The ESV's good literal translation suggests that the "faith" and "love" are qualities that are found "in Messiah Jesus." This would suggest that the grace of our Lord overflowed in the sense of his "faithfulness" and "love." This is very similar to the thoughts in Gal 2:20 where Paul wrote: "but what now I live in flesh, I live in/by [the] faithfulness of the Son of God, who loved me and gave himself on my behalf" (my translation). Love is overtly expressed while faithfulness is implicitly expressed by the phrase "gave himself on my behalf," meaning death on the cross as an atonement for the sins of the world.

Paul's personal testimony (1 Tim 1:12–17) emphasized the grace of God in his life, and thus faithfulness and love "constitute the outworkings of grace and not responses to it."[92] Wallis admitted that both "outworkings" and "responses" could be at work here, for Paul began his testimony with the words "he [Christ Jesus our Lord] judged me faithful" (1:12). The former was the predominate idea here because Paul wrote further: "I received mercy because I had acted ignorantly in unbelief" (1:13b). The Lord Jesus took the initiative in Paul's life, an initiative that included faithfulness and love on Jesus' part. Consequently, Paul was "entrusted" with the gospel (1:11). Even, Knight, who does not necessarily agree with the subjective genitive interpretation as expressed in Romans and Galatians, wrote: "By saying that ἀγάπη and πίστις are ἐν Χριστῷ Ἰησοῦ, Paul indicated that their sources are in Christ because of his being in Christ. . . . It was when he acknowledged Jesus of Nazareth to be the Christ that he moved from unbelief to belief and from hatred to love."[93]

First Timothy 3:13—"For those who serve well as deacons gain a good standing for themselves and also great confidence in the faith that is in Christ Jesus." Again, as in 1:14, "great confidence in the faith that is in Christ Jesus" suggests that the "faithfulness" of the Messiah Jesus is what the well-serving deacon has confidence in. Christ's personal qualities are pronounced in the two letters to Timothy: "perfect patience" (1:16); making the "good confession" before Pontius Pilate (6:13; also 2 Tim 1:8); and his "sound words . . . teaching that accords with godliness" (6:3; also 2 Tim 1:13), the norm for all teaching. Thus, Jesus is the source for "love"

---

92. Wallis, *Faith of Jesus Christ*, 135.
93. Knight, *The Pastoral Epistles*, 99.

(2 Tim 1:13); "faith[fulness]" (1 Tim 1:14; 3:13; 2 Tim 1:13; 3:15) and "grace" (2 Tim 1:9; 2:1; Titus 1:4; cf. 2 Tim 4:22).[94]

Jesus' faithfulness, as expressed in Romans, Galatians, Philippians, and Ephesians, has to do with his doing God's will by going to the cross and dying on behalf of the whole world. In the pastorals, faith[fulness] has as its source, content, and object in Messiah Jesus. It goes beyond the one act of obedience to the cross (see Rom 5:19). In the Pastorals, the faithfulness of Jesus is of the risen Messiah Jesus who remains faithful to believers, who participate by faith in the risen life of Jesus, presently reigning at God's right hand.

In light of the above, the content of faith (that which is believed) was important to the author: deacons holding "the mystery of the faith" (3:9); "some will depart from the faith" (4:1); "being trained in the words of the faith" (4:6); whoever does not provide for his family has "denied the faith" (5:8); the love of money has caused some to have "wandered away from the faith" (6:10); "fight the good fight of the faith" (6:12); and "some have swerved from the faith" (6:21). This may have been the meaning when Paul wrote of Timothy as "my true child in the faith" (1:2), or in the opposite direction when he wrote that "some have made shipwreck of their faith" (1:19). Both of these latter references may have the idea of "trust."

Most often *pistis* is used for a virtue, meaning "trust, fidelity, and faithfulness." Paul qualified "the stewardship of God" with an article "the" and "by faith" (1:4). Here the meaning is a "trust." Knight commented that the "in faith" that describes the "stewardship of God" is the "trust relationship that is the seedbed in which God works and produces growth."[95] The next verse, v. 5, mentioned "a sincere faith," which is part of the sources for Paul's charge to Timothy: "The aim of our charge is love that issues from a pure heart and a good conscience and a sincere faith" (1:5). Knight described this faith: "Πίστις here has the general NT and Pauline meaning of trust in God and reliance on him (cf. the two previous usages, 1:2 and especially 1:4)."[96] "Holding faith" in 1:19 means "trusting" to the point of being loyal. In 2:7 the "in faith" is similar to 1:2, 4, 5 above. It is how Paul instructed gentiles. It is his "trust." He must communicate "truth."

---

94. Wallis, *Faith of Jesus Christ*, 138.
95. Knight, *The Pastoral Epistles*, 76.
96. Knight, *The Pastoral Epistles*, 78.

"Faithfulness" appears the meaning in several passages: "Yet she will be saved through childbearing—if they continue in faith[fulness]" (2:15, whatever that means!); "set the believers an example . . . in faith[fulness]" (4:12); and "pursue . . . faith[fulness]" (6:11).

A less frequent meaning for *pistis* is found in 5:12: here young widows who wish to marry are not to be enrolled because they "incur condemnation for having abandoned their former faith." The meaning surely is "pledge" in this context. The NRSV and NIV translate the term "pledge." Also, 2 Tim 4:7 will have the same meaning as will be explained below.

Pistos, the adjective "faithful," is used in a variety of ways in 1 Timothy. The most interesting is the quotation-commendation formula: πιστὸς ὁ λόγος (*pistos ho logos*) which means "a faithful/trustworthy saying" (used five times in the Pastorals: 1 Tim 1:15; 3:1; 4:9; Titus 3:8; 2 Tim 2:11). Knight explained: "So when Paul states that the λόγος is πιστός, he is saying that it is a faithful presentation of God's message (cf. 2 Tim 2:2)."[97] The "trustworthy saying" in 1:15, "Messiah Jesus came into the world to save sinners" (my translation), is worthy of note. In 3:1 the saying is: "If anyone aspires to the office of overseer, he desires a noble task." At 4:9 the saying precedes the phrase (v. 8): "for while bodily training is of some value, godliness is of value in every way, as it holds promise for the present life and also for the life to come." Second Timothy 2:11 and Titus 3:8 will be examined below.[98]

Another use of *pistos* is the adjective used as a nominal or noun idea—"faithful one," meaning "believer," usually in the plural form. In 1 Tim 4:3 the ESV translates *tois pistois* as "by those who believe," but that is equal to "believers." First Timothy 4:10 has "especially of those who believe" (ESV). Knight suggested that the word "especially" (*malista*) should be understood as "that is," thus the phrase in 4:10 should be read: "that is, believers."[99] The ESV does translate the absolute form, τῶν πιστῶν, *tōn pistōn*, "believers" in 4:12. The ESV is true to form in 6:2 translating the first use of *pistos* "believing masters," but translates the second plural use as "believers."

A final use of *pistos* is simply "faithful." The wives of deacons are to be "faithful" in all things (3:11). At 5:16 the word is in a feminine form,

---

97. Knight, *The Pastoral Epistles*, 99.
98. See Knight, *The Faithful Sayings*.
99. Knight, *The Faithful Sayings*, 203.

meaning "believing woman." It could just as well be translated as "faithful (woman)," as "believing masters" at 6:2a could be "faithful masters." The negative of *pistos* (*apistos*) is used at 5:8 for "unbeliever." Another negative, *apistia*, "unbelief," is used as a description of Paul before his conversion/commissioning experience on the Damascus road (1 Tim 1:13): "I had acted ignorantly in unbelief."

The verb, *pisteuō*, "to believe," is used three times in 1 Timothy. In a past tense form (aorist) of the passive voice means "be entrusted with" (1 Tim 1:11). Paul was entrusted with the gospel. Secondly, Paul sees himself "as an example to those who were to believe in him for eternal life" (1 Tim 1:16). Here the meaning could also be "trust in him for eternal life." Finally, in 3:16 the same verb form of 1:11 (aorist passive) is used, but it should be understood as a simple passive, "be believed," or perhaps "be trusted." The only other use of this word in this form was in 2 Thess 1:10 (see above). The ESV translation is: "believed on in the world."

Titus

It is conjectured that 1 Timothy was written to Timothy while he was in Ephesus, and the situation in Ephesus accounts for the particular content of the letter. The letter to Titus has Titus in Crete where apparently Paul had worked with Titus and others to establish churches on that island (Titus 1:5). Paul gave Titus the unfinished work of selecting qualified leadership for the churches. Above all, Paul was concerned about false teaching that was proliferating among the churches (house churches). Paul considered proper Christian living an essential concern for Crete and Ephesus, and thus his emphasis on real godliness in everyday life. Of course, the Cretan culture was counter to all of Paul's instructions for Titus to accomplish. The reputation of Cretans was "Cretans are always liars, evil beasts, lazy gluttons" (Titus 1:12). It is only a guess as to whether Titus was written after or before 1 Timothy c. AD 61–62, after Paul was released from a Roman imprisonment and after an acquittal of Jewish charges (Acts 28). As expected, Titus has a limited usage of the *pistis* word group due to the small size of the letter.

While each pastoral letter should be considered independently from the others because of the unique purpose and background for each, the pastorals are bound together by the "trustworthy sayings" found in them: see 1 Tim 1:15; 3:1; 4:9; Titus 3:8; and 2 Tim 2:11. The text of Titus 3:8

reads: "The saying is trustworthy, and I want you to insist on these things, so that those who have believed in God may be careful to devote themselves to good works." Most of the "trustworthy sayings" come after the term (1 Tim 1:15; 3:1; and 2 Tim 2:11). The "saying" is before the term in 1 Tim 4:9 and almost certainly Titus 3:8, though scholars debate as to how many verses are part of the saying.[100] Knight reviewed the debate and settled on vv. 4–7 as the possible saying, but this is not certain.

Pistos is used twice more in Titus: 1:6, 9. Titus 1:6 is used as a noun: "believers." In Titus 1:9 the ESV properly translates *pistos* as "trustworthy" describing "word as taught." The negative of *pistos* (*apistos*) is used once: Titus 1:15—"To the pure, all things are pure, but to the defiled and unbelieving, nothing is pure; but both their minds and their consciences are defiled." The ESV translated the word as it is, an adjective, but it could have also been used as a noun, that is, an "unbeliever."

The verb *pisteuō*, "to believe," is used only twice: 1:3 and 3:8. Titus 1:3 is the aorist passive, meaning "I have been entrusted." The verse reads: "and at the proper time manifested in his word through the preaching with which I have been entrusted by the command of God our Savior." This usage is the same for 1 Tim 1:11. Titus 3:8 has a perfect active participle (*pepisteukotes*) with the object being "God." Titus 3:8: "A trustworthy saying (previous vv. 4–7), indeed, concerning these things I want you to insist in order that those who have trusted in God may be careful to be engaged in good works. These things are good and profitable for people" (my translation).

Pistis, the noun, is used six times. Twice it is used of what is believed, perhaps doctrine. Titus 1:4—"To Titus, my true child in a common faith" (see 1 Tim 1:2). Titus 1:13—"This testimony is true. Therefore, rebuke them sharply, that they may be sound in the faith." The former could possibly mean "a common trust," but it probably means that which is believed. Most of the usages seem to be "faithfulness," or "trust." Titus 1:1 does not use the article before *pistin*. Titus 1:1—"Paul, a slave of God, indeed an apostle of Jesus the Messiah according to [the] faithfulness of [the] elect of God and knowledge of truth, the [truth] according to godliness" (my translation).

In Titus 2:2 Paul exhorts Titus to teach "sound (healthy) doctrine." This included the older men be "sound (healthy) in faith." This was part of a list of virtues and thus can be translated as "faithfulness" or "trust."

---

100. Knight, *The Pastoral Epistles*, 347–50.

In Titus 2:10, Titus was to teach that slaves (bondservants) are to not to pilfer but to show "all good faith." The idea here is reliability and faithfulness in terms of being honest and dependable.

Finally, Paul's greeting and benediction at the end of the letter refers to "the faith" as in 1:4 (see 1 Tim 1:2): "Greet those who love us in the faith" (3:15). However, there is no article before *pistei* in the Greek text. It is therefore possible to read this greeting differently: "Greet those who love us in faithfulness." In other words, Paul had enemies in Crete and Paul wants Titus to be sure and greet those who were trustworthy and faithful to Paul's ministry and work on the island of Crete, those who truly had warm loving feelings (*phileō*) for the apostle.

Second Timothy

Second Timothy is probably Paul's last letter to Timothy or anyone else, because he was once again imprisoned in Rome and expected nothing less than execution (2 Tim 4:6–8). Since Nero's persecution of Christians began c. AD 64, Paul's last letter could have been written sometime between AD 64–67. With all the detailed instructions to Timothy, Paul seemed to be confident that he would survive at least the winter but not the spring (2 Tim 4:21). The letter is emotional and yet encouraging to Timothy to remain steadfast and faithful to his duties realizing that he must "pick up the mantle" of his mentor. This letter is more general in nature in contrast to the specifics of the first letter to Timothy. However, like Titus, Paul was concerned about "false teachers," presumably at Ephesus (2 Tim 2:14—3:9) and addressed this critical issue with Timothy.

Because of the circumstances of the letter and its purpose, Paul used the *pistis* word group aggressively. "Faithfulness" could very well be the theme of the letter, which lists God, the Lord Jesus Christ, Paul, Timothy, and many others as being faithful. In fact, Paul mentioned by name many of those whom he deemed faithful (Lois and Eunice, grandmother and mother of Timothy, Onesiphorus, Crescens, Titus, Luke, Mark, Tychicus, Carpus, Prisca and Aquila, Erastus, Trophimus, Eubulus, Pudens, Linus, and Claudia) and many who were unfaithful (Phygelus, Hermogenes, Hymenaeus, Philetus, Jannes and Jambres,[101] Demas, and Alexander the coppersmith). The *pistis* word group, due to the small size of the letter,

---

101. Early extrabiblical Jewish literature listing these magicians who opposed Moses used them as illustrations of unfaithfulness.

is scattered throughout the letter with some interesting statements that contribute to the *pistis Christou* debate.

Pistos, the adjective "faithful," is used three times. The first use was when Paul encouraged Timothy to teach faithful men who will be able to teach others and thus keep the people of God on an ever-growing maturity toward salvation: 2 Tim 2:2—"and what you have heard from me in the presence of many witnesses entrust to faithful men who will be able to teach others also." I have often called this the "222 Club." No one fully learns anything until that person is able to teach someone else what he or she knows. That is the principle Paul is encouraging, but it must be done by *faithful* men (and women)!

The second use of *pistos* is the "trustworthy saying" that characterized and bound together the Pastoral Epistles. This "saying" followed the term: 2 Tim 2:11–13—"The saying is trustworthy for: If we have died with him, we will also live with him; if we endure, we will also reign with him; if we deny him, he also will deny us; if we are faithless, he remains faithful—for he cannot deny himself." Scholars are all over the place with regard to this saying or hymn. I simply want to show that the saying or hymn was appropriate for Paul to use because of his emphasis on endurance (2:10) and faithfulness (1:5, 13; 2:2). The saying offered much teaching concerning the Christian faith. We die with Christ in baptism but are raised out of the water to walk in a newness of life (cf. Rom 6:4). If Christians endure to the end, then after death (whether naturally or by martyrdom) we shall reign with Christ (cf. Rev 2:10; 3:21; 14:12; 20:6).[102] If any believer denies who Jesus is, he or she will be denied by Jesus (cf. Matt 10:32–33). Finally, the saying/hymn suggested that even when we are faithless (and here the verb *apisteuō* is used), Jesus remains faithful (the third use of *pistos*). Paul apparently added: "for he [Jesus] cannot deny himself." Knight gives us some insight on this last phrase of the saying or hymn:

> This fourth line of the saying is demonstrated in Christ's faithfulness to Peter even though Peter was so unfaithful that he denied Jesus (Jn. 21:15ff.; Lk. 22:31–32). While the apodoses in the first three lines of the saying result from the corresponding protases, here the apodosis is not the result but the opposite

---

102. Christians reign with Christ now (Eph 2:6). However, Revelation presents the assurance of martyrs reigning with Christ at their death. These two ideas can be reconciled. See comments on Revelation in chapter 7.

of the protasis. In the fourth statement in the saying, εἰ means "although," not "if."[103]

Pistis, the noun "faith," is used eight times. The references that seem to support the *pistis Christou* phrases, interpreted as subjective genitives, will be examined first. Having already commented on 1 Tim 1:14 and 3:13, it was declared above that "faithfulness" and "love" belonged to Jesus and it is from him that we can be faithful and loving. In 2 Tim 1:13 the same phrase is found: "Follow the pattern of the sound words that you have heard from me, in the faith and love that are in Christ Jesus." The phrase is translated the same way as above: "in the faithfulness and love that are in Messiah Jesus." The source of these two qualities is initially found in the Messiah, and as one participates in his life, one acquires the very same qualities or virtues in one's life.

The strongest argument for the subjective genitive comes with 2 Tim 3:15. The context, 2 Tim 2:8-13, indicated that the theme is "the faithfulness of Jesus the Messiah" (2:8). David Downs commented on this context: "In this regard, the author of Second Timothy, while highlighting the subjective aspect of Christ's own saving fidelity, locates 'faith that is in Christ' not solely in the narrative of the life and death of the earthly Jesus but also in the continuing faithfulness of the risen Christ for those who are saved through participation in him."[104] In this context Paul exhorted Timothy vigorously to be faithful to his task (2 Tim 2:14-26 and 3:10—4:8), interrupted only by an elaborate critique of false teachers (2 Tim 3:1-9). These future false teachers were men who "oppose the truth," who are "corrupted in mind" and "disqualified regarding the faith" (3:8). "The faith" probably refers to the whole practice of the Christian faith (Christianity). Paul wanted Timothy to follow his example in every way, one of which is "my faith," (3:10) which I interpret to be Paul's faithfulness or his trust in God the Father and Jesus the Messiah.

Paul continued to exhort Timothy to "continue in what you have learned and have firmly believed, knowing from whom you learned it" (3:14). "Firmly believed" is a translation of the word *pistoō* ("prove oneself faithful to something," "become convinced"). All of the above context sets up Paul's words at 2 Tim 3:15: "and how from childhood you have been acquainted with the sacred writings, which are able to make you wise for salvation through faith in Christ Jesus." Most commentators consider

---

103. Knight, *The Pastoral Epistles*, 407.
104. Downs, "Faith(fulness) in Christ Jesus," 145.

Christ to be the object of faith expressed in this text. However, the phrase is perfectly ambiguous. It could possibly refer to human faith in Christ or to faith as a characteristic of the Christ. Downs argued that it is important to note how often the Pauline phrase "in Christ Jesus" was used in 2 Timothy (1:1, 9, 13; 2:1, 10; 3:12, 15). This indicated the importance of participation in Christ for salvation. Downs noted: "A key dimension of Pauline soteriology is the notion that, in some mysterious way, believers participate in Christ and in his story—that is, in Christ's crucifixion and resurrection (Gal 2:19–20; 1 Corinthians 15). The incorporative character of Christian existence is present also in the 'in Christ' language of Second Timothy."[105] After reviewing all the "faith" language in 2 Timothy as well as the "in Christ" passages, Downs concluded his arguments:

> Given how the language of being "in Christ" functions elsewhere in the epistle, and given the emphasis on the faithfulness of the risen Christ in 2 Tim 2:8–13, the locution διὰ πίστεως τῆς ἐν Χριστῷ Ἰησοῦ also evokes a salvation that is made possible by faith(fulness) that resides in Christ Jesus. In this sense, πίστις in 2 Tim 3:15 is subjective in that it is a quality characteristic of the risen Christ Jesus himself. It is the faithfulness of the resurrected Christ that empowers and characterizes the faithfulness to which Timothy is called by Paul throughout the epistle.[106]

The single use of the verb, *pisteuō*, "to believe," is Paul's introductory statement to all that he would say following: "But I am not ashamed [of suffering], for I know whom I have believed and I am convinced that he is able to guard until that Day what has been entrusted to me" (2 Tim 1:12). The verb is a perfect form, meaning that his belief continues to the present and into the future and thus turns into a life of faithfulness. That set the stage for the discussion above.

Four usages of *pistis* remain. In 2 Timothy 1:5, at the beginning of his letter, Paul referred to Timothy's great advantage in his maternal family's faithfulness: "I am reminded of your sincere faith, a faith that dwelt first in your grandmother Lois and your mother Eunice and now, I am sure, dwells in you as well." This faith or faithfulness was "without hypocrisy" (*anupokritos*, usually translated "sincere" using a positive word; cf. 1 Tim 1:5). Paul will mention Demas later in the letter as one who showed insincere or hypocritical faith(fulness), having loved "this present world"

---

105. Downs, "Faith(fulness) in Christ Jesus," 153.
106. Downs, "Faith(fulness) in Christ Jesus," 160.

(4:10). "Paul is thankful to God that he can remember Timothy as one in whom (ἐν σοί) there was a faith that neither wavered nor was double-minded, a genuine trust in God (cf. by analogy Jas. 1:6–8)."[107] Timothy's mother, Eunice, was not named but mentioned by Luke in Acts 16:1 as "a Jewish woman who was a believer, but his [Timothy's] father was a Greek." It seems that Timothy's father was not a believer or a Christian. The key feature of this faith turns out to be true faithfulness, a genuine trust in God in the midst of hardship, suffering, and political and cultural pressure.

In 2 Tim 2:18c Paul wrote: "They are upsetting the faith of some." He names the "they" as Hymenaeus and Philetus, who were saying that the resurrection had already occurred (2:18b). Paul called this a "swerving from the truth" (2:18a) and considers it "iniquity" (2:19c). Not all were taken in by this heretical teaching (from a Christian doctrinal point of view). So, "the faith of some" referred to personal faith, but a faith that includes teaching about the resurrection of believers at Jesus' *Parousia* (1 Cor 15:12, 13, 21, 42). The worldview of the Christian is contingent on belief in the resurrection of Jesus, first of all (2 Tim 2:8a), and then the resurrection of all true believers at the appearance (*Parousia*) of Jesus on the last day, the day of judgment (2 Tim 2:10). Without the resurrection as a firm conviction and a historical truth or fact, there is no exalted Messiah at God's right hand, no gospel to preach; faith[fulness] is in vain and futile; we are still in our sins; and the dead have no hope of eternal life and have perished (1 Cor 15:12–19). The resurrection is at the heart of all Christian belief, a doctrine or teaching to be trusted. True faith is believing that God has raised Jesus the Messiah from the dead (cf. Rom 4:17, 24, 25).

However, at 2 Tim 2:22, Paul lists "faith" as a virtue along with other virtues: "So flee youthful passions and pursue righteousness, faith, love, and peace, along with those who call on the Lord from a pure heart." As a virtue, *pistis* should be translated "faithfulness." It includes the idea of reliability. Paul is encouraging Timothy to persevere under extreme difficulties facing false teachers and obstinate people of every type (see 2 Tim 1:15; 2:23—3:9; 4:3–5).

The fourth use of *pistis* is Paul's last use of the word in this letter, which is not without some significance. It is one of the most interesting usages of *pistis* by the author of the Pastorals. The apostle Paul knows he will more than likely be executed by Nero, one of the first Caesars to persecute Christians by imposing the death sentence (c. AD 64–66).

---

107. Knight, *The Pastoral Epistles*, 369.

Paul has no doubt about this scenario fatefully awaiting. It had to be an emotion-filled moment for Timothy to read the finality in Paul's words: "For I am already being poured out as a drink offering, and the time of my departure has come. I have fought the good fight, I have finished the race, I have kept the faith. Henceforth there is laid up for me the crown of righteousness, which the Lord, the righteous judge, will award to me on that Day, but not only to me but also to all who have loved his appearing" (2 Tim 4:6–8). What did Paul mean when he wrote "I have kept the faith"? On the surface it certainly can mean the entire life of the Christian, living by faith, exhibiting faithfulness, and holding fast to every sound doctrine of faith from Scripture; i.e., being true to Christianity (see 1 Tim 1:2, 19; 3:9; 4:1, 6; 5:8; 6:10; Titus 1:4, 13; 2:2; 2 Tim 2:18; 3:8, among other references). However, I think Paul used *pistis* here as a double entendre; i.e., there is another meaning added to this word meriting attention.

Paul used several metaphorical thoughts in this passage. First of all, he referred to his life as a "drink-offering," a well-known Jewish practice (Exod 29:40–41; Lev 23:13; Num 15:5–10; 28:7–8). The image of his life "being poured out" is striking in that it is complete, gone, unretrievable. Yet, it is an offering to YHWH in praise and thanksgiving along with sacrifices that are meant to atone, reconcile, and put one in right relationship with God. The passive voice perhaps indicated that God is the one doing the pouring! The second metaphorical idea is that of a ship about ready to "loose" its moorings, a departure out to sea. This became a figurative statement for death or dying. The time (*kairos*, "appropriate time") is neither immediate nor is it a definite time, but it is soon enough. It is critical time. He encouraged Timothy to come "soon" (4:9), indeed, "before winter" (4:21). The third metaphorical idea is athletic terminology. Interpreted in this light, it will make plain the understanding of this double entendre.

Paul was anxious to get to Corinth after leaving Athens (see Acts 17–18). In April or May of AD 51, the Corinthians prepared for the Isthmian Games, about ten miles south of ancient Corinth. Crowds gathered every two years between the two harbors of Cenchreae and Lechaion for this event. It was a great opportunity for Paul and his associates (including the tentmakers, Priscilla and Aquila) to sell tents and to preach the gospel. At this event a bull was sacrificed at the altar to the god Palaimon. The athletes took an oath at the altar of Poseidon (god of the sea) that they would compete honestly according to the rules. Five years later, Paul wrote from Ephesus to Corinth recalling the athletes' training for the foot race and the boxing match to illustrate the severe self-control to which he subjected himself: "Do you not know that in a race all the runners run, but only one receives the prize? Do run that you may obtain it. Every athlete exercises self-control in all things. They do it to receive a perishable wreath, but we an imperishable. So I do not run aimlessly; I do not box as one beating the air. But I discipline my body and keep it under control, lest after preaching to others I myself should be disqualified" (1 Cor 9:24–27). It is clear that Paul was well aware of the athletic games in his day, in his case, the Isthmian Games. He would have been well aware of the Olympic games in Athens and many others, such as the Nemean and Pythian.[108]

Given the above, Paul gave us a hint to his meaning of *pistis* (4:7) at the beginning of his letter: "An athlete is not crowned unless he competes according to the rules" (2 Tim 2:5). What does this mean? Look at the Corinthian correspondence. Paul twice commented: "For we are not, like so many, peddlers of God's word, but as men of sincerity, as commissioned by God, in the sight of God we speak in Christ" (2 Cor 2:17). "But we have renounced disgraceful, underhanded ways. We refuse to practice cunning or to tamper with God's word, but by the open statement of the truth we would commend ourselves to everyone's conscience in the sight of God" (2 Cor 4:2). Phillip's translation or paraphrase of the above text makes the formal translations clear: "We use no hocus-pocus, no clever tricks, no dishonest manipulation of the Word of God."

Thus, when Paul wrote "I have kept the faith," he meant "I have kept *the pledge* to compete honestly according to the rules." In Paul's case that imagery meant preaching the gospel in an honest and open way, without charge, with sincerity of faithfulness to the word of God, while presenting the truth about God's great salvation offered to humanity. False teachers and the so-called "super apostles" (in Corinth) did the opposite! Also, one should note that each verb in 4:7 is a perfect active indicative, meaning that Paul is saying something about his entire ministry, including up to the present as he awaited a certain execution. When Paul wrote "I have kept (with abiding results) the *pledge*," he can talk about the "crown of righteousness" that will be awarded to himself and all who love the appearing of the Lord. These three verbs and three phrases made a powerful statement of confidence in the Lord's faithfulness to him!

---

108. Broneer, "Paul and the Isthmian Games," 404.

Oscar Broneer, several years ago now, presented the archaeological and literary background for this statement. At the end of his presentation he paraphrased 2 Tim 4:7–8:

> "I have competed in the good athletic games; I have finished the foot race, I have kept the pledge [i.e. to compete honestly, with reference to the athletic oath]. What remains to me is to receive the crown of righteousness, which has been put aside for me; it will be awarded to me by the Lord, the just umpire, on that day" (an allusion to the last day of the games when, presumably, the prizes were handed out to the winners).[109]

Thus, Paul's last use of *pistis* in his last letter referred both to his entire ministry of faithfulness to the Lord, his Christian faith, and to the *pledge* to compete honestly (athletic metaphor) by preaching the word without peddling it or using dishonest means of reaching people with the gospel ("no hocus pocus, no clever tricks, no dishonest manipulation of the word of God"). In essence Paul challenged Timothy with his perfect tense verbs: "I competed!" "I finished the competition!" "I competed according to the rules!" "Therefore, I await (present tense) the crown!" "This is a powerful analogy of Paul's faithful life of service, his integrity with the gospel message, his disciplined commitment to souls he had ushered into the kingdom, and his expectation of meeting his master at the finish line."[110]

This concludes the discussion of the *pistis Christou* debate (Romans, Galatians, Philippians, and Ephesians) as well as the *pistis* word group in the rest of the traditional Pauline letters (Colossians, Philemon, 1–2 Thessalonians, 1–2 Corinthians, and the Pastorals). Chapter 5 will cover the general epistles, excepting the letters of John (Hebrews, James, 1–2 Peter, and Jude).

---

109. Broneer, "Paul and the Isthmian Games," 420 (brackets Broneer's). The "perishable wreath" mentioned in 1 Cor 9:25 may be a reference to the withered celery leaf crown awarded to winners in the events at the Isthmian games. See p. 404. Paul's expected crown would be eternal and lasting: a "crown of righteousness."

110. A *crowning* statement by Dr. Tom Ewald.

5

The General Epistles

> "All that the pastor has said about the full sufficiency of Jesus to atone for sin and bring the faithful into God's presence is encompassed in the all-inclusive phrase 'the Pioneer and Perfecter of the faith.'"
> —GARETH LEE COCKERILL[1]

HAVING SURVEYED THE TRADITIONAL Pauline epistles for the *pistis Christou* phrases (giving the subjective genitive interpretation) and the *pistis* word group (verb, noun, and adjective), the general epistles, minus the Johannine letters (1–3 John), will now be examined. Hebrews, James, 1–2 Peter, and Jude will yield some interesting and substantial thoughts on "the faithfulness of Jesus the Messiah." In fact, the major theme of Hebrews *is* "the faithfulness of Jesus."

Hebrews: "Come to the Mountain!"

Authorship

The Epistle "to the Hebrews" is one of the most profound epistles in the New Testament. Its content can be overwhelming to the neophyte who makes a first attempt at digesting its message. But it is not impossible, for it was written to be clearly understood and acted on: "I appeal to you,

---

1. Cockerill, *Hebrews*, 606. Cockerill calls the author of Hebrews "the pastor."

brothers, bear with my word of exhortation, for I have written to you briefly" (Heb 13:22). If this is a "brief" letter, what would this author's "lengthy" letter be? However, no one knows the author of this letter.[2] How the authorship was lost is impossible to know, yet many have made guesses. Perhaps the most famous and common is Martin Luther's guess that it was Apollos, since Apollos was eloquent, competent in the Scriptures, and fervent in spirit. While he taught accurately about Jesus, he only knew about the baptism of John. Priscilla and Aquila met him in Ephesus and taught him "the way of God more accurately" (Acts 18:24–26).

Apollos, then, began a great ministry to Jews who did not believe in the Messiah. He went to Corinth. "When he arrived, he greatly helped those who through grace had believed, for he powerfully refuted the Jews in public, showing by the Scriptures that the Christ was Jesus" (Acts 18:27b–28). Such a person could have written this "word of exhortation." In more recent years, T. W. Manson made the same guess. For many years, because of the KJV which had added the title "The Epistle of Paul the Apostle to the Hebrews," the letter was thought to be by Paul. Few today accept that view, though it has had a long history. Manson gave a new title to the epistle by calling it "The Epistle of Apollos to the Churches of the Lycus Valley."[3] Manson thought that Apollos, the Hellenistic Jew from Alexandria, was well acquainted with the Colossian heresy and addressed those issues with this letter of exhortation.

William Lane wrote: "In antiquity, the names of Paul, Barnabas, Luke, and Clement of Rome were mentioned in certain church centers as the author of Hebrews. In current scholarship, Apollos, Silvanus, the deacon Philip, Priscilla and Aquila, Jude, Aristion, and others have found their proponents."[4] Ruth Hoppin has argued vigorously for Priscilla's authorship of the letter.[5] It is still a guess.

It is difficult to understand how the author of a theological letter such as Hebrews, with emphasis on the high priesthood of Jesus, could have been lost to those who selected the canon of the New Testament. Perhaps the best that one can say about authorship of Hebrews is what

---

2. From this point I will refer to the author of Hebrews as "author" and to the "book of Hebrews" as "Hebrews."

3. Manson, "Epistle to the Hebrews," 1.

4. Lane, *Hebrews 1–8*, xlix.

5. Hoppin, *Priscilla's Letter*. While her arguments are clever and extensive, they are not convincing. We will never know the author until that Day! Note: a masculine participle is employed in Heb 11:32 which argues against female authorship.

Lane wrote: "Although the writer is presumably within the Pauline circle and expects to travel with Timothy 'our brother' (13:23), it is certain that he is not Paul, but one who numbered himself among those to whom the immediate hearers of the Lord had delivered the gospel (2:3–4)."[6] The author had to have been a learned Greek scholar, for the Greek of Hebrews is sophisticated in terms of grammar and vocabulary. Perhaps Hebrews made it into the canon because of the power of its message about the faithfulness of Jesus the Messiah as our high priest.

The Recipients

Most early commentators on Hebrews took for granted that the recipients of the letter were ethnic Jews who had become Christian and were in danger of reverting back to Judaism, either because they were being persecuted by Roman officials who did not recognize their legitimacy as a "religion," such as Judaism enjoyed, or because they simply became lethargic toward their own faith in Jesus as Messiah and sought to go back to the splendor and majesty of Jewish worship at the temple (at least to support it). Just as there has been a move among Pauline scholars to see the recipients of the Epistle to the Romans as exclusively gentile, so too the recipients of Hebrews. David DeSilva has argued strongly for this opinion. He wrote:

> Gentile Christians would be subject to the "discipline" of their Greco-Roman neighbors on account of their flagrant violation of the values of piety, gratitude, and civic unity; Jewish Christians would come under pressure from their non-Christian Jewish family and associates. The goal of all non-Christians was the same—to correct the dangerous and vicious errors of their former colleagues by any means necessary.[7]

DeSilva made a strong case for the recipients being gentile Christians, but the argument of William Lane seems better: "The social and religious roots of this community are almost certainly to be traced to the Jewish quarters and to participation in the life of a Hellenistic synagogue."[8] He argued well for the recipients to be mainly Jewish Christians in Rome.

---

6. Lane, *Hebrews 1–8*, xlix.

7. DeSilva, *Perseverance in Gratitude*, 12. See his full discussion on pp. 2–23.

8. Lane, *Hebrews 1–8*, liv. For his full discussion on recipients, see his "Introduction," pp. xlvii–lxvi.

The historical background to the persecution of this group would be "the edict of Claudius" in AD 49 (the expulsion of Jews from Rome) and the Neronian persecutions that started c. AD 64–66.[9]

Of all the commentaries available today, the most beneficial was Gareth Cockerill's commentary (*The New International Commentary on the New Testament*). He took a "middle of the road" position on recipients. After much exposition on possible recipients, he wrote: "'Jewish Christian' describes both Jews and Gentiles who give allegiance to Christ while insisting on or feeling the need of various Jewish associations or practices."[10] While he is cautious to not be dogmatic about such things, he suggested that the recipients were probably "Jewish Christians" (meaning both Jews and gentiles) who were in a "house church" amongst a larger community of Christians in Rome. They certainly were Hellenistic in background and understood their Scriptures from a version or versions of the Septuagint. Regardless of what position one holds about authorship and the recipients, Cockerill's comments are appropriate: "One can understand Hebrews without identifying either the name of its author or the location of the recipients. One cannot, however, interpret Hebrews without taking a position as to whether the recipients were Jewish or Gentile believers."[11] Cockerill is vague in his own arguments here by putting both Jew and gentile Christians as recipients of this letter. But the edge is of "Jewish Christians" who are attracted to their previous commitments to the synagogue, thus the Jewish temple worship.

Cockerill thinks that the author of Hebrews "tips his hand" at Heb 13:9–10 by saying to his house church not to live according to the old order but to go "outside the camp" (13:13): "The pastor's intention has been to encourage his hearers clearly to distinguish themselves from those who still live by the provisions of that former order. To go 'outside the camp' (13:13) is to separate from these people."[12]

Hebrews will forever remain a mystery as to authorship and its recipients. Every interpreter must stay humble before this mystery.

---

9. See Lindars, *Letter to the Hebrews*, 18. He wrote: "But two events in Rome would be likely to leave a mark on Hebrews, if it were sent to Rome. One is the expulsion of Jews from Rome by the emperor Claudius in AD 49 (Acts 18.2), which was not revoked until the accession of Nero in 54. The other is the persecution of Christians following the great fire of Rome (which Nero blamed on the Christians) in 64."

10. Cockerill, *Hebrews*, 20.

11. Cockerill, *Hebrews*, 19.

12. Cockerill, *Hebrews*, 21.

However, like DeSilva (gentiles) or Lane (Jews) or Cockerill (Jews and gentiles), it is necessary to declare how one is approaching the text in order to make sense of it in a given context. For the purposes of this brief look at Hebrews, in light of the *pistis* word group, I am in favor of supporting Lane's opinion but allowing for a minority of gentiles as espoused by Cockerill. Rome is probably the destination of the letter, but, again, that is not without its problems. The date cannot be certain either, but I prefer a mid-60s date: AD 63–67. The content and message of this great "word of exhortation" are much more certain.

The "Word of Exhortation": Its Motifs and Themes

The author of Hebrews pled for his listeners to "bear with my word of exhortation" (Heb 13:22). Indeed, the letter is more a sermon than a letter. The letter form is not found except at the end—Heb 13:18–25, with a request for prayer for present circumstances, a benediction, and a final greeting. Hebrews 1–12 holds together as a well-crafted sermon of exposition of Scripture and interspersed with five exhortations or warnings. These could be the hindering "sin which clings so closely" as Christians attempt to run the race of life (12:1):

1. Drifting away from our salvation (2:1–4)
2. The hardening of the heart (full text, 3:7—4:13; specific text, 4:12–13)
3. Laziness in hearing (full text, 5:11—6:12; specific text, 6:4–8)
4. High-handed sin (full text, 10:19–39; specific text, 10:26–31)
5. Bitter root (full text, 12:12–29; specific text, 12:25–29).

If one were to pull out these five exhortations and squeeze the letter together, it still would be an exposition of Jesus as the faithful Son of God who is our great high priest with the aim that we be faithful as well. The following motifs and themes enhance the message of the faithful Messiah. Each major theme and motif will find its climax in chapter 12.

- A major theme in the letter is the encouragement to "draw near to God" (using the verb προσέρχομαι, *proserchomai*, "to draw near, approach, come to"). It is a word used in the Septuagint (LXX) for "entering covenant relationship with God and approaching him in worship.... It can be used of priestly ministry (Lev 9:7; 21:17; 22:3) or of congregational worship (Exod 16:9; Lev 9:5)."[13] The theme is introduced at Heb 4:16 and continues throughout the sermon (7:19 using ἐγγίζω, *engizō*, "draw near," a synonym; 7:25; 10:1, 22; 11:6), climaxing at Heb 12:18, 22 with the closing of the sermon itself. The subtitle "Come to the mountain!" captures a major theme of this letter sermon.

- Another major theme is "Sonship," also climaxing in chapter 12 (1:2, 3, 5; 2:10, 11; 3:6; 5:5, 8; 6:6; 7:28; 10:29; and 12:5–11).

- The theme of Jesus' high priesthood is, likewise, a major theme. The word, "high priest" (ἀρχιερεύς, *archiereus*), is used seventeen times with special references to Jesus (3:1; 4:14, 15; 6:20).

- The theme of "faithfulness" can be found throughout (see 2:10, 13; 3:2; 3:7—4:13, its opposite "unfaithfulness"; 5:5–9; 11:1–40 the "by faith" chapter; and 10:38–39 with 12:1–3 for the faithfulness of Jesus. This major theme will be explored in more detail later.[14] The terms of "trust" or "trustworthiness" could be used for many of these references.

- A theme related to the above is usually translated as "perfect" or "to be perfect," but this idea from τέλειος, *teleios* (Heb 9:11), can also be thought of as "complete" or "mature" (see 5:14). The noun, τελειότης, *teleiotēs*, is used once for "maturity" or "completeness" (6:1). The verb, τελειόω, *teleioō*, is used frequently (2:10; 5:9; 7:19, 28; 9:9; 10:1, 14; 11:40; and 12:23). It can be translated as "complete, bring to an end, finish." It can also mean "bring to full measure, fulfill." Another noun, τελείωσις, *teleiōsis*, is used once (7:11) and translated as "perfection" in ESV. It is possible to see this as "completion." A related noun, τελεωτής, *teleiōtēs*, is used only once (12:2) and is translated "perfecter" in ESV. However, it can also be translated as "completer." The idea of being "complete" is best used in

---

13. Cockerill, *Hebrews*, 227.

14. See Marohl, *Purpose of Hebrews*. Marohl gives various insights into the comparisons and contrasts found in Hebrews. He wrote: "However, when social identity theory, and in particular the theories of shared life story and prototypicality are related to Hebrews, the meaning of such comparisons is made clear. Jesus is described as the prototype of faithfulness. In return, all other faithful members of God's house are described in relation to Jesus. While the addressees and the 'great cloud' are faithful, their faithfulness is understood only in relation to the prototypical faithfulness of Jesus. In addition, the author integrates both Jesus and the addressees into an ongoing story of faithfulness" (148).

reference to Jesus (5:9), rather than the ESV "perfect." This term is applied to Christians as well.

- The overall theme of the letter (as a sermon) is "in these last days he [God] has spoken to us by [his] Son" (Heb 1:2a, my translation). Since there is no article with the word "son," the text could be translated "one who is a Son" or simply "Sonship." This theme is pervasive throughout Hebrews. The following texts only highlight the theme: 1:2; 4:12–13; and 12:25–29. One can discern in the sermon that God speaks (1:5–13; 5:6; 7:21; 10:37–38; 12:5–6, 26), the Son speaks (2:12–13; 10:5–7), and Holy Spirit speaks (3:7–11; 10:15–18). Of course, this theme is more complex than the above points, for there are others who speak in this sermon as well, but they are all speaking "the word of the Lord."[15] The final exhortation is: "See that you do not refuse him who is speaking" (Heb 12:25a). This theme controls all the others.

- A major motif is the use of the word "better": a better name (1:4); better things that belong to salvation (6:9); the lesser is blessed by the better (7:7); a better hope (7:19); a better covenant (7:22); a covenant he mediates is better (8:6); better promises (8:6); better sacrifices (9:23); a better possession and abiding one (10:34); a better country (11:16); a better life (11:35); something better for us (11:40); and a better word than the blood of Abel (12:24).

- Another major motif is the throne of God (1:3, 8; 8:1; 10:12; and 12:2, 28; see Rev 3:21).

- A minor motif, but important one, is the thought of fixing our eyes/thoughts on Jesus (2:9; 3:1; and 12:2).

Before leaving the motifs and themes completely, mention must be made as to how Hebrews presents the "superiority of Jesus the Messiah" over against all the old covenant era institutions and people, a message appropriate for a Jewish audience:

- Jesus is superior to old covenant revelation (1:1) because "in these last days he [God] has spoken to us by (One who is a Son), i.e., Sonship" (1:2a, my translation).

---

15. According to George H. Guthrie in his article "Hebrews," 921. God is the speaker for twenty-three quotations, while four are placed on the lips of the Christ and four are attributed to the Holy Spirit.

- Jesus is superior to angels because he is God's Son (1:4–14; 2:5–16).
- Jesus is superior to sinful humanity because he was perfect/complete/mature (*teleioō, teleios*) man, man as man was meant to be, who fulfilled the human vocation of Ps 8 (2:9).
- Jesus, by dying on behalf of humanity's sin, is superior to the devil himself because he destroyed the devil who had the power of death (2:14).
- Jesus is superior to Moses because Jesus is a Son over God's house rather than a servant within God's house (3:3–6).
- Jesus is superior to the Joshua of the old covenant because unlike him, Jesus (*Joshua*) of the new covenant does lead his people to the promised rest (4:1–3; cp. 2:10; 12:1–2).
- Jesus is superior to Aaron, the old covenant high priest, because Jesus' priesthood is "after the order of Melchizedek" (5:6–10; 7:1–28).
- Jesus has entered the true sanctuary, heaven itself, rather than an earthly sanctuary (8:1–2; 9:11–12).
- Jesus has mediated a better covenant based on better promises in contrast to the old covenant (8:6–7; 9:15).
- Jesus has offered himself as the perfect sacrifice for the sins of the world in contrast to the old covenant sacrifices of bulls and goats which could never take away sins (9:26b–28; 10:4–14).
- Jesus is superior to the old covenant priesthood because his priesthood is permanent, and besides that he lives forever (7:23–24).
- Jesus is superior to the old covenant priests because he is "holy, innocent, unstained, separated from sinners, and exalted above the heavens" (7:26).
- Jesus is superior even to all the faithful because he is "the trail blazer and completer of faithfulness" (12:2, my translation). As Ron Simkins has written: "It is this daily human living throughout his thirty plus years of life that gives Jesus' faithfulness in the face of an unjust execution its deep meaning."[16]
- Finally, Jesus is superior to the old covenant concept of kingdom because he gives a kingdom that cannot be shaken in judgment (12:25–29; cp. 9:28b).

16. Comment by Simkins, reader of my rough drafts.

Indeed, Jesus is superior over all old covenant institutions and people.

Structural Outline of Hebrews

William Lane has an excellent introduction to the structural analysis of Hebrews.[17] Gareth Cockerill also presents a good overall introduction to the "rhetorically effective structure" of the epistle.[18] In spite of so much scholarly work done on the structure of Hebrews, there is no consensus among them. Cockerill surveyed the best ideas on the subject and presented his own approach to its structure. He took the "best" of others and added his own insight into his presentation, especially the center section of Heb 8:1—10:18.[19] Cockerill showed how the "symphony in three movements" (8:1–13; 9:1–22; 9:23—10:18) on the themes of "sanctuary" (8:1–2; 9:1–10; 9:23–24), "sacrifice" (8:3–6; 9:11–15; 9:25—10:14), and "covenant" (8:7–13; 9:16–22; 10:15–18) developed the main theme of Jesus as our faithful and merciful high priest (Heb 5–7). He revealed that the climactic point of these texts is Heb 10:5–10, the heart of the third movement. He wrote: "These verses affirm that Christ's effective sacrifice is the willing offering of himself unto death as an obedient human being."[20] The following is essentially Cockerill's outline with slight changes, showing the chiastic structure.

A. God Has Spoken in His Son (1:1—2:18) [From the Mountain]
   In His Son (1:1–4)
      Through the Eternal Son (1:5–14)
         Don't Neglect "So great a salvation" (2:1–4) [*First Warning*]
      By the Suffering Son (2:5–18)
B. Avoid the Disobedient (3:1—4:13) [Pilgrimage to the Promised Home]
   The Faithful Son (3:1–6)
      The Unfaithful Generation (3:7–19)
      Avoid Them (4:1–11)

---

17. Lane, *Hebrews 1–8*, lxxv–ciii. See especially lxxxix, a chart for nine scholarly opinions on the structure of Hebrews. Lane also admires and presents Guthrie's *Structure of Hebrews*, xc–xcviii.

18. Cockerill, *Hebrews*, 60–81.

19. See Cockerill, "Structure and Interpretation."

20. Cockerill, "Structure and Interpretation," 179.

The General Epistles

[*Second Warning*] (4:12-13) [Prepare for Christ's High Priesthood, 4:14-16]

C. Christ's High Priesthood (4:14—10:18) [Enters the Tent]

    The New High Priest and the Old (5:1-10)

        Reverse Your Unnatural Regression (5:11—6:3)

            Avoid the Danger of Apostasy (6:4-6) [*Third Warning*]

            Shun Apostasy and Embrace the Community of the Faithful (6:9-12)

                Trust God's Promise Verified by God's Oath (6:13-20)

    Melchizedek Is Greater than Levi (7:1-10)

        The Priest in "the likeness of Melchizedek" Displaces Aaron (7:11-25)

        This Priest is Exactly the Kind of Priest We Need (7:25-28)

            Our High Priest's All-Sufficient Sacrifice: A Symphony in Three Movements (8:1—10:18)

            First Movement: The New Promised (8:1-13) [sanctuary 8:1-2; sacrifice 8:3-5; covenant 8:6-13]

            Second Movement: The Old Antiquated; the New Foreshadowed (9:1-22) [sanctuary 9:1-10; sacrifice 9:11-15; covenant 9:16-22]

            Third Movement: The New Explained (9:23—10:18) [sanctuary 9:23-24; sacrifice 9:25—10:14; covenant 10:15-18]

B¹ Join the Faithful (10:19—12:3) [Entering the Tent]

    Appropriate Christ's High Priesthood (10:19-25)

        [*Fourth Warning*] (10:26-31)

            Join Them (10:32-39)

                The Past Faithful (11:1-40)

                    The Exalted Son (12:1-3)

A¹ God Speaks/Will Speak in His Son (12:4-29) [From the Mountain]

    The Suffering of Legitimate Sons and Daughters (12:4-13)

        Don't Fall into Apostasy (12:14-17)

Through the Son from Heaven (12:18–24)

At the Judgment: [*Fifth and Final Warning*] (12:25–29)

The Letter Ending: Final Exhortations and Benediction (13:1–25)

The Community of the Faithful and the Life of Gratitude and Godly Fear (13:1–6)

The Unbelieving World and the Life of Gratitude and Godly Fear (13:7–17)

A Sermon Sent as a Letter (13:18–25)

The Message of Hebrews and Its Use of the *Pistis* Word Group

The following is where the *pistis* word group is found in Hebrews:

> *Pistos*, the adjective "faithful" (Heb 2:17; 3:2, 5; 10:23; and 11:11).
>
> *Pisteuō*, the verb "to trust/believe" (Heb 4:3; 11:6).
>
> *Pistis*, the noun, "trust/trustworthy/faith/faithfulness" (Heb 4:2; 6:1, 12; 10:22, 38, 39; 11:1, 3, 4, 5, 6, 7^2, 8, 9, 11, 13, 17, 20, 21, 22, 23, 24, 27, 28, 29, 30, 31, 33, 39; 12:2; and 13:7).
>
> *Apistia*, the negative noun "unbelieving, unbelief" (Heb 3:12, 19).

With these references in mind, the message of Hebrews and its usage of the adjective *pistos*, "faithful" (2:17; 3:2, 5; 10:23; and 11:11), and the negative noun *apistia*, "unbelief" (3:12, 19), will be examined.

The message of Hebrews is clearly centered on Jesus, who is called "the apostle and high priest of our confession, who was *faithful* to him who appointed him" (Heb 3:1b–2a, my emphasis). The author contrasts Moses as a servant *in* (ἐν, *en*, Greek) God's house (Israelites) with Jesus as a Son *over* (*epi*, Greek) God's house (Jews and gentiles who believe). "But Christ [Messiah] is *faithful* [implied] over God's house as a son. And we are his house if indeed we hold fast our confidence and our boasting in our hope" (Heb 3:6, my insertions and emphasis). Dennis Hamm prefers the passive meaning "trustworthy" rather than the active meaning "trusting," and, therefore, "faithful."[21] Jesus is trustworthy in his role as high priest. In a nutshell this is the heart of the message of Hebrews.

Hebrews 1:1–14 established the fact that "in these last days he [God] has spoken to us by One who is a Son" (my translation). As stated earlier,

---

21. Hamm, "Epistle to the Hebrews," 281

there is no article with "Son" in the Greek text and thus the quality of sonship is being expressed here in terms of God's revelation of himself to the world. God speaks to us through that Sonship. He is the divine Son, through whom God created the world, the radiance of the glory of God, the exact imprint of God's nature, upholding the universe by the word of his power (Heb 1:2b–3b). That is why he is "heir of all things" (Heb 1:2a). Yet, a hint of his "humanity" and purpose for coming to earth is given: "After making purification for sins, he sat down at the right hand of the Majesty on high, having become as much superior to angels as the name he has inherited is more excellent than theirs" (Heb 1:3c–4). This pregnant phrase will be explored throughout the rest of the "word of exhortation" (13:22).

Hebrews 1:1–4 is the introduction (*exordium*) to the entire letter sermon. But it is also a part of a chiasm for vv. 5–14. Victor Rhee has shown this in his study of Heb 1:1–14:[22]

A The function of the Son: God's final spokesperson (vv. 1–2a).

  B The Son in his exaltation: heir of all things (v. 2b).

    C The Son in his preexistence: bearer of God's nature, creator, and sustainer of the world (vv. 2c–3b).

      D The Son in his incarnation: purifier of sins (v. 3c).

        E The Son in his exaltation: he sat down at the right hand of God, with the result that he became superior to the angels (vv. 3d–4).

        E¹ The Son in his exaltation: because of God's enthronement of the Son at the right hand, he is superior to the angels (v. 5).

      D¹ The Son in his incarnation: the Son who is brought into the world is superior to the angels because they worship him (v. 6).

    C¹ The Son in his preexistence: the Son is superior to the angels because he is God (vv. 7–12).

  B¹ The Son in his exaltation: the Son is superior to the angels because the Father has exalted him at his right hand (v. 13).

A¹ The function of the angels: the Son is superior to the angels because they are the ministering spirits for the sons who will inherit salvation (v. 14).

---

22. Rhee, "The Role of Chiasm," 342.

Rhee has shown how this "carefully designed chiasm" emphasizes the "three stages of Christ's existence" (preexistence, incarnation, exaltation).[23] He concluded his article by showing how these three existences of the Messiah are presented throughout Hebrews:

> The three aspects of Christ's existence are crucial for the author because they are the basis for exhorting the readers to continue in faith in God. For this reason he introduces these concepts in 1:1–4, repeats them artistically in 1:5–14 in an inverted order, and further delineates them in other parts of the epistle (e.g., preexistence: 2:9; 10:5; 13:8; incarnation: 2:5–18; 5:7–8; 12:2–3; exaltation; 5:5–6, 9; 8:1; 12:2–3; 13:12) to encourage his audience not to forsake Christ, who is the author and perfecter of faith.[24]

Using mainly psalm passages from a Septuagint version, the author supported his exposition in Heb 1:5–14 (Ps 2:7; 2 Sam 7:14; Ps 97:7 or Deut 32:43; Ps 104:4; Ps 45:6–7; Ps 102:25–27; and Ps 110:1). After a brief exhortation to "pay much closer attention to what we have heard" (Heb 2:1), the author exclaimed "how shall we escape if we neglect such a great salvation" (2:3a)! At this point the author quoted Ps 8:4–6 LXX (Heb 2:6–8a) in order to give the true purpose of the Son's incarnation (see D and D¹ above). Psalm 8 is being used in a double sense of a mandate for all humankind and as a "messianic" passage. The author explained in this manner: "Now in putting everything in subjection to him [humankind], he left nothing outside his [humankind's] control. At present, we do not yet see everything in subjection to him [humankind]. But we see him [Jesus] who for a little while was made lower than the angels, namely Jesus, crowned with glory and honor because of the suffering of death, so that by the grace of God he might taste death for everyone" (Heb 2:8b–9, my insertions).

In other words, sinful humanity has never fulfilled the human vocation of proper oversight over the creation. But "we see Jesus" who, indeed, did fulfill the mandate. One can point to the gospel reports (see the Gospel of Mark) of how Jesus healed various diseases, cast out demons, calmed a storm, raised people from the dead, multiplied fish and bread, walked on water, experienced a transfiguration, cursed a fig tree, predicted his betrayal by Judas and a denial by Peter, and even predicted his own death and subsequent resurrection.

---

23. Rhee, "The Role of Chiasm," 361.
24. Rhee, "The Role of Chiasm," 362.

These actions by Jesus revealed how his true humanity has fulfilled Ps 8. Jesus is "bringing many sons (and daughters) to glory" (Heb 2:10b). Jesus is the "founder of their salvation," having made their salvation "perfect through suffering" (Heb 2:10). The term "founder" (ESV) (*archēgon*) can be understood as "originator," "leader, ruler, prince";[25] "pioneer" (RSV); "author" (NIV). Lane's suggestion sought to take the entire paragraph into consideration. He commented: "A translation of ἀρχηγός sensitive to the cultural nuances of the term in Hellenism and appropriate to the literary context of v 10 is 'champion.' . . . Jesus is 'the champion' who secured the salvation of his people through the sufferings he endured in his identification with them, and more particularly through his death."[26]

The only other place in Hebrews where this word is used of Jesus is Heb 12:2, the climax of the author's exhortation to faithfulness. Lane translated this verse accordingly: "fixing our eyes upon Jesus, the champion in the exercise of faith and the one who brought faith to complete expression, who rather than the joy set before him endured a cross, disregarding the disgrace, and has now taken his seat at the right hand of the throne of God."[27] Another word may encompass both the idea of "champion" and "pioneer," which is "trailblazer." Jesus, indeed, was the *trailblazer* (*archēgon*) of faithfulness as well as the *completer* (*teleiōtēn*) of faithfulness (Heb 12:2).[28]

The incarnation of the Son was essential in order to save mankind from death. In fact, as Simkins expressed it, "Demeaning Jesus' humanness leads to diminishing his amazing faithfulness."[29] "Since therefore the children share in flesh and blood, he himself likewise partook of the same things, that through death he might destroy the one who has the power of death, that is, the devil" (Heb 2:14). Jesus' resurrection vindicated him as God's Son (see Rom 1:4) and thus he became the firstfruits for all believers who die (1 Cor 15:20). The devil can no longer hold death over humankind since the resurrection of Jesus and his subsequent exaltation. The author of Hebrews continued his thoughts: "Therefore he had to be made like his brothers in every respect, so that he might become a

25. "*archēgon*," in BDAG 138–39.
26. Lane, *Hebrews 1–8*, 57.
27. Lane, *Hebrews 9–13*, 397.
28. A suggestion offered by Ron Simkins. I agreed.
29. Comment by Ron Simkins.

merciful and *faithful* high priest in the service of God, to make propitiation for the sins of the people" (Heb 2:17, my emphasis). On this use of *pistos* (2:17) and at 3:2, Hamm comments:

> Since both passive and active meanings ("trustworthy" and "faithful") are available in the adjective *pistos*, it seems reasonable that, in climaxing his treatment of Jesus' solidarity with humankind (2:17), our author should invoke the dimension of "faithful," and then, in introducing the section of Jesus' dependable authority (3:2), he should use the same word to refer to the exalted Christ as "trustworthy." That one word, *pistos*, should serve both meanings makes the transition all the more graceful.[30]

Jesus was man as man was meant to be, true man, and it is this status that allowed him to become the "merciful and faithful high priest in the service of God." This is the first statement that began the exposition of Jesus' high priesthood (see 1:3c).

Jesus was and is faithful to God, who appointed him as "apostle and high priest" (Heb 3:1–2). The author did not denigrate Moses, for he wrote: "Now Moses was faithful in all God's house as a servant, to testify to the things that were to be spoken later, but Christ [Messiah] *is faithful* [implied in Greek] over God's house as a son. And we are his house if indeed we hold fast our confidence and our boasting in our hope" (Heb 3:5–6; my comments in brackets).

Twice more *pistos*, the adjective "faithful," is used of God. "Let us hold fast the confession of our hope without wavering, for he who promised is faithful" (Heb 10:23). On this verse Lane commented: "The community possesses the strongest incentive for fidelity in the faithfulness (πιστός) of God who does what he has promised (v 23b). The formulation πιστὸς γὰρ ὁ ἐπαγγειλάμενος, 'for he who promised is faithful,' is confessional in character."[31] The other reference is found at Heb 11:11—"By faith Sarah herself received power to conceive, even when she was past the age, since she considered him [God] faithful who had promised." Thus, in Hebrews, *pistos* is used of God (three times), Jesus (once and implied once), and Moses (once).

After having established the divinity and the true humanity of the Son as the basis for Jesus' merciful and faithful priesthood, the author explained the superiority of the Son over Moses. Moses led God's people out

---

30. Hamm, "The Jesus Factor," 282.
31. Lane, *Hebrews 9–13*, 289.

of Egypt as a servant, not as a son. Jesus is the Son who now leads God's people to glory (2:10). But first, the author will give a lengthy warning (Heb 3:7—4:13) about unbelief or unfaithfulness to God as exemplified in the first generation of Israelites, who exited Egypt with Moses as their leader. He quoted Ps 95:7–11 LXX to support the warning. That generation had an "evil, unbelieving heart" that led them "to fall away from the living God" (Heb 3:12). They were "hardened by the deceitfulness of sin" (3:13). They "rebelled" (v. 16), "sinned" (v. 17), and were declared "disobedient" (v. 18). "So we see that they were unable to enter because of unbelief" (Heb 3:19). This is the second use of *apistia*, "unbelief," and it functioned as an *inclusio* to bind vv. 12–19 together.

The verb, *pisteuō*, "to trust/to believe" is used only twice (Heb 4:3 and 11:6). In Heb 4:1–11 the author discussed the fact that a "promised rest" still remained for the people of God, for the Joshua of the old covenant did not give the people rest (4:1, 8–9). But he boldly stated: "For we who have believed enter that rest" (4:3a). The implication was that *those who trust the God of power and promises* will enter the rest of God. Even though the first generation were disobedient and could not enter God's rest, the author encouraged his listeners: "therefore it remains for some to enter it" (4:6a) and "there remains a Sabbath rest for the people of God" (4:9). He then concluded and exhorted: "Let us therefore strive to enter that rest, so that no one may fall by the same sort of disobedience" (4:11).

What does the "rest" mean? Walton has argued persuasively that "rest" meant finishing the "temple" (the creation of the earth) and then entering into the ongoing work of the "temple." The Psalms and Hebrews carried this idea forward to show that Jesus was opening the way to the work of being the fulfillment of God's great human temple project begun at creation (Gen 1–3). God is ruling over his creation in his "rest" and his people are to join him in that "rest" as we are commanded to have dominion, dress, till, keep, fill up, and subdue the earth (Gen 1:26–28). We must strive to enter that "rest."[32]

"Striving" is equivalent to obedience and living in faithfulness to God. Surveying *pistis/pisteuō* outside of Heb 11, Hamm summarized in this way: "Faith is obedience to divine initiative. It involves trust in God who will keep his promises. It is the opposite of *apistia* ('infidelity'), *apeitheia* ('disobedience'), and *hypostolē* ('apostasy'). It expresses itself in patience, perseverance, and a bold confidence in the face of trials. Faith

---

32. Walton, *Lost World of Genesis One*, 72–92.

is bold to 'approach' God (presumably, given the liturgical connotation of the word for 'approach', in community worship)."[33]

In Heb 11:6 the author showed the importance of trusting God's existence and his power to reward the faithful: "And without faith it is impossible to please him, for whoever would draw near to God *must believe* that he exists and that he rewards those who seek him" (Heb 11:6, my emphasis).

Pistis, "faith/faithfulness," is used thirty-two times in Hebrews. Hebrews 11 (the great "faith" chapter) includes twenty-four references. Only eight references are found outside chapter 11. Barnabas Lindars made the observation about *pistis* that "in Hebrews faith does not mean the content of the Christian confession, i.e. what I believe, but the quality of faithfulness in living in accordance with the Christian confession, i.e., what I do as a believer. Thus, the outcome of the life of these evangelists was their life of faith based on the confession."[34] Simkins explained: "Trust in the person of Jesus leading to trustworthy actions is the only proper response."[35]

The first use is found at Heb 4:2 in the context of the "unbelief" of the generation that exited Egypt: "For good news came to us just as to them, but the message they heard did not benefit them, because they were not united by faith with those who listened." This statement anticipated the use of *pistei* in chapter 11, those who did live the "good news" *by faith*. Certainly, Joshua and Caleb could be added to the list of the Hebrew heroes of chapter 11 (see Num 13:25—14:10).

The next two usages (Heb 6:1, 12) are in the context of an exhortation and warning (5:11—6:20; particularly 6:4-8) against possible apostasy. The author charged his recipients (listeners) with being "dull of hearing" (5:11). He wanted them to "leave the elementary doctrine of Christ and go on to maturity, not laying again a foundation of repentance from dead works and of faith toward God" (6:1). This is the foundational teaching of trusting in God's sovereignty over creation and his love for all humankind. It is very close to the idea expressed at 11:6: "And without faith it is impossible to please him, for whoever would draw near to God must believe that he exists and that he rewards those who seek him."

---

33. Hamm, "The Jesus Factor," 276.
34. Lindars, *Letter to the Hebrews*, 8–9.
35. An added critique by Ron Simkins.

Thus, the believer ought to go beyond this fundamental belief toward God (*pisteōs epi theon*) and move toward maturity.

At Heb 6:12 there is an obvious word used (νωθροί, *nōthroi*, "dull" or "sluggish") to bind the first three parts of the exhortation together (Shaming, 5:11—6:3; Warning, 6:4-8; and Consolation, 6:9-12). In the midst of a dire warning against possible apostasy (6:4-6), the author exhorted "so that you may not be sluggish, but imitators of those who through faith and patience inherit the promises" (6:12). This *pistis* ought to be understood as "faithfulness" since it is combined with "patience" and the end result is "inherit[ing] the promises." These thoughts build to a climax as unfolded in Heb 10:19—12:29, particularly the list of Hebrew heroes in chapter 11 and Jesus as the "trailblazer (champion? pioneer?) and completer (finisher? perfecter?) of faithfulness" (Heb 12:2). After the author gave assurance of hope to his listeners (6:13-20), he launched into a detailed exegesis of Ps 110:4b: "You are a priest forever after the order of Melchizedek" (Heb 7:1-28). The consequences of Jesus being a high priest "after the order of Melchizedek" are recounted in Heb 8:1—10:18 in what Cockerill labeled "a symphony in three movements."[36]

The author compared and contrasted three major ideas in three different places in the same order: *sanctuary* (8:1-2; 9:1-10; 9:23-24); *sacrifice* (8:3-6; 9:11-15; 9:25—10:14); and *covenant* (8:7-13; 9:16-22; 10:15-18). At the conclusion of these great expositions of the heavenly sanctuary, the perfect sacrifice, and the new covenant, the author invited his listeners to enter into the very presence of God, "the holy place(s)." By the blood of Jesus (his death on the cross), we now have access to God's presence "by the new and living way that he opened for us through the curtain, that is, through his flesh" (10:19b-20). While there is some ambiguity in this statement, it is clear that all Christians now have "a great priest over the house of God" (10:21; cp. 1:3b; 2:17; 3:1, 6; 4:14-16; 5:5-10; 6:20; 7:1-28; 8:1-2; 9:11-12, 14, 24-26; 10:5-10, 12-14).

Consequently, the author exhorted his listeners to do three things: 1) "Let us draw near"; 2) "Let us hold fast"; and 3) "Let us consider" (10:22a, 23a, 24a). The first exhortation is an invitation for worship: "Let us draw near with a true heart in full assurance of faith, with our hearts sprinkled clean from an evil conscience and our bodies washed with pure water" (10:22). The "true heart" is in contrast to the "evil heart" (3:12) of the wilderness generation. Also, the context of Jesus' obedience (10:5-10) and

---

36. See his commentary: Cockerill, *Hebrews*, 345-460.

the new covenant promise of God's law being placed in the heart (10:16; Jer 31:33), the double reference to "heart" in v. 22 is to be clearly understood in like manner. Fullness or full assurance of faith included the idea of a lifetime commitment to Messiah in terms of faithfulness. Forgiveness by his blood (10:17–18) cleanses us from an evil conscience, beginning with baptism ("our bodies washed with pure water," see Acts 2:38).

The last two usages of *pistis* in Heb 10 have to do with an Old Testament quote, so special attention will be given to these (Heb 10:38, 39). In Heb 10:32–39 the author encouraged his listeners to remember when they, earlier in their Christian life, were faithful in the midst of persecution (vv. 32–34). He then exhorted them to endure to the end, doing the will of God, in order to receive what God had promised (vv. 35–36). In other words, don't renounce your faith because of outside evil forces that seek to punish your non-conformance to their lifestyle. Stay faithful! The author, then, like in all his other exhortations, quoted Scripture.

But he did something special: he selected a beginning text from Isa 26:20, "Yet a little while." The context in Isaiah is about the apocalyptic city, the "New Jerusalem," which God will accomplish. Even though Israel has failed, the "faithful Israelite" will see a resurrection (Isa 26:19). Like Passover night, the people are to enter their rooms and shut the doors and hide "for a little while" (Isa 26:20). It is the promise that God will deliver them in their greatest need. Be patient, the persecution will not last long before God delivers, the Hebrews author is saying.

Secondly, the author reversed the last two lines of the text from Hab 2:3–4 LXX: "and the coming one will come and will not delay; but my righteous one shall live by faith, and if he shrinks back, my soul has no pleasure in him." The author added an article to "coming one" from the LXX to emphasize "the coming one" as the Messiah. "The righteous one" is parallel to this phrase. Both terms were understood to refer to the Messiah as promised by God. I have argued in Romans and Galatians that Hab 2:4b is used messianically throughout. Of course, the phrase can refer to those who trust God's provision for salvation through the faithful Messiah and thus can become "righteous ones" who live out of faithfulness as the Messiah did. That is the case here.

Hebrews 10:39 is the key to understanding the application of this text to the listeners: "But we are not of those who shrink back and are destroyed, but of those who have faith and preserve their souls." This ESV translation is typical of most English versions on this verse. My translation is quite different: "But we are not of 'shrinkers back' toward destruction, but of 'faithfulness' toward a living treasure (prized possession)." The following is how I came to this translation and interpretation.

Some years ago I did a word study on the Hebrew word סְגֻלָּה, *segullah*.[37] It is found only eight times in the Hebrew Scriptures (Exod 19:5; Deut 7:6; 14:2; 26:18; Ps 135:4; 1 Chr 29:3; Eccl 2:8; and Mal 3:17). The Septuagint (LXX) will use two nouns as synonyms to translate *segullah* in these texts: περιούσιος (*periousios*) and περιποίησις (*peripoiēsis*).[38] The literal meaning of *segullah* is "a king's most-prized treasure," usually silver and gold (see 1 Chr 29:3 and Eccl 2:8). All the other references in the Hebrew Scriptures are metaphorically applied to God's people. The two Greek words, as synonyms, are found in only six references in the New Testament (Titus 2:14; 1 Pet 2:9; Eph 1:14; Heb 10:39; 1 Thess 5:9; and 2 Thess 2:14). There is a verbal form of one of these synonyms found at Acts 20:28, relevant to my study. In all of these New Testament references the contexts indicated that the idea of *segullah* was behind the Greek words, especially in 1 Pet 2:9 (alluding to Exod 19:6), Titus 2:14, and Eph 1:14. First and Second Thessalonians can be questioned, but I have argued for *segullah* in both references: "a saved treasure" (1 Thess 5:9) and "a glorious treasure" (2 Thess 2:14), both referring to God's people. The question is: does Heb 10:39 refer to *segullah* as well or is it to be understood as ESV and other English versions translate the Greek word *peripoiēsin*?

I used this for a bible study one Sunday morning in a church in Pittsburgh, Pennsylvania. My audience was a number of college students, primarily from the University of Pittsburgh. When I had covered all the New Testament references and argued for *segullah* being behind the two Greek synonyms, I questioned my interpretation for Heb 10:39, for no English version or commentary viewed it as such. Instead, they all "turned" the noun into a verbal idea, "preserve," and translated it as saying: "preserving their souls." By the way, "their" is not in the Greek New Testament!

Unfortunately, the word "soul" is usually misunderstood in the Platonic concept: the immaterial part of man that is "immortal." The Jewish concept of "soul" is holistic. The Hebrew *nephesh* and the New Testament Greek *psuchēs* refer to personhood including all that defines personality: body, spirit, mind, heart, and maybe even flesh. Soul is close to but not exactly what we mean by "personality," which is everything

37. See Zorn, "Segullah." This is an academic presentation of the word *segullah*.

38. The study is more complicated than these two words, but essentially it is correct. See my study above.

that comprises who we are. Even if one were to translate it as "person" or "self" or even "life," it would not help the understanding of the phrase. The students responded as if this was the first time they ever heard of this definition of "soul"!

A young lady raised her hand and declared that she was in a PhD program and was studying "ancient metallurgy." She said that the context fit what she was learning in that class; i.e., that the context of Heb 10:32–39 is couched in the image of ancient metallurgy, that is, the art of purifying precious metals. The author of Hebrews reminded his readers they have only lost their "real estate," immovable treasure: "For you had compassion on those in prison, and you joyfully accepted the plundering of your property, since you knew that you yourselves had a better possession and an abiding one" (Heb 10:34). Indeed, they had more "lasting possessions" than that! They, themselves, were God's living treasure, his *segullah*! How is this presented?

Jesus, "the coming one," is the model of one who did not "shrink back" but held firmly to the task of living by faith(fulness). Jesus is "my righteous One" of the Habakkuk passage, which has been convoluted, that is, the lines were reversed, in order to emphasize the messianic content ("the coming one"). While the author applied this to the Messiah's Second Coming, the author referred to Messiah's incarnation and exaltation at Heb 12:1–3, presenting Jesus as the "pioneer/trailblazer and perfecter/completer of faithfulness," the paradigm for all Christians. Thus, Heb 12:1–3 and 10:37–39 became a "Jesus" *inclusio* for the great "by faith" listing of Hebrew heroes (Heb 11).

The student, Ann Joyce, had written notes on a pamphlet and she gave it to me at the conclusion of the class. This is what she wrote:

> v. 27—raging fire—purification, removal of impurities (enemies of God). Vv. 32, 33—example of standing fast as God's *segullah*. V. 34—confiscation of *property*, better and lasting *possessions*. The writer of Hebrews discusses three ideas about treasure: (1) *You have lost material treasures* vv. 35–36. (2) *You are promised eternal treasures.* V. 38—"shrink back"—the response of dross to heat. V. 39—Shrink back and are destroyed—a perfect visual description of the gold-refining process. This is exactly what dross does as it floats to the surface, pulls away from the pure metal towards the sides, and is completely consumed, leaving pure metal, which 'stands fast.' Those who believe and are God's *segullah*. (3) *YOU ARE GOD'S TREASURE!*" (Ann's emphasis)

In my article I wrote:

> In the process of purifying precious metals (such as silver and gold), the dross under a very hot fire rises to the top and shrinks back to the sides of the cauldron. The purified metal (silver or gold or any other precious metal) is then poured out for safe keeping, while the dross is scraped off the sides of the cauldron and thrown away. This is the imagery of the verse. The Hebrew Christians to whom this letter is addressed may lose their property (immovable possession) due to persecution, but through this purification process (the testing of fire), they have been found faithful with the result that they have become a *living* (movable) treasure to God. This reality one day will be "a great reward" (v. 35b). So there is a sense in this passage that Christians are God's *segullah* now, but they continue to be "purified" by trials and even persecution so that ultimately they will forever be God's purified "gold and silver," his prized treasure, a "living" *segullah*.[39]

That is why I translate Heb 10:39 with the understanding of *segullah* for the Greek word περιποίησιν (*peripoiēsin*) and then interpret ψυχῆς (*psuchēs*) as "living." So, my translation and interpretation of Heb 10:39 is: "But we are not of 'shrinkers back' toward destruction, but of 'faithfulness' toward a living treasure (prized possession)."

The next use of *pistis* is at Heb 11:1 where a definition of "faith" is given by the author as he begins a series of "by faith" statements of Hebrew heroes: "Now faith is the assurance of things hoped for, the conviction of things not seen." The ESV and many other English translations choose to translate the words *hupostasis* and *elegchos* in a subjective manner: "assurance" and "conviction," respectively. Cockerill argued effectively that these words should be understood in an objective manner. Cockerill translated Heb 11:1: "Now faith is the *reality* of things hoped for, the *evidence* of things not seen" (my emphasis).[40] His translation has sound semantic merit.

With this "rhetorical" definition, the author launched into a great listing of ancient Hebrew heroes. Hebrews 11 is divided into four sections: Heb 11:1–7 (The Primeval History—Gen 1–11); 11:8–22 (The Patriarchal History—Gen 12–50); 11:23–31 (The Moses Story and Entrance to the Promised Land); and 11:32–40 ("And what more shall I say?"—a

---

39. Zorn, "*Segullah*," 50.

40. Cockerill, *Hebrews*, 520–21. Many good resources support Cockerill's translation.

rhetorical account of acts of faith designed to evoke the emotions of the listeners). Eighteen times the author used *pistei* ("by faith") to begin his litany. What did they all have in common? They "did not receive what was promised" (Heb 11:39b).

However, with the coming of the "merciful and faithful high priest," Jesus, God has brought us to "perfection/completion" along with the ancient Hebrew heroes. It is clear that "by faith" in this chapter is to be understood as "faithfulness" in the fact that all who lived by "faith" did not actually see "the reality of the things hoped for." "Faith" becomes "faithfulness" when faith is exercised over time, enduring all kinds of cruel treatment from the unbelieving world (vv. 35–38). These Hebrew men and women of faithfulness have now been made "perfect," or better, "complete" along with believers in the Messiah, because Jesus is the "pioneer/trailblazer and perfecter/completer of faithfulness" (Heb 12:2a).

As already mentioned, Heb 12:1–3 formed an *inclusio* with 10:37–39. The author of Hebrews sought to encourage his listeners that Jesus is "the coming one" and he will come back. Therefore, don't "shrink back" toward destruction but rather by faithfulness be God's living treasure as God intended Israel to be in the first place (see Exod 19:5–6). But the listeners not only anticipate the future coming of Christ, they should look to Jesus for what he has already done in his incarnation and exaltation: "looking to Jesus the pioneer/trailblazer and perfecter/completer of faithfulness, who over against the joy that was set before him endured the cross, despising the shame, and is seated at the right hand of the throne of God" (Heb 12:2, my translation).

The words "pioneer" and "trailblazer" are good words for ἀρχηγὸν (*archēgon*), but other translations are available. Lane is insistent that the word as found in Heb 2:10 should be understood the same in 12:2. Lane writes:

> (. . . Jesus is 'the exemplar, the champion of faith'). In 2:10–16 Jesus' solidarity with the family of faith was presented under the aspect of cosmic struggle with the devil (2:14–15). In 12:2–3 his struggle is recalled in its personal aspect as the enduring of shame and of hostility from sinful men. The comparison of Jesus' experience with that of believers in 12:1–4 also suggests a leadership motif: Christ's conduct has exemplary value for his people in their own engagement with the demands of persevering faith.[41]

---

41. Lane, *Hebrews 9–13*, 411.

Cockerill prefers "pioneer": "As Pioneer of his people's salvation (2:10), Christ opened the way for their ultimate entrance into the presence of God by becoming their all-sufficient High Priest, able to cleanse them from sin. . . . 'Pioneer' and 'Perfecter/Completer' are reminiscent of the words for 'beginning' and 'end' respectively."[42] Both translations, "champion" and "pioneer," make good sense and it is difficult to decide one or the other. However, I prefer the ideas of "pioneer" or "trailblazer" along with the words "perfecter" or "completer." Jesus blazed the trail of faithfulness and brought it to completion or perfection, thus bringing all God's faithful people (both old and new covenant) to glory with him (Heb 2:10). As Wallis expressed it: "Jesus is, thus, the first to reach faith's heavenly goal and, as a result of the way in which this was accomplished, has enabled others to follow in his footsteps."[43] Jesus' faithfulness leads to our faithfulness. Jesus has led us to a new level of completion (Heb 2:10; 5:9; 7:28), not perfection as such. Jesus brings his people "to completion—a maturity of other human beings as well (Heb 6:1; 10:14; 11:40; 12:23)."[44] In other words, God completed Jesus, Jesus completes us!

In most English versions they interpret *pistis* in Heb 12:2 as "our faith." Only an article is in the Greek text: "the pioneer and completer of the faith." This refers back to Heb 11 ("by faith") and all those who are subsequently faithful after the Messiah's death, burial, resurrection, and exaltation. There is continuity between the old covenant people of God and the new covenant people of God (now made up of Jews and gentiles). They all manifest the same "faithfulness" as Jesus pioneered and completed it. This "faith" was paraphrased by Cockerill: "Faith is living in accord with the reality of things hoped for," or "faith is living as if the things hoped for are real."[45] This way of living affects all that we think, say, and do.

A final observation is whether "the joy set before him" is renounced by Jesus, translating the word *anti* as "instead of, over against," or embraced, thus the ESV "for." Lane made a good argument for the former and thus his translation: "who rather than the joy set before him endured a cross, disregarding the disgrace, and has now taken his seat at the right

---

42. Cockerill, *Hebrews*, 607.
43. Wallis, *Faith of Jesus Christ*, 157.
44. This insight was shared with me by Ron Simkins.
45. Cockerill, *Hebrews*, 521.

hand of the throne of God."[46] The author of Hebrews drew out the implications of this kind of faith for the people of God. It is a matter of endurance in the face of persecution and the author called it the "discipline" of a loving Father (Heb 12:3–17). In contrast to the wilderness generation, the author exhorted: "See to it that no one fails to obtain the grace of God" (Heb 12:15a). If we persevere in faith[fulness], we have already arrived (*proserchomai*, "draw near") at "Mount Zion and to the city of the living God, the heavenly Jerusalem" (Heb 12:22a). Only "acceptable worship" will bring us to what we yet cannot see (Heb 12:28). Already, we have come to the mountain! When Jesus returns, we, as faithful followers of Jesus, will experience Mount Zion in reality!

The final use of *pistis* in Hebrews is found at Heb 13:7, where the listeners of the author are encouraged: "Remember your leaders, those who spoke to you the word of God. Consider the outcome of their way of life, and imitate their faith." Apparently, these were their past leaders who had led them to accept Jesus as Lord and Messiah (Anointed King and High Priest). Having gone through some persecution along with these early leaders, the author wished for his listeners to "do it again." That is why he demanded: "Obey your leaders and submit to them, for they are keeping watch over your souls, as those who will have to give an account. Let them do this with joy and not with groaning, for that would be of no advantage to you" (Heb 13:17). Their present leaders have been neglected in terms of discipline and warnings with regard to their faith. To be faithful is to obey.

Conclusion

At the heart of the message of Hebrews is the "merciful and faithful high priest" (Heb 2:17). Indeed, "Christ (the Messiah) is faithful over God's house as a son" (Heb 3:6). Jesus is the apostle [sent by God] and high priest of our confession (Heb 3:1). On the basis of the divine Son of God (Heb 1) and the fact of his true humanity (Heb 2), Jesus is our high priest "after the order of Melchizedek" (Heb 5–7). With all of these facts established, the implications are enormous for one who would be faithful to this high priest: we have a new covenant (Heb 8), a heavenly sanctuary (Heb 9), and a perfect sacrifice, Jesus himself (Heb 10). We are invited to enter into the very presence of God in the heavenly holy of

---

46. Lane, *Hebrews 9–13*, 397.

holies (Heb 10:19–25). We are not to lose this great salvation by unbelief (Heb 3:7—4:11) but rather being surrounded by "so great a cloud of witnesses" (Heb 11), we are to look to Jesus, the pioneer/trailblazer and perfecter/completer of faithfulness, and follow him (Heb 12:1–17). If we do, we will have already arrived at the mountain of God—"Mount Zion, the city of the living God, the heavenly Jerusalem" (Heb 12:18–24). God, one day, will shake heaven and earth in judgment, and all that will be left is the "unshakable kingdom," which we are now receiving. Therefore, we should "offer to God acceptable worship with reverence and awe, for our God is a consuming fire" (Heb 12:25–29).

James: "Faith and Deeds"

James' uniqueness stands out among New Testament writings. It is the only letter that could possibly be labeled a "wisdom" genre. The author, James, is given, but which James? Tradition, rightly so, has presented this small letter as a message from James the Lord's brother, who became one of three leaders in the early Jerusalem church (see Acts 12:17; 15:13–21; 21:17; Gal 1:19; 2:9). There are others named "James" to consider, but James, the Lord's brother, is the best candidate. To keep this introduction to James brief, I will simply quote the evaluation of Patrick Hartin with whom I partly agree:

> In summary, the best reading of the evidence points to James of Jerusalem as the authority behind this circular or encyclical letter to the believers from the world of Israel ("the twelve tribes in the Dispersion") found scattered throughout the Roman world. This letter is sent in the name of James shortly after his death in order to remind communities in the Diaspora of his teachings and the relevance they hold for building themselves up as "the first fruits of his (God's) creatures" (1:18). This would date the letter somewhere in the late sixties of the first century C.E.[47]

While I agree with the author being James the Lord's brother, the letter could easily have been written much earlier, not necessarily published after his death (c. AD 62, according to Josephus). However, the author and date need not affect our understanding of its content.

The structure of James is difficult to discern, but most see Jas 2:14–26 as the central theme of the brief letter. "In 2.14–26 the overriding

---

47. Hartin, *James*, 25.

theme is that faith without works is dead and useless. This recurs as a constant, hammer-like refrain throughout the section (2.17, 20, 26). It is illustrated first (14–17) by an example very close to that in 2.1–7; that is the discrepancy between the faith that is claimed and the action which fails to correspond to it."[48] Chester earlier wrote: "The themes that are prominent, indeed notorious, in it have already been introduced and discussed earlier in the letter, especially 1.19–26; 2.1–13 (cf. also 1.2–4, 5–9), and are taken up subsequently (if less directly) in 3.13–18, 4.11–12 (cf. 4.13–17)."[49]

Pistis is used sixteen times in the letter (1:3, 6; 2:1, 5, 14², 17, 18³, 20, 22², 24, 26; 5:15). The verb, *pisteuō*, is used three times (2:19², 23). One can immediately see that most of these references are found in the section 2:14–26 (all but five!) with its theme of "faith" and "works." Leading up to Jas 2:14–26, James used *pistis* four times that help us understand this major theme.

James 1:3—"for you know that the testing of your faith produces steadfastness." And if one lacks wisdom, simply ask God "in faith" (1:6).

> For the letter of James faith means a total and complete trust in God that enables believers to withstand every form of testing and ultimately to survive the final eschatological test. This emerges clearly in 2:5 in the description of the faith of the poor: "Has not God chosen the poor in the world to be rich in faith and heirs of the kingdom that he has promised to those who love him?" The faith of the poor, their total trust and confidence in God, enables them to pass through trials and testing and become fellow members of God's twelve-tribe kingdom which will attain fulfillment in the future.[50]

The fourth use of *pistis* directly informs my thesis: the faithfulness of Jesus the Messiah—"My brothers, show no partiality as you hold the faithfulness of our Lord Jesus Christ, [the Lord] of glory" (Jas 2:1, my translation). The ESV and most all English versions translate the phrase as an objective genitive: "as you hold the faith in our Lord Jesus Christ." Most commentaries hold to this opinion, but the opinion and argument of Hartin supports my own opinion for the subjective genitive reading:

---

48. Chester and Martin, *Theology*, 22.
49. Chester and Martin, *Theology*, 20.
50. Hartin, *James*, 30.

However, the *subjective* genitive is more probable: "the faith of our Lord Jesus Christ." In the letter of James faith is directed toward God, the Father, rather than to Jesus (see 2:19, 23). In this sense (a subjective genitive) the faith to which James refers is Jesus' faithfulness to his Father's will through the obedience of his life. This faithfulness operates as an example for the lives of believers: a faithfulness demonstrated in actions. . . . In 2:1 the basis for avoiding favoritism is Jesus' faithfulness, the example of a life that embraced all people.[51]

The above four usages of *pistis* (Jas 1:3, 5; 2:1, 5) set the stage for the intensive discussion of *pistis* in Jas 2:14–26, a major theme in James. Basically, James is saying that genuine faith is always accompanied by "works" (better, "deeds"). If any believer does not take care of the needs of the poor, he or she is holding to a "false" faith. "So also faith by itself, if it does not have works, is dead" (2:17). Believing that God is one (Deut 6:4) is no better than demons believing! Verse 19 included two of the uses of the verb *pisteuō*, "to believe."

The other use is in reference to Abraham believing (trusting) in God (v. 23). James argued that faith can only be seen by accompanying "works" (v. 18). He wrote: "Faith apart from works is useless" (v. 20b). James combined Gen 15:6 and 22:9–18 to show Abraham's faith. "You see that faith was active along with his works, and faith was completed by his works (v. 22). Making his point even more strongly, James wrote: "You see that a person is justified by works and not by faith alone" (v. 24). This is the verse that allowed Luther, the great reformer, to call James a "straw epistle." He saw conflict between Paul's "justification by faith *alone*" and James' statement. Luther rejected James as a canonical letter. But this is clearly a mistake. Paul and James actually *agree*! For Paul, faith (including obedience) saves. Thus, faith becomes faithfulness in terms of that obedience (see Rom 1:5; 16:26 for "the obedience of faith"). For James, faith plus works ("deeds," *see below*) of obedience saves. Thus, proper deeds always accompany genuine faith and is part of faithfulness.[52]

Perhaps the use of the English word "works" for the Greek term *erga* skewed the understanding of the phrase. It would be much more to the original idea of James if it were translated "deeds." As Hartin has noted:

---

51. Hartin, *James*, 117.

52. The comparison of Paul and James with the idea of "faith/faithfulness" was shared with me by Dr. Carl Bridges, a dear friend and critical reader of this book in its rough draft.

"The *erga* ('works') to which James refers are understood as 'good deeds' (see, e.g. Matt 5:16; John 3:21) and not *erga nomou* ('works of the law')."[53] In other words, good deeds are the natural outworkings of a genuine faith. Otherwise, it is no faith at all or at best a "false" faith—"dead" or "useless." In light of that, Chester makes a good observation that James is referring in this paragraph to two different kinds of faith:

> It ["faith"] is used positively, in the sense of "true" faith, in 1.3, 6; 2.1, 5; 5:15, and also negatively, in the sense of "claimed," that is, *false*, faith, in 2:14–26. This distinction appears complicated by the fact that 2.14–26 has something of an "overlap" of usage. Thus 2.22 twice uses faith in the sense of genuine faith, on the part of Abraham. In fact, however, this passage helps to clarify the point at issue. Thus 2.24, 26, along with 2.22, show that "faith" can only be properly what it claims to be when, as in the case of Abraham, it is *shown* by "works." That is, proper action in Abraham's case *demonstrates* his complete *trust* in God.[54]

Besides Abraham's deed of sacrificing Isaac according to God's command (Gen 22), James referred to Rahab and her deeds to illustrate his discussion of faith (v. 25). James concluded: "For as the body apart from the spirit is dead, so also faith apart from works [good deeds] is dead" (my interpretation of "works"). Understanding "works" as good deeds is very similar to the apostle Paul's concept of "the obedience of faith" (Rom 1:5; 16:26). Paul would not have disagreed with James, although I think the two letters are talking about two different ideas: Paul used "faith" as both the initial response to the gospel and the continuing faith which is called "faithfulness." Paul sought the "obedience of faith" among the gentiles/nations. James, on the other hand, wrote about faith as genuine only when it is accompanied by "good deeds," not in order to be saved but simply because that is the way genuine faith operates. The whole letter of James bears out this thought. Salvation could possibly be jeopardized if there is no genuine faith that results in "good deeds" (see Jas 2:14 and 5:20).

James will not mention *pistis* again until the conclusion of his letter. "And the prayer of faith will save the one who is sick, and the Lord will raise him up. And if he has committed sins, he will be forgiven. Therefore, confess your sins to one another and pray for one another, that you may be healed. The prayer of a righteous person has great power as it is working" (Jas 5:15–16). This "prayer of faith" is the prayer of the elders,

---

53. Hartin, *James*, 150.
54. Chester and Martin, *Theology*, 25.

anointing the sick with oil, asking for the Lord to work his power over evil that attacks us bodily and spiritually. Our bodies need healing and our sins need forgiveness. The "prayer of faith" is indeed a good deed!

There are only two explicit references to Jesus the Messiah in James (1:1 and 2:1). James 2:1 referred to the "faithfulness of our Lord Jesus [the] Messiah," as Christians imitate his life by not showing partiality, especially between the rich and poor, the oppressors and the oppressed (see Matt 19:16–22; ch. 23–the seven woes). The title "Lord" is possibly used of Jesus beyond the explicit passages (see Jas 5:7, 8, 14, 15). God is the referent for "Lord" in Jas 1:7; 4:10, 15; 5:4, 10, 11^2. The word "God" is used sixteen times in James and would support its theocentric emphasis (Jas 1:1, 5, 13^2, 20, 27; 2:5, 19, 23^2; 3:9; 4:4^2, 6, 7, 8).

First Peter: "A Living Hope"

First Peter is similar to Hebrews in that it is addressed to believers who are experiencing some kind of persecution (compare Heb 10:32–39 and 1 Pet 4:12–19). Such persecution apparently was local and sporadic, although some type of persecution was to be expected by Christians everywhere (1 Pet 5:9). Peter, the apostle, is plainly the author of the letter (1 Pet 1:1a) and perhaps Silvanus as his secretary and/or letter bearer (1 Pet 5:12). The letter was written from Rome, referred to as "Babylon" (1 Pet 5:13), and sent to mainly gentiles (1 Pet 2:12; 4:3) in the northern part of Asia Minor (Pontus, Galatia, Cappadocia, Asia, and Bithynia—see 1 Pet 1:1), all north of the Taurus mountains. The date is uncertain, but if Peter is the author, then the date would have to be c. AD 62–63, before his writing of 2 Peter (if he is the author) and his traditional date of martyrdom c. AD 64–67.

One of the best early commentaries on the Greek text of 1 Peter was by Edward G. Selwyn.[55] However, since his commentary, many scholars have rejected Peter's authorship and have considered the letter to be pseudonymous.[56] They date the letter later than AD 70, after the destruction of the temple and Jerusalem and before the end of Diocletian's reign as emperor c. AD 95. Since none of these views, either conservative or

---

55. Selwyn, *First Epistle of St. Peter*.

56. See Elliott, *Home for the Homeless*, 197–223; Michaels, *1 Peter*, lxii–lxvii; and Davids, *Theology*, 102, 121. Even Ralph P. Martin considers 1 Peter to be authored by a later group of Peter followers in Rome. See his theological assessment in Chester and Martin, *Theology*, 90–94.

critical, is certain, one must consider the contents of the letter for the theme of "the faithfulness of Jesus the Messiah."

Most commentaries and scholars give an outline of 1 Peter similar to the one below:

Opening greeting (1:1–2)

Who we are as the people of God (1:3—2:10)

Living as aliens in a hostile world (2:11—4:11)

How to suffer as a Christian (4:12—5:11)

Final greetings and benediction (5:12–14)

The initial greeting of the letter is typical of ancient letter writing. Peter described himself simply as "an apostle of Jesus Christ." The recipients were called "elect exiles of the dispersion," a very Jewish way of addressing Christians living in the outskirts of the Roman Empire, the northeast part of Asia Minor (1 Pet 1:1). These Christians seem to be mainly gentiles (2:10–12; 4:1–4). Finally, the greeting included a trinitarian blessing with information that helped to explain how the people of God came to be in the Messiah (1 Pet 1:2a). It concluded with a blessing prayer—"May grace and peace be multiplied to you" (1 Pet 1:2b).

Almost all English versions translate the "trinitarian blessing" similar to the ESV: "according to the foreknowledge of God the Father, in the sanctification of the Spirit, for obedience to Jesus Christ and for sprinkling with his blood." The NIV is slightly different: "according to the foreknowledge of God the Father, through the sanctifying work of the Spirit, for obedience to Jesus Christ and sprinkling by his blood." The statements on the surface seem perfectly fine until one looks closely at the Greek text. The Greek text is violated both by structure and grammar with both the ESV and NIV.

First, note the structure. The verse is a typical apostolic trinitarian formula in an introductory statement (compare Eph 1:3–14). Peter is saying something about each of the Persons of the Trinity using different prepositions:

elect ones . . .

kata ("according to") foreknowledge of God [the] Father,

en ("by") [the] sanctifying [work] of [the] Spirit,

eis ("unto, toward the view of") obedience and sprinkling of the blood of Jesus Christ.

The Rheims New Testament shows the parallel structure well: "according to the foreknowledge of God the Father, unto (?) the sanctification of the Spirit, unto obedience and sprinkling of the blood of Jesus Christ" (my question on the "unto" for *en*, should be translated as "by"). The point is, most translations in English seem to shy away from any thought of Jesus having "faith" or "obeying." In this text each prepositional phrase is saying something about the Person of the Trinity—God's foreknowledge, the Spirit's sanctifying work, and Jesus' obedience understood as his shedding of blood on the cross which effects our cleansing from sin. But it is certainly not about *our* obedience and then *his* sprinkling of blood. The genitive of the proper noun, *Iesou Christou*, modifies both nouns in the phrase *eis hupakoen kai hrantismon haimatos Iesou Christou* (translated: "unto/toward obedience and sprinkling of the blood of Jesus Christ").

As Francis Agnew observed: "The *eis* phrase (1:2c) is brought into perfect parallelism with the *kata* phrase (1:2a) and the *en* phrase (1:2b) where the 'activity' involved is clearly ascribed to Father and Spirit. All that benefits the elect sojourners is attributed to the 'trinitarian' subjects of the triadic formula."[57] Thus, it is Jesus' obedience and sprinkling of his blood that has brought salvation to humankind in concert with the Spirit's sanctifying work and God's foreknowledge; i.e., God's redemption plan and determination from before the creation (cp. Eph 1:4). Jesus' obedience is nothing new (see Rom 5:19; Heb 5:8–9).

Strangely, Michaels argued: "To attempt to link 'Jesus Christ' both to 'obedience' and 'blood' would create difficulty by making it an objective genitive in relation to the first (i.e., obedience to Jesus Christ) and a possessive in relation to the second (i.e., Jesus Christ's blood)."[58] What Michaels wants to do is make the noun "obedience" an absolute term, not related to "sprinkling of blood," meaning "obedience [to the gospel]," as he translated the phrase. It is a difficulty only if one rejects the arguments by Agnew.

In fact, Michaels listed Agnew's article but never mentioned it in his commentary otherwise. Agnew is correct when he stated: "*Iesou Christou* stands as a subjective genitive in both parts of the *eis* phrase."[59] The two phrases go together in the sense that the "obedience" of Jesus was the Father's will that he go to the cross and shed his blood (see Phil 2:6–11; Rom

---

57. Agnew, "1 Peter 1:2," 70.
58. Michaels, *1 Peter*, 11, and many others.
59. Agnew, "1 Peter 1:2," 70.

5:12–19; Heb 5:7–10; 10:5–10). The shedding of Jesus' blood allowed the cleansing or purification from sin (see Exod 24:3–8; Heb 9:18–21; 12:24). This model of obedience can be found in the Synoptics (Mark 14:32–36 // Matt 26:36–39 // Luke 22:39–43) and in John (4:35; 5:30; 6:38, etc.).[60] Agnew cited 1 Pet 1:18–19, 2:18–25, 3:18, and 4:13, which draw out the implications of Jesus' obedience for the salvation of God's people (1:14, 22). "Christians are 'children of obedience' (1:14) and manifest 'obedience to truth' (1:22) because of their redemption by 'the blood of Christ' (1:18–19).... The obedient Christian lives by the attitude of obedient Jesus."[61] This interpretation is substantiated by the contents of the letter itself.

The *pistis* word group is not used extensively in this brief letter:

> *Pistis*, the noun, "faith/faithfulness," is used at 1:5, 7, 9, 21; 5:9.
>
> *Pistos*, the adjective, "faithful/believer," is used at 1:21; 4:19; and 5:12.
>
> *Pisteuō*, the verb, "to believe/trust," is used at 1:8; 2:6, 7.
>
> The negative verb, *apisteuō*, "not believing," is at 2:7.

Immediately one notices that most of the noun, *pistis*, is used in the first chapter (four of five references). It is clear that Peter wished to establish the importance of faith/faithfulness in the context of suffering because of persecution from the powers of government and the culture of a pagan society who worshiped gods and their idols to support the political state. Even though Peter's letter is theocentric, Jesus the Messiah is at the center and heart of most of the thoughts throughout the letter. Jesus is the one through whom God works salvation for the people of God, made up of Jews and gentiles. There are at least sixteen sections or paragraphs where Jesus is mentioned in some form, mainly concerning his sufferings, glory, and exaltation. Peter's use of the *pistis* word group can be found in several of these sixteen sections:

1. I have already considered the trinitarian presentation of 1 Pet 1:2 where I interpreted the last phrase: "the obedience and sprinkling of the blood of Jesus the Messiah." It is on this understanding that the rest of the letter will comment about Jesus the Messiah and his faithfulness in spite of the fact that the *pistis* word group is not mentioned in 1 Pet 1:2.

---

60. Agnew, "1 Peter 1:2," 71.
61. Agnew, "1 Peter 1:2," 72.

2. First Peter 1:3–9: The first use of *pistis* at 1:5 is significant in light of what was discussed in the "trinitarian blessing" above. Peter is blessing God the Father for causing us to be "born again to a living hope" through the resurrection of Jesus the Messiah from the dead (v. 3). Those who have been born again have an inheritance that is "imperishable, undefiled, and unfading, kept in heaven" (and is still there!). God's power guards our salvation *dia pisteōs* (through the Trinity's faithfulness), a salvation ready to be revealed in the last time (καιρῷ, *kairō*, "the appointed time"). In other words, it is God the Father, the Spirit, and the Son's faithfulness to God's determined plan to save the world.

   Jesus' obedience to the cross, his shed blood for our forgiveness, and the sanctifying work of the Spirit in every believer's life enables every believer to experience salvation. Through trials and various forms of persecution, our *faith*, or better, *trust*, in God the Father and his Son, Jesus the Messiah, is "tested by fire" (v. 7). As the ESV translated: "so that the tested genuineness of your faith . . . may be found to result in praise and glory and honor at the revelation of Jesus Christ" (v. 7). Our faith becomes *faithfulness* in the end! Even though we do not yet see Jesus with our mortal eyes, we love him and continually believe in (trust) [a present participle] him, "obtaining the outcome of your faith, the salvation of your souls" (v. 9). I would translate the ESV's "outcome" as "goal"; "faith" as "faithfulness"; and "souls" as "lives" or "being," thus reading it: "obtaining the goal of your faithfulness—salvation of [your] lives."

3. First Peter 1:13–21: Verse 21 included two *pistis* words: the adjective *pistos* used as a noun—"believers"—and the noun *pistis*. Just as in Romans that our faith is in God (see Rom 4:24), so also Peter expressed the same thought: "who through him [Jesus] are believers in God, who raised him from the dead and gave him glory, so that your faith (trust) and hope are in God." Ralph Martin wrote: "Probably no document in the New Testament is so theologically oriented as 1 Peter, if the description is taken in the strict sense of teaching about God. The epistle is theocentric through and through, and its author has a robust faith in God which he seeks to impart to the readers."[62] Martin showed that Peter is charting out the character of God in such a way as to encourage those who are suffering for their

---

62. Chester and Martin, *Theology*, 104.

faith: 1) God as sovereign in human affairs; 2) Christ the model believer in God; 3) the holy character of God; and 4) God as Protector.[63] Thus, *pistis* in v. 21 should be understood as "trust," which becomes faithfulness over the lifetime of the one trusting.

4. First Peter 2:4–10: Jesus is the "living stone," rejected by men but "chosen and precious" by God the Father. Likewise, followers of the Christ are "living stones," being built up as a "spiritual house" to be a "holy priesthood," to offer "spiritual sacrifices acceptable to God through Jesus Christ" (v. 5). To support these ideas Peter quotes Isa 28:16 (LXX) (cf. Rom 9:33; 10:11) and Ps 118:22 with Isa 8:14. In these texts are found the last two uses of the verb *pisteuō*, "to believe or trust," and the negative word *apisteuō*, "not believe or trust." "And whoever believes in him [the stone] will not be put to shame" (v. 6c). "So the honor is for you who believe, but for those who do not believe, 'The stone that the builders rejected has become the cornerstone' and 'A stone of stumbling, and a rock of offense'" (vv. 7–8). Reading this section, one cannot help but think of the "spiritual house" as a "temple" where God dwells in the midst of his people (see Eph 2:18–22).[64] Peter never forgot Jesus' nicknaming him *Cephas* (Aramaic for "rock, stone"; the Greek equivalent, *petros*, hence, "Peter," see John 1:42; Matt 10:2; 16:18–20).

Peter concluded this section with a cascade of Hebrew texts that label the new covenant people of God, made up of Jews and gentiles, as God's "new Israel." Peter used terms applied to ancient Israel in Exod 19:5–6. They are "a royal priesthood, a holy nation" (Exod 19:6). However, he sandwiched these two terms with the word *segullah* (Hebrew, סְגֻלָּה, meaning "a king's most-prized treasure," usually silver and gold, Exod 19:5) and the word "chosen." In almost every reference to this term in the Hebrew Scriptures, a synonym, "chosen," is found (see Exod 19:4–6; Deut 7:1–8; 14:1–2; 26:16–19; Ps 135:4; 1 Chr 29:1–5; Eccl 2:8; Mal 3:16–18; also in the LXX, Exod 23:22 and Isa 43:21). Thus, God's people are "chosen," a "royal priesthood," a "holy nation," and "God's most-prized treasure." He, then, included terms from Isa 43:21 (LXX), Hos 1:6, 9; and 2:23—"that you may proclaim the excellencies of him who called

---

63. Chester and Martin, *Theology*, 105–7.

64. Chester and Martin, *Theology*, 100–101. Michaels critiques Elliott's insistence that "spiritual house" does not mean a "temple." See Elliott, *Home*, 197–233, for a different interpretation.

you out of darkness into his marvelous light. Once you were not a people, but now you are God's people; once you had not received mercy, but now you have received mercy" (1 Pet 2:10).[65] Faithfulness is the unstated expectation of those who trust the "Stone."

5. First Peter 4:12-19: This passage is the heart of the apostle Peter's thoughts on how to suffer as a Christian. We are never to forget that the Messiah suffered and that we share in his suffering, a glorious thing, because one day we shall share in his glory! Just as in the beginning of the letter with the trinitarian comments, so now the Trinity is involved in the life of the believer: "If you are insulted for the name of Christ, you are blessed, because the Spirit of glory and of God rests upon you" (v. 14).

Whereas the name "Christian" may have been a derogatory term directed toward believers or disciples of Christ, now it has become a good thing to suffer for that name—"Yet if anyone suffers as a Christian, let him not be ashamed, but let him glorify God in that name" (v. 16). Proverbs 11:31 provided the clinching argument: "If the righteous is scarcely saved, what will become of the ungodly and the sinner?" First Peter 4:19 gave us the second use of the adjective *pistos*, "faithful": "Therefore let those who suffer according to God's will entrust their souls to a faithful Creator while doing good." God is faithful to the suffering and faithful Christian.

6. First Peter 5:6-11: In these final exhortations (over thirty imperatives in 1 Peter), Peter urged his listeners, whoever they may be, to "resist him [the devil], firm in your faith, knowing that the same kinds of suffering are being experienced by your brotherhood throughout the world" (v. 9). Again, I prefer to translate "faith" as "faithfulness," for it is a faith undergoing adversity and some form of persecution. When faith is exercised against such, it becomes faithfulness.

---

65. Michaels' interpretation that "a people unto (God's) possession" should be understood as "a people destined for vindication" by appealing to LXX Isa 43:21 is intriguing (*1 Peter*, 109) but avoids the fact that both Greek words, *peripoiēsis* and *periousios*, were used in the LXX for the Hebrew *segullah*. The reference is from Exod 19:5, even though Isa 43:21 is echoed later in the verse at 2:9b. "Chosen" and "prized treasure" are the synonym words, not "destined for vindication," though that may be true. See my study on "*Segullah*" above (chapter 3 in *Deuteronomy: The Prophets and the Life of the Church*). See also my exegesis of Heb 10:39 above.

7. First Peter 5:12–14: Peter referred to Silvanus as "a faithful brother." He is probably the secretary of Peter's letter or simply his letter bearer, or perhaps both. He concluded: "Peace to all of you who are in Christ" (v. 14b). The faithfulness of Jesus the Messiah was expressed throughout 1 Peter by drawing out the implications of Jesus' sufferings, his death, resurrection, and exaltation to God's right hand, with all authority and power subject to him. By virtue of being "in Christ" are we saved. It is clearly a relationship description ("in Christ").

Second Peter: "Participating in the Divine Nature"

Second Peter and Jude have been like "orphan children" among the New Testament letters. Both letters have been relegated to late dates, even into the second century AD. Authorship by Peter and Jude (Judah) is denied to both letters.[66] Usually most conservatives take the author titles at face value and proceed. The main concern will be the content of each letter where there is mostly agreement among scholars, although recipients and background understanding are hotly debated because of authorship and dating issues. Second Peter's content can be outlined in the following manner:

> Greetings (1:1–2)
>
> Letter Opening Exhortation to Confirm Your Calling (1:3–15)
>
> The Body of the Letter: Four Issues Addressed (1:16—3:13)
>
> (1) The Parousia is a myth (1:16–19)
>
> (2) Appeal to OT prophecy is vain (1:20–21)
>
> (3) False teachers exposed (2:1–10)
>
> [Digression on their immorality] (2:10–22)
>
> (4) The Parousia will not happen (3:1–13)
>
> Letter Body Closing (3:14–16)
>
> Letter Closing (3:17–18)[67]

---

66. Most critical commentaries will give full information to these issues. For convenience and up-to-date information that includes both conservative and critical information concerning authorship and date of the two letters of 2 Peter and Jude, even their relationship to each other, see the following: Wright and Bird, *New Testament*, 749, 763–69, 777–83; Davids, *Theology*, 190–208, 251–65; and Chester and Martin, *Theology*, 65–67, 81–86, 134–51.

67. Adapted from Davids, *Theology*, 202–3.

The noun, *pistis*, "faith/faithfulness," is only used twice (2 Pet 1:1, 5). The verb and adjective are not used at all. The opening phrase is remarkable in many ways: "To those who have obtained a faith of equal standing with ours by the righteousness of our God and Savior Jesus Christ" (1:1b). The "faith of equal standing" is the commitment[68] or allegiance that has come about by "the righteousness of our God and Savior Jesus Christ." Davids wrote: "The implied readers are not designated by name or location, but are designated by their commitment: they have received a faith or commitment, like receiving a grant from a ruler, that is 'equally honorable' to the commitment that 'we' (probably meaning 'we delegates [*apostoloi*] of Jesus') have."[69] Wright and Bird commented: "Here 'righteousness' is not Christ's obedience or saving work, but his moral rectitude. Jesus is seen as the divine patron, acting justly, to grant faith to his clients (1.1–2)."[70]

If *pistis* in this context is closer to the idea of commitment, then one can safely view it as including the idea of "faithfulness." The remarkable part of the phrase is how Jesus is referred to as "our God and Savior," which the Greek text suggests. There is only one article before the word "God" so that the term "Savior" is referring to the same person (known as the Granville Sharp rule). Some do not think that "God" ought to refer to Jesus, but there are other such references in the New Testament (see Titus 2:13; 1 John 5:20; Rom 9:5; 2 Thess 1:12; and possibly Heb 1:8). The argument against this designation for Jesus is the very next verse which separates God from Jesus: "May grace and peace be multiplied to you in the knowledge of God and of Jesus our Lord."

But the next opening exhortation supports the fact that Jesus as "God" is the essential part of the "divine nature" in which we as believers must participate in order to prevent us "from being ineffective or unfruitful in the knowledge of our Lord Jesus Christ" (1:8b). Thus, the readers/listeners to Peter's message are exhorted "to make every effort to supplement your faith with virtue, and virtue with knowledge, and knowledge with self-control, and self-control with steadfastness, and steadfastness with godliness, and godliness with brotherly affection, and brotherly affection with love" (vv. 5–7). These virtues are essential for making our "calling and election sure, for if you practice these qualities you will never

---

68. Davids' implication, *Theology*, 209.
69. Davids, *Theology*, 209.
70. Wright and Bird, *New Testament*, 778.

fall" (v. 10). Davids concluded: "The foundation that they [the virtues] are built on is commitment (πίστις, *pistis*)—commitment to the royal person of Jesus, the Anointed One, 'our Lord' or 'our Lord and Savior' (1:8, 11). But commitment needs to be expressed in imitation and obedience, and that is what we see in this passage, expressed in terms that for the most part were common in Hellenistic philosophy."[71]

Second Peter referred to two events, one in the past and one in the future, about Jesus that demonstrated his faithfulness to God the Father and his will in terms of being the Savior of the world: 1) Peter's eyewitness account of the transfiguration (2 Pet 1:16–18) (see Mark 9:2–8; Matt 17:1–8; Luke 9:28–36), which event revealed to Peter, James, and John that Jesus indeed was God's Son; and 2) the surety and promise of Jesus' Second Coming (2 Pet 3:1–13).

And now 2 Peter's final exhortation: "But grow in the grace and knowledge of our Lord and Savior Jesus the Messiah" (2 Pet 3:18a, my translation). If "grace" belongs to the Messiah and he gives it to us and we are to grow in it, then "knowledge" also belongs to Jesus and he gives that to us (see 1:5–6) as a virtue which we are to seek with "every effort" (1:5; cp. Eph 4:13).

Jude

Enough has been said about authorship and date for Jude (Judah or Judas), the Lord's brother along with James, Joseph, and Simon (Matt 13:55; Mark 6:3). There is a close relationship in the two letters of 2 Peter and Jude. Many think that 2 Peter is following some of the content of Jude and not vice versa:

2 Peter	Jude	Subject
2:1–3	4	The false teachers will face judgment.
2:4	6	God will judge rebellious angels.
2:6	7	God has judged Sodom and Gomorrah.
2:10	8	The false teachers defile the body and despise authority.

---

71. Davids, *Theology*, 213.

2 Peter	Jude	Subject
2:11–12	9–10	The false teachers are irrational animals who blaspheme what they do not understand.
2:15	11	The false teachers follow the way of Balaam and seek reward.
2:13, 17	12–13	The false teachers share meals with acute irreverence, are 'waterless' sources, and will be kept in darkness.
2:18	16	The false teachers are driven by desire.[72]

Perhaps Jude set out to write to his recipients (whoever they are) about "our common salvation" (v. 3a), but he found it necessary that he change course and exhort them "to contend for the faith that was once for all delivered to the saints" (v. 3b). The chart above shows Jude is concerned about false teachers who were surreptitiously perverting "the grace of our God into sensuality and deny[ing] our only Master and Lord, Jesus Christ" (v. 4b).

Verse 3 marked the first use of *pistis* in Jude. It will only be used once more at v. 20. What is the meaning of *pistis* in this context? On the surface it means that body of teaching given through the apostles about Jesus. It is fixed and knowable. It was not to be changed in any way. Wright and Bird commented:

> This "faith" is not the stale dogma of a so-called "early Catholicism." Rather, it is the apostolic testimony to God's saving action in Jesus Christ and its immediate implications. By referring to this apostolic "faith" as being given "once for all," Jude underscores its implicit Christological foundation: what God did in Jesus the Messiah he did once and for all, with neither the need nor the possibility of the achievement being repeated or added to. The "faith" in question is thus permanent, effective, and rooted in the primary work of the spirit.[73]

Jude placed the "false teachers" among them as in the position of the ancient Israelites who left Egypt but were "destroyed" by God because

---

72. Wright and Bird, *New Testament*, 780.
73. Wright and Bird, *New Testament*, 749–50, using the thoughts of McKnight.

they "did not believe" (v. 5). They did not trust God to protect and be with them as they entered the promised land (Num 14:20–25). Instead, they mutinied and wanted to go back to Egypt (to slavery?). This is the only use of the verb *pisteuō*, "to believe, trust," in Jude.

Jude concluded his rebukes of the false teachers and exhortations toward his recipients with these words: "But you, beloved, building yourselves up in your most holy faith and praying in the Holy Spirit, keep yourselves in the love of God, waiting for the mercy of our Lord Jesus Christ that leads to eternal life" (vv. 20–21). This second and last use of *pistis* in Jude is very much the same as it is in v. 3. It functions much like an *inclusio* for the letter (vv. 3 and 20). This "faith" is more than content, it is "commitment" to Jesus personally, it matures by reaching toward "the love of God" in Christ and ultimately finding by patience the "mercy of our Lord Jesus Christ that leads to eternal life," referring to Jesus' Second Coming.

So ends our review of the "general letters" of the New Testament. We turn now to the Synoptic Gospels and Acts.

6

The Synoptic Gospels and Acts

"The synoptics indicate that in Gethsemane Jesus prays a prayer of faith, that after he drinks the cup the Father will not abandon him forever to the desolation of wrath and judgment for sin but, as he has promised Israel in the last days, will remove the wrath of God from him, resurrecting and restoring him."

—CRAIG A. BLAISING[1]

Introduction: Jesus and Faith

WHY HAVE MODERN ENGLISH versions of the New Testament been reluctant to recognize that Jesus may have had faith, and consequently at the end of his life on earth to have been faithful (i.e., his faithfulness)? I think the answer lies in part with our view of Jesus' humanity and even the nature of faith itself. As two Catholic scholars, O'Collins and Kendall, have observed: "Any attempt to discuss the faith of the earthly Jesus and reach solidly founded conclusions (either for or against attributing faith to him) requires reflection in at least three areas: the nature of faith, the question of Jesus' human knowledge, and NT data that bears on claims about Jesus' faith."[2] The first two points will be considered before examining the Synoptic Gospels and Acts to continue the study of "faith/faithfulness" in relationship to Jesus.

1. Blaising, "Gethsemane," 342.
2. O'Collins and Kendall, "The Faith of Jesus," 405.

On the nature of faith one can get into quicksand very quickly! The more one explains the less one may understand. At the risk of doing so, allow me to simply give my view of faith. I take Abraham to be a paradigm for faith. Paul quoted Gen 15:6 when he wrote: "But Abraham believed in God, and it was reckoned to him unto righteousness" (Rom 4:3, my translation). Later in this same letter Paul makes a reasonable argument that he has been sent to preach the gospel. When people hear this gospel, they are capable of believing it, and therefore they call upon the name of the Lord for salvation (see Rom 10:14, 15). Against most Protestant views that faith is a gift from God, the context of Rom 10 does not suggest it. The text reads: "So faith comes from hearing, and hearing through the word of Christ." It is possible to translate this verse differently by translating the word ἀκοή (akoē) as "that which is heard, i.e., the message." I translate it: "So faith [comes] from the message, and the message through the spoken word about the Messiah." There is no hint that faith is a gift from God, as if God must somehow give a person the ability to believe. "For everyone who calls on the name of the Lord will be saved" (Rom 10:13).

Faith includes knowledge, knowledge about God in Abraham's case and knowledge about the gospel (good news about Jesus) in the case of all human beings since Pentecost. Faith also includes assent, saying "yes" to the content of faith. But having content to one's faith and saying "yes" to it is still not enough to say one has faith. As mentioned in the last chapter, James writes about this one-dimensional kind of faith when he says: "You believe that there is one God. Good! Even the demons believe that—and shudder" (Jas 2:19). The third ingredient of faith is "trust." Most church doctrinal positions on faith would agree that genuine faith includes knowledge, assent, and trust. (This is a good Lutheran doctrinal presentation!) I would add that "trust" should lead to obedience, as Paul expressed it: "the obedience of faith" (Rom 1:5; 16:26). Genuine faith must include obedience (Jas 2:14–26). Clearly from a New Testament perspective, if one does not "act" or produce "deeds" in line with his/her professed faith, it is not genuine faith. Or as Jesus said according to the Gospel of John: "By this my Father is glorified, that you bear much fruit and so prove to be my disciples" (John 15:8).

Faith (*pistis*) is foremost a relational word, meaning that we should translate it more often as "trust" or "trustworthy/trustworthiness." The English word "faith" does not often conjure up the idea of "trust" in the mind. We must force ourselves to see the relational idea of *pistis* by using the idea of trust. One can see this as we work through the New Testament with the *pistis* word group.

However, all who believe and trust in the God who raised Jesus from the dead and profess Jesus to be Lord and Savior do not always obey. Sin is still prevalent among God's believing people. As John expressed it: "If we say we have no sin, we deceive ourselves, and the truth is not in us. If we confess our sins, he is faithful and just to forgive us our sins and to cleanse us from all unrighteousness. If we say we have not sinned, we make him a liar, and his word is not in us" (1 John 1:8–10). To say one believes does not mean one is perfect in obedience.

The above leads me to say that all human beings, no matter how corrupt or sinful, can respond by faith to the gospel. Admittedly, that is an "Arminian" position, but whatever position it may be, I believe it to be biblical. On the other hand, I do not rule out the Spirit's work in convicting the sinner of sin—universally (John 16:8–11). But to say that means I think that a person can say "yes" or "no" to the Spirit's promptings. Again, what I am saying is that faith is not a gift from God. It is a "gift" only in the sense that had God not acted initially in his Son, Jesus, there would be no gospel and thus nothing to believe or trust. There is a "measure of faith" that is given to certain Christians in relationship to spiritual gifts (see Rom 12:3), a gift to be used for the entire body of believers. God desires that all persons be saved (1 Tim 2:4) and therefore all are capable of responding in faith to God's good news when it is proclaimed accurately and clearly.

The doctrine that God must put "faith" in someone's heart in order for that person to be saved is not a biblical teaching. I simply do not see it in Scripture. That teaching denies my free will to choose to believe or not believe. I maintain that the subjective genitive view of interpretation in our passages above, already discussed, offers support for an Arminian soteriology. At the expense of repetition, allow me to emphasize this point once again.

Usually Eph 2:8 is offered as evidence for faith being a gift from God for salvation. In light of all the texts above treated as subjective genitives, I see the same for Eph 2:8: "For by grace you have been saved through faith, and this is not from you, [it is] God's gift" (my translation). The word "this" is neuter (τοῦτο, *touto*, in Greek), which is referring to the entire phrase: "salvation by grace through faith," not to "faith" (*pistis*) itself which is feminine in form (essential to note in the Greek text). While the phrase "through faith" may refer to our faith, I prefer to understand it as referring to God's faithfulness in his love for us by raising Jesus from the dead. After all, this is the context of the phrase "by grace you have been saved" in vv. 4–6: "But God being rich in mercy, through his great love which he loved us, and while we being dead in trespasses he made us alive together with Christ—by grace you have been saved—and he raised [us] up and enthroned [us] in the heavenlies in Messiah Jesus" (my translation). Therefore, Eph 2:8 is saying: "For by grace you have been saved through [God's, and thus Christ's] faithfulness." Because this is true, Paul can emphasize: "This [is] not from you, [it is] God's gift," referring to our salvation. Note: none of my interpretation takes away the necessity for our hearing the gospel and responding to it by an obedient faith (see Eph 1:13, 14).

O'Collins and Kendall go into much more detail about the nature of faith and its complexities. They discuss the essential "parts" of faith as "cognitive content" and "voluntary commitment." In other words, faith is oriented toward meaning and truth. They write:

> It is a distinction between [a] firmly holding to be meaningful and true the Christian message as revealed by God, and [b] entering a loving, obedient, and trusting relationship with the God who graciously forgives us and gives us life. We could distinguish two aspects of (b): on the one hand, faithful commitment here and now (b^1); on the other hand, a persevering confidence that entrusts our future to God's hands (b^2). Just as the cognitive content of faith (a) can be seen to have two aspects, so also with faith's voluntary commitment (b).[3]

The two aspects of the "cognitive content of faith" are: (1) believing that God exists; and (2) believing what God has revealed. In other words, "faith" includes knowledge of truth, human will, and commitment, trust or belief, which results in faithfulness. These scholars include one other aspect that must be considered. Faith is believing in that which is unseen: Heb 11:1—"Now faith is the reality of things hoped for, the evidence of things not seen" (my translation). Now we must ask how this definition of faith affects the idea of Jesus having faith and being faithful. Is it different from human faith described above?

On the second point, the question of Jesus' human knowledge is just as difficult as defining faith. "Aquinas and the subsequent Catholic theological tradition held that in his human mind Jesus enjoyed the beatific

---

3. O'Collins and Kendall, "The Faith of Jesus," 405.

vision and hence lived by sight, not by faith."[4] While Protestants may not hold such a view, for all practical purposes worshipers in the Protestant churches seem to view Christ more as "divine," in the gnostic view, rather than truly human. This is a strong accusation, but after teaching in the local church for over fifty years, I am convinced many Christians do not understand Jesus' true humanity. Otherwise, how could Jesus suffer genuinely (Heb 5:7–10) or have free will to obey or not obey during times of testing (see Mark 1:12–13; Luke 22:28; Heb 2:18; 4:15)?

There had to be some limit on the human knowledge of Jesus if he was truly human. True human knowledge grows and develops by experience. Jesus is no exception (e.g., Mark 5:30–32; 13:32). Granted, Jesus manifested great powers, but it was God's power working through the perfect and complete humanity of Jesus. Jesus, however, was conscious of his divine identity as Son of God (Matt 16:16) as well as his destiny in fulfilling God's redemptive mission (Luke 2:49, 50). It seems that the early church had more of a problem viewing Jesus as somehow "divine," while the present-day church has a problem of seeing the true "humanity" of Jesus. In light of this, a couple of points N. T. Wright has made bear upon the humanity and divinity of Jesus:

> The Christian doctrine of the incarnation was never intended to be about the elevation of a human being to divine status. That's what, according to some Romans, happened to the emperors after they died, or even before. The Christian doctrine is all about *a different sort of God*—a God who was so different to normal expectations that he could, completely appropriately, become human in, and as, the man Jesus of Nazareth. To say that Jesus is in some sense God is of course to make a startling statement about Jesus. It is also to make a stupendous claim about God.[5]

> What I have argued for elsewhere, not to diminish the full incarnation of Jesus but to explore its deepest dimension, is that Jesus was aware of a call, a vocation, to do and be what, according to the scriptures, only Israel's God gets to do and be. That, I believe, is what it means to speak about Jesus being both truly divine and truly human. And we realize, once we remind ourselves that humans were made in God's image, that this is not a category mistake, but the ultimate fulfillment of the purpose of creation itself.[6]

4. O'Collins and Kendall, "The Faith of Jesus," 407.
5. Wright, *Who Was Jesus?* 52.
6. Wright, *Simply Christian*, 118.

O'Collins and Kendall make six statements against the Catholic idea that "Jesus' human knowledge embraced the beatific vision."[7] First, how could Jesus have genuinely suffered if through his human mind he had a constant vision (beatific) of God? Second, such a vision raises a problem for the free operation of Jesus' human will. The beatific vision rules out human free will in this life. The exercise of freedom requires limited knowledge. Third, Jesus is described by the New Testament as having remained obedient to the Father despite trials and temptations (see Mark 1:12–13; Luke 22:28; Heb 2:18; 4:15). Otherwise, Jesus' struggles would have been only a "show." Fourth, the beatific vision cannot be reconciled with the way human knowledge grows and develops through experience, but always remains limited. To think that Jesus knew everything about every creature on earth presents him as superhuman, not the truly human knowledge of the world. Fifth, the Synoptic Gospels admit that there were some limits to Jesus' human knowledge (see Mark 5:30–32; 13:32). "Sixth, the ontological fact of the hypostatic union (the two natures of Christ united in the second person of the Trinity) does not as such necessarily imply something special, let alone something unique like the beatific vision, about the range of Jesus' human knowledge."[8] Given these six arguments, one must still maintain that Jesus was conscious of his divine identity as Son of God and his "Israel formed" mission of redemption, not only for Israel but for the world (Gen 12:3).

The third and final point O'Collins and Kendall make is to review the New Testament data that bears on the claims of Jesus' faith. We have already reviewed many of the texts outside the Gospels. The Synoptic Gospels and Acts will add much to the understanding of Jesus and his faith and faithfulness. But, first, the nature of these books of the New Testament must be explored.

The Synoptic Gospels

So far, this study has considered mainly one genre (type of literature), that is, the letters of the New Testament. Even there, it was discovered that Hebrews was a combination of a sermon and a letter (only in its conclusion). Paul's letters were very consistent as letters and, yet, each letter had its own purpose and circumstances (occasional in nature). James,

---

7. O'Collins and Kendall, "The Faith of Jesus," 407–8.
8. O'Collins and Kendall, "The Faith of Jesus," 408.

even though addressed to the "twelve tribes in the Dispersion," was a "wisdom" tract, designed to exhort toward practical Christian living for believers (Jewish?) in Messiah. But now the Gospels, specifically, the Synoptic Gospels (Matthew, Mark, and Luke) are unique in their presentation of the Messiah—his life and ministry.

The Gospels are biographies[9] about Jesus, who he was, where he came from, his ministry, and especially his last week, which included his death, burial, resurrection, and exaltation. The Gospels are meant to generate faith in the reader/listener simply by knowing who Jesus was and his claims upon the human race. Indeed, the story of Jesus is the culmination of Israel's story and they cannot be separated, as the Gospels reveal. Even the book of Acts (a selected history of the early church with mainly the chronicling of the leadership of the two apostles of Peter and Paul) is a continuation of the ministry of Jesus through his apostles and by the power of the Holy Spirit (Acts 1:1–5).

The Synoptic Gospels are called such because they can be displayed in parallel, noting their similarities and differences. They tell the story of Jesus in the same order and time frame. This order apparently comes from the Gospel of Mark. The theory that Mark is prior to the other two Gospels of Matthew and Luke still prevails. Almost 90 per cent of Mark can be found in Matthew and about 50 per cent in Luke. Many years ago, D. A. Carson (a Trinity Seminary scholar) said to me: "Until we have a better theory, the priority of Mark is the best way to study the Synoptics." In spite of Mark's position as prior to Matthew and Luke, and the "borrowing" by the latter two, each Gospel has its own plan, structure, and presentation to the story of Jesus. It may be that Matthew, as an eyewitness to Jesus' ministry, did not borrow Mark so much as that he had the same material of Jesus' teaching memorized as did Mark's source (Peter?). We simply don't know.

"The gospel of Mark is a densely packed, fast-paced, action-filled narrative about Jesus of Nazareth, his life and teachings, his divine identity and human vulnerability, God's kingdom breaking in through him, and the Judean and Roman opposition mounted against him."[10] Mark begins his story of Jesus abruptly without a birth narrative and ends it in mystery pointing toward his resurrection. Mark's Gospel is theocentric and apocalyptic. Apocalyptic means that "Mark highlights the notion of a

---

9. Not in the traditional sense of that word. They each have a similar purpose and it is more theological in nature.

10. Wright and Bird, *New Testament*, 554.

secret to be penetrated, of a mystery to be explored and grasped by faith."[11] Tradition says that Mark's Gospel is the result of Mark's remembering of Peter's teaching about Jesus and what we have is essentially Peter's "Jesus-traditions." This may account for how the Gospel of Mark moves from one event to another in telling the story of Jesus by the use of εὐθύς, *euthus* ("immediately, at once, then, so then"). This small word is used fifty-one times in the New Testament, but it is found in Mark forty-one times! When reading Mark, this word simply moves from one event to another, not necessarily in chronological order, but simply to be understood in its weakened form as "then."

Matthew is written from a very Jewish perspective. "Matthew," or whoever the author was, presents Jesus as the "new Moses." This is supported by the five discourses of Jesus scattered throughout the gospel, suggesting perhaps the five books of Moses.[12] These five teaching discourses in Matthew are marked at the conclusion of each one: Matt 7:28; 11:1; 13:53; 19:1; 26:1). However, these five discourses do not correspond to the content of the five books of Moses.

Jesus is the Davidic deliverer who ushers the kingdom to the earth. He is the Savior who has forgiven the sins of God's people, Israel, and of the whole world. In the end Jesus has all authority and sends every disciple out to the nations to disciple, baptize, and teach (Matt 28:18–20). Matthew pinpoints prophesies, primarily in the prologue, that are fulfilled in Jesus' life and ministry (see Matt 1:22–23; 2:5–6, 15, 17–18, 23; 3:3; 4:14–16). While Matthew presents Jesus as the "Davidic King," he shows that only the common people in Israel recognize him as such, who "see" and "confess" that Jesus is the Son of David, Israel's Messiah.[13] Matthew's presentation of Jesus is to emphasize the fact that Jesus as Messiah is indeed the "Son of God" and the only proper representative of Israel. Carmen Imes commented: "Jesus is also the one who models covenant faithfulness for Israel by representing the Father perfectly."[14] Matthew's

---

11. Wright and Bird, *New Testament*, 555.

12. This suggestion is not widely accepted today among NT scholars on the Gospel of Matthew. Rather than the five teachings of Jesus being the structural framework of Matthew, R. T. France argues for a geographical framework based on the Gospel of Mark: Jesus' ministry in three phases—A Prologue (1:1—4:11); Galilee (4:12—16:20), journey to Judea from Galilee (16:21—20:34), and in Jerusalem (21:1—28:15); An Epilogue (28:16-20). See France, *Matthew*, 3.

13. Kingsbury, "Title 'Son of David,'" 599.

14. Imes, *Bearing God's Name*, 148.

gospel became the most popular among the four. It became a great handbook for disciples following the Lord.

Tradition says that Luke, the physician, who accompanied Paul at various times in his travels, is the author of the Gospel of Luke. If this is true, then Luke was also the author of the book of Acts, the only "historical" book in the New Testament. The Gospel of Luke and Acts make up over one quarter of the New Testament. That fact is significant in terms of their importance to New Testament studies. Luke wrote in well-polished Greek and was truly the first "historian" of the Christian faith. Luke uniquely presented Jesus as the "Lord's Messiah." Luke's major theme was "salvation" for all mankind, especially the down and out, the poor and rich, the sick and the well, the ignorant and the educated. In the two-volume work Luke begins in Nazareth and ends in Rome. A brief review of the critical issues with regard to Luke-Acts can be found in the newly published work of Wright and Bird.[15] In light of the above discussion on the nature of faith, Jesus' human knowledge, and a brief look at the Synoptic Gospels and Acts, we now turn to each of the Synoptic Gospels and Acts to see if they have anything to offer our study on "the faithfulness of Jesus the Messiah."

Mark: "Jesus—'The Son of Man'"

The *pistis* word group is used moderately in Mark's short Gospel. Including the variant for the ending of Mark (16:9–20), the verb, *pisteuō*, is used fourteen times. The noun, *pistis*, is used only five times, while the adjective is not used at all. The negative forms are used six times.

Mark opens his gospel with "Jesus Christ, the Son of God," a spoiler of a storyteller if ever there was one! But surprisingly the declaration "Son of God" is announced only from demons (Mark 3:11 and 5:7) and again by the centurion (Mark 15:39). God's voice is heard to say "You are my beloved Son" (Mark 1:11, Jesus' baptism) and "This is my beloved Son" (Mark 9:7, transfiguration). Jesus' self-designation is "Son of Man," which is a divine title from Dan 7:13. The Daniel passage declared, "There came one like a son of man"—clearly a human being but with divine attributes—"with the clouds of heaven" (Dan 7:13). This suggests the true humanity and true divinity of Jesus, the exalted Lord. The "Son

---

15. Wright and Bird, *New Testament*, 607–16.

of Man" saying is a major theme in Mark and is found fourteen times (Mark 2:10, 28; 8:31, 38; 9:9, 12, 31; 10:33, 45; 13:26; 14:21², 41, 62).

Mark has Jesus beginning his ministry after John is arrested (and later executed), going to Galilee: "Now after John was arrested, Jesus came into Galilee, proclaiming the gospel of God, and saying, 'The time is fulfilled, and the kingdom of God is at hand; repent and believe in the gospel'" (Mark 1:14–15). Jesus is heralding the good news of God that it is time for God's reign to begin on earth as it is in heaven! All has been fulfilled (according to the Hebrew Scriptures) and thus God's people, the Jews, are called upon to repent (not only from sin but their old way of thinking about the kingdom of God) and believe (trust) in the good news of God. Faith in what God was doing in Jesus to bring all this about is absolutely necessary for belonging to the people of God.

The second use of *pisteuō* is in the context of a powerful act by Jesus (Mark 5:36). Jairus, a ruler of a synagogue, had a dying daughter and implored Jesus to heal her before she died. As Jesus obligingly went with him to his home, a woman who had been sick with "a discharge of blood for twelve years" (Mark 5:25), at her wit's end, approached Jesus in a crowd and "touched his garment," (v. 27) probably meaning a tassel. Jesus felt a sensation of power emanating from his body as the woman was healed by the mere touching of the hem of his garment. The woman confessed what she had done "in fear and trembling." She had made all unclean who had possibly touched her (Lev 15:19–27), including Jesus. But just the opposite happened! Jesus acknowledged her saying: "Daughter, your faith has made you well; go in peace, and be healed of your disease" (v. 34). Faith or trust in Jesus' power to heal was the key to the woman's ability to experience healing of her discharge.

The delay to Jairus' house brought bad news! Jairus' daughter was already dead. But this report did not deter Jesus. He said to Jairus: "Do not fear, only believe" (v. 36). The implication is that not only must Jairus believe, but Jesus himself believed that God could raise this young child from the dead. Jesus' statement may have been a mocking moment toward those who did not believe: "Why are you making a commotion and weeping? The child is not dead but sleeping" (v. 39). In turn, they laughed and perhaps mocked! But Jesus allowed the parents to enter with him, along with his inner circle (Peter, James, and John). Jesus took the little girl by the hand and said (in Aramaic): "*Talitha, cumi*" (v. 41), which Mark interprets: "Little girl, arise." Actually, the Greek text has "*cum*," not "*cumi*," though that is accurate. Also, Mark adds "I say to you" to the

Aramaic words. Regardless, the child of twelve years of age rose up and began to walk around. Did this take great faith on Jesus' part? Certainly, Jesus told Jairus, "Only believe." Recording the Aramaic words of Jesus implies a good eyewitness (Peter?) of this event to Mark.

The next two usages of the verb *pisteuō* lead us to think in terms of Jesus' own faith (Mark 9:23, 24). The same inner circle of Peter, James, and John had been with Jesus on a high mountain, what we call "the mount of transfiguration" (Mark 9:2–13). After this "mountain-top experience," they came down the mountain to meet with the rest of the disciples. The disciples were arguing with the scribes and a great crowd were gathered. Jesus asked what they were arguing about. A man addressed Jesus: "Teacher, I brought my son to you, for he has a spirit that makes him mute. And whenever it seizes him, it throws him down, and he foams and grinds his teeth and becomes rigid. So I asked your disciples to cast it out, and they were not able" (Mark 9:17–18).

Jesus rebukes his own disciples for not being able to cast out the unclean spirit: "O faithless generation, how long am I to be with you? How long am I to bear with you? Bring him to me" (v. 19). Immediately the unclean spirit recognized Jesus and "convulsed the boy, and he fell on the ground and rolled about, foaming at the mouth" (v. 20b). Jesus asked the father how long this had been happening. The father said: "From childhood. And it has often cast him into fire and into water, to destroy him. But if you can do anything, have compassion on us and help us" (vv. 21c–22). At this point Jesus became exasperated and exclaimed: "If you can! All things are possible for one who believes" (v. 23). The father cried out: "I believe; help my unbelief!" (v. 24). Jesus, before a growing crowd, rebuked the unclean spirit: "You mute and deaf spirit, I command you, come out of him and never enter him again" (v. 25). The unclean spirit left but not without one last convulsion of the boy. He seemed dead to the crowd, but Jesus, with the same gesture as with the little girl, "took him by the hand lifted him up, and he arose" (v. 27).

Later, in a private home, the disciples asked: "Why could we not cast it out?" (v. 28). Jesus' response is interesting in that he applies his response to himself: "This kind cannot be driven out by anything but prayer" (v. 29). A variant reading adds "and fasting." Either way, the implication is that great faith or trust in God's power to overcome such evil is necessary and Jesus had that kind of trust (see also Matt 17:20 and Luke 17:5).

The article by O'Collins and Kendall quoted from a German scholar, Joachim Gnilka, who wrote: "For the miraculous healings not only the faith of the one who received help but also the faith of Jesus is relevant . . . In that Jesus was open to God in a unique way he showed his unique faith . . . When Jesus according to Mark 9:23 says to the father of the epileptic [sic] boy, 'All things are possible to him who believes,' that is an invitation to share in his faith."[16] O'Collins and Kendall, themselves, made the following observation:

> In this episode Jesus complains of his contemporaries as being "a faithless generation" (Mark 9:19). They have "little faith" (Matt 6:30 = Luke 12:28) and should learn to trust in divine providence. He reproaches his disciples as a group and Peter in particular for having "little faith" (Matt 8:26; 14:31; 17:20). He promises that God will hear those who ask in prayer (Matt 7:7–12 = Luke 11:9–13). Some, or probably much of this language goes back to Jesus himself. He speaks about faith as an insider, one who knows personally what the life of faith is and wants to share it with others (see 2 Cor 4:13).[17]

Peter Bolt considered this text (Mark 9:23) important as well for understanding the "faith of Jesus." He wrote: "The flow of the action in this account strongly suggests that Jesus was able to do what the disciples could not do, because he is the one who epitomizes 'the one who believes,' and so he does the impossible. . . . He is able to work these mighty powers because he himself is a believer."[18]

Mark 11:20–25, concerning the withered fig tree, has much in common with Mark 9 above, although a totally different circumstance. Jesus had cursed a fig tree because it did not have any fruit (Mark 11:13, 14). Later, when Peter drew attention to the withered fig tree, Jesus' response is instructive: "Have faith in God" (ESV). Note that there are other possible ways to translate this phrase. One interpretation is: "Reckon upon God's faithfulness."[19] It could be interpreted as an encouragement: "You have

---

16. O'Collins and Kendall, "The Faith of Jesus," 416–17.
17. O'Collins and Kendall, "The Faith of Jesus," 417.
18. Bird and Sprinkle, *Faith of Jesus Christ*, 215.

19. This phrase initiated D. W. B. Robinson's study of the subjective genitive interpretation as he explained: "Many years ago, as a schoolboy, I gave my autograph book to a visiting preacher who wrote in it three Greek words from Mark xi.22, *echete pistin theou*, with this rendering, 'Reckon on God's fidelity.' I knew that this was not the usual rendering of the text, which in most versions is 'Have faith in God.' But when in later years I came to the serious study of the Greek Testament I found myself wondering whether perhaps the text could indeed be about *God's faithfulness*. I transferred my curiosity to another phrase, more frequently found in the New Testament, *pistis*

the faithfulness of God," a suggestion by Lane's commentary on Mark. Robinson suggested: "Be firm as God is firm."[20] In other words, Jesus was encouraging his disciples to depend upon the covenant promises of God to fulfill his word concerning the coming kingdom and its establishment upon the earth. These things would be accomplished by Jesus' own impending death, burial, resurrection, and exaltation.

Jesus continued: "Truly, I say to you, whoever says to this mountain, 'Be taken up and thrown into the sea,' and does not doubt in his heart, but believes that what he says will come to pass, it will be done for him. Therefore I tell you, whatever you ask in prayer, believe that you have received it, and it will be yours" (Mark 11:23-24). It is possible to see this as Jesus' statement about his own faith in this sense. Notice that Mark recorded the cursing of the fig tree at 11:12-14, told the story of Jesus "cleansing" the temple at 11:15-19, and then gave the lesson about the withered fig tree (11:20-26). This is called "Intercalation." Wallis instructs us: "Intercalation is a characteristically Markan technique and here it encourages the reader to view the cursing alongside Jesus' conduct in the temple as judgement upon the corrupt cultus. Further, when Jesus illustrates the power of faith in terms of levelling τῷ ὄρει τούτῳ [this mountain], attention is once again drawn to the temple mount and to the seat of corruption."[21]

One of the earmarks of faith is the prayer life of the disciple. So, it is with Jesus. His prayer life was impeccable (see Mark 1:35; 6:46; 14:22, 23, 32-42; Matt 11:25; 14:23; 26:36-46; Luke 3:21; 4:42 [implied]; 5:16; 6:12; 9:18, 28, 29; 10:21-22; 11:1-4; 18:1; 22:32, 40-46; 23:34, 46). "Praying like that expressed a deep sense of dependence and trust—in other words, a strong relationship of faith in God."[22]

Ever since leaving Caesarea Philippi (Mark 8:27), Jesus predicted and prophesied at least three times about his impending death, burial, and resurrection (Mark 8:31 [Matt 16:21; Luke 9:21]; 9:31 [Matt 17:22, 23; Luke 9:44]; and 10:33, 34 [Matt 20:18, 19; Luke 18:32, 33]). Jesus was reckoning upon God's faithfulness by repeating the phrase: "after three

---

Iesou Christou, and wondered whether it, likewise, might be referring to a quality possessed by Jesus, his faith or his faithfulness, rather than our faith in him"(Robinson, "Justification and the Faith of Jesus," in *Verdict: A Journal of Theology* 2.4 [1979] 15). The original article appeared in another journal: Robinson, "'Faith of Jesus Christ.'" Reading this article is what started my career-long study of the *pistis Christou* debate.

20. Bird and Sprinkle, *Faith of Jesus Christ*, 212.

21. Wallis, *Faith of Jesus Christ*, 42.

22. O'Collins and Kendall, "The Faith of Jesus," 417.

days he will rise." Such statements require genuine faith. Jesus' prediction of the temple's destruction (Mark 13) is in this same category. The temple and Jerusalem were destroyed by the Romans in AD 70.

The rest of the usages of the verb, *pisteuō*, do not add to our arguments. Now, the noun, *pistis*, must be considered. The first is Mark 2:5. In Capernaum, Jesus was "at home" and crowds had gathered so large that there was no room for anyone to get close to him. Four friends of a paralytic broke apart the roofing and let the poor man through on his pallet in front of Jesus. "And when Jesus saw their faith, he said to the paralytic, 'Son, your sins are forgiven'" (Mark 2:5). The faith of these four men was manifested by their action, as difficult as it was to climb to a roof, tear it apart, and let down a grown man on a pallet. Jesus' response is somewhat ironic. He first forgave the man's sins, knowing what the scribes were thinking! "Only God can forgive sins!" Then he said: "Why do you question these things in your hearts? Which is easier, to say to the paralytic, 'Your sins are forgiven,' or to say 'Rise, take up your bed and walk'? But that you may know that the Son of Man has authority on earth to forgive sins—he said to the paralytic—'I say to you, rise, pick up your bed, and go home'" (Mark 2:8b–11). Jesus does what only God can do—forgive sins! He also healed a paralytic—perhaps something only God can do, but he does it through this one perfect and complete man, the Messiah, the Son of Man.

At another time Jesus, with the twelve, were crossing the Sea of Galilee (Mark 4:35–41). Jesus, being very tired, fell asleep on the cushions in the stern. A storm arose and was about to sink the boat. His disciples woke him and said: "Teacher, do you not care that we are perishing?" Jesus awoke and, apparently calmly, rebuked the wind and the sea saying: "Peace! Be still!" And so it happened! But what Jesus said afterward is significant for understanding the faith of Jesus: "Why are you so afraid? Have you still no faith?" (Mark 4:40). The implication is that Jesus had all the faith he needed to rebuke the wind and sea. The disciples did not.

Comments have already been made about Mark 5:34 (the woman with the discharge of blood) and 11:22 ("Reckon upon God's faithfulness"). Only Mark 10:52 remains. In this story Jesus healed Bartimaeus, a blind beggar in Jericho. Bartimaeus apparently knew that Jesus was the promised Messiah, the Son of David (see 2 Sam 7:16). He would not stop saying: "Jesus, Son of David, have mercy on me!" (Mark 10:47, 48). Finally, with the disciples and the crowd looking on, Jesus replied to Bartimaeus: "Go your way, your faith has made you well." The text reads: "And immediately he recovered his sight and followed him on the way" (Mark 10:52b). "Your faith has made you well" is the same for the woman in Mark 5:34. Jesus had said: "All things are possible for one who believes!" Surely this can be applied to Jesus as well as to the ones who needed healing and forgiveness.

Many years ago, the late D. S. Cairns wrote about the faith of Jesus: "The faith of Jesus in the Almighty Father, like all faith, is woven of three strands—faith in God's power and reality, faith in His love, and faith in His perfect liberty to help men."[23] These words by Cairns are confirmed by the use of the *pistis* word group in the Gospel of Mark.

Matthew: "Jesus—'The Son of God'"

I have always admired R. T. France's independent thinking about the Synoptic Gospels, his commentary on their content and dating. Most scholars late-date the Gospels after the destruction of Jerusalem and its temple of AD 70, primarily because they do not believe that Jesus or the Gospel writers could have predicted such a destruction (see Matt 24; Mark 13, Luke 21). By contrast, France sided with those who believe that such a prediction was not only possible, but could have been easily discernible in the years leading up to AD 70. Without going through the arguments, France suggested that Mark's Gospel was the first to be written while Peter was still living, perhaps in the late 50s, then Matthew would have been written sometime in the mid-60s or even a little earlier, while Luke-Acts would have been written at approximately the same time frame: the Gospel of Luke before Paul's Roman imprisonment and the book of Acts at the close of Paul's Roman imprisonment (perhaps his release c. AD 62). Of course, this is a minority view but just as viable as other conjectures. France wrote:

> Moreover, there are a number of passages in the gospel which presuppose that the temple is still standing (see below [in his commentary] on 5:23–24; 17:24–27; 23:16–22), and while it is of course possible that Matthew has preserved such sayings even after they have ceased to be applicable, in at least one case this would have been to risk significant misunderstanding by post-70 readers [a reference to the "temple tax" at 17:24–27 of which France makes comment on p. 668, n. 15].[24]

23. Cairns, "The Faith of Jesus," 217.
24. France, *Matthew*, 19.

If Matthew used Mark as a basis for his gospel (90 per cent of Mark!), it is remarkable how different Matthew presents the story of Jesus. The *pistis* word group does not even begin in Matthew's Gospel until the eighth chapter, and the usages of these words follow well the use by Mark.[25]

For the size of Matthew's Gospel compared to Mark, the *pistis* word group is used moderately as well. The verb, *pisteuō*, is used eleven times, but four of those are in one episode where John the Baptizer is the object of the verb (Matt 21:25, 32³). Jesus is the object of the verb several times where it means "to believe or trust" that Jesus is able to heal or perform similar miracles (Matt 8:13; 9:28; 21:22). Twice it is used as "believing in" Jesus, once by "little ones" (Matt 18:6) and once by Jesus' enemies at the cross (Matt 27:42). Twice it is used of "believing" in the report of false messiahs (Matt 24:23, 26).

Matthew 21:20–22, which includes a verb and noun for "faith," finds its parallel in Mark 11:12–14. Jesus taught his disciples about the power of prayer by saying "if you have faith and do not doubt" and "whatever you ask in prayer, believing, you will receive" (Matt 21:21, 22, my translation). As said earlier, Jesus may be referring to his own faith in prayer and its power.

The noun, *pistis*, "faith," is used eight times (Matt 8:10; 9:2, 22, 29; 15:28; 17:20; 21:21–22; 23:23). Most of these are parallel in Mark. In Matt 23:23 Jesus chastised the scribes and Pharisees for neglecting the weightier matters of the law such as "justice and mercy and faithfulness." The ESV has correctly translated *pistis* as "faithfulness." I would translate the word "mercy" (*eleos*) as "covenant loyalty," based on the fact that the Greek word *eleos* is used always to translate the Hebrew חֶסֶד (*chesed*). All three words relate to being faithful to God!

One of the more interesting features of Matthew's Gospel is how he elaborated on the story of Jesus walking on water (sea of Galilee). Mark's account (Mark 6:45–52) is straightforward and does not mention any discussion between Peter and Jesus and Peter's attempt to walk on water (Matt 14:22–33). When Peter begins to sink in the water due to his fear,

---

25. However, we should note in the "sermon on the mount" that Jesus refers to those who are anxious about the necessities of life as having "little faith" (*oligopistoi*), Matt 6:30. The implication is that Jesus himself is not anxious about such things and has "great faith" in his heavenly Father. A similar thought is found in Matt 7:11. Again, the implication is that Jesus' requests in prayer have been answered! See also Matt 17:20 in parallel with Mark 9:19.

Jesus mildly rebukes Peter: "O you of little faith (*oligopiste*), why did you doubt?" (Matt 14:31b). The implication is that Jesus had great faith while Peter had practically speaking none.

In light of the above discussion, Ian Wallis makes an insightful conclusion:

> It may well be, therefore, that in addition to the christological focus of faith in his Gospel, Matthew also wished to acknowledge the place of Jesus' faith within the performance of miracles and to exploit its exemplary function for the life of the community. If this was the case, Matthew did not consider faith in Jesus and the faith of Jesus to be mutually exclusive. A disciple must follow Jesus' example in the life of faith; but even where faith comes to expression in performatory miracle-working conduct, its source and object is still the person of Jesus who is messiah, Lord and son of God.[26]

Finally, the adjective, *pistos*, "faithful," is used three times (Matt 24:45; 25:21, 23). Jesus commends the "faithful servant" who is faithful as a steward in God's kingdom in light of the coming of the Lord (his *Parousia*).

The negative words of *apistos* ("faithless") and *apistia* ("unbelief") are used once each: Matt 17:17 and 13:58. The former has already been commented on, but the latter is interesting, for it is Matthew's description of Jesus' rejection in his own home town of Nazareth: "And he did not do many mighty works there, because of their unbelief" (see Mark 6:6a).

It is obvious that an idea can be expressed without necessarily using the words for the idea such as the *pistis* word group. An example is found in Matt 27:41–43 where the chief priests, with the scribes and elders, mocked the crucified Jesus by saying: "He saved others; he cannot save himself. He is the King of Israel; let him come down now from the cross, and we will believe in him. He trusts in God; let God deliver him now, if he desires him. For he said, 'I am the Son of God.'" The phrase: "He trusts in God" (πέποιθεν ἐπὶ τὸν θεόν, *pepoithen epi ton theon*) suggested that even Jesus' enemies understood the character of Jesus in terms of his preaching and healing ministry. While Jesus' enemies did not believe their own mocking statement, Matthew certainly did. Matthew used the word "he trusts" rather than the word in the Septuagint (LXX), "he hoped." The word can also mean "he relied upon" or "he depended on."

---

26. Wallis, *Faith of Jesus Christ*, 41.

This is equivalent to "he has faith in/believes in/trusts God." After more detailed observations and arguments, Peter Bolt concluded:

> When we realize that "he trusts in God", or "he trusted in God", is an almost exact equivalent of the expression "the faith of Jesus Christ"—with the genitive understood subjectively—and that Matthew appears to summarize the Messiah's ministry in exactly these terms, then we see that this kind of substructure could certainly be deeply embedded in the gospel message and so also underlie the Pauline expression.[27]

More possibilities such as the above will be discussed after probing the uniqueness of the Gospel of Luke.

Luke: "Jesus—'Savior of the World'"

The Gospel of Luke presented Jesus as the world's Savior. "Luke, as a historian, inhabited the worlds of both Judaism and Hellenism. As a theologian, he remained firmly Jewish while claiming to address the world of paganism."[28] While Matthew used 90 percent of Mark, Luke only used about 50 percent. This makes Luke's Gospel unique from Matthew. None of the Gospel writers present their stories in a strict chronological order, but all three Gospels present Jesus' ministry without regard to the time frame of his entire ministry (in contrast to John's Gospel of three-plus years, marked by Jesus' visits to Jerusalem's festivals). Since Luke only used approximately half of Mark, his Gospel presents more materials that are uniquely Luke's, presumably by his own research (Luke 1:1–4).

The unique material includes the following texts in Luke: 3:10–14; 4:25–27; 7:11–15, 36–47; 10:30–37, 39–42; 11:5–8; 12:16–20, 35–38; 13:1–5, 6–9, 10–17, 31–32; 14:1–5, 8–10, 12–14, 28–32; 15:4–6, 8–9, 11–32; 16:1–8, 19–31; 17:7–10, 12–18; 18:2–8, 10–14; 19:1–10.[29] This fact makes Luke's Gospel more interesting in how he combines this material with Mark and possibly Q (?). Most of the unique passages in Luke do not

---

27. Bolt, "Faith of Jesus Christ," 217.
28. Wright and Bird, *New Testament*, 604.
29. Wright and Bird, *New Testament*, 606. Note that this list from Wright and Bird omits the story of the boy Jesus in the temple (Luke 2:41–51). This story is not found in the other Gospels. Surely it should be added to the list as unique to Luke ("Special Luke"). It also omits the resurrected Jesus with the two on the road to Emmaus (Luke 24:13–35), unique to Luke.

add to our idea of the faithfulness of Jesus, with a few exceptions which will be commented on below (see Luke 4:25–27; 16:1–8; 18:2–8; and 19:1–10).

For Luke's size, he used the *pistis* word group moderately in comparison to the other two Gospels. The verb, *pisteuō* ("to believe, trust"), is used nine times: 1:20, 45; 8:12, 13, 50; 16:11; 20:5; 22:67; 24:25. The noun, *pistis* ("faith, faithfulness, trustworthiness"), is used eleven times: 5:20; 7:9, 50; 8:25, 48; 17:5, 6, 19; 18:8, 42; 22:32. The adjective, *pistos* ("faithful"), is used five times: 12:42; 16:10, 11, 12; 19:17. The negative words are used twice each: the verb, *apisteuō* ("disbelieve, not believe"), in 24:11, 41 and the adjective, *apistos* ("unfaithful, faithless"), in 9:41; 12:46.

In comparison to Mark and Matthew, Luke shortened the story of the boy with an unclean spirit and did not emphasize the conversation with the father of the boy about "faith." Neither did he recount subsequent discussion with his disciples about the need for "prayer [and fasting]" (Mark 9:14–29; Matt 17:14–21). The faithfulness of Jesus can be found in his temptations in the wilderness as already mentioned in Matthew (Matt 4:1–11). Luke reversed the last two temptations (Luke 4:5–12) and added the comment: "And when the devil had ended every temptation, he departed from him until an opportune time" (Luke 4:13). The devil will test the faithfulness of Jesus many times over!

Luke's account of Jesus' rejection in his hometown of Nazareth (Luke 4:16–30) added significant information about that rejection. First of all, Jesus' reading of Isa 61:1–2a and his statement that "today this Scripture has been fulfilled in your hearing" (Luke 4:21b) indicated Jesus' faithfulness to the Father's will that such a ministry should occur with regard to his Son. Luke's unique material recounted Jesus referring to gentiles (widow of Zarephath and Naaman the Syrian, vv. 25–27) as receiving a measure of God's grace. This is what incited the synagogue "worshipers" to attempt to execute Jesus, by charging him with blasphemy.

In Luke 4:43 Jesus said to those who sought him out even in a desolate place: "I must preach the good news of the kingdom of God to the other towns as well; for I was sent for this purpose." This was a not so subtle hint of Jesus' faithfulness to the Father's will in terms of his preaching, teaching, and healing ministry, a fulfillment of Isa 61:1–2a.

Several times Jesus' healing ministry required faith on behalf of the sick. Luke made a comment about what allowed Jesus to heal the sick: "And the power of the Lord was with him to heal" (Luke 5:17c). A variant reading is possible: "And the power of the Lord was present to heal them." When this is coupled with the verse above (v. 16—"But he would withdraw to desolate places and pray"), it implied that Jesus was very close to the power of God through constant praying. His faithfulness to the Father and his ability to perform healings and exorcisms came from this source. Apart from so-called miracles, Jesus spent all night in prayer just before choosing his twelve apostles (Luke 6:12–16). Luke suggests that something within Jesus himself was at work during his sessions of healing and exorcisms: "And all the crowd sought to touch him, for power came out from him and healed them all" (Luke 6:19).

If Jesus expected his disciples to be faithful, it meant he himself must be faithful. One such teaching highly suggested this: "A disciple is not above his teacher, but everyone when he is fully trained will be like his teacher" (Luke 6:40). Jesus fully expected his fellow Jews to have faith in him as Messiah. When a gentile exhibited such faith as the centurion who sought healing for his servant, even from a distance, Jesus exclaimed: "I tell you, not even in Israel have I found such faith" (Luke 7:9b).

When John the Baptist wavered while he was in prison and sent a servant saying, "Are you the one who is to come, or shall we look for another?" Jesus responded with a litany of acts in fulfillment of Isa 61:1–2a (Luke 7:18–23) and concluded his words to the servant: "And blessed is the one who is not offended by me" (v. 23). The term "not offended" in ESV is stronger in the Greek: μὴ σκανδαλισθῇ, *mē skandalisthē*, "not scandalized." This word is the opposite of *pistis*, meaning "lose faith."[30] Jesus had the anointing of the Holy Spirit and he was accomplishing all the deeds Isaiah proclaimed would occur with the coming of Messiah. Like other stories found in Mark, Luke shortened the story of calming the storm with a word (Luke 8:22–25). Luke had Jesus say: "Where is your faith?" without any elaboration. Again, it is implied that Jesus had great faith in the midst of the storm.

Jesus' faithfulness to the Father can be seen in Luke's account where Jesus made a decision to go to Jerusalem and expose himself to the authorities. "When the days drew near for him to be taken up, he set his face to go to Jerusalem" (Luke 9:51). "Taken up" can have multiple meanings such as "taken up" on a cross or "taken up" to the Father's right hand in exaltation after his resurrection. From that point in Luke's Gospel, Jesus confronted all around him with a warning about the kingdom of God: "No one who puts his hand to the plow and looks back is fit for the kingdom of God" (Luke 9:62). At one point along the way to Jerusalem, Jesus

---

30. This insight was shared with me by Dr. Carl Bridges, reader of my rough drafts.

taught his apostles not to be anxious about anything (Luke 12:22–34), a virtue Jesus certainly demonstrated explicitly. In the midst of this teaching Jesus described them: "O you of little faith!" (Luke 12:28c). This implied Jesus' faith to be without anxiety. It is interesting that Luke recorded the names of the women who helped support Jesus' ministry (Luke 8:1–3). Surely Jesus trusted his God that such women of wealth and faith would support his ministry.

One of the more interesting yet puzzling of Jesus' parables was given by Luke's unique contribution (Luke 16:1–8): the story of the dishonest manager. Regardless of how one interprets this passage, Luke added an application of this parable in Jesus' own words: "One who is faithful in a very little is also faithful in much, and one who is dishonest in a very little is also dishonest in much. If then you have not been faithful in the unrighteous wealth, who will entrust to you the true riches? And if you have not been faithful in that which is another's, who will give you that which is your own? No servant can serve two masters, for he will be devoted to the one and despise the other. You cannot serve God and money" (Luke 16:10–13). Again, the implication is that Jesus is himself the model for faithfulness in regard to his commitment to the will of God and the kingdom.

A passage that seemed out of place in the midst of Luke's unique material has the apostles asking Jesus to increase their faith (Luke 17:5). Jesus' response was perhaps sardonic, at best ironic: "If you had faith like a grain of mustard seed, you could say to this mulberry tree, 'Be uprooted and planted in the sea,' and it would obey you" (Luke 17:6). Jesus' trust in the Father's power through the Holy Spirit enabled him to be successful in his preaching, teaching, and healing ministry. In one of the unique texts of Luke (Luke 18:1–8), the parable of the persistent widow, Jesus made the point that praying to God should always be persistent and that we should not lose heart, for God in his righteousness will give to his faithful ones justice. Luke's account has Jesus end the parable by saying: "Nevertheless, when the Son of Man comes, will he find faith on earth?" (Luke 18:8b). In other words, faithfulness requires a persistent prayer life of which Jesus was the model par excellence.

The use of "Son of Man" is Jesus' subtle way of identifying himself with the "Son of Man" of Dan 7:13 who is exalted at God's right hand and given "dominion and glory and a kingdom" (Dan 7:14a). He will make reference to this prophetic text after his arrest and as he stands before the council: "'If you are the Christ, tell us.' But he said to them, 'If I tell you,

you will not believe, and if I ask you, you will not answer. But from now on the Son of Man shall be seated at the right hand of the power of God'" (Luke 22:67–69).

Luke's story of Jesus and Zacchaeus, the chief tax collector (Luke 19:1–10), is one of the well-known unique texts in Luke. At the end of the story Luke recorded the words of Jesus: "Today salvation has come to this house, since he also is a son of Abraham. For the Son of Man came to seek and to save the lost" (Luke 19:9–10). Jesus is here seen as being faithful to his mission as the Son of Man.

Among all the Gospels, Jesus was portrayed as having "seven sayings" from the cross. Mark was sparse: "My God, my God, why have you forsaken me?" (Mark 15:34). He added that Jesus "uttered a loud cry and breathed his last" (Mark 15:37). Matthew, too, was sparse following Mark's account with the quote from Ps 22:1 and recording Jesus' last breath: "And Jesus cried out again with a loud voice and yielded up his spirit" (Matt 27:50). Luke's account is more full, if a variant is accepted: "Father, forgive them, for they know not what they do" (Luke 23:34a); "Truly, I say to you, today you will be with me in Paradise" (Luke 23:43, addressed to a repentant criminal); and finally Luke puts words to Jesus' "loud cry" or "loud voice": "Father, into your hands I commit my spirit!" (Luke 23:46). The other three sayings are found in John: "Woman, behold, your son!" (John 19:26) and to the disciple "Behold, your mother!" (John 19:27); "I thirst" (John 19:28); and "It is finished!" (John 19:30b).

Luke's account spoke to the thesis that Jesus had complete trust and faith in the Father. At the point of death Jesus placed himself in the hands of God the Father. Through a life of prayer and commitment to God's mission for himself, Jesus completed that mission by saying in his struggle on the Mount of Olives: "Father, if you are willing, remove this cup from me. Nevertheless, not my will, but yours, be done" (Luke 22:42; see Isa 53:10). Jesus' complete trust in God was expressed by these words: "Into your hands I commit my spirit!" In light of the mission of Jesus the Messiah, Peter Bolt wrote:

> Each person must exercise faith in the context of the unique circumstances of life given to them by God. Jesus was more than just an ordinary Israelite; he had the special vocation of the Servant of the Lord—and the Christ, the Son of Man, the Son of God. For him to exercise faith was to embark upon a mission that ended only in one place: the death of the Servant as a ransom for many. This is not a destiny that can be shared

or imitated by anyone else, for his role was unique in God's purposes for redeeming a lost world.[31]

Luke recorded his unique story of Jesus with the two on the road to Emmaus (Luke 24:13–35). The humor of the story is found with Cleopas' question: "Are you the only visitor to Jerusalem who does not know the things that have happened there in these days?" (Luke 24:18). "These two Emmaus men thought they knew what had happened in Jerusalem. They didn't know. Jesus knew and he knew they didn't know and he knew they thought they did know. In God's great universe only Jesus knew! No one else in Jerusalem knew! No one!"[32] After much discussion on the events surrounding the resurrection of Jesus, Jesus finally reprimanded the two: "'O foolish ones, and slow of heart to believe all that the prophets have spoken! Was it not necessary that the Christ should suffer these things and enter into his glory?' And beginning with Moses and all the Prophets, he interpreted to them in all the Scriptures the things concerning himself" (Luke 24:25–27). What a wonder it would be to have the content of that discussion! Yet, we do have it, for we know some of the most important passages in the Hebrew Scriptures that speak of the Messiah and his suffering on behalf of the world (e.g., Isa 42, 49, 50, 53, 61, 63). There is no doubt that Jesus presented himself before the two on the road to Emmaus as the Servant of the Lord. Bolt concluded on this thought: "As this occurs [Jesus as the Servant of the Lord], the message of the Synoptics and Acts provides a serious picture of the faithfulness of Jesus Christ, and this may well provide a narrative substructure which supports, or even demands, a subjective reading of the genitive in πίστις Χριστοῦ."[33]

Conclusion

The Synoptic Gospels and even the Gospel of John present the life of Jesus in a very unbalanced way, although what is presented makes sense. While the birth of Jesus received various stories (Matthew and Luke), both Mark and John basically omit it or limit it to a phrase: "And the Word became flesh and dwelt among us" (John 1:14a). But all of the Gospels give more attention to the last week of Jesus' life on earth, from Jesus' triumphal entry to the post-resurrection events (see Mark 11–16;

---

31. Bolt, *Faith of Jesus Christ*, 218–19.
32. Comment by Dr. Tom Ewald.
33. Bolt, *Faith of Jesus Christ*, 222.

Matt 21–28; Luke 19–24; and John 12–21). This emphasis revealed the faithfulness of Jesus to his mission as the Messiah of the Jewish nation on behalf of the whole world. These last-week events of Jesus became in essence the heart of the gospel (see Acts 2:23–36; Rom 3:21–26; and 1 Cor 15:1–11). Focus on the last week of Jesus' ministry as it unfolded in and around Jerusalem revealed the faithfulness of Jesus the Messiah, starting from his deliberate preparations to enter Jerusalem riding on a donkey in a literal fulfillment of Zech 9:9b—"Behold, your king is coming to you; righteous and having salvation is he, humble and mounted on a donkey, on a colt, the foal of a donkey"—to his deliberate manifestation of his resurrection appearances to his disciples. Reading these chapters in all the Gospels gives the believer great hope in a future resurrection based on Jesus as a "firstfruits" of the resurrection.

The Acts: "The Acts of the Holy Spirit"

The book of Acts is selective history of the early church and is usually called "The Acts of the Apostles," although it mostly considered Peter (Acts 1–12) and Paul (Acts 13–28). In reality the Acts is about the acts of the Holy Spirit as he descends at Pentecost and continues throughout the narrative as the gospel is spread from Jerusalem and Judea to Samaria and ultimately Rome. The Spirit is the one who prompts the apostles to continue the ministry of Jesus in terms of preaching, teaching, and healing.

If Luke is the author, then he is the author of both books: Luke, volume one, and Acts, volume two. Although these two books are anonymous, it is likely that Luke, the beloved physician[34] (Col 4:14), is the author due to the "we" passages in Acts beginning at Acts 16:10. This would make Luke a companion of Paul in his later missionary work. Apparently, Luke attended to Paul during some of his imprisonments (see Phlm 24

---

34. The medical knowledge and terms in Luke support the author was well educated in Hippocratic medicine. At least four hundred medical terms are used exclusively in Luke and Acts or more frequently there than in any other New Testament books. Yet, Luke does not make the erroneous "humoral" theory of Hippocrates in his two volumes. Hippocrates advocated the healing properties of balancing the four humors: black bile, yellow bile, blood, and phlegm. Nothing of this can be found in Luke or Acts! Many of Luke's medical terms have equivalents or transliterations in contemporary medicine. Luke even rejected the Rabbinic teaching that sin causes sickness. The study to support this information about the "beloved physician" was done by Dr. Ewald.

and 2 Tim 4:11). Some suggest that Luke is probably a gentile, converted God-fearer who had gained much of his education in Scripture (the Hebrew Bible) from attendance at the Jewish synagogue.

Both books are dedicated to Theophilus ("Lover of God"), perhaps a recent convert and a patron for Luke's research and writing. Acts 1:1 referred to volume one as "all that Jesus began to do and teach." Volume two was supposedly the continuing work of Jesus through his apostles and others who were empowered from the beginning by the Holy Spirit. Both books cover approximately thirty years each for Jesus' life and the progress of the early church.

The Acts can be structured in different ways. One way is geographical by taking Acts 1:8 as the key: "You will be my witnesses in Jerusalem and in all Judea and Samaria, and to the end of the earth." Thus, the outline would be: Acts 1–7 (Jerusalem); 8–12 (Judea and Samaria); 13–28 (the end of the earth = Rome). Another outline could be found by focusing on the theme of "witnesses" from the same text (1:8).[35] In that case the following makes good sense:

    I. Preparation for Witness (1:1—2:13)

    II. The Witness in Jerusalem (2:14—5:42)

    III. The Witness beyond Jerusalem (6:1—12:25)

    IV. The Witness in Cyprus and Southern Galatia (13:1—14:28)

    V. The Jerusalem Council (15:1–35)

    VI. The Witness in Greece (15:36—18:22)

    VII. The Witness in Ephesus (18:23—21:16)

    VIII. The Arrest in Jerusalem (21:17—23:35)

    IX. The Witness in Caesarea (24:1—26:32)

    X. The Witness in Rome (27:1—28:31)

Acts can be considered a bifid—that is, a biblical book that is divided into two equal parts: Acts 1–12 (mainly about Peter) and Acts 13–28 (mainly about Paul).

Luke punctuated the volume with "church growth reports" after narratives of activities of the disciples of Jesus. There seem to be minor

---

35. John B. Polhill's outline in the ESV Study Bible, 2077–79.

reports (parentheses) and major reports (italics): (2:41, 42); 2:47; (4:4); 5:14; (6:1); 6:7; 9:31; (11:21, 24); 12:24; 16:5; 19:20; and 28:31.

One might guess that the *pistis* word group would be used even more profusely than in the Gospels.[36] That guess is correct. The verb, *pisteuō* ("to believe, trust"), is used thirty-seven times (thirty-nine with a couple of variants, Acts 8:37). The noun, *pistis* ("faith[fulness], trust"), is used fifteen times. The adjective, *pistos* ("faithful"), is used four times. The negative words are used only once each: *apisteuō* ("disbelieve, not believe") at Acts 28:24 and the adjective *apistos* ("unfaithful, faithless") at Acts 26:8, translated "incredible," meaning "unbelievable" in terms of God raising the dead.

The verb was used primarily to describe various individuals and groups who came to believe in the Lord Jesus as the Messiah. Sometimes the verb was not used, rather a synonymous phrase: "So those who received his word [equivalent to "those who believed," see v. 44] were baptized" (Acts 2:41). Usually when it was recorded that a person or persons believed and/or repented, they were immediately baptized in the name of the Lord Jesus Christ (see Acts 2:38, 41; 8:12, 13, 16, 35–38; 9:18; 10:43, 47–48; 16:15, 31–34; 18:8 ["Corinthians"], 25–26 [implied]; 19:2–5; 22:16). This indicated that when only the word "believe" was used of those who were added to the church, baptism was a natural and necessary part of the process of becoming a "believer" and was often not expressed (Acts 2:44; 4:4, 32; 9:42; 11:17, 21; 13:12, 39, 48; 14:1, 23; 15:7, 11; 17:4 [implied], 12, 34; 18:8 ["Crispus"], 27; 19:2; 21:20, 25; 22:19). These usages implied that those who believe have joined themselves to the Lord's new people of God (made up of both Jews and gentiles, the new family of God, the church).

The use of the participle as substantive (noun, "believers") and in the absolute state had some overlap with the above: 2:44; 4:32; 5:14; 11:21; 13:39; 15:5; 18:27; 19:18; 21:20, 25. The rest of the usages of *pisteuō* have more or less the idea of "trust": Acts 9:26 (disciples in Jerusalem did not trust Paul); 13:41 (a quote from Hab 1:5 with the idea of "trust"); 27:25 (Paul trusted God's message that he and his many companions will be saved in a shipwreck); 24:14 (Paul witnessed to Felix of his believing, perhaps better "trusting," in the Scriptures, that there will be a resurrection and a reckoning on Judgment Day). The final use of *pisteuō* was Paul's question to King Agrippa: "Do you believe the prophets? I know

---

36. Darrell L. Bock does a brief word study on *pisteuō* and *pistis* in Luke-Acts in his book *A Theology of Luke and Acts*, 267–68.

that you believe" (26:27). Agrippa could not complete what faith he had with a commitment.

The noun *pistis* is used in a variety of ways. The most used is *pistis* with the article to indicate "the faith," i.e., Christianity: Acts 6:7; 13:8; 14:22; 16:5; 24:24 ("about the faith in Messiah Jesus"). Acts 26:18 is difficult. Verse 18b is translated: "that they may receive forgiveness of sins and a place among those who are sanctified by faith in me." Paul recounted his commission by the resurrected Jesus to go to the gentiles and preach the Gospel so that they may receive forgiveness and belong to those who are sanctified—either as translated in most English versions, "faith in me," or perhaps another possibility is: "by faithfulness, the [faithfulness] in/unto me." Possible. Another usage was the idea of "commitment": Acts 6:5 ("Stephen, a man full of faith and of the Holy Spirit"); 11:24 ("Barnabas ... a good man, full of the Holy Spirit and of faith"); both of the above (6:5 and 11:24) may refer to the spiritual gift of faith as understood in Rom 12:3; 1 Cor 12:9; and 13:2.

We continue with Acts 15:9 (gentiles "having cleansed their hearts by faith"); and 20:21 ("testifying both to Jews and to Greeks of repentance toward God and of faith in our Lord Jesus Christ"). Acts 14:9 had Paul healing a man crippled from birth. It was similar to some of Jesus' healings, for Paul "[saw] that he had faith to be made well." Paul gave the command "Stand upright on your feet!" The context indicates that God was the source of the healing. When Paul returned to Antioch he reported the results of his first missionary journey: "they declared all that God had done with them, and how he had opened a door of faith to the Gentiles" (14:27). An unusual use of *pistis* is found at 17:31 translated as "assurance" in the ESV: "because he has fixed a day on which he will judge the world in righteousness by a man whom he has appointed; and of this he has given assurance to all by raising him from the dead." *Pistis* in this context can be understood as "confidence" or "assurance." One last usage was found at Acts 3:16 which is important for this study, but it will be considered after a comment on the adjective.

The adjective, *pistos* ("faithful"), is only used four times. Twice it is used as a noun: "And the believers (*pistoi*) from among the circumcised who had come with Peter were amazed, because the gift of the Holy Spirit was poured out even on the Gentiles" (Acts 10:45). Timothy's mother is called "a Jewish woman who was a believer (*pistēs*), but his father was a Greek" (16:1). At 13:34 the ESV translated *ta pista* as "sure" in a quotation from Isa 55:3: "I will give you the holy and sure blessings of David."

The idea of "firm" could have been used here. The final use is the basic meaning of *pistos* ("faithful"). After Lydia and her household had been baptized, she urged Paul: "If you have judged me to be faithful (*pistēn*) to the Lord, come to my house and stay" (16:15).

Finally, we come to our main verse in Acts—Acts 3:16 and its use of *pistin* (twice). The context is Peter's healing of a lame beggar at the gate called the Beautiful Gate. The man had no faith to be healed, he was just expecting a little money (alms). "But Peter said, 'I have no silver and gold, but what I do have I give to you. In the name of Jesus Christ of Nazareth, rise up and walk!'" (Acts 3:6). A great crowd gathered in Solomon's portico, close to the temple proper. Peter used the occasion to explain that the healing was done by the God of our fathers who had glorified Jesus by his resurrection. Boldly Peter accused the people of having "killed the Author of life," of which Peter and John had been witnesses. Then he said: "And his name—by faith in his name—has made this man strong whom you see and know, and the faith that is through Jesus has given the man this perfect health in the presence of you all" (3:16). It is a difficult verse to interpret from the Greek text. Most interpreters and commentaries interpret similarly to Luke Timothy Johnson's comments:

> Not only does this statement as a whole interrupt Peter's "kerygmatic statement," (thereby linking the healing even more directly to the event of Jesus' resurrection), but it is garbled in Greek. The translation places this phrase within dashes in order to indicate its parenthetic character: it serves to qualify the bald statement, "his name has strengthened." The next statement about faith, however, is almost as confusing, "the faith that comes through him." The author is struggling, it appears, to join the objective power of "the name" working through the apostles, with the subjective necessity of "faith" to make that power operative. For the relationship of faith to salvation in Luke-Acts, see Luke 5:20; 7:9, 50; 8:12, 25, 48, 50; 17:19; 18:42; Acts 14:9; 15:11.[37]

Not much light is produced by this commentary. The fact that the lame man did not have faith before his healing contradicts the references given in Luke and Acts above. Johnson does not address the issue, merely presents it.

Another interpretation is suggested by Douglas Campbell. Campbell comments in note 14 for his chapter 16 concerning a series of so-called "objective genitives" in Paul's writings (2 Thess 2:13; Phil 3:8–9; Rom

---

37. Johnson, *Acts of the Apostles*, 68.

10:2; and Acts 3:16): "I am, incidentally, not convinced that Acts 3:16 does supply an objective genitive construction, but suggest rendering its two instances of πίστις in terms of 'proof,' and the genitive consequently more as one of content—the proof of God's saving activity in Christ that is supplied by the miraculously healed cripple."[38] Thus, Douglas would translate Acts 3:16 in this manner: "And upon the proof of his name—his name made strong whom you see and know—and the proof through him (Christ) was given to him (the lame man) this wholeness in the presence of all of you" or something similar.

A better interpretation was given by Shuji Ota. He observed also that the man had no faith before his healing. "By faith in his name" is not a good or even possible translation. Ota wrote: "Furthermore, when referring to someone's faith in Jesus the author of Acts uses the preposition εἰς, *not a genitive construction*."[39] He, then, gives three Acts references to illustrate this point: 20:21; 24:24; and 26:18. Ota elaborates on the meaning of the "name of Jesus" in this text:

> The "name of Jesus" is considered to be a metonym of Jesus Christ that embraces all that belongs to him: his identity, authority and power, and working at the right hand of God (including his messiahship, resurrection from the dead, pouring-out of the Holy Spirit, provision of human agents and missionaries, healing, exorcism, miracles, and salvation above all.[40]

Several times Luke recounted Peter's statements with regard to the "name of Jesus": See 2:38; 4:7, 10, 12, 30; 9:14, 15–16, 21; 10:43. Thus, Ota took the genitive case of "his name" in 3:16 to be understood subjectively and "the faith" preceding it in the sense of "trustworthiness," "truthfulness," or "faithfulness."[41] Hence, "*Jesus' name is trustworthy, truthful, and even faithful for human beings*" (emphasis is Ota's).[42] Ota's conclusion connects these thoughts to the "subjective genitive" debate:

> I believe that the genitive case in Paul's πίστις Χριστοῦ formulation does not so much denote Christ's own faith or faithfulness to God as *Christ's faithfulness toward humanity* in the

---

38. Campbell, *The Deliverance of God*, 1101–2.
39. Ota, "*Pistis* in Acts," 2.
40. Ota, "*Pistis* in Acts," 3.
41. Ota, "*Pistis* in Acts," 4.
42. Ota, "*Pistis* in Acts," 4.

sense of Christ's being steadfast, truthful, and trustworthy as God's Christ.[43]

This gives a slightly different twist to the subjective reading of the *pistis Christou* phrases, but it certainly works for Acts 3:16. Hence, I would translate with Ota Acts 3:16 in this manner: "And because of *the trustworthiness of his name, his name* has made this man strong, whom you see and know; and *the faith that is through him* (or it [= his name]) has given him this perfect health in the presence of all of you."[44] I would have translated the second *pistis* as "trustworthiness" as well.

One last observation about the "faithfulness of Jesus the Messiah" in the book of Acts needs attention. Acts included many speeches, mainly from Peter and Paul. The speeches that can be labeled "missionary speeches," even in a summary form by Luke, manifest an emphasis on Jesus' faithfulness as Messiah, who through his death, burial, resurrection, and exaltation had brought salvation to the world. In the first fifteen chapters of Acts, nine speeches are attributed to Peter. Five are missionary speeches: 2:14-36, 38-40 (Pentecost); 3:12-26 (Solomon's portico); 4:8-12 (Jewish council); 5:29-32 (high priest and council); and 10:34-43 (Cornelius' household). In each speech emphasis is placed upon Jesus' crucifixion, his burial, and resurrection, and often his exaltation as Lord and King. This harmonizes with the understanding of "the faithfulness of Jesus the Messiah" theme in Paul's writings, which referred to Jesus as our "means of atonement through [his] faithfulness at the cost of his blood" (Rom 3:25).

The same can be said of Paul's missionary speeches in Acts: 13:16-41(Antioch in Pisidia, synagogue); a summary in 17:3 (Thessalonica); 17:22-31 (Areopagus); 22:3-21 (Paul's testimony of his conversion and commission); 23:6 (summary only); 24:10-21 (testimony before Felix); 26:2-23, 25-29 (testimony before King Agrippa); and 28:17-20, 25-28 (Jews in Rome). The same emphasis on the gospel is found: the death, burial, and resurrection of Jesus. Of course, there are elaborations and differences in Paul's speeches, but that is primarily due to the circumstances and the people to whom he was speaking. The faithfulness of Jesus to God the Father in bringing salvation to the world through his passion and exaltation is the crowning message of Peter and Paul as well as the minor players found in Acts.

---

43. Ota, "*Pistis* in Acts," 4.
44. Ota, "*Pistis* in Acts," 2.

Our final survey of the New Testament comes with a look at the "Johannine Literature": the Gospel of John, the Letters of John, and the book of Revelation. This body of New Testament literature will surprise us even more concerning "the faithfulness of Jesus the Messiah."

7

The Johannine Literature

"As Christ comes to us, there is always an element of surprise that will cause us to cry out in delight, 'So that is what he meant.'"

—EUGENE H. PETERSON[1]

THE JOHANNINE LITERATURE CONSISTS of the Gospel of John, the three Letters of John, and Revelation. All three are different genres: gospel (biography), letter, and apocalyptic. All three have been greatly studied by scholars throughout the centuries right up to the present day. Of course, the critical issues of each are debated to the extent that a vast library is required to house all the books, monographs, and articles that have been written about this literature—questions of authorship (which John?), date, provenance, and purpose still rage for each and a consensus is difficult to achieve. However, there are certain parameters and possibilities for these issues. Useful background information will be given to put the *pistis* word group in a viable context. Each genre will be presented separately: first the gospel, then the letters, and finally the apocalypse.

---

1. Peterson, *Reversed Thunder*, 194.

The Gospel of John: "The Word Became Flesh"

Introductory Concerns

The Gospel of John is unique among the Gospels in that it is not like the Synoptic Gospels in telling the story of Jesus, although in broad outline they are the same. John's prologue (John 1:1-18) is poetic in nature and theologically loaded. Some scholars see the prologue in chiastic arrangement with vv. 10-14 about the incarnation of the Word at its center:

A. The Word's activity in creation (1:1-5)
  B. John's witness concerning the light (1:6-9)
    C. The incarnation of the Word (1:10-14)
  B^1. John's witness concerning the Word's preeminence (1:15)
A^1. The final revelation brought by Jesus Christ (1:16-18)[2]

John is saying the very Word that brought the creation into existence and brought life to all, "the life of men," is none other than Jesus, the Son of God, the incarnate Word. The creative Word is now a real human being that we know, for we have seen his glory, "glory as of the only Son from the Father, full of grace and truth" (v. 14). Verse 18 further explains: "No one has ever seen God; the only God, who is at the Father's side, he has made him known." A variant suggests the word "Son" instead of "God" in reference to Jesus. Also, "in the bosom of the Father" can be translated "at the Father's side" (ESV), which parallels the beginning words "and the Word was with (*pros*) God" (v. 1b).

The body of John's Gospel will develop the major themes found in the prologue:

1. Jesus (the Word made flesh) is presented as speaking many "words" in the great discourses of this gospel.

2. Jesus will prove to be the life of men (climaxed in the raising of Lazarus, John 11). Of course, his resurrection will assure the same.

3. A major theme is v. 5: "The light shines in the darkness, and the darkness has not overcome it." The play on these words will be found throughout the body of the gospel. The term "overcome" (κατέλαβεν, *katelaben*) in v. 5 can also mean "understood." D. A. Carson suggested translating it "mastered" to capture the dual

---

2. Köstenberger, *Encountering John*, 57.

sense of "understood" and "overcome."³ I prefer the term "apprehend" to do the same. The term will be used a couple of significant times (1:5; 8:3, 4 [some MSS omit]; 12:35).

4. The narrative of the Gospel of John will reveal how dark the world is and how the world did not know Jesus. Indeed, his own people, as a whole, did not receive or accept him as the Messiah.

5. However, a few, that is, those "who believed in his name," were given the right to become children of God. These are those who are born from above (see John 3 and the story of Nicodemus).

6. Seeing Jesus' miracles (works) is seeing his glory. Seven "signs" are given throughout the body of this Gospel (see 2:1–11; 2:13–22; 4:46–54; 5:1–15; 6:1–15; 9:1–41; and 11:1–44)⁴ to reveal who Jesus is—the Messiah, the Son of God (John 20:31).

7. The stories of Jesus' healings (miraculous acts) and especially his death on the cross will demonstrate his "grace heaped upon grace." But beyond that, those who truly *believe* (a major word) will experience eternal life now!

8. Jesus will make known to all who have eyes to see and ears to hear who God is—"whoever has seen me has seen the Father" (John 14:9b). Jesus emphasized: "Trust me that I am in the Father and the Father is in me, or else trust because of the works themselves" (John 14:11, my translation).

9. Finally, Moses gave the Law, but Jesus' incarnation brought the great Old Testament ideas of "grace and truth," which stand for the two Hebrew words: חֶסֶד וֶאֱמֶת *chesed veemeth*), which should be properly understood as "covenant love/loyalty and truth."⁵ Jesus will demonstrate in his life and ministry his covenant loyalty and his faithfulness (truth) to God the Father. Only by Jesus' perfect fulfillment of the purposes of God the Father for his life could Jesus say (as John witnessed) just before he died: "It is finished!"

---

3. Blomberg, *Historical Reliability*, 74. Blomberg is referring to Carson, *Gospel according to John*, 138.

4. Wright and Bird see Jesus' crucifixion as the seventh sign and thus deleting Jesus' walking on water to still give seven signs. See Wright and Bird, *New Testament*, 666.

5. See Koehler and Baumgartner in English, *Hebrew and Aramaic Lexicon*, 1:68–69 for the word *emeth*; for the more complex word of *chesed*, see 1:336–37. Also, *TDOT* 5:44–64.

Controversy surrounds the attempt to "discover" sources for John's Gospel, begun by the great Rudolf Bultmann (1971). He postulated "a 'signs' source, a 'discourse' source and a 'passion' source to account for a sizeable percentage of John's unique material."[6] Scholars, since, have postulated even more to the point that the approach is being continually scrutinized due to the difficulty of establishing good arguments one way or the other. Some have now shifted to a more literary approach, analyzing the narrative as is. Scholarly work on the Gospel of John continues to this day unabated with no consensus in sight, and there probably will never be.[7]

However, a simple outline of the Gospel of John is given by a good number of scholars, one of which appears below:

Prologue (1:1–18)

I. The Book of Signs (1:19—12:50)

II. The Book of Glory (chs. 13–20):

Jesus' Passion and Preparation of the New Covenant Community

Epilogue (ch. 21)[8]

Before proceeding with the *pistis* word group found in the Gospel of John, it is necessary to produce a rationale for a traditional position regarding authorship. The key question is: Who is the historical "John" to be considered? The traditional and longstanding view has been that the apostle John, son of Zebedee, one of the Twelve, is the author of the Gospel of John, the Letters of John, and the book of Revelation.[9] Whoever wrote the Gospel is usually credited with the three Letters of John, if not also Revelation. The language and ideas between the two (Gospel and letters) are significant. From this perspective the apostle John is identified with "the beloved disciple" in the Gospel of John.

---

6. Blomberg, *Historical Reliability*, 45.

7. See Thatcher, *What We Have Heard*. This book includes articles from the major players in the study of the Gospel of John, their contributions and how minds have changed, and where the inquiries are headed in the future. It is a very informative and insightful volume, but it only covers up to 2007. A good source that updates the study of John to 2013 is the article by Keener on "John, Gospel of" in *Dictionary of Jesus and the Gospels*, 419–36.

8. Köstenberger, *Encountering John*, 32. His outline is more detailed but the above is the main outline.

9. For the traditional view many sources can be found. I offer only two: Blomberg, *Historical Reliability*, 22–41 and Köstenberger, *Encountering John*, 22–25.

However, critical scholarship has questioned whether John the apostle, son of Zebedee, is the author of this Gospel. Recent scholarship has opted for "John, the elder" of 2 John 1 and 3 John 1. Even though there is slim evidence, many hold this opinion. Wright and Bird make every effort to identify this "John, the elder" with the unnamed "beloved disciple" in the Gospel of John (see John 13:23; 19:26, 27; 21:24; 20:8; 21:7).[10] They write about four "Johns": John the son of Zebedee, John the evangelist (author/redactor of the Gospel), John the elder (author of the letters and perhaps the Gospel), and John of Patmos (author of Revelation).[11] These scholars postulate John the elder as author/redactor of the Gospel of John and the Letters of John. For the book of Revelation, they suggest a different John—John the Seer (a prophet in the church at Ephesus). Again, these critical matters will be debated *ad nauseum*. The traditional view is as compelling as the others and all their variety of approaches. This debate will only continue but it need not prevent addressing the use of the word *pistis* in the Gospel.

The *Pistis* Word Group

One of the unique features of the Gospel of John is its use and non-use of the *pistis* word group. The verb, πιστεύω (*pisteuō*), "to believe, trust," is used ninety-eight times, much more than all the Synoptic Gospels put together. The noun, πίστις (*pistis*), "faith[fulness]," is not used at all! Andreas J. Köstenberger suggested: "It appears therefore that John's primary purpose is to engender in his readers the *act* of believing, of placing their trust in Jesus Christ" (his emphasis on *act*).[12] This seems to be true because of John's purpose statement in writing this Gospel: "But these are written so that you may believe [trust] that Jesus is the Christ [Messiah], the Son of God, and that by believing [trusting] you may have life in his name" (John 20:31, my annotations in brackets). The adjective, πιστός (*pistos*), "faithful," is used only once along with its negative word ἄπιστος (*apistos*), "unfaithful," in a context of Jesus' rebuke of Thomas for not trusting in Jesus' resurrection: "Put your finger here, and see my hands;

---

10. Wright and Bird, *New Testament*, 659. For the view of "John the evangelist," also see Beasley-Murray, *John*, lxvi–lxxv. Beasley-Murray calls him "John the Evangelist," the redactor of the Gospel.

11. Wright and Bird, *New Testament*, 655.

12. Köstenberger, *Encountering John*, 56.

and put out your hand, and place it in my side. Do not be unfaithful, but [be] faithful" (my translation). The ESV translated these adjectives as verbs: "Do not disbelieve but believe." I prefer the word "be trustful." Once, a related word to the *pistis* word group is used: πιστικός (*pistikos*), which is translated "pure" to describe the nard used by Mary on Jesus' feet (John 12:3).

In light of the above, an analysis of the use of the verb *pisteuō* ("to believe, trust") will now be given. First, note the direct objects of the verb. There are a variety of direct objects in terms of what is believed or trusted: 2:22—"the Scripture and the word that Jesus had spoken"; 4:50— "the word that Jesus spoke to him"; 5:47^2—"his [Moses'] writings . . . my words"; 8:24—"that I am he (ἐγώ εἰμι, *ego eimi*)"; 9:18—"that he had been blind"; 11:27—"that you are the Messiah, the Son of God"; 11:42—"that you sent me"; 12:38—"what he heard from us" (Isa 53:1); 13:19—"that I am he (ἐγώ εἰμι, *ego eimi*)"; 14:10—"that I am in the Father and the Father in me"; 16:27—"that I came from God"; 16:30—"that you came from God"; 17:8—"that you sent me"; 17:21—"that you have sent me"; and 20:31—"that Jesus is the Messiah, the Son of God" (I usually translate "Christ" as "Messiah"; it is a title, not part of Jesus' name.).

Often, *pisteuō* should be translated as "to trust," especially when it refers to Hebrew Scripture or the words of Jesus (2:22; 4:50; 5:47; and 12:38). One of the important concepts that will be discussed in more detail later is the fact that Jesus was sent from God the Father (presumably with a mission—11:42; 16:27, 30; 17:8, 21). Twice, Jesus is reported to have used a term for himself that is similar to the name of YHWH ("I AM"—8:24 and 13:19). This strong identification with YHWH is expressed in another way: "that I am in the Father and the Father in me" (14:10). Twice, *pisteuō* is used with what amounts to a confession of faith—"that Jesus is the Messiah, the Son of God" (11:27 and 20:31, my translation). While most of the above usages can have the idea of "trust" in terms of its object, one reference probably means "believe"—"that he had been blind" (9:18), the story of Jesus' healing of the blind man and the fact that "the Jews" did not believe he had been born blind. This would be merely mental belief. On the other hand, it could mean that they did not *trust* the fact he had been born blind—that he was faking it!

About twenty-six times *pisteuō* is used in an absolute form with no object or indirect object. In most of these references the idea of "trusting" should be understood. For example, John 6:64^2 can be translated: "But there are some of you who do not trust. (For Jesus knew from the beginning who those were who did not trust, and who it was who would betray him.)" The same could be said of the following: 1:50; 3:12[2]; 4:41, 42, 48, 53; 5:44; 6:36, 47, 64[2], 69; 9:38; 10:25, 26; 11:15, 40; 12:39; 14:29; 16:31; 19:35; 20:8, 25, 29[2]. "Trust" implies a relational idea with the one being trusted. A few of these absolute forms imply an object or a prepositional phrase after it. Again, for example, John 6:35, 36—"whoever believes/trusts in me shall never thirst. But I said to you that you have seen me and yet do not believe/trust." The last use of *pisteuō* in these verses suggests that the prepositional phrase "in me" is implied.

In fact, *pisteuō* is used with the prepositional phrase εἰς, *eis* ("in, into"), "in me" or "in him" about twenty-nine times (referring to the Messiah). Three times "in his name" (1:12; 2:23; 3:18). Twice "in the Son/Son of Man/Son of God" (3:36 and 9:35). Once each to "Jesus" (12:11), "God" (14:1), and "light" (12:36). Once the preposition ἐν, *en* ("in"), is used with the pronoun "him" referring to "the Son of Man." Once διὰ, *dia*, with the genitive is used: "through him [John the Baptist]" (1:7). Once with διὰ, *dia*, with the accusative (14:11—"trust on account of the works themselves," my translation). John does not use ἐπί, *epi* ("upon"), with *pisteuō* in his Gospel. Several times John will only use the dative of persons (4:21; 5:24, 38, 46; 6:30; 8:31, 45, 46; 10:37, 38; 14:1), which is the same as using the prepositions εἰς, *eis* ("in, into, unto"), or ἐν, *en* ("in").

Six times the perfect form of *pisteuō* is used meaning the *act* of believing or trusting having occurred in the past and continuing right up to the present. Where these are found, their contexts are interesting: John 3:18—"The one continually trusting in him is not condemned, but the one not trusting is already condemned, because *he has not trusted* (with continuing results) in the name of the only Son of God" (my translation and perfect form in italics throughout these references); John 6:69—"and *we have trusted* (with continuing results) and have come to know that you are the Holy One of God"; John 8:31–32—"Therefore, Jesus said to the Jews *who had trusted* in him, 'If you abide in my word, truly you are my disciples, and you will know the truth, and the truth will set you free'" (the subsequent conversation suggests that these Jews really did not have genuine faith or trust in Jesus as the Son of God); John 11:27—"She says to him, 'Yes, Lord, *I have believed/trusted* (and continue to trust) that you are the Messiah, the Son of God, the one coming into the world" (Martha is speaking to Jesus about the death of Lazarus); John 16:27—"For the Father himself loves (φιλεῖ, *philei*) you (as a friend), because *you have loved* (πεφιλήκατε, *pephilēkate*) me and *have trusted* (πεπιστεύκατε, *pepisteukate*) that I came from God" (Jesus is speaking to his now eleven disciples); finally, John 20:29—"Jesus says to him, 'Because *you have seen me, you have believed/trusted*? Blessed are the ones having not seen and *believed/trusted*" (Jesus is speaking to Thomas who had seen the Lord and all others who have not seen the resurrected Lord).

The fact that *pistis* does not occur in John and neither does the *pistis Christou* phrase as found in Paul's epistles, one could ask how the Gospel of John contributes to "the faithfulness of Jesus the Messiah" theme. Also, the fact that Jesus is mostly the object of the usages of *pisteuō* in John and never the subject makes the issue suspect. However, there is one use of *pisteuō* not mentioned: John 2:24–25—"But Jesus on his part did not entrust (ἐπίστευεν, *episteuen*) himself to them, because he knew all people and needed no one to bear witness about man, for he himself knew what was in man." This is highly enlightening. Willis H. Salier offered the following insight into this text:

> The believer entrusts himself or herself to Jesus in a way that Jesus would not entrust himself to human beings (2:24). An interesting contrast is thereby set up. Jesus would not entrust himself to human beings because he knew them and what was in their hearts. By the end of the gospel, the readers of the gospel are invited to entrust themselves to Jesus because they have seen what is in the heart of Jesus; they have seen the revelation of the Father and his love and can therefore entrust themselves to both with confidence. If this insight has any truth, then the Fourth Gospel presents a classic dynamic of faith being engendered in response to the faithful work of the Son.[13]

The Mission and Work of the Son of God

Salier has expressed a truism I discovered years ago as a seminary student: "One does not always need specific vocabulary to mark the presence of a concept, and it can be seen that the Fourth Gospel has a contribution with respect to the broader concepts involved in the subjective/objective genitive debate."[14] I worked on a master's thesis paper on "Worship in the New Testament." I did all the groundwork of word studies using all the words for "worship," but soon discovered the New Testament can reveal

---

13. Salier, "The Obedient Son," 235.
14. Salier, "The Obedient Son," 223.

concepts of worship without necessarily using "words" for worship. My theology professor agreed wholeheartedly, thankfully.

A good example is how the apostle Paul wrote about preaching Jesus. He wrote: "But we preach Christ crucified" (1 Cor 1:23a) and "For I decided to know nothing among you except Jesus Christ and him crucified" (1 Cor 2:2). Without using the phrase, Paul's underlining idea is "the faithfulness of Jesus the Messiah." Another good example can be found in John's Gospel: "If you keep my commandments, you will abide in my love, just as I have kept my Father's commandments and abide in his love" (John 15:10). "Keeping the Father's commandments" is the same as saying "the faithfulness of Jesus the Messiah." The same is true here. Salier has presented, in his excellent chapter, two concepts found in John that mark the presence of "the faithfulness of Jesus the Messiah": 1) the mission of the faithful Son, and 2) the work of the Son (in terms of his obedience to the Father).

First, consider the mission of the Son. As mentioned earlier, when Jesus cried out from the cross, "It is finished!" (τετέλεσται, *tetelestai*), and then expired, the question needs to be asked: "What was finished?" John's use of the word τελειόω, *teleioō*, is instructive. John 4:34: "Jesus said to them [the disciples], 'My food is to do the will of him who sent me and to *accomplish* his work.'" (ESV with my brackets and emphasis). The idea is to "complete/finish" the work of the Father. John 5:36: "But the testimony that I have is greater than that of John. For the works that the Father has given me *to accomplish*, the very works that I am doing, bear witness about me that the Father has sent me" (my emphasis). "Accomplish" is a very good translation as long as we remind ourselves that the Greek word is "to complete/finish" something. John 17:4: "I glorified you on earth, *having accomplished* the work that you gave me to do" (my emphasis). John 17:23: "I in them and you in me, that they may become *completely* one, so that the world may know that you sent me and loved them even as you loved me" (my emphasis). In this verse the verb is a perfect participle coupled with the "is" verb: literally—"in order that they may be *completed/perfected* into one." The ESV has turned it into an adverb and modified the word for "one." Note that this unity, heavily emphasized, is the key to the world trusting that God sent his Son into the world because he loved the world. Finally, John 19:28: "After this, Jesus, knowing that all was now *finished*, said (to fulfill the Scripture), 'I thirst'" (my emphasis). It is not clear if Jesus is the one fulfilling Scripture (Ps 69:21 or 22:15) or if John is interpreting what Jesus said as fulfilling Scripture. Regardless, with his thirst briefly quenched, Jesus was able to say, "It is finished!"

From this word study on *pisteuō*, one of the direct objects of trusting/believing was "that you sent me" (11:42; 17:8, 21) and "that I came from God" (16:27, 30). The fact that the Father *sent* the Son is emphasized in John using two Greek terms, πέμπω, *pempō*, and ἀποστέλλω, *apostellō*, both translated "to send." The well-known text is John 3:16–17: "For in this manner God loved the world, so that he gave his only (unique) Son, in order that everyone who believes in him may not perish but have eternal life. For God did not send (*apostellō*) the Son into the world in order to condemn the world but in order that the world through him might be saved" (my translation). John 5:23b: "Whoever does not honor the Son does not honor the Father who sent (*pempō*) him." One more example is John 5:30b: "I seek not my own will but the will of him who sent (*pempō*) me." The other references are similar: 5:36; 10:36; 12:49; 14:24; 17:3, 18, 21, 23, 25; 20:21. Just as the Father sent the Son on a mission, so Jesus sends his disciples on a mission: John 20:21: "Jesus said to them again, 'Peace be with you. As the Father has sent (*apostellō*) me, even so I am sending (*pempō*) you."

What was the purpose of the Father sending the Son? What was his mission? The primary purpose was for salvation of the world, at least, for those who would accept it (John 3:16–17). Equally important was his mission to reveal and make known the Father (John 1:14, 18). In somewhat an ironic way Jesus was sent for judgment of the world (John 9:39)—"For judgment I came into this world, that those who do not see may see, and those who see may become blind" (Jesus' healing of a blind man on the Sabbath). The combination of *saving* and *judging* in the proper context can be found at John 12:47–48—"If anyone hears my words and does not keep them, I do not judge him; for I did not come to judge the world but to save the world. The one who rejects me and does not receive my words has a judge; the word that I have spoken will judge him on the last day." Jesus came to give life, even life abundantly, eternal life (John 10:9–10; 6:33, 40, 44, 50–58). In so doing, Jesus challenges those who serve him to indeed follow him (John 12:26)—"If anyone serves me, he must follow me; and where I am, there will my servant be also. If anyone serves me, the Father will honor him." Jesus came to gather God's scattered sheep into a unity (John 10:16; 11:51, 52).

The Father initiates and the Son responds.[15] Jesus brings glory to the Father by obedience (5:23; 7:18). He does the Sender's will (4:34; 5:30, 38; 6:38–39). Jesus speaks the Sender's words (3:34; 7:16; 12:49; 14:10b, 24). Jesus does the Sender's works (5:36; 9:4). He is accountable to the Sender (see all of John 17—the so-called "High Priestly Prayer"). Jesus represents the Sender accurately (12:14–15; 13:20; 15:18–25). He bears witness to the Sender (5:36; 7:28). Jesus has the Sender's glory uppermost in mind (11:4; 12:28; 13:31; 14:13). Jesus' "food" is to do the will of the Father and accomplish (finish) his work (4:34). While on the earth Jesus is continually doing the "work" of the Father (5:17; 9:4). Jesus is able to work only in the power of the Father (5:19–20). His words emanate from the Father (7:16; 12:48–50; 14:24). In fact, Jesus "is faithful in this task because he completes the work the Father has given him, the obedient Son."[16] Salier refers to A. E. Harvey's thoughts when he says "only the son, an only son beloved by the Father, could be fully trusted to promote the interests of the Father and perfectly fulfill his will."[17]

The overall mission of Jesus was to fulfill the biblical narrative of Israel's purpose and the promises of God in the Hebrew Scriptures. From the opening verses of the Gospel of John in his prologue, he refers to the creation motif ("In the beginning"—Gen 1:1) and moves to Israel (1:11) and God's tabernacling in the midst of his people (1:14) and finally to Moses and the Law (1:17). John is showing how Jesus is greater than Moses because he gives grace heaped upon grace and he truly gives us covenant love/loyalty and truth/faithfulness (1:17). Jesus is greater than Abraham (8:58). He is greater than Israel/Jacob (1:51). To love, obey, know, and see in John 14:15–24 resonates with Exodus and Deuteronomy. The theme of Isa 40–66 is echoed throughout John's Gospel. Jesus replaces the temple (2:18–22). He came to fulfill the wider plans of God for his people and the world (1:10–13; 12:20–23).

All of the "I am" passages proclaim Jesus as the only way one will see God the Father: see the absolute "I am" statements (6:20; 8:24, 28, 58; 18:5); "I am the bread of life" (6:35, 48, 51); "I am the light of the world" (8:12; 9:5); "I am the door of the sheep" (10:7, 9); "I am the good shepherd" (10:11, 14); "I am the resurrection and the life" (11:25); "I am the way, the truth, and the life" (14:6); and "I am the true vine" (15:1).

---

15. At this point I am summarizing Salier's discussion of Jesus' obedience and dependence upon the Father. See his article "The Obedient Son," 226.

16. Salier, "The Obedient Son," 226.

17. Salier, "The Obedient Son," 227.

This last statement clearly replaces an unbelieving Israel with his own faithfulness to the Father on behalf of his people.

Second, beside the mission consider the work of the Son himself. The question again is: What is finished? While there is much overlap on the mission and work of the Messiah, look at the word "work" (ἔργον, *ergon*) in the singular (John 4:34; 17:4) and in the plural (5:20, 36). Jesus is actually doing the "works of God" (6:28; 9:3, 4; 10:37–38). He is testifying and revealing the Father (10:25, 38) in order to bring about a trusting response (10:38; 14:11). Jesus showed the people "many works" of the Father (10:32). These works clearly included the signs given in John after having enumerated the first two, but readers must discern the rest: 1) changing water to wine (2:1–11); 2) healing the official's son (4:46–54); 3) healing the invalid (5:1–15); 4) feeding the multitude (6:5–13); 5) walking on the water (6:16–21); 6) healing the man born blind (9:1–7); and 7) raising Lazarus (11:1–44). Some scholars, noted above, have deleted "walking on the water" and taken the cross/resurrection as the seventh sign. This makes good sense in the overall scheme of the Gospel of John. These signs were to awaken a faith and trust that Jesus was indeed the Messiah of the Jews and king over God's kingdom.

The "works" (plural) included fulfillment of Scripture, even to the last breath (19:28)! They included Jesus preparing a "dwelling place" for his disciples and all who would follow afterward (14:2–3). Jesus' discourse in John 14 is not about "preparing a place in heaven when we die," rather he is referring to the dispersion of the Holy Spirit (14:23) that would soon take place on the Day of Pentecost, the establishment of the church, the new temple of God![18] That is what Jesus was "preparing" and doing the "works" necessary for (cross, resurrection, and exaltation). In this manner Jesus was the "way" to the Father (14:6). The "works" included giving life to the dead and executing judgment (John 5). The major work of Jesus was to reveal the Father, bringing life to believers and showing God's love for humankind through the cross and atonement (17:1–5).

The latter is important in terms of Jesus' works. He came as "the Lamb of God, who takes away the sin of the world" (1:29), a key text for understanding Jesus' atoning sacrifice, substitutionary in nature. The "hour" motif pointed toward this crucial moment (2:4; 7:40; 8:20; 12:23, 27, 38; 13:31; 17:1). Jesus spoke of his "being lifted up" (3:14–15; 8:28; 12:32–34). He received death threats (5:18; 8:37, 40; 17:1, 19). Twice he

---

18. See McCaffrey, *House with Many Rooms*. Also, Kerr, *Temple of Jesus' Body*.

was threatened with stoning (10:31–33; 11:8). The cross always hovered as the shadow over the life and work of Jesus (1:29; 19:14, 29, 36). Indeed, Jesus was the Paschal Lamb (18:28, 39; 19:14, 29, 31–37). Sin was even the problem from beginning (1:9–10) to the end (20:23) and Jesus dealt with it as the "Good Shepherd" (10:11, 15, 18) who lays down his life for the sheep—a king who dies for the kingdom! As Salier wrote: "The Father who is revealed by the Son is the Father who has sent the Son to reveal and to be the Lamb of God that takes away the sin of the world."[19]

It is important to note that all of the above concerning the mission and work of the Son required believers to see Jesus as a real human being, with all the characteristics of what it means to be human ("the Word became flesh"). No passage in the Gospel of John "demands an interpretation which impugns the true humanity of Jesus."[20] Salier added: "John shows us one who in true humanity obeyed and loved to the end—but always within the context of his identity as the Son who has come, been sent, into the world from above."[21] The king of the kingdom of God, even the universe, stooped down to wash the feet of quarreling men who had followed him for three years (John 13:3–12). How God the Father completed all this through his Son, Jesus the Messiah, is unfathomable. Yet, Isaiah has captured the sentiment very well: "For my thoughts are not your thoughts, neither are your ways my ways, declares the LORD. For as the heavens are higher than the earth, so are my ways higher than your ways and my thoughts than your thoughts" (Isa 55:8–9). John would affirm his Gospel is about "the faithfulness of Jesus the Messiah." On that basis one needs to trust that Jesus is the Messiah, the Son of God. That trust can only lead to eternal life by the grace of God.

Letters of John: "Assurance of Eternal Life"

Authorship of 1 John is anonymous, but tradition holds that John the apostle wrote this letter as well as the small letters we call 2 and 3 John, sometime during Domitian's reign (AD 81–96). In the latter two letters the author calls himself "the elder" (2 John 1; 3 John 1). For this reason and others, many scholars today argue for a different author of both the

---

19. Salier, "The Obedient Son," 233.

20. Thompson, *The Incarnate Word*, 117. Salier quoted this in his text and gave the foregoing reference (p. 236).

21. Salier, "The Obedient Son," 236.

Gospel of John and the Letters of John, i.e., the "elder" John. Whether the author is the apostle John or an "elder" called John, many are saying that whoever wrote the Gospel also wrote these letters. For those who take the "elder" John as different from the apostle John because he doesn't call himself an apostle, note should be taken that Peter referred to himself as a "fellow elder" in 1 Pet 5:1, even though he was certainly an apostle. The debate will be the same for the book of Revelation.

Regardless of authorship, 1 John is technically not a letter in the purest sense of the word. It is more like a tract on "the assurance of salvation" for those who are being greatly criticized and even deceived by a group characterized by an early form of Gnosticism. At one time they were part of the Christian community but have now pulled away (1 John 2:19). The mature form of Gnosticism from the second through the fifth centuries AD suggested that 1 John is combatting similar ideas.[22] John (whether the apostle and/or the elder) gave his purpose for writing: "I write these things to you who believe in the name of the Son of God that you may know that you have eternal life" (1 John 5:13). John wanted to give his readers the assurance (παρρησία, parrēsia, "boldness, confidence") of their salvation: 2:28—boldness at Jesus' *Parousia*; 3:21—boldness if our heart does not condemn us; 4:17—boldness for the day of judgment; and 5:14—boldness to ask God anything according to his will. This purpose for writing offsets the attacks made by these "worldly" people who had apparently left the church community but were still around!

These early Gnostics, if we may label them as such, were saying such things as: "We have no sin!" (1 John 1:8); "We have not sinned!" (1 John 1:10); "We have fellowship with God" (1 John 1:6); and "I know him (God)!" (1 John 2:4). Yet, having said these things, they denied that Jesus was the Messiah (1 John 2:22). Thus, they were also denying the Father of our Lord and Savior Jesus the Messiah. Above all, they were denying that Jesus had come in the flesh and was a genuine human being (1 John 4:2). Apparently, these people were claiming a superior "knowledge" about the flesh (humanity) and the material world, supposing that it was evil in itself and therefore did not matter in terms of human conduct. On that basis they could deny having any sin. They could hate the true believers (John's community of believers) and not have a guilty conscience about it (1 John 2:11). They could claim fellowship with God but walk in darkness (1 John 1:6). At best they were deceivers of those who would trust Jesus to

---

22. See Wright and Bird, *New Testament*, 162–63, for a simple explanation of the philosophical and theological underpinnings of gnostic thought.

be the Messiah, the Son of God, having come in flesh (1 John 4:2; see also 2 John 7). They lived disobedient and lascivious lives due to their denial of a "good" creation by a "good" God. They were saying "I love God" and at the same time were "hating their brothers and sisters" (1 John 3:11–15; 4:20–21). These early Gnostics were loving the world (1 John 2:15–17), ironically while denying the fact that "the whole world lies in the power of the evil one" (1 John 5:19).

It is difficult to outline this small letter tract. Robert Law's classic commentary gave a spiral outline that many have followed. Law insisted that John gave his Christian community, the true believers, three tests at three different levels. The first level is about "walking in the light" tested by (1) "righteousness," first negatively by confessing sin (1 John 1:5–10) and second positively by keeping Christ's commandments (1 John 2:1–6); (2) "love," first positively by loving one's brothers and sisters in the faith (1 John 2:7–11) and second negatively by not loving the world (1 John 2:15–17); and (3) "true belief," first negatively by knowing the anti-Christ (1 John 2:18–22) and second positively by confessing the Son so as to have the Father as well (1 John 2:23–25). The second level is determining whether or not one has been born of God and hence belongs to God as his child. This level is tested in the same order: "righteousness" (1 John 2:29—3:10); "love" (1 John 3:11–24); and "true belief" (1 John 4:1–6). The third level is different in that the same three tests are not given in the same order, rather John is showing the interrelationship of love, true belief, and righteousness (1 John 4:7—5:12) based on the first two levels. Law's outline breaks down at the third level and most scholars have tried to modify his work in order to produce a more productive outline. The quest is still ongoing. Too bad ancient writers did not outline the way we Westerners do!

The *Pistis* Word Group

The use of the *pistis* word group in John's three letters (tract and two letters) is similar to their use in the Gospel. *Pisteuō* ("to trust, believe") is used nine times (3:23; 4:1, 16; 5:1, 5, 10³, 13). When looking closely at the context of each of these usages, the idea of "trust" is prevalent rather than simply "believe." The noun, *pistis*, is used only once (remember the Gospel of John never used the word): 1 John 5:4: "For everyone who has been born of God overcomes the world. And this is the victory that has overcome the world—our faith." *Pistis* in this context should be translated "faithfulness." It is our faithfulness (to the end) that has overcome the world. Many have lost such faithfulness by being deceived by the so-called early Gnostics. They have left the fellowship but continue to bedevil the community of faith in John's care. The adjective, *pistos*, is used twice: once in 1 John 1:9 where God is referred to as "faithful and just to forgive us our sins and to cleanse us from all unrighteousness." Of course, God does this through the atoning work of his Son, Jesus the Messiah (1 John 1:7). The other use is in 3 John 5–6a: "Beloved, it is a faithful thing you do in all your efforts for these brothers, strangers as they are, who testified to your love before the church." Gaius is being praised for his faithfulness in showing hospitality to traveling missionaries (3 John 5–8) such as Demetrius (v. 12) in contrast to the rascal Diotrephes (vv. 9–10).

Just as was discovered in the Gospel of John, in 1 John the phrase "faithfulness of Jesus the Messiah" is not used. Yet, the idea of Jesus' faithfulness can be found throughout the letter tract. Disregarding any outline to this text and simply reading through it, one will discover that Jesus is at the center of most if not all of the units of thought in this small letter tract. Various ideas about who Jesus is, what he has done and continues to do, his relationship to God the Father, and how we relate to him will be found. This unique letter tract is now surveyed.

Jesus: "The Word of Life"

Much like the beginning of the Gospel of John ("In the beginning"), so this text: "That which was from the beginning" (1 John 1:1a). With perfect tenses John emphasized that "we have heard" and "we have seen" the word (*logos*) of life. That experience continued to the present for John. With aorist tenses (completed action) John wrote, "We gazed upon and have touched with our hands" (1:1, my translation). The physical ability to relate to Jesus no longer prevailed but John can testify that the "word of life" that was manifested to him (and presumably the other apostles or disciples) was "with the Father" (1:2). John emphasized the close relationship of the Father (YHWH God) with the Son Jesus the Messiah and how that relationship is now a part of Christian experience—"that our joy may be complete" (1:4). John has immediately established the complete and full humanity of Jesus the Messiah. All else one may think about Jesus is based upon this fact.

In 1 John 1:5–10 John informed us that to walk in the light is to walk "as he (Jesus) is in the light." This means that we can have fellowship with one another because we have been cleansed from all sin by the atoning blood of Jesus on the cross (think Rom 3:21–26). The faithfulness of Jesus to the cross was the great turning point in history, or as N. T. Wright put it, "the day the revolution began."[23] Without the cross and resurrection, of course, salvation from sin would not be possible. God has taken care of the world's sin problem by sending his Son to bear our sins (see Isa 53:4–6). John wrote: "You know that he appeared to take away sins, and in him there is no sin" (3:5). Jesus was man as man was meant to be (without sin! See Heb 4:15 and 7:26). As a genuine Christian, one must continually confess sins knowing that the Father is "faithful and just to forgive us our sins and to cleanse us from all unrighteousness" (1:9). No doubt this is what John meant in the Gospel: "And from his fullness we have all received, grace upon grace" (John 1:16).

In 1 John 2:1–2, John is realistic about Christians struggling to live without sin (as Jesus did!). Christians do sin! But when they do, they have "an advocate (παράκλητον, *paraklēton*, "lawyer, advocate, comforter") with the Father, Jesus [the] Messiah, [the] Righteous One" (2:1b, my translation). John made plain what was written in 1:7 about the "blood of Jesus": "And he himself is [the] propitiation (ἱλασμός, *hilasmos*) concerning our sins, and not concerning ours alone but also concerning [the sins] of the whole world" (2:2, my translation and insertions). The word "propitiation" was also used at 4:10 in a similar context.[24] Jesus' willingness to go to the cross allowed God to concentrate as it were the sins of the whole world for all time upon him. As Paul the apostle expressed it for his own ministry: "For our sake he made him to be sin who knew no sin, so that in him we might become the righteousness of God" (2 Cor 5:21).

First John 2:3–6 included a possible statement by the early Gnostics: "I know him!" Yet, that claim must be backed up by keeping his (Jesus') commandments. Clearly this is not the Ten Commandments of the old covenant. It is the word of Jesus as v. 5 indicated: "But whoever keeps his word, in him truly the love of God is perfected. By this we may know that we are in him." The commandment is the word of Jesus about loving our brothers and sisters in the Lord (2:8–10) and its opposite, not loving

---

23. Wright, *The Day the Revolution Began*.

24. The word for "propitiation" as used here (twice) is only used in other forms in a few NT passages: see Luke 18:13 (*hilasthēti*); Heb 2:17 (*hilaskesthai*); Rom 3:25 (*hilastērion*); Heb 9:5 (*hilastērion*); Matt 16:22 (*hileōs*); and Heb 8:12 (*hileōs*).

the world (2:15-17). The key part of this paragraph is John's statement: "Whoever says he abides in him ought to walk in the same way in which he walked" (2:6). This is taking the human nature of Jesus seriously. Jesus' faithfulness to the cross is only a pinpoint of Jesus' life on earth. While the cross is important as stated above, it would have been meaningless if Jesus had not been faithful to the Father for his entire life and ministry on earth. Jesus is the complete human that we are to imitate—"walk in the same way in which he walked" (2:6b). Being cleansed of all unrighteousness (1:9), we are able to walk in righteousness, love, and faithfulness—just like Jesus did!

The next paragraph about Jesus is 1 John 2:18-27. John encouraged his Christian family to realize the Holy Spirit's anointing in their lives in knowing the truth about Jesus. He indeed is the Messiah (the Anointed One). The Holy Spirit testified within the Spirit-filled Christian about Jesus as Messiah and his close relationship to the Father as Son of God. What they had "heard from the beginning" takes us back to 1 John 1:1-4 where the full humanity of Jesus was affirmed and must not be denied. Those who were denying Jesus was God's Son and Messiah, and denying he had come in the flesh, were making every attempt to deceive John's true Christian community (2:26). Instead, they are to abide in the Holy Spirit. (2:27d).

One of the most fascinating paragraphs in John's letter tract is 1 John 2:28—3:3. It is the first appearance of the word παρρησία, *parrēsia*, "boldness, confidence." The ESV used the word "confidence" to translate this Greek word. Abiding in the Messiah meant letting the Holy Spirit have full sway in our lives in terms of living the righteous life. John wrote: "And now, little children, abide in him, so that when he appears we may have *confidence* and not shrink from him in shame at his coming. If you know that he is righteous, you may be sure that everyone who practices righteousness has been born of him" (2:28-29, my emphasis). Living in a shame culture such as was the Roman Empire toward the end of the first century AD, this statement highlighted the importance of imitating the "righteousness" of the Messiah. There will be a Second Coming of the Messiah called *Parousia* (his Presence or his Appearance).

In the pagan environment of the Roman Empire, followers of the Messiah were susceptible to ridicule at such a notion (not unlike in parts of America today!). John assured his listeners/readers that being God's children has more for us even than what we have now in terms of the quality of life, which he calls "eternal life" (1:2). He explained why we should not be ashamed at Jesus' Second Coming: "Beloved, we are God's children now, and what we will be has not yet appeared; but we know that when he appears we shall be like him, because we shall see him as he is. And everyone who thus hopes in him purifies himself as he is pure" (3:2–3). Jesus is glorified and complete man, the way God intended all of us to be from the beginning. But our sins have devastated God's plan. However, God has raised Jesus from the dead and exalted him to his right hand, giving him full authority, power, honor, and glory over all creation. He is still the human we were meant to be! When Jesus returns, we shall see him as he is (exalted and glorified man), and we shall be in turn resurrected with new bodies, glorified bodies, and exalted to a new creation ("the new heaven and new earth," Rev 21:1). In anticipation of that event, every follower of Jesus purifies (makes holy, sanctifies) himself or herself just as Jesus is already pure (holy, sanctified). It is strange that the modern church (of all brands!) does not emphasize this more. The usual proclamation gives the idea of "going to heaven when we die" in some kind of spiritual existence apart from this material earth. John exclaims, "Not so!" We will become like Jesus in every way.

A brief word must be given concerning the paragraph of 1 John 3:4–10. John made two statements about Jesus in this paragraph: two sides of one coin—1) Jesus appeared the first time to take away sin, and 2) Jesus (the Son of God) also appeared to destroy the works of the devil. With one event, Messiah's death on the cross, God made atonement for the sins of the world and destroyed the works of the devil (see Heb 2:14–15). The devil's lies brought death to the world and he has used that power ever since, but in Jesus the power of death is broken and his people never need to fear death at all. The children of the devil are always sinning (lying as in Gen 3) and doing lawless deeds (3:11–15), while the children of God are always practicing righteousness as Jesus is righteous (3:7b). Christians must continually imitate the Messiah, for one day they shall become just like him!

First John 3:16–24 is quite a challenge. "By this we know love, that he laid down his life for us, and we ought to lay down our lives for the brothers" (3:16). This is a good interpretation of Jesus' own words when he said: "And whoever does not take his cross and follow me is not worthy of me. Whoever finds his life will lose it, and whoever loses his life for my sake will find it" (Matt 10:38–39). And again: "Then Jesus told his disciples, 'If anyone would come after me, let him deny himself and take up his cross and follow me. For whoever would save his life will lose it, but whoever loses his life for my sake will find it" (Matt 16:24–25). In essence, John said the same thing, for dying to self means serving others in need (1 John 3:17). John's challenge is this: "Little children, let us not love in word or talk but in deed and in truth" (3:18). By serving others regardless of background, ethnicity, gender, religious or not, the follower of Jesus experiences a heart that does not condemn. Here is the second use of *parrēsia* (boldness or confidence): "Beloved, if our heart does not condemn us, we have confidence before God; and whatever we ask we receive from him, because we keep his commandments and do what pleases him" (3:21–22). And what is his commandments? "That we believe in the name of his Son Jesus Christ and love one another" (3:23). This is the first use of *pisteuō* in John's letter tract, about halfway through! This word can be translated "trust": "that we trust in the name of his Son Jesus the Messiah and love one another" (my translation). I. Howard Marshall has written: "Belief in the name of Jesus means believing that his name contains the power which it signifies, so that the question is not simply one of right belief, but of *trust* in the One who is the object of the Christian confession" (my emphasis).[25] By trusting Jesus and loving others one knows that God abides in Christians by means of his Holy Spirit (3:24).

In 1 John 4:1–6, the topic returned to the true humanity of Jesus. False prophets have taught that Jesus did not come in the flesh and John calls them "antichrists" (4:1–3). Those who are genuine followers of the Messiah confess that Jesus "has come in the flesh," that is, he is and continues to be a real human being just like us, only without sin (4:2). But there were those who were already denying that Jesus was the Messiah (see 1 John 2:18, 22). These "antichrists" are denying that Jesus was a real human being. That is why John wrote at the beginning: "Beloved, do not believe every spirit, but test the spirits to see whether they are from God, for many false prophets have gone out into the world" (4:1). Again, *pisteuō* should be understood as "trust": "Beloved, do not trust every spirit." This makes better sense in terms of its nuance and what was going on among the churches for which John felt responsible. John declared that the "Spirit of truth" was in those who confessed Jesus to be a real human being, whereas "the spirit of error" was in those who denied the same.

John gives us a long paragraph about love—1 John 4:7–21. Jesus is at the very center of this teaching. John begins with his proposition:

---

25. Marshall, *The Epistles of John*, 201.

"Beloved, let us love one another, for love is from God, and whoever loves has been born of God and knows God" (4:7). How does one know love is from God? He sent his only Son to be the propitiation (ἱλασμός, *hilasmos*) for our sins. This is the second and last use of this important word in John (see 2:2). This reminds one of the several times the author of the Gospel of John used the same phrase of "sending" (John 11:42; 16:27, 30; 17:8, 21). Because God loved us in this manner, we should love one another. John writes: "No one has ever seen God; if we love one another, God abides in us and his love is perfected in us" (4:12). The term "perfected" is best understood as "completed," since Jesus has been described in other places as the "completed" man. One completes love by loving others the way Jesus loved others, even the whole world!

Verse 16 used *pisteuō*: "So we have come to know and to believe the love that God has for us." The verbs in this verse are perfect forms so I would translate the phrase in this manner: "So we have come to know [with abiding results] and have trusted [with abiding results] the love that God has for us" (my translation with insertions). John continued: "By this [the fact that God is love] is love perfected (completed) with us, so that we may have *confidence* for the day of judgment, because as he is so also are we in this world" (4:17, my additions and emphasis). This is the third use of *parresia* (boldness, confidence). When love is completed in us as it is in Jesus, we have boldness to stand on the day of judgment. I translate John's phrase: "Complete love casts out fear. For fear has to do with punishment, and whoever fears has not been completed in love" (1 John 4:18, my translation). John continued: "We love because he first loved us" (4:19). The meaning is probably: "We have *the capacity* to love because he first loved us." How did he love us? By sending his only Son to die on our behalf and thus take away what destroys us—sin! Thus, no one can say, "I love God," and hate his brothers or sisters. John penned a great passage: "For he who does not love his brother [or sister] whom he has seen cannot love God whom he has not seen" (4:20b). Sometimes in 1 John it is difficult to determine when he is referring to God or to Jesus, but clearly he is referring to Jesus in this last phrase: "And this commandment we have from him [Jesus]: whoever loves God must also love his brother [and sister]" (4:21, my additions).

First John 5:1–5 began and ended with the word *pisteuō*. In both cases they should be translated as "continually trust," since both are present participles: v. 1—"Everyone who continually trusts that Jesus is the Messiah has been born of God, and everyone who loves the Father loves whoever has been born of him"; v. 5—"Who is it that overcomes the world except the one who continually trusts that Jesus is the Son of God?" It is not just head knowledge or assent that Jesus is the Son of God, rather it is a total trusting commitment that is required. Verse 4 has already been commented on, which read: "And this is the victory that has overcome the world—our faithfulness" (my translation), the only use of *pistis* in 1 John. Such faithfulness is in imitation of Jesus' faithfulness (see John 16:33).

The paragraph represented by 1 John 5:6–12 has been a puzzle for many, but it is not impossible to understand. John wrote: "This is he who came by water and blood—Jesus the Messiah; not by the water only but by the water and the blood. And the Spirit is the one who testifies, because the Spirit is the truth. For there are three that testify: the Spirit and the water and the blood; and these three agree" (5:6–8). Can one make sense of this?[26]

The old covenant law required two or three witnesses to establish a case (Deut 17:6). John declared that in the new covenant there are three witnesses with regard to Jesus: the "water" may refer to his baptism and at his baptism the Spirit descended upon Jesus with a voice from heaven declaring him to be the Son of God: "This is my beloved Son, with whom I am well pleased!" (Matt 3:16); the "blood" probably represented Jesus' death on the cross which cleansed us from all unrighteousness (see 1 John 1:7). "This is the testimony of God that he has borne concerning his Son" (5:9b). The *faithfulness* of Jesus to be immersed by John the Immerser to fulfill all righteousness (Matt 3:15) also gave him the power of the indwelling Holy Spirit to accomplish his mission and work. Completing that mission by going to the cross was appropriately signified by Jesus' last words on the cross as recorded by John: "It is finished!" (John 19:30). Thus, God's testimony is to be *trusted*!

Three times in v. 10 John used the word *pisteuō* which has been translated as "trust": "The one trusting in the Son of God has the witness/ testimony in himself; the one not trusting in God has made him [with abiding result] a liar, because he has not trusted [with abiding result] in the witness/testimony which God witnessed/testified [with abiding result] concerning his Son" (my translation with insertions, the insertions

---

26. First John 5:7–9, ESV, reflects the best manuscript evidence. These verses include a variant in the Textus Receptus which is reflected in the KJV among others, probably added by a later copyist. The textual witnesses are weak for the variant. My explanation is based on the Greek text behind the ESV.

indicate perfect tenses of the verbs). Marshall opined: "It is inconsistent to profess belief in God, as John's opponents did, and yet to disbelieve what God has said. Belief in God and in his Son, Jesus Christ, are inseparably joined."[27]

The witness/testimony has a final goal: "And this is the testimony, that God gave us eternal life, and this life is in his Son. Whoever has the Son has life; whoever does not have the Son of God does not have life" (5:11–12). John has come full circle in his thoughts from 1:2. He finished with a closing purpose statement for the entire letter tract: "I write these things to you who believe in the name of the Son of God that you may know that you have eternal life" (5:13). Again, translating *pisteuō* as "trust" implies a personal relationship to Jesus in total commitment to his mission and work. John wanted us to walk *in his steps* (2:6).[28]

Finally, John's last statement clinched the essential ideas broadly speaking concerning Jesus the Messiah—the main character of his letter tract. "But we know that the Son of God has come, and he has given [with abiding results] to us understanding in order that we might know the genuine [One]. Indeed, we are in the genuine [One], in his Son, Jesus the Messiah. This one is the real [genuine] God and eternal life" (5:20, my translation and insertions). In contrast to the antagonists of John's community who said they "knew the Lord" (2:4) and had perhaps "special knowledge" (*gnosis*), John repeated his earlier thoughts by saying that the Son of God has come and it is he who has given Messiah's people true understanding about the most genuine Person who ever lived on the earth—Jesus the Messiah, Son of God. Jesus, as genuine glorified man, is the only one who manifests God in his character ("the Word in flesh") and gives eternal life to his people. What a powerful thought! To think otherwise is to worship an idol of God; hence, his final phrase: "Little children, keep yourselves from idols [false views of God]" (5:21, my insertion).

Revelation: "Triumph of the Slain Lamb"

The last book of the New Testament, "Revelation," is self-proclaimed as an "apocalypse of Jesus the Messiah," which God gave him to show to his

---

27. Marshall, *The Epistles of John*, 241.

28. This is the title of a classic Christian novel that takes seriously "walking in the steps of Jesus"—*In His Steps* by Charles Sheldon.

servant (δοῦλος, *doulos*) John by means of an angel (Rev 1:1). The purpose was to reveal "the things that must soon take place" which is done through the "word of God" and the "testimony of Jesus the Messiah" (1:2). Thus, the communication chain began with God, then went to the Messiah, then to an angel, then to John, then to the church at large (represented in the seven churches). While the genre of Revelation is clearly apocalyptic, there is a letter form imposed upon it as a frame (1:4–8, 22:20–21). A third genre, and perhaps the most important, is that it is a prophecy (see 1:3; 22:6–7, 10, 18–19). A blessing is pronounced upon everyone who hears and obeys this prophecy (1:3; the first of seven blessings, 14:13; 16:15; 19:9; 20:6; 22:7, 14). The genre of apocalypse for the book of Revelation should be labeled a "Christian" apocalypse, for unlike many apocalypses of the day, this revelation is not pseudonymous, for it names the author as John, a servant of Jesus. The question again is: Which John is it?

A cursory look at the authorship for Johannine literature finds modern scholarship all over the board on the issue. Wright and Bird, in their newly published book entitled *The New Testament in Its World*, have settled on "the elder John" (2 John 1 and 3 John 1) as the possible author of the Gospel of John and the Letters. They posit a different John for the Apocalypse whom they call "John the Seer" or prophet. Hence, there are several "Johns" to consider: 1) John the apostle, son of Zebedee; 2) John the elder; 3) John the prophet; and 4) "John" as a pseudonym for Revelation. Of course, tradition has John the apostle as author of all the literature: gospel, letters, and apocalypse.[29] The traditional view is held by most conservatives, but arguments against it are not irrational. G. K. Beale wrote: "While the Apostle may well have written the book, another John also could have written it. The issue is not important to settle since it does not affect the message of the book."[30]

Since the book of Revelation is such a controversial New Testament book as to its message, it is best to be up front about my own view. I take an amillennial view of the book, though that term is easily misleading. There is a millennium (one thousand years), but it is a symbolic number like all the other numbers in the book. Taking the apocalypse genre seriously,

---

29. See Wright and Bird, *New Testament*, 653, 812. Also, for the traditional view and the acceptance of that view see the conservative commentary by Wilder et al., *Faithful to the End*, 251–55.

30. Beale, *Revelation*, 35. However, Beale continued to say: "It is probable that John should be socially identified with a group of early Christian itinerant prophets" (36). This is in line with Wright and Bird.

and seeing the message given in symbolic and metaphorical language with grotesque visions difficult sometimes to comprehend in the mind's eye, I interpret the thousand years as simply a long period of time, but complete time (perhaps the time between the first coming of the Messiah until his Second Coming, as other symbolic numbers seem to suggest).

This also affects the way one interprets the book as a whole. I prefer not a linear (in time) interpretation, but rather a series of recapitulations of the symbolic presentation of history over which Jesus is Lord. The opening of the seals (Rev 6) revealed the mystery of what is taking place in heaven as well as on earth, for the two are interrelated. The seventh seal opened up to the blowing of seven trumpets, a recapitulation of the same period of time but in an increasing intensity (Rev 8–9), and finally the pouring out of the wrath of God from seven bowls (Rev 16) revealed the same time frame. The end finally comes and judgment day is described after that for the characters of evil (Satan, the two beasts, and Babylon—Rev 17–20) and the characters of good (Jesus' victory revealed at his *Parousia* and the revealing of the New Jerusalem—Rev 19, 21–22). Between the latter two is a "freehand" (lacking overtly the sevens) presentation of the same thing, which is placed in the center of the apocalypse (the introduction of the dragon and two beasts—Rev 12–14). These chapters are the most important for understanding the whole as well as what was immediately revealed (Rev 4–11). By the end one is assured of the sovereignty of God to accomplish his will through the church on earth, but not without great sorrow and tribulation, persecution and martyrdom, trials and temptations for the "martyr church" on earth. These recapitulations, "though spiraling toward a genuine end of the beginning and beginning of the future, are a completion of character, community, and creation just as Paul promised in less symbolic terms in Romans 8. Renewal and completion of character, community, and creation are always God's goals."[31]

The genre of prophesy is preeminent throughout the book because the message is prophetic. The key verse is Rev 19:10: "For the testimony of Jesus is the spirit of prophecy." John himself is referred to as a "prophet" among others (22:9). He is told to prophesy (10:11) as well as the church in the symbol of the "two witnesses" (11:3). The term "prophets" is mentioned many times, especially the latter half of the book: (10:7; 11:10, 18; 16:6; 18:20, 24; 22:6). At the very beginning of the Revelation, the content is called "the words of this prophecy" (1:3). The church's main

---

31. An insightful comment shared with me by Ron Simkins.

responsibility is to prophesy; that is, to give a testimony about "the word of God and the testimony of Jesus" (1:1:6). The book will end with an emphasis on "prophecy": "Blessed is the one who keeps the words of the prophecy of this book" (22:7); "Do not seal up the words of the prophecy of this book, for the time is near" (22:10); "I warn everyone who hears the words of the prophecy of this book: if anyone adds to them, God will add to him the plagues described in this book" (22:18); and "if anyone takes away from the words of the book of this prophecy, God will take away his share in the tree of life and in the holy city, which are described in this book" (22:19). For the book of Revelation, the genres consist of three: the book is framed as if a letter, the message is a prophecy, and its mode of communication is apocalyptic.

The following is a chiastic outline of Revelation from an amillennial viewpoint:

A. 1:1–8. Prologue
  B. 1:9—3:21. Imperfect Church (Seven Letters)
    C. 4:1—8:1. Seven Seals
      Prelude: 4:1—5:14. Throne of God
      Vision: 6:1-17; 8:1. Seven Seals (four horses)
      Interlude: 7:1-17. (Sealed Saints)
    D. 8:2—11:18. Seven Trumpets
      Prelude: 8:2-6. Prayers of the Saints
      Vision: 8:7—9:21; 11:14-18. Seven Trumpets
      Interlude: 10:1—11:13. (Two Witnesses)
      E. 11:19—14:20. War of the Ages
      Prelude: 11:19. Presence of God revealed
      Vision: 12:1—13:18. Woman, Child, Dragon
      Interlude: 14:1-20. (Three Angels/Harvest)
    D¹. 15:1—19:10. Seven Bowls
      Prelude: 15:1-8. Song
      Vision: 16:1-21. Seven Bowls
      Interlude: 17:1—19:10. (Whore vs. Bride)
    C¹. 19:11—21:8. Triumphal Procession
      Prelude: 19:11-16. Divine Warrior (white horse)
      Vision: 19:17—20:15. Unholy Trinity Destroyed

Interlude: 21:1–8. (New Heavens and New Earth)
B¹. 21:9—22:5. Perfect Church (The bride, wife of the Lamb)
A¹. 22:6–27. Epilogue[32]

Most scholars date Revelation to AD 96, near the end of Domitian's reign as Caesar of the Roman Empire. John (whether the apostle or a prophet in the same circle) was exiled on the island of Patmos, around forty miles from Ephesus, the leading city in Asia Minor. Patmos was a place where political prisoners were exiled. John was exiled on this small island for preaching "the word of God" and giving "the testimony of Jesus" (1:9). Hence, he considered himself "a partner in the tribulation" that the saints were having to endure for the sake of the kingdom, represented by the seven churches in Asia Minor (Ephesus, Smyrna, Pergamum, Thyatira, Sardis, Philadelphia and Laodicea—chapters 2–3). When one peers into the content of Revelation, one discovers that Jesus is the leading character in the drama of history that unfolds. What the Revelation will reveal about Jesus and his role in this drama may surprise.

The *Pistis* Word Group

In contrast to the Gospel of John, the verb *pisteuō* (to trust/believe) is not used at all! However, *pistis*, the noun (faith/faithfulness/trustworthiness), is used four times (2:13, 19; 13:10; 14:12), while the adjective, *pistos* (faithful/trustworthy), is used eight times (1:5; 2:10, 13; 3:14; 17:14; 19:11; 21:5; 22:6). Once, the negative adjective, *apistos* (faithless/unfaithful), is used (21:8). This is a small number for the size of the book of Revelation, but one must remember its main communication genre is apocalyptic. While the *pistis* word group is used judiciously throughout the book, the noun and adjective are critical to understanding the overall content of the book. These relatively few references reveal much about the faithfulness of Jesus the Messiah and thus his trustworthiness.

---

32. This outline is an adaptation of Beale's outline in his Greek commentary, *Revelation*, 131, which in turn is an adaptation of Meredith G. Kline's notes, a course taught at Gordon-Conwell Theological Seminary, Summer, 1992, called the "Minor Prophets." See Beale, *Revelation*, 131, n. 97.

"The Faithfulness of Jesus"

In the initial greeting of the letter form (Rev 1:4–5), John used unusual trinitarian terminology (cp. Eph 1:3–14; 1 Pet 1:2). God was referred to as "him who is and who was and who is to come." This is an echo of God's revelation of his name to Moses in Exodus: "I AM" or "I AM WHO I AM" (Exod 3:14). Of course, even this is a "play" on God's personal name, the tetragrammaton (יהוה, YHWH). The Holy Spirit was presented as "the seven spirits who are before his throne." Beale explained: "the expression is more likely a figurative designation of the effective working of the Holy Spirit, since this is the characteristic identification of πνεῦμα in the NT when found in conjunction with or as part of an apparent formula with God and Christ."[33] Finally, Jesus was described: "and from Jesus Christ the faithful witness, the firstborn of the dead, and the ruler of kings on earth." All of these descriptions need further explanation.

"Christ" should be understood as Jesus' title which is "Messiah." Jesus is the Jewish Messiah (Anointed One), which placed him in the role of king over a kingdom (v. 6), exalted by God on his throne and will come again (v. 7, referring to Dan 7:13). Ultimately, Jesus will come again with this name on his robe and thigh: "King of kings and Lord of lords" (19:16).

"The faithful witness" was a key term for Jesus in this apocalyptic prophesy. The term "witness" was translated "testimony" in ESV in reference to Jesus at the beginning: "He made it known by sending his angel to his servant John, who bore witness to the word of God and to the testimony of Jesus Christ, even to all that he saw" (vv. 1b–2). The word "faithful" (*pistos*) was emphasized in this phrase "the faithful witness": ὁ μάρτυς ὁ πιστός (literally, "the witness, the faithful one"). Later, the adjective "faithful" will be better translated in this context as "trustworthy." "Faithful" is not out of the question, but Jesus as a "trustworthy witness" has a better nuance than the former. The word for "witness/testimony" came to refer to one who dies for his/her witness/testimony and thus is called "martyr," a transliteration of the word. See this in one of the letters (to the church in Pergamum): "Yet you hold fast my name, and you did not deny my faith even in the days of Antipas my faithful witness, who was killed among you, where Satan dwells" (2:13). Antipas was listed as the first "martyr" among the seven churches. More Christians will die because of their witness (see 11:7 and 17:6). I translate "my faith" (*pistis*) as "my faithfulness" referring to Jesus' faithfulness in this context. Holding

---

33. Beale, *Revelation*, 189.

fast to the name of Jesus is to hold fast to his faithfulness as Messiah.[34] This faithfulness will be revealed fully in Rev 5 but is already hinted at in the immediate context.

"The firstborn of the dead" referred to Jesus' resurrection from the dead. He inaugurated a new creation by his resurrection. Jesus is preeminent among all who one day will be resurrected, a "primogeniture" ("especially in the context of royal succession," see 3:14 and Col 1:18).[35] "The ruler of kings on earth" is a phrase indicating Jesus' victory over antagonists and enemies of God's kingdom, both human powers of government and "the satanic forces behind these kingdoms."[36] All three phrases or ideas can be found in Ps 89:23, 27, 37. It also echoed the content of Ps 2:2–9.

John concluded this greeting by making special reference to what Jesus had done for his people: "To him who loves us and has freed us from our sins by his blood and made us a kingdom, priests to his God and Father, to him be glory and dominion forever and ever. Amen" (vv. 5b–6). Motivated by love Jesus gave himself up to death on a cross so that sins may be atoned for, forgiven by the mercy of God the Father. As a consequence, followers of Christ are made a kingdom, priests to God the Father. The role of ancient Israel (Exod 19:5–6) is now brought to a new fulfillment in and through the church, those who are "in Christ," made up "from every nation, from all tribes and peoples and languages" (7:9). This was God's next step in the covenant with Abraham. Gentiles must always remember that they were "grafted in" (Rom 11:17) the olive tree. The natural branches (the Jews) can be easily grafted back in and become part of God's further fulfillment of Israel's destiny. The church did not replace the Jews (ancient or modern! See Rom 9–11).

John then described how he was exiled on an island, Patmos, because of his preaching of the "word of God" and holding or preserving the "testimony of Jesus" (v. 9). It is interesting that John referred to himself as "your brother and partner in the tribulation and the kingdom and the patient endurance that are in Jesus" (v. 9a). The Greek is more direct: "the tribulation and kingdom and endurance in Jesus." John was saying that when disciples follow Jesus, they find themselves in a kingdom but will be persecuted requiring faithfulness in terms of faithful endurance—all

---

34. Contra Beale, 246, who views this phrase as objective genitive: "faith in me."
35. Beale, *Revelation*, 191.
36. Beale, *Revelation*, 191.

patterned after Jesus himself. This is not at all what Jews were looking for in their expectation of Messiah or the kingdom.

Almost immediately the problem of theodicy is found in Revelation. The issue was the justice of God's handling of the reality of evil in the world. As expressed by so many: "How can a good God allow so much evil in the world?" What is going to be unveiled in this apocalypse is how God through Jesus' faithfulness has unmasked the real face of evil; and secondly, Jesus will be faithful in his full disclosure of God's character. The same sentiment came from those who were actually martyred for their faith, who cried out: "O Sovereign Lord, holy and true, how long before you will judge and avenge our blood on those who dwell on the earth?" (6:10).

John was told by a voice to write down what he sees in a book and send it to the seven churches in Asia Minor (1:10–11). When John turned to see the voice, he saw "seven golden lampstands" (the seven churches) and in the midst of the lampstands was one like "a son of man" (a reference to Dan 7:13). The very human Jesus was the glorified "Son of man" and he was described as God was described in the Hebrew Scriptures (Dan 10:16; 10:5; 7:9; 10:6; Ezek 1:7; 43:2; and Isa 11:4; 49:2; 60:1–2, 19). John fell to his knees in awe and this glorified "Son of man" laid his right hand on John and said: "Fear not, I am the first and the last, and the living one. I died, and behold I am alive forevermore, and I have the keys of Death and Hades" (1:17–18). The living Messiah was in the midst of his churches and he had a message for them. Every phrase was weighty with ideas that were about to unfold.

The messages to the seven churches are fascinating but I will only comment on those places where the *pistis* word group is found and not yet commented on (*pistis* in 2:19 and *pistos* in 2:10, 13; 3:14). In Rev 2:19 Jesus commended the church in Thyatira before he revealed where it is lacking: "I know your works, your love and faith and service and patient endurance, and that your latter works exceed the first." Because each of these terms has something to do with perseverance and a period of time undergoing some form of pressure from outside, I would translate "faith" as "faithfulness." Indeed, the Christians in Thyatira were enduring the cultural pressure of a "Jezebel" who called herself a "prophetess." She was tempting members of the church to "eat food sacrificed to idols" and thus participate even in "sexual immorality." She was teaching the so-called "deep things of Satan." Jesus pronounced judgment upon her and all who were being seduced by her. But to those who refused the temptation and remained "faithful," Jesus exhorted: "Only hold fast what you have until I come" (2:25).

To the church in Smyrna Jesus instructed: "Be faithful unto death, and I will give you the crown of life" (2:10). Apparently, the Jewish synagogue, at least its leaders, were persecuting Christians who perhaps had attended at one time the same synagogue. Jesus warned: "Do not fear what you are about to suffer. Behold, the devil is about to throw some of you into prison, that you may be tested, and for ten days you will have tribulation" (v. 10). The Greek term in v. 10c suggests much harsher testing: "Be faithful until death." It can possibly have two meanings: faithful in martyrdom or faithful until one dies of old age or some other cause. The following phrase suggested martyrdom rather than any kind of death: "and I will give you the crown of life." Just as Jesus was raised from dead ones, so those who give their lives for the kingdom's sake will be raised from dead ones as well. This will happen when Jesus returns (see Rev 20:11-14).

Each of the letters was addressed by Jesus, who was described by seven different phrases taken from Rev 1:5, 6, 7, and 13-16, the description of Jesus as the glorified "Son of man." "The faithful witness" in 2:13 and 3:14 was exactly like 1:5 in terms of its emphasis on "faithful." There were two "Amens" given at the end of 1:6, 7. But these were saying "Amen" to a praise of redemption and a warning about Jesus' Second Coming. Perhaps these mirrored the two "Amens" in 22:20, 21. Certainly here in this text (3:14), Jesus was called the "Amen," a Hebrew word whose root means "to be firm, trustworthy, safe." The Hebrew idea behind all the *pistis* word group allows one to translate mostly by "to trust/to believe" for the verb, "trustworthiness/faithfulness" for the noun, and "trustworthy/faithful" for the adjective. "The beginning of God's creation" does not mean that Jesus is the first of creation; rather, he is the first in terms of God's new creation, referring to his resurrection, which guaranteed the resurrection with new bodies of those whose names are written in the book of life and the renewal of creation itself—"a new heaven and new earth" (see Rev 21:1). For the text to call Jesus the "Amen" is to say he is reliable, trustworthy, the true One (beyond the references above, see Rev 5:14; 7:12; and 19:4).

The way Jesus is addressed in Rev 1-3, mainly "a faithful/trustworthy witness," gives strong hints as to what was happening throughout the Apocalypse. John was shown an "open door in heaven" and he entered "in the Spirit" (4:1-2). It was a throne-room scene! God is on his throne and he is constantly praised by guardians of the throne who cry out: "Holy, holy, holy is the Lord God Almighty, who was and is and is to come!" (4:8; cp. Isa 6:2–3). The "twenty-four elders" (the church) fall down in worship, casting their crowns before the throne and extolling God as "worthy" to receive "glory and honor and power," for he is Creator and Sustainer of all things (vv. 10–11). In God's right hand was a scroll, written front and back, sealed with seven seals.

The idea of "worthiness" is taken up by a "strong angel" who proclaimed: "Who is worthy to open the scroll and break its seals?" (5:1–2). Silence! No one! John weeps until an elder said: "Weep no more; behold, the Lion of the tribe of Judah, the Root of David, has conquered, so that he can open the scroll and its seven seals" (v. 5, cp. Gen 49:8–12; Isa 11:1, 10; Luke 1:32). Jesus was the king of Davidic descent (Rom 1:3) and like David has come to "conquer." However, his conquering is quite different from the first King David. What John *heard* was a lion, what he *saw* was a lamb standing as having been slaughtered! The lamb (ἀρνίον, *arnion*) has great power ("seven horns"), for he has conquered by dying and thus redeeming people for God. When the Lamb took the scroll to open its seals, the creatures around the throne and twenty-four elders sang a new song:

> Worthy are you to take the scroll and to open its seals,
> for you were slain, and by your blood you ransomed people for God
> from every tribe and language and people and nation,
> and you have made them a kingdom and priests to our God,
> and they shall reign on the earth. (Rev 5:9–10)

Then the myriad of angels that surround the throne said with a loud voice: "Worthy is the Lamb who was slain, to receive power and wealth and wisdom and might and honor and glory and blessing!" (5:12). As a response every living creature in heaven and on earth said: "To him who sits on the throne and to the Lamb be blessing and honor and glory and might forever and ever!" (5:13). "And the four living creatures said, 'Amen!' and the elders fell down and worshiped" (5:14).

Richard Bauckham wrote: "When the slaughtered Lamb is seen 'in the midst of' the divine throne in heaven (5:6; cf. 7:17), the meaning is that Christ's sacrificial death *belongs to the way God rules the world*."[37] And how does God rule the world? Strange indeed! The angel took John on a visionary journey that opens up his eyes to what is really going on around him: "Write therefore the things that you have seen, those that

---

37. Bauckham, *Book of Revelation*, 64. Emphasis is his.

are and those that are to take place after this" (1:19). "Come up here, and I will show you what must take place after this" (4:1b; cp. Dan 2:28, 45). Revelation is about what is reality—past, present, and future. Specifically, Revelation is concerned about the *truth* of God. The worthiness of the One who sits on the throne depends on the worthiness of the Lamb. And by the same token what Christ does, God does![38] Jesus is worthy (qualified) to open the seals.

The first four seals are opened (6:1–8) and there is no surprise at all—it is all old news! Conquests, bloodshed, famine, and death had been the hallmark (or low-mark!) of human beings from time immemorial. "It was given to him" (ἐδόθη αὐτῷ, *edothē autō*) suggested that this is an activity of an evil power. It showed itself for what it is and it is allowed by God! The freedom to commit evil is a problem for Christian martyrs and the holy council around the throne of God (5:1–4; see Isa 29:10–11, 18; Dan 12:9–10). In the opening of the fifth seal they cried out: "O Sovereign Lord, holy and true, how long before you will judge and avenge our blood on those who dwell on the earth?" (6:10). Tonstad has written: "If the theodicy in the book of Revelation is thought of in strict dictionary terms as 'vindication of God's justice in tolerating the existence of evil,' God has, in the figure of the slaughtered Lamb, prevailed."[39] The martyrs were not given an answer. They were only told to wait. Others are yet to be killed!

What Revelation revealed is a cosmic conflict that included heaven and earth. This cosmic conflict can only be solved *in God's way, not man's*! A. T. Hanson wrote: "Christ and the saints conquer by dying; Satan and the powers of evil by physical force."[40] So true!

The sixth seal revealed a world so terrible that the main characters who have brought this on themselves hid among the mountains and rocks and cried out: "Fall on us and hide us from the face of him who is seated on the throne, and from the wrath of the Lamb, for the great day of their wrath has come, and who can stand?" (6:16–17).

But what about the Christians who are also suffering and dying? The answer was a so-called "Interlude" between the sixth and seventh seals,

---

38. Bauckham, *Book of Revelation*, 63.

39. Tonstad, *Saving God's Reputation*, 219. I am following Tonstad's thoughts on Revelation in this section because I think he has correctly assessed what is going on with the opening of the seals, blowing of the trumpets, and the pouring out of the bowls. His thoughts and emphasis on Revelation 12–14 seem to be exactly right in order to properly understand the apocalyptic/prophetic message of Revelation.

40. Hanson, *Wrath of the Lamb*, 165.

a needed pause before the end to give assurance to God's people. Revelation 7:1–17 was the "sealing of the saints." The 144,000 represented God's army in this cosmic conflict. John *heard* the number but what he *saw* was "a great multitude that no one could number, from every nation, from all tribes and peoples and languages, standing before the throne and before the Lamb, clothed in white robes, with palm branches in their hands, and crying out with a loud voice, 'Salvation belongs to our God who sits on the throne, and to the Lamb!'" (7:9–10). As before, John *heard* a Lion but *saw* a Lamb. Here John *heard* the number but *saw* a multitude. "These are the ones coming out of the great tribulation. They have washed their robes and made them white in the blood of the Lamb" (7:14). Martyrdom cannot keep them away from the presence of God nor from the shepherding care of the Lamb (7:15–17). We are witnessing a *martyr church*!

When the seventh seal was opened, there was silence in heaven for about a half hour (8:1). Could this be the silence of shock? (see Isa 52:14–15). In Isaiah the "kings shall shut their mouths because of him" (Isa 52:15b). He "shall startle many nations" (Isa 52:15a)[41] is parallel to the second phrase just stated. Why? And who is "he"? They are shocked into silence by "a man of sorrows," "smitten by God, and afflicted," "crushed for our iniquities" (Isa 53:3b, 4c, 5b). Just as kings shut their mouths because of this "servant," this "servant" never opened his mouth: "He was oppressed, and he was afflicted, yet he opened not his mouth; like a lamb that is led to the slaughter, and like a sheep that before its shearers is silent, so he opened not his mouth" (Isa 53:7). This is "slaughterhouse language" (σφάξω, *sphaxō*). As Tonstad commented: "Only the Lamb (slaughtered) could have solved the cosmic conflict this way."[42]

The seventh seal opened up the seven trumpets (Rev 8:2—11:19). The seven trumpets recapitulated the seven seals, only this time the intensity is increased from one-fourth to one-third destruction. It is patterned after the Egyptian plagues, only on steroids! The imagery of the plagues of Egypt will continue with the bowls of wrath with complete intensity (Rev 16). The first four trumpets paralleled the four horsemen

---

41. Most English versions use the word "sprinkle" here, but the other possibility is "startle," which keeps the parallelism with "kings shall shut their mouths because of him." The Hebrew is difficult.

42. Tonstad, *Saving God's Reputation*, 218. There are other interpretations of the "silence in heaven," and the one that has the best possibility is Peterson's view: "It was in order to hear those prayers that there was silence in heaven" (Peterson, *Reversed Thunder*, 87).

(Rev 8:6–12). The next three trumpets will be called "Woes" (8:13). The fifth angel blew his trumpet and the description was surely of demonic activity climaxed by 9:11: "They have as king over them the angel of the bottomless pit. His name in Hebrew is Abaddon, and in Greek he is called Apollyon." The Hebrew word means "destruction" and the Greek name "destroyer." What was somewhat veiled here will be revealed clearly at Rev 12–14.

Once again, between the sixth trumpet and the seventh is an "Interlude" designed to pause to give the saints a better understanding of what God is doing for them. It is a strange "doing" of God. The interlude (10:1—11:13) revealed what God will do for his people who are killed for their prophesying and witnessing (11:3, 6, 7). The "beast" that arose from the bottomless pit came out of the blue, but more will be learned about this beast in chapter 13. In spite of the desecration of their dead bodies (11:8), they are "resurrected" to new life and are whisked to heaven to be with God and the Lamb. More martyred saints are added to those of 6:10! When will it end? Well, the seventh angel blew the seventh trumpet and it did end: "The kingdom of the world has become the kingdom of our Lord and of his Christ, and he shall reign forever and ever" (11:15b). Worship was once again offered by the twenty-four elders (the church) and the presence of God was manifested at the end by the "ark of the covenant" and the accompaniment of God-like phenomena, "flashes of lightning, rumblings, peals of thunder, an earthquake, and heavy hail" (11:19; cf. Exod 19:16–18; Rev 4:5; 8:5; and 16:18).

Revelation is a bifid, meaning it is divided into two equal halves (Rev 1–11 and 12–22), each half reflecting on the other, but progression is to be found in the second half. Rev 12–14 is the crucial and climactic presentation of the cosmic conflict that John is witnessing (see the chiastic outline). The proper context and understanding of this cosmic conflict are found in this text. John dropped his sevens scheme, or better was revealed to him apart from a seven scheme (seals, trumpets, and later bowls). In "freehand"[43] a picture was drawn to reveal what was truly happening on earth and heaven. This scene was in heaven and John saw three characters: a red dragon, a magnificent pregnant woman, and a male child born of the woman. The woman was described in breathtaking terms: "clothed with the sun, with the moon under her feet, and on her head a crown of twelve stars," and pregnant (12:1). This was a "great

---

43. "Freehand" is a term used by Vernard Eller, *Most Revealing Book*, 125.

sign." Another sign was the appearance of a "great red dragon" (12:3–4). The red dragon sought to devour the child about to be born.

These three characters represented three persons or entities that were well known. I will take them in reverse order. First, the child. The child was described as "one who is to rule all the nations with a rod of iron, but her child was caught up to God and to his throne" (12:5). This was clearly a reference to Ps 2:9. He can be none other than the promised Messiah, the Davidic king who is coming. His destiny was to rule the nations. But the next phrase has the child "caught up to God and to his throne" (see Rev 4–5). This was the Lamb (slaughtered!) "in the midst" of the throne of God (5:5–6). He is now reigning at God's right hand (Ps 110:1). By God's power and intervention, the red dragon cannot reach him.

Second, the red dragon. It was described clearly in the next paragraph as "that ancient serpent, who is called the devil and Satan, the deceiver of the whole world" (12:9). These were ancient biblical terms used for the "adversary" and "accuser" of humanity throughout the ages. It suggested by "that ancient serpent" that it began in the garden of Eden with the deception of Adam and Eve (Gen 3:1). "Satan" is *ha-satan* (the adversary, accuser) whose work of accuser was clearly seen in Job 1–2 (Job 1:9 and 2:5; also see Zech 3:1; 1 Chr 21:1). The devil (*diabolos*) is a Greek name meaning "slanderer," which was used in the Septuagint to translate *ha-satan*.

Third, the pregnant woman. In this case, the symbol was not as clear, but multi-faceted. She can possibly symbolize Eve of Gen 3 where the prophesy of Gen 3:15 made sense of this text: "I will put enmity between you [the shrewd serpent] and the woman [Eve], and between your offspring [seed] and her offspring [seed]; he shall bruise your head, and you shall bruise his heel" (my additions). The apostle Paul applied this verse in a unique way (see Rom 16:17–20). But the woman can also stand for Israel (see Joseph's dream, Gen 37:9), which indeed produced the Messiah (Rom 9:5). No doubt the woman could also stand for Mary, the mother of Jesus. Giving birth to Jesus in a manger was a trial and the danger of her child being killed by a Satanic monster (King Herod) was real (see Matt 2:1–18). Finally, the woman, when she fled into the wilderness "where she has a place prepared by God" (12:6; cp. John 14:1–2?) for protection, suggested a symbolism of the New Israel (the church). This same scenario was described at 12:14–17. The dragon became frustrated and so he "went off to make war on the rest of her offspring" (true Christians) (12:17b), "those who keep the commandments of God and hold to the testimony of Jesus" (12:17c). Thus, through this symbolism John revealed that the church, God's genuine people, is still susceptible to "persecution, deception, and corruption."[44]

Revelation 12 had three sections: vv. 1–6 (birth of a male child); vv. 7–12 (war in heaven); and vv. 13–18 (the dragon's pursuit of the woman). The same can be said about Rev 14: vv. 1–5 (the Lamb on Mt. Zion; vv. 6–12 (the three angels' messages); and vv. 13–20 (the harvest). Tonstad has given insight into these two chapters by showing the narrative sequence was not the chronological progression. The chronological progression was: vv. 7–12 (war in heaven); then vv. 1–6 (birth of male child); and vv. 13–18 (dragon's pursuit of the woman). In Rev 14 the chronological progression is: vv. 6–12 (the three angels' messages); 13–20 (the harvest); and finally, vv. 1–5 (the Lamb on Mt. Zion). The "war in heaven" was the story of the casting down of Satan and his angels (demonic spirits, unclean spirits?) from heaven to earth. Satan could not and did not thwart God's ability to fulfill his goal of rescuing the human race and his creation from destruction. How did he do this? A great voice from heaven (martyred saints? angels?) told us:

> Now the salvation and the power and the kingdom of our God and the authority of his Christ have come, for the accuser of our brothers (and sisters) has been thrown down, who accuses them day and night before our God. And they have conquered him by the blood of the Lamb and by the word of their testimony, for they loved not their lives even unto death. Therefore, rejoice, O heavens and you who dwell in them! But woe to you, O earth and sea, for the devil has come down to you in great wrath, because he knows that his time is short! (Rev 12:10–12)

Jesus is the "faithful/trustworthy martyr (witness)" (Rev 1:5) who shed his blood for the salvation of the world. The saints now participate in that same martyrdom (witness) by upholding the word of their testimony (witness) and giving their lives to be faithful to the Messiah and his word. Of course, not everyone will die for their faithfulness to the Messiah, but everyone must be faithful *until death*. Those who follow Jesus must become a *martyr church*.

Revelation 13 revealed two beasts that the dragon will use in his pursuit of the saints: the first is from the sea (abyss, 13:1–10) and second from the land (13:11–18). Beale wrote: "The depiction of the two beasts

---

44. Beale, *Revelation*, 627.

in ch. 13 is based in part on Job 40–41, which is the only OT depiction of two Satanic beasts opposing God."[45] "Beasts" in Daniel represented evil kingdoms (see Dan 2, 7). John was referring to the Roman imperial power. Revelation 13:1–10 described the political deception of the day. In many ways this beast was a parody of the Messiah himself. At the end of this description was a poem with an exhortation: The poem—"If anyone is to be taken captive, to captivity he goes; if anyone is to be slain with the sword, with the sword must he be slain." Certainly, this referred to the Christian martyrs who have been slain and those who will be slain. The exhortation—"Here is a call for the endurance and faith of the saints." I would translate "faith" as "faithfulness," since it is coupled with endurance. A similar exhortation at the end of Rev 14 will be seen, but first, the second beast.

The second beast was from the land (earth). Revelation 13:11–17 described this beast as a "religion," indeed, a false religion. It was called a "false prophet" (20:10). It described the local governments who pay homage to Rome and to Caesar. Contests existed about each local city, building a better temple to Roma/Caesar in each of their little principalities. This was participation of the imperial cult (worship). Domitian demanded that he be called "Lord and God." When Christians could not do this, presumably they were declared "treasonous" and executed, at least potentially. However, there is very little evidence from historical resources of this persecution during Domitian's reign. Such persecution was probably local and sporadic, depending upon the depth of evil of the protectors of the imperial cult. Mangina has well summarized this chapter:

> The beast from the sea attempts to mimic Christ the Lamb, and together the dragon, beast, and false prophet constitute an entire demonic Trinity parodying God, the Lamb, and the Spirit. As God gives life, generously and with overflowing abundance, so the dragon reeks of death. As Christ comes bearing the peace of God, so the beast embodies every kind of violence and bloodshed and exploitation. As the prophetic Spirit exposes the truth in all things, so the false prophet spins a web of lies, inviting us to debase ourselves by worshiping the beast rather than the Creator.[46]

---

45. Beale, *Revelation*, 682.

46. Mangina, *Revelation*, 166. Also, see Davis, *Revelation*, 278–79 for an extensive chart on this parody of God vs. Satan, Christ vs. Beast from the sea, and Holy Spirit vs. Beast from the land.

The last verse of Rev 13 has been greatly controversial to the present day. A very simple explanation of this verse can be given: "This calls for wisdom: let the one who has understanding calculate the number of the beast, for it is the number of a man, and his number is 666" (13:18). *Gematria* was commonly used in Jewish literature where names of people were reduced to a numerical value for various purposes. Most interpretations seek an answer to this number by posing the myth of *Nero redivivus* (Nero revived) and giving number values to his name, but this can't be done without adding an "n" to the end of Nero's name and moving into the Hebrew letters. Not quite kosher! The simple solution is to take the name of beast in the Greek (θηρίον, *thērion*) and use the equivalent Hebrew letters: תריון, thus the following—Th = 400; r = 200; y = 10; o = 6; n = 50 > total 666. "The number 666, or the number of its [the beast's] name (Rev 13:17 and 15:2), should be interpreted as a cipher for 'beast.'"[47] In other words, the number of the beast is simply 666, the number of a man, which is less than the perfect number of 777 (perfection? God?). This makes sense and is simple enough!

Chapter 14 is like the so-called "interludes" of the seals (7:1–17) and the trumpets (10:1—11:13), designed to give encouragement and hope to those who are being persecuted and martyred for their allegiance to the kingdom of God and its king, Jesus. The 144,000 (YHWH's army) has the name of the Lamb and the Father on their foreheads for their protection and ownership. They are bearing God's name to the nations. Carmen Imes made this application: "People either bear the divine name or the name of the beast on their foreheads, indicating the object of their worship and allegiance. . . . Because of the faithfulness of Jesus, we can be marked with God's name and participate in his mission to bring blessing to all nations."[48] "It is these who follow the Lamb wherever he goes" (14:4b).

While this paragraph (14:1–5) was first, it was last in chronological progression with the Lamb and the 144,000 standing on Mt. Zion singing a new song about their redemption. The second paragraph (14:6–13) was first in chronological progression with the messages of the three angels. The first angel announced that everyone must fear God and worship him, for judgment was coming: "The hour of his judgment has come" (14:7c). The second angel announced the demise of "Babylon" ("Fallen, fallen is

---

47. Wood, "Simplifying the Number of the Beast (Rev 13:18)," 140.
48. Imes, *Bearing God's Name*, 181.

Babylon the great," 14:8b), presumably the Roman Empire or any state that took on the agenda of Satan and his two beasts. The third angel announced that all who follow the beast and have its mark on them will experience the terrible wrath of God forever and ever (14:9–11).

Now comes the key text at the climactic point of the cosmic conflict—Rev 14:12: "Here is a call for the endurance of the saints, those who keep the commandments of God and their faith in Jesus." The ESV is no different from most major English translations. They all preferred the objective genitive, either "faith in Jesus" or "faithfulness to Jesus." I have already commented on Rev 13:10, which is a similar phrase: "Here is a call for the endurance and faithfulness of the saints" (my translation). One should notice that there are several doublets throughout Revelation:

> Rev 1:2—"to the word of God and to the testimony of Jesus Christ"
>
> Rev 1:9—"the word of God and the testimony of Jesus"
>
> Rev 6:9—"the word of God and the witness they had borne"
>
> Rev 12:17—"on those who keep the commandments of God and hold to the testimony of Jesus"
>
> Rev 14:12—"those who keep the commandments of God and their faith in Jesus"
>
> Rev 20:4—"for the testimony of Jesus and for the word of God"

When one examines these doublets, it is obvious that there is overlap in meaning with "the word of God" and "the commandments of God." Also, "witness" and "faithfulness" go hand in hand. It is best to see "faithfulness" as a circle within a bigger circle of "the word of God." Some have suggested that the *kai*, the Greek "and," can be epexegetical, i.e., meaning the second phrase adds ideas to the first word, so one would translate the *kai* as "even," "namely," "that is," or "in fact." If this is so, and it probably is, then one needs to take another look at the text in the ESV. In light of the fact that all the phrases are subjective genitives, considered such even by the ESV, then it stands to reason that given the above arguments so far, the phrase "their faith in Jesus" should be understood rather as a subjective genitive and translated in this way: "and/even the faithfulness of Jesus." One could translate it "the faith of Jesus," but this is putting the emphasis on the personal faith of the human Jesus, which is not part of the overall story line of Revelation.

Tonstad[49] has given at least three good arguments for the interpretation of "the faithfulness of Jesus": 1) There is the conditioning of the story line. The question of *means* to set things right (5:6) is the clear beginning of this story line. The heavenly council (5:1–3) and the victims of injustice (6:10) are puzzled as to what is reality. What is going on around them says that God is unfaithful! The answer is not to defeat evil by physical force as one would expect the "Lion of Judah" to do, and most thought the Messiah would be just like the ancient lion himself, King David. No, the strange work of God is to bring forth only a "slaughtered Lamb," who alone could break the seven seals (5:5–6). This is how (*means*) God overcomes evil. The unfolding of history revealed that the kingdom was all about freedom, and freedom meant that evil can have its way as well. With the opening of the seals, the blowing of the trumpets, and the pouring of the bowls, we saw evil intensifying and increasing, until God finally brought it all to a halt with a cry: "It is done!" (16:17). Judgment will finally have its Day (Rev 17–20). At the very climactic point of these three recapitulations, retold in the "freehand" of Rev 12–14, came the exhortation: "Under these circumstances is the endurance of the saints, those who keep the commandments of God and the faithfulness of Jesus" (my translation). Jesus' faithfulness to the word and will of God also affirmed God's faithfulness and vindicated him. At the same time the faithfulness of Jesus was for human imitation (see 13:10). It fits the story line.

2) The explicative quality of τὴν πίστιν Ἰησοῦ has already been revealed by observing the doublets, the subjective genitives throughout the phrases, and how they covered the same territory whether or not there was an epexegetical use of *kai*.

3) Tonstad argued that the Christology of Revelation suggested the subjective genitive reading. What was declared in Isaiah, for instance, for YHWH God (Isa 44:6—"I am the first and I am the last"; 48:12—"I am he; I am the first, and I am the last") was declared of Jesus in Revelation (Rev 1:17–18—"I am the first and the last"; 2:8—"the words of the first and last, who died and came to life"; 22:13—"the first and the last"). "What God does is expressed and reflected in the faithful life and death of Jesus."[50] Again, Tonstad stated: "When 'the faithfulness of Jesus' is held up as the lodestar for those who face the contested issue in the climax of

---

49. Tonstad, *Saving God's Reputation*, 159–61. I am only briefly summarizing his thoughts and arguments here.

50. Tonstad, *Saving God's Reputation*, 265.

the cosmic conflict (14:12), it is because 'faithfulness' encapsulates the contested issue in the conflict from the very beginning."[51]

Jesus was called the "Amen, the faithful and true witness" (3:14). When Jesus returned in victory over evil at his *Parousia* (19:11), he was called "the Faithful and True." This was in line with the emphasis on YHWH God being the "God of truth" (Isa 65:16). The three root letters of the Hebrew word אמן mean "reliability, true, trustworthy." The word "truth" is אֱמֶת, *emeth*. "Faithfulness" is related, of course, to these words, in Hebrew, אֱמוּנָה, (*'emûnâ*ʰ]. This latter word of "faithfulness" was used by the apostle Paul in Romans (Rom 1:17) as he quoted a portion of Hab 2:4b—"The righteous (One) shall live out of his faithfulness" (my translation). This was God's answer to Habakkuk who, too, had cried out like the martyrs, "How long, O Lord?" (Hab 1:2). In fact, the Letter to the Romans was a theodicy where Paul was having to defend the way God had brought salvation to the world through Jesus the Messiah. What has been said about Romans can also be said about Revelation.

Revelation was a theodicy explaining how and by what means God was dealing with evil in the world—through a "Lamb standing, as though it had been slain" (Rev 5:6). What a strange battle! A Lamb against a red dragon. The Lamb prevailed precisely in being slain. In his resurrection he can no longer be slain, for he lives forever. Death itself died! The faithfulness of this Lamb was his going to the slaughter, silently, obediently, and willingly. Christians are to imitate this faithfulness in their lives. The very next verse proclaimed: "And I heard a voice from heaven saying, 'Write this: Blessed are the dead who die in the Lord from now on.' 'Blessed indeed,' says the Spirit, 'that they may rest from their labors, for their deeds follow them!'" (Rev 14:13).

When the seven bowls of wrath were poured out (Rev 16), the judgment of all evil finally came. The great prostitute, Babylon, and the beast upon which she sat had made themselves "drunk with the blood of the saints, the blood of the martyrs of Jesus" (17:6). But that was how the Lamb and the saints conquered: "They will make war on the Lamb, and the Lamb will conquer them, for he is Lord of lords and King of kings, and those with him are called and chosen and faithful (*pistoi*)" (17:14, my parenthesis). The long-awaited vindication of God and his judgment against the real evil of this world was now drawn out in detail by Revelation.

---

51. Tonstad, *Saving God's Reputation*, 254.

John saw the "fall of Babylon" (Rev 18), a great multitude rejoicing over her fall (19:1–5), and the marriage supper of the Lamb (19:6–10). A key verse in Revelation is given: "For the witness of Jesus is the spirit of prophecy" (19:10d, my translation). Jesus' *Parousia* will be his victory march with his army (144,000 = the church). The text described that "he is clothed in a robe dipped in blood," presumably his enemies' blood (Isa 63:1–6), but I suggest tentatively it was his own blood that was actually seen (Rev 1:5, 18). This was how God conquered evil, by a slain Lamb.

We saw the two beasts thrown into the lake of fire (19:17–21). Finally, the red dragon called by many names will be destroyed likewise, but not without being released for a little while (20:7–10). Yet, one more to come: "Death and Hades" were also thrown into the lake of fire, the second death! (20:11–15). Those whose names were written in the book of life were given entrance into the New Jerusalem, located on a "new heaven and new earth." John had to write all this down, "for these words are trustworthy and true" (21:5). With the reversal of Gen 3, the so-called fall of humankind, Revelation concluded with an emphasis on these words of prophesy (22:6, 7, 9, 10, 18, and 19). Again, John was apprised: "These words are trustworthy and true" (22:6a). The adjective *pistos* is usually translated "faithful," but in these two passages (21:5 and 22:6) it is appropriate to translate as "trustworthy."

But why just these two references for the ESV? Perhaps the translators thought that *pistos* should be "faithful" only for people, while inanimate things such as "the word of God" could be "trustworthy." After reviewing the use of *pistos* in Revelation, I am convinced that from the beginning of the Revelation Jesus the Messiah is referred to as "the trustworthy witness" (1:5). This idea includes the next reference to Jesus: "the words of the Amen, the trustworthy and true witness" (3:14). Finally, the reference to the victorious *Parousia* of Jesus is called "Trustworthy and True" (19:11). Certainly, each of these references can include the idea of being "faithful," no doubt, but being faithful also allows one to be trustworthy, that is, worthy to be trusted! This does not at all deter me from translating the noun *pistis* as "faithfulness" at Rev 14:12. The other references to the use of *pistos* as "faithful" are appropriate as well (see 2:10, 13; 17:14).

Solving the problem of theodicy in Revelation will not become a reality until there is a reversal of the problem of evil in the world and the complete fulfillment of salvation on the earth. The resurrection (20:13; 21:4) will overcome death. The curse of Gen 3 must be nullified (22:3). Estrangement between God and humankind must be reconciled (22:4).

All suffering must end (21:4). Tears will be wiped away (7:17; 21:4). Only then will God be vindicated, his reputation restored, and the theodicy of Revelation realized!

One last word is left, the negative word *apistos*, "faithless." John gave fair warning to those who capitulated to persecution, deception, and corruption: "But as for the cowardly, the *faithless*, the detestable, as for murderers, the sexually immoral, sorcerers, idolaters, and all liars, their portion will be in the lake that burns with fire and sulfur, which is the second death" (21:8, my emphasis). The first two words, "cowardly" and "faithless," are addressed especially to former Christians who could not overcome their fear of rejection or separation from economic prosperity or even the fear of persecution to the point of martyrdom. Loving the present world can cause one to leave the faith (example, 2 Tim 4:10). I conclude with Tonstad's own conclusion: "In Revelation the faithfulness of Jesus in the form of the slaughtered Lamb is the means by which God wins the war that began in heaven and the means by which believers must prevail through the climax of the cosmic conflict."[52] Amen.

---

52. Tonstad, *Saving God's Reputation*, 348.

8

Conclusion

> "Justification is by means of God's faithfulness expressed in love, demonstrated in Christ's act of faithfulness expressed in love, to which humans, enabled by the Spirit, respond in faithfulness expressed in love —i.e., in co-crucifixion."
>
> —MICHAEL J. GORMAN[1]

"What Is at Stake?"[2]

HAVING RESEARCHED THE ENTIRE New Testament for its usage of the *pistis* word group and the specific use in the traditional Pauline letters of the *pistis Christou* passages, it is appropriate at this point to summarize the most important issues that are at stake as a result of this study. I have taken the position that the *pistis Christou* passages in the traditional Pauline Epistles should be translated "the faithfulness of Jesus the Messiah." I found these statements are Pauline phrases found primarily in Romans and Galatians, but also in Philippians and Ephesians. The two letters of Romans and Galatians have much in common and thus helped to solidify my interpretation, especially with the "catchphrase" *ek pisteōs*, "from/out of *his* faithfulness," taken from the Hab 2:4b passage.

---

1. Gorman, *Cruciform God*, 104.
2. This is the subtitle of Hays' article "ΠΙΣΤΙΣ and Pauline Christology," 35, 55.

The *pistis* word group has been found to have alternative interpretations such as "trusting," "trustworthy," "trustworthiness," and "pledge," over against the usual "believing," "faith," and "faithfulness." Every use and context of each word dictated its nuance. Just as one word can have different meanings according to context, so also when applied to the *pistis* word group. Whereas we use different English words to communicate the nuances of *pistis*, the Greek mind only heard the word *pistis*. Could they discern slightly different ideas from that one word? I think so, not unlike English or any other language. The context always matters. Finally, the question must be asked as I began: What difference does it make? Or, better as Hays expressed it: "What is at stake?" Hays articulated five different theological issues that are at stake.[3] I will comment about each of these and add a few of my own.

1. Source of Salvation

Hays referred to this issue as a "relation between Christology and soteriology in Pauline theology." More precisely, how does the death of Jesus become the source of our salvation? I don't think anyone in this debate, whether accepting the subjective or objective genitive, would disagree that somehow the death of Jesus on the cross has brought salvation to humanity, all people for all time. There is wide agreement that Jesus is the source of our salvation. Disagreement occurs regarding how the apostle Paul expressed that idea. Those who accept the subjective genitive interpretation, as advocated in this book, place the emphasis of Paul's gospel on the faithfulness of Jesus the Messiah as the source and means of our salvation. The strongest argument for this is that all the *pistis Christou* phrases in Paul's letters implied and sometimes expressed explicitly the human response to the gospel in its immediate context (see Rom 3:22, Gal 2:16, 3:22, and perhaps Phil 3:9) as well as the faithfulness of Jesus. Those who accept the objective genitive interpretation emphasize the human response to the gospel. In several passages this approach clearly revealed duplications as well as confusion as to means and goal of salvation.

Yet, no one rejects the fact that somehow the death of Jesus on the cross is the source of our salvation. To think otherwise would be heretical. However, if one can establish the original understanding of the *pistis Christou* phrases in Paul, that understanding is the one we should heed in

---

3. Hays, "ΠΙΣΤΙΣ and Pauline Christology," 55–57.

terms of preaching and teaching the gospel. I am convinced beyond the shadow of a doubt that Paul's emphasis in his gospel is upon the faithfulness of Jesus to the Father's will. When Jesus went to the cross and gave himself on behalf of sinful humankind, he was motivated by love. *The epigraph above expresses this idea completely.* The human response of an "obedient faith" to the gospel is necessary to receive this wonderful gift of salvation, but what really saves us is what God has done already through his Son, Jesus the Messiah.[4] His blood (death) shed on the cross is the atoning sacrifice for our sins and that alone can save. All we humans can do is say "yes" to that fact and then live the "cruciform" life.

We must add that the resurrection of Jesus vindicated him as the Son of God and has given us assurance of that objective nature of salvation (see Rom 1:3–4). That seems to be the meaning of the enigmatic phrase of Paul's in Rom 1:17: "out of faithfulness unto faithfulness," i.e., "from Jesus' faithfulness unto our faithfulness." I don't think the objective genitive adherents would disagree with this. They simply don't think that is Paul's point. They emphasize the traditional anthropological exegesis, the NIV's "faith from first to last." I hold that the emphasis in Paul's gospel is Christological, which is the best way to understand the *pistis Christou* phrases in the traditional Pauline letters. That is the first thing that is at stake. We lose that emphasis otherwise.

2. Jesus' Humanity

In the early church, especially the first two centuries, Gnosticism was the most perilous threat to the rise of Christianity. The New Testament authors (mainly apostles) had to wrestle with both philosophical and theological ideas that dismissed the possibility of Jesus' bodily presence and his manhood. Later, we will demonstrate the New Testament's emphasis on Jesus' true humanity.

The "faithfulness of Jesus the Messiah," of necessity, implied the true humanity of Jesus. This teaching ought to be self-evident but it is true that many Christians have a "docetic view of Christ."[5] Such Christians cannot see Jesus as a human being who believed or trusted as human

---

4. Paul's phrase "obedience of faith" (Rom 1:5; 16:26) is very important as a human response. Ron Simkins, a reader of my book, commented that "it is important, but it is our response to being loved not our way of becoming loved, our willingness to receive a gift not our way of obtaining a gift."

5. See Pollard, "The 'Faith of Christ,'" 225, and Hooker, "ΠΙΣΤΙΣ ΧΡΙΣΤΟΥ," 322.

beings do. Because we worship Jesus as our Lord and Messiah, Savior of the world, it is difficult to see him as a real human being, someone who is like us, only without sin. Doceticism (a form of Gnosticism) held Jesus' body was illusory or absent. Robert Clyde Johnson put the heresy of a docetic Christ in an understandable way: "There are three classic types of Christological heresy:

1. *A Manlike God (but not really a man)*
2. *A Godlike Man (but not really God)*
3. *God/Man (but neither really God nor really man).*[6]

His conclusion was to affirm the creedal statement that Jesus is both "very God and very Man."

The book of Hebrews, perhaps better than any other New Testament book except the Gospels, presented Jesus' humanity as real, genuine, and essential:

- Heb 2:14: "Since therefore the children share in flesh and blood, he himself likewise partook of the same things, that through death he might destroy the one who has the power of death, that is, the devil."
- Heb 2:17–18: "Therefore he had to be made like his brothers in every respect, so that he might become a merciful and faithful high priest in the service of God, to make propitiation for the sins of the people. For because he himself has suffered when tempted, he is able to help those who are being tempted."
- Heb 3:6a: "But Christ is faithful over God's house as a son."
- Heb 4:15: "For we do not have a high priest who is unable to sympathize with our weaknesses, but one who in every respect has been tempted as we are, yet without sin."
- Heb 5:7–10: "In the days of his flesh, Jesus offered up prayers and supplications, with loud cries and tears, to him who was able to save him from death, and he was heard because of his reverence. Although he was a son, he learned obedience through what he suffered. And being made perfect, he became the source of eternal salvation to all who obey him, being designated by God a high priest after the order of Melchizedek."

---

6. Johnson, *The Meaning of Christ*, 70, 73, 75.

- Heb 7:26: "For it was indeed fitting that we should have such a high priest, holy, innocent, unstained, separated from sinners, and exalted above the heavens."
- Heb 9:14: "How much more will the blood of Christ, who through the eternal Spirit offered himself without blemish to God, purify our conscience from dead works to serve the living God."
- Heb 9:26b–28: "But as it is, he has appeared once for all at the end of the ages to put away sin by the sacrifice of himself. And just as it is appointed for man to die once, and after that comes judgment, so Christ, having been offered once to bear the sins of many, will appear a second time, not to deal with sin but to save those who are eagerly waiting for him."
- Heb 10:5c, 7a (paraphrased from LXX Ps 39:7–9 [40:6–8]): "But a body have you prepared for me; . . . Then I said, 'Behold, I have come to do your will, O God.'"
- Heb 10:19–20: "Therefore, brothers, since we have confidence to enter the holy places by the blood of Jesus, by the new and living way that he opened for us through the curtain, that is, through his flesh . . ."
- Heb 12:2: "Looking (away) to Jesus, the pioneer (trailblazer) and perfecter (completer) of faithfulness, who over against the joy that was set before him endured the cross, having despised the shame, he was enthroned [seated with abiding results] at the right hand of the throne of God" (my translation with annotations).
- Heb 13:12: "So Jesus also suffered outside the gate in order to sanctify the people through his own blood."
- Heb 13:20–21: "Now may the God of peace who brought again from the dead our Lord Jesus, the great shepherd of the sheep, by the blood of the eternal covenant, equip you with everything good that you may do his will, working in us that which is pleasing in his sight, through Jesus Christ, to whom be glory forever and ever. Amen."

Hebrews presented Jesus as "one of us"—a genuine human being, yet without sin. His faithfulness to the Father in all things meant that in his flesh he obeyed perfectly and completely, but had to suffer and ultimately to shed his blood as an atonement for the sins of the world. He prayed for deliverance from death and was answered with his resurrection on the third day. He was exalted to the right hand of God to rule as king and high priest. He continually intercedes on our behalf to this day. He will one day return to save all who wait for him, to experience a resurrection like his, to enjoy the "new heaven and new earth," the New Jerusalem. Jesus blazed the trail of faithfulness and completed it to God's satisfaction. Jesus is now "our Man in heaven,"[7] our high priest with whom we have access in time of need (Heb 4:16). Without Jesus' true humanity, none of the claims above could have come to pass.[8]

John's Gospel is well known:

- John 1:14a: "And the Word became flesh and dwelt among us."
- John 1:18: "No one has ever seen God; the only God, who is at the Father's side, he has made him known."
- John 19:5: "So Jesus came out, wearing the crown of thorns and the purple robe. Pilate said to them, 'Behold the man!'"

First John began with a similar idea:

- 1 John 1:1: "That which was from the beginning, which we have heard, which we have seen with our eyes, which we looked upon and have touched with our hands, concerning the word of life."
- 1 John 3:2–3: "Beloved, we are God's children now, and what we will be has not yet appeared; but we know that when he appears we shall be like him, because we shall see him as he is. And everyone who thus hopes in him purifies himself as he is pure."
- 1 John 4:2–3a: "By this you know the Spirit of God: every spirit that confesses that Jesus Christ has come in the flesh is from God, and every spirit that does not confess Jesus is not from God."

These phrases from John's first letter encouraged the most widely held doctrine concerning who Jesus is—a real human being. If we do not believe that, we cannot claim to be genuine Christians, that is, "from God." When Jesus comes again, we shall be transformed in the resurrection to be like his resurrected body and glorified as he is now glorified in God's presence.

---

7. Edward Fudge's title to his commentary on Hebrews—*Our Man in Heaven*.

8. See Ron Simkins' new book, *Jesus Is One of Us* (forthcoming from Wipf and Stock).

The apostle Paul taught us the same about Jesus. I will mention only a few passages:

- Acts 17:31: "Because he has fixed a day on which he will judge the world in righteousness by *a man* whom he has appointed; and of this he has given assurance to all by raising him from the dead" (my emphasis).
- Rom 1:3–4: "Concerning his Son, who was *descended from David* according to the flesh and was declared to be the Son of God in power according to the Spirit of holiness by his resurrection from the dead, Jesus Christ our Lord" (my emphasis).
- Rom 8:3b: "By sending his own Son in the likeness of sinful flesh and for sin (or a sin offering), he condemned sin in the flesh" (my addition).
- 1 Cor 15:21: "For as by *a man* came death, by *a man* has come also the resurrection of the dead" (my emphasis).
- Phil 2:5–8: "Have this mind among yourselves, which is yours in Christ Jesus, who, though he was in the form of God, did not count equality with God a thing to be grasped [or to be taken advantage of], but made himself nothing, taking the form of a servant, being born in the likeness of men. And being found in human form, he humbled himself by becoming obedient to the point of death, even death on a cross" (my addition).
- Gal 4:4–5: "But when the fullness of time had come, God sent forth his Son, born of woman, born under the law, to redeem those who were under the law, so that we might receive adoption as sons."

These texts from Paul clearly presented Jesus as a real human being, born of a woman, descended from David, and even though he was the divine Son of God he did not take advantage of that fact. He suffered death like every human being, but his death was upon a cross for the salvation of the world. He was faithful to the Father's will. Consequently, God has raised him from the dead, exalted him to his right hand, and he now reigns as Lord to the glory of God the Father. One day we shall be glorified with him.

The concept of "the faithfulness of Jesus the Messiah" required that we understand him to be "one of us," a genuine and true human being, now glorified and reigning at God's right hand. When people make the statement "Well, I'm only human!" after making a "mess of things," they do not understand the purpose of God's creation of human beings. "To be truly human is to be Christlike, which is to be Godlike."[9] That is exactly what the Second Epistle of Peter meant in the opening statement:

> His divine power has granted to us all things that pertain to life and godliness, through the knowledge of him who called us to his own glory and excellence, by which he has granted to us his precious and very great promises, so that through them you may become *partakers of the divine nature*, having escaped from the corruption that is in the world because of sinful desire. (2 Pet 1:3-4, my emphasis)

The true humanity of Jesus is the goal and/or the completion of every follower of Jesus. Paul wrote: "For those whom he foreknew he also predestined to be conformed to the image of his Son, in order that he might be the firstborn among many brothers. And those whom he predestined he also called, and those whom he called he also justified, and those whom he justified he also glorified" (Rom 8:29-30).

The Synoptic Gospels present Jesus as a genuine human being. Both Matthew and Luke trace Jesus' genealogy back through David to Abraham (see Matt 1:1, 2, 6 and Luke 3:31, 34), and Luke takes it all the way back to Adam. In the book of Acts the apostle Paul experienced Jesus in his glorified form, but nevertheless the real and genuine Jesus (see Acts 9:5). Much more could be said about the humanity of Jesus, but it will suffice to see its prevalence in the New Testament. Without this teaching the faithfulness of Jesus is robbed of its power.

3. Individualism vs. Corporateness

Hays calls this idea "experiential-expressive vs. 'narrative' theology." These terms need some clarification. Those who emphasize the individual faith of the believer by adhering to the objective genitive interpretation are in danger of reducing the gospel to an "individual religious experience." In a strange way they turn "faith" into a "work" in order to obtain salvation. They juxtapose human "works of the law" with human "faith in Christ." In other words, the human act of believing brings about our salvation. As Hays expressed it: "The narrative account of salvation as won ὑπερ ἡμῶν ('for us') through the faithfulness of Jesus attempts to preclude this theological

---

9. Gorman, *Cruciform God*, 39.

misstep, emphasizing ... its public, corporate character."[10] There is no doubt that people become Christians as "individuals," one at a time. We see this in the book of Acts quite clearly: Acts 8:26–39 (the story of the baptism of the Ethiopian eunuch) and Acts 9:1–19 (the conversion and commission of Paul). But usually there is a public and corporate nature to these conversions: see Acts 10 (Cornelius and his household); Acts 16:13–15 (Lydia and her household); and Acts 16:25–34 (the Philippian jailor and his household). Salvation that Jesus brought to the earth by his faithfulness to the cross was for more than merely an "individual experience."

The scope of Jesus' salvation is cosmic in nature. He came to save not only human beings but the entire universe (see Rom 8:18–23). In the end there will be a resurrection of our bodies in order to dwell upon a "new heaven and new earth" (Rev 21–22). Our salvation has a corporateness to it, for we are the "body of Christ" on earth (see Eph 1:22, 23; 2:16, 22; 4:4, 16, 25; 1 Cor 12:27 and many other references!). This "corporateness" is seen clearly in how the church as a whole is to make known the "manifold wisdom of God" to the "rulers and authorities in the heavenly places" (see Eph 3:10). The subjective genitive interpretation allows exegetes to emphasize this aspect of salvation. There is no question that a person is not saved apart from a human response to what God has done in Christ for our salvation. But it is also clear that the objective nature of our salvation is based upon the faithful action of God through his Son, Jesus the Messiah. Our human response is meant to draw us into a new community, the family of God (Gal 6:16—"The Israel of God"). Salvation is individual, yes, but also corporate and cosmic.

4. "The Cruciform Character of Christian Obedience"[11]

Our comments above flow into this section, whereby the concept of being a Christian is to become truly human as God intended us to be in the first place—to reflect the "image of God" (Gen 1:26–27). Recent scholarship has taken up this idea, particularly by Michael J. Gorman in his theological thinking.[12] Gorman argues that "justification is by co-crucifixion: it is participation in the covenantal and cruciform narrative identity of Christ, which is in turn the character of God; thus justification

---

10. Hays, "ΠΙΣΤΙΣ and Pauline Christology," 56.
11. Hays' words in "ΠΙΣΤΙΣ and Pauline Christology," 56.
12. See Gorman, *Cruciformity*; *Cruciform God*; and *Apostle of the Crucified Lord*.

is itself theosis."[13] Gorman unpacked this concept starting with an exegesis of Phil 2:5–11.[14] Two passages from Gorman's work explained this term more clearly:

> A close reading of Gal 2:15–21 and Rom 6:1—7:6, in connection with other passages in Paul (especially Rom 5:1–11; 2 Cor 5:14–21; and, once again, Phil 2:6–11), reveals that the apostle understands faith as co-crucifixion, and "justification by faith" as new life/resurrection via crucifixion with the Messiah Jesus, or "justification by co-crucifixion," and therefore as inherently participatory.[15]

> To be more specific, Paul has not *two* soteriological models (juridical and participationist) but *one*, justification by co-crucifixion, meaning restoration to right covenant relations with God and others by participation in Christ's quintessential covenantal act of faith and love on the cross; this one act fulfilled both the "vertical" and "horizontal" requirements of the Law, such that those who participate in it experience the same life-giving fulfillment of the Law and therein begin the paradoxical, christologically grounded process of resurrection through death. That is, they have been initiated into the process of conformity to the crucified Christ (cruciformity, Christification), who is the image of God—and thus the process of theoformity, or theosis.[16]

Gorman accepts the subjective genitive interpretation and uses it to support his own special vocabulary for justification.[17] I think many have said the same as Gorman, only with different vocabulary. God, indeed, "is incorporating us into an already existing family, community, brother/sisterhood people, kingdom, assembly in which we immediately are taught to pray 'Our Father.'"[18] When a person accepts Jesus as Lord, confessing him as the Messiah, the Son of God, having repented of past sins, and is baptized into the Messiah, that person is identifying with the death, burial, and resurrection of Jesus (see Rom 6:1–4). Sins, thus, are forgiven and above all, the gift of the Spirit is given to the believer (Acts 2:38). The apostle Paul gives a clear exposition of the gift of the Holy

---

13. Gorman, *Cruciform God*, 2.
14. Gorman, *Cruciform God*, 9–39.
15. Gorman, *Cruciform God*, 44.
16. Gorman, *Cruciform God*, 45.
17. Gorman, *Cruciform God*, 58–63.
18. Comments by Ron Simkins.

Spirit and his purpose in our lives in Rom 8:1–17. This is justification by participation in the Messiah. Not only is it judicial (8:3–4) but also clearly ethical (8:12–13). Beyond that, it is eschatological (8:16–17). In addition, Paul wrote: "provided we suffer with him in order that we may also be glorified with him" (8:17b). "Co-crucifixion" was certainly a part of the apostle Paul's life (see Col 1:24 and 2 Cor 11:21–29).

As Hays expressed it: "From a practical point of view, this has the distinct disadvantage of summoning us to live lives of costly self-sacrificial burden-bearing."[19] This was Peter's point throughout his epistle, expressed in this verse: "For to this you have been called, because Christ also suffered for you, leaving you an example, so that you might follow in his steps" (1 Pet 2:21). The broader context indicated that suffering is a necessary part of the Christian life, if we truly follow Jesus. Peter continued: "But rejoice insofar as you share Christ's sufferings, that you may also rejoice and be glad when his glory is revealed" (1 Pet 4:13). Peter's conclusion is: "Therefore let those who suffer according to God's will entrust their souls to a faithful Creator while doing good" (1 Pet 4:19). Since Jesus' faithfulness inherently included suffering, even death, the believer must also live the "crucified" life in faithfulness to the Spirit, Son, and Father. *The cruciform character of Christian obedience is summarized by the epigraph above.*

5. The Meaning of the Righteousness of God

The faithfulness of Jesus the Messiah is necessarily connected to the idea and meaning of the "righteousness of God." Paul began his Roman epistle: "For in it [the gospel] the righteousness of God is revealed from faith for faith, as it is written, 'The righteous shall live by faith'" (Rom 1:17). I have interpreted this thematic phrase as supporting the subjective genitive interpretations of the *pistis Christou* phrases in the traditional Pauline letters. The gospel (good news) is about the revelation of God's righteousness through the faithfulness of Jesus to the cross (Rom 3:22, 25). The phrase "righteousness of God" is a term implied by Rom 3:20, an allusion to Ps 143:2. When one observed the context of this psalm, it was appealing to God's righteousness to deliver the psalmist from dire trouble (Ps 143:11). The psalmist wanted an answer "in your [God's] righteousness (Ps 143:1). The same kind of circumstances are found in

---

19. Hays, "ΠΙΣΤΙΣ and Pauline Christology," 56.

Isaiah 40–66. From these texts and others, the apostle Paul drew his vocabulary. Thus, the "righteousness of God" is the characteristic of God that desires to rescue humanity from its dire circumstances—to put us in a right relationship with God and with one another. In essence the righteousness of God is his covenant faithfulness in action.

N. T. Wright, in his commentary on Romans, elaborates the meaning of the righteousness of God by declaring it included three very Jewish ideas: covenant, law court, and apocalyptic.[20] First of all, the righteousness of God included the idea that God will keep his promises made to the patriarchs, the promise of restoration of the nation in full control of their own destiny, a temple with a legitimate priesthood, and a return to the great golden age under the kingships of David and Solomon. The fact that Israel had rebelled in idolatrous activities, declined as a nation, and was eventually exiled, did not take away Israel's desire for a coming Deliverer to restore all things (see John 4:25, Acts 1:6). Even Paul made the strong point that the faithlessness of some of the Jews did not nullify the faithfulness of God (Rom 3:3). Would God keep his promises to Abraham, the initial promise? Most certainly (Gal 3:7–14). Paul emphasized this point in Romans 3 by stating three characteristics of God in succession: his "faithfulness" (v. 3), his "righteousness" (v. 5), and his "truth" (v. 7). God's righteousness is a righteousness that fulfilled his promises to Israel. That was the climactic point Paul was making in Rom 9–11! Perhaps this idea is given its full force in the Second Coming of Jesus as described in apocalyptic terms in Rev 19:11: "Then I saw heaven opened, and behold, a white horse! The one sitting on it is called Faithful and True, and in righteousness he judges and makes war." I have chosen to translate "Faithful" as "Trustworthy." God's righteousness is revealed (at least partly) by Jesus' faithfulness, hence his trustworthiness (Rom 3:21–26).

Secondly, the righteousness of God entails a judicial element, the imagery of the Jewish law court. As Wright expressed it: "'Righteousness' was the status of the successful party when the case had been decided."[21] The appropriate word to use for either the accuser or the defendant, if the case was won, is "vindicated." Their status in the eyes of the court would be "righteousness." The term also was understood to apply to the judge who was supposed to judge impartially (see Rom 2:11). God is the judge,

---

20. Wright, *Romans*, 398.
21. Wright, *Romans*, 399.

but on judgment day, he will judge through the Messiah: "On that day when, according to my gospel, God judges the secrets of men by Christ Jesus" (Rom 2:16). Jesus is in a position to know those who are his own (John 10:14). In summary, God's righteousness was seen in terms of covenant faithfulness and putting things right (like in a law court).

Thirdly, the righteousness of God was revealed, that is, it comes as God's last act in history, invading it so to speak, with the goal of vindicating Israel. Paul has used the very word that expressed this at Rom 1:17: ἀποκαλύπτεται, *apokluptetai*, "is revealed." This was the plan of God from the very beginning (Eph 1:5–14). At just the right time God invaded the earth with "his Son, born of a virgin, born under the law, to redeem those who were under the law, so that we might receive adoption as sons" (Gal 4:4–5). Paul used a close synonym for *apokluptetai* at Rom 3:21 meaning essentially the same, πεφανέρωται, *pephanerōtai*, "has been manifested [with abiding results]." Thus, God's righteousness has been manifested [with abiding results] through the faithfulness of Jesus the Messiah (Rom 3:21–22a). That was the apocalyptic nature of God's righteousness—manifested through Jesus' faithfulness to the cross. This is how God will bring "justice" to the world. Wright concluded that the apostle Paul "quickly came to regard the events of Jesus' death and resurrection as the apocalyptic moment for which he and others had longed, and he rethought his previous way of viewing the story of Israel and the world as a result."[22] If I have any criticism of Wright at this point, it is he downplays the ultimate goal and end-time event that has not yet occurred: the subjection of all things under the feet of Jesus, even death, and then delivering the kingdom to the Father without grasping after it or seeking some benefit from it, but rather submitting himself to the Father so that "God may be all in all" (see 1 Cor 15:24–28).[23] An enormously important eschatological event yet awaits us in the future!

When Paul wrote Romans, he was vindicating the righteousness of God by showing how God fulfilled his promises to Israel in covenant faithfulness, justifying both Jews and gentiles on the same basis (Rom 3:27–31), and doing all of this through the faithfulness of Jesus the Messiah, an apocalyptic act. Thus, one can say that the righteousness of God

---

22. Wright, *Romans*, 401. Also, see Wright, *The Day the Revolution Began*.

23. However, Wright has given more detail to his thinking about this eschatological event in his latest published book, *History and Eschatology*, the result of the Gifford Lectures. See Wright, *History and Eschatology*, 138, 141, 143, 265, and 272 for comments on the critical passage of 1 Cor 15:28 and its context.

is essentially God's covenant faithfulness that seeks to save his people. These are presently controversial ideas, but the next issue deserves more detail, for it is connected to both covenant and apocalyptic ideas. These first five issues are at stake according to Hays. However, I add a few more concerns I think are at stake as well. Some are theological in nature, but others have a more practical application.

More Is at Stake!

6. Climax of a Covenant or Apocalyptic Invasion?

What more is at stake? For one, scholars are divided as to how to approach the Pauline texts in light of the subjective genitive interpretation. This doesn't seem to be the case with the traditional objective genitive approach. Therefore, it is relevant to mention at least this one example of such a disagreement.

This issue is currently an ongoing battle among highly touted theologians such as N. T. Wright, J. Louis Martyn, and Douglas Harink. All three support the subjective genitive interpretation of the *pistis Christou* passages of Paul. Yet, they differ on how to interpret Paul's presentation of his gospel. Edwin Chr. van Driel has written an insightful article giving a critique of all of these theologians' emphases on the gospel—salvation-historical (Wright) and apocalyptic readings (Martyn and Harink). Van Driel's article articulates the relevant problem:

> The theological issue at stake is the place that Christ has in Paul's narrative. On a salvation-historical reading, Christ is presented as the climax of an extended covenantal history of God and God's people. But if this is so, then the story of Jesus appears to be only a subplot in the story of Israel, a notion that seems inconsistent with what Beverly Roberts Gaventa calls "the singularity of the gospel." On an apocalyptic reading, Christ's coming is understood as God's apocalyptic invasion in this world. But then God's act in Christ seems to abrogate the previous salvific presence of God in and through Israel.[24]

Edwin van Driel's critique is that "they both [Wright and Martyn] conceive of Christ as accidental to the divine intent for creation, a notion

---

24. van Driel, *Climax of the Covenant*, 8.

that falls short of the robust Christology that Paul adheres to."[25] Before I offer van Driel's so-called solution to this issue, I will give an extended discussion on both positions.

First, I will take N. T. Wright's position of a salvation-historical account: Christ the climax of the covenant. Wright placed all of his writings in the context of what one might call "the story." He called it the "single continuous narrative" of Scripture which moved from Adam to Abraham to Israel reaching its climax in the Christ. Let's take a journey through that "story."

The Story

"The faithfulness of Jesus" is the short form for "the story," the story of God's choice of Israel. The purpose of the choice of Abraham was to reverse the curse of Adam upon the world. The story of Israel began with God's call to Abraham to leave his country, kindred, immediate family, and go to a land unseen and unknown (Gen 12:1). God promised Abraham that he would become a great nation by being blessed and having his name (reputation) become great. A command was given: "Be a blessing!" (Gen 12:2). Finally, more promises and then a prophecy: "I will bless those who bless you, and him who makes light of you, I will curse, and in you all the ethnic families of the earth shall be blessed" (Gen 12:3, my translation). From this calling a family (Gen 12–50) became a small nation, destined to be a "kingdom of priests" and "a holy nation," God's "most prized treasure" (Exod 19:5–6). Israel's failure to "be a blessing" to the nations did not deter God's sovereign plan of recovering a rebellious world and renewal of all creation.

If one might read Galatians backward,[26] Jesus was born "in the fullness of time" (Gal 4:4–7) to bring about that which Israel was unable to do because of her sin and rebellion—taking upon himself the "curse of the law" (Gal 3:13). By so doing the "blessing of Abraham came to the nations in Messiah Jesus, so that we might receive the promise of the Spirit through [Jesus'] faithfulness" (Gal 3:14, my translation). As Paul understood this, he wrote: "But I live, yet not I, indeed Messiah lives in me; but what now I live in flesh, I live by the faithfulness of the Son of God who loved me and handed himself over on my behalf" (Gal

---

25. van Driel, *Climax of the Covenant*, 8.
26. See Scot McKnight's unique book, *Reading Romans Backwards*.

2:20, my translation). At the beginning of this letter, Paul expressed the gospel in this way: the Lord Jesus the Messiah "gave himself for our sins to deliver us from the present evil age, according to the will of our God and Father" (Gal 1:4).

Jesus' loving act of going to a cross by the will of God in order to release not only the Jews but the whole world from the bondage of sin was capsulated in the one phrase "the faithfulness of Jesus the Messiah." Paul summarized all these thoughts at Gal 3:25-29: "But 'faithfulness' having come, we are no longer under a pedagogue; for you all are sons of God through the 'faithfulness' in Messiah Jesus. For as many of you as were immersed into Messiah, were clothed with Messiah; there is neither Jew nor Greek, neither slave nor free, no male and female, for you are all one in Messiah Jesus. And if you are Messiah's, then you are Abraham's seed, heirs according to promise" (my translation).

The story of Israel was always imperative in the telling of the gospel, and that is why the apostle Paul agonized over his people's intransigence, for they were "Israelites, and to them belong the adoption, the glory, the covenants, the giving of the law, the worship, and the promises. To them belong the patriarchs, and from their race, according to the flesh, is the Messiah who is God over all, blessed forever. Amen" (Rom 9:4-5, ESV, my change of "Christ" to "Messiah"). Without a proper understanding of Israel's story, one cannot appreciate and understand who Jesus the Messiah really is and what he accomplished while on this earth. The story must be told, over and over again, until it begins to sink in.

The story of the old covenant is what structures our understanding of the new covenant, both in comparison and contrast. We see this in the book of Hebrews, but also in every other New Testament book. Indeed, the way Paul put it: "the Jews were entrusted with the oracles of God. What if some were unfaithful? Does their faithlessness nullify the faithfulness of God? By no means!" (Rom 3:2b-4a). Thus, God's righteousness (covenant faithfulness) has been manifested through Jesus' faithfulness (Rom 3:21) and the old covenant Scriptures testified to it. We knew it all along but didn't understand. We must tell the old story again.[27] This, I think, is Wright's position on "the story," or according to the title of his first major book, "the climax of the covenant."

---

27. Much more could be said about "The Story," and it should be understood for a better understanding of the New Testament. This is the emphasis in N. T. Wright's first two volumes in his series: *The New Testament and the People of God* and *Jesus and the Victory of God*.

Van Driel's critique is that the way Wright tells the story is not adequate. He claims: "On Wright's narration, Christ is accidental to the 'single plan' of salvation. The very thing Christ does could have been accomplished by another agent—Israel; in fact, it should have been accomplished by Israel, and it would have been, had Israel not fallen into disobedience.... Jesus is really plan B."[28] I will look at van Driel's "solution" later, but now I move to Martyn's apocalyptic reading of Paul.

The Apocalyptic

J. Louis Martyn has advocated that Galatians is an apocalyptic presentation of the gospel. Many have missed this idea because of the traditional reading of the *pistis Christou* phrases as objective genitives. He argued that the traditional position forced Paul's theology to be a circular exchange—"this for that." This was what the "agitators" in the Galatian churches were advocating. They wanted the Galatian Christians to obey the "works/deeds of the law" such as circumcision in order to be accepted by God. Faith in Christ was necessary but not enough. In other words, the divine gift of salvation was God's response to something human beings do. Martyn argued against this. He wrote: "From the epistle's beginning to its end, Paul draws contrasts not between two human alternatives, such as works and faith, but rather between acts done by human beings and acts carried out by God (1:1; 6:15). According to Gal 2:15–16a, what is known about God's way of making things right is that a person is rectified not by observing the Law, but rather by the faith of Christ, that is to say, his faithful deed of dying on the cross in our behalf."[29]

Martyn contends, against most commentaries on Galatians, that Galatians contained a number of apocalyptic motifs throughout the letter. He listed and commented on the following: "The present evil age" (1:4), "the new creation" (6:15), "to free us" (5:1), "to liberate from slavery" (3:13), "to be under the power of" (4:5). He concluded: "In short, *the human tragedy is universal oppression, ubiquitous enslavement to the powers of the present evil age. And in Christ, God's deed is the cosmic act of liberation, deliverance from that slavery.*"[30] He described the gospel in this way: "God has elected to invade the realm of the wrong—'the present

---

28. van Driel, "Climax of the Covenant," 12.
29. Martyn, "Apocalyptic Gospel," 250.
30. Martyn, "Apocalyptic Gospel," 254.

evil age' (1:4)—by sending God's Son and the Spirit of the Son into it from outside it (4:4-6).... The gospel is not about human movement into blessedness (religion); it is about God's liberating invasion of the cosmos (theology)."[31] This redemptive movement was seen particularly in Gal 3:23-25 and 4:4-6. All of these texts were considered more in depth in his now influential commentary on Galatians.[32] I must add that Martyn's support of the subjective genitive is not dependent upon his apocalyptic approach to Paul in Galatians.

While Wright emphasized the "time" element in the gospel story, Martyn emphasized "space." "For him, the incarnation is not the apex of a long history, but the invasion of an occupied territory. The image that shapes Martyn's interpretation is that of a twice-invaded world."[33] It was first invaded by "sin," not necessarily personal but rather spiritual powers that have enslaved the world. To counter that, God has invaded the corrupt world by means of his Son, Jesus the Messiah, to set free those enslaved to sin. The apostle Paul called this "invasion" *apocalyptic* (Gal 1:12; 2:2). The end result of this approach is that the church, as the new creation, is "fundamentally cruciform. The bodily shape of the new creation ... is the church, and this church is 'cross-bearing.'"[34] From this approach one can see the development of Michael Gorman's concept of "the cruciform God."

Van Driel's major critique of Martyn is that his "apocalyptic reading" is also "Plan B," like Wright's. The incarnation of Jesus was dependent upon the sin that invaded the world, not the original plan, thus, "Plan B." Harink, who sides with Martyn, has been critical of Wright and accused him of "supersessionism," meaning that the church has replaced Israel. Harink's criticism of Wright is basically this: "Israel is not elected for its own sake, but for the sake of God's plan to save the world."[35] The question is: what is the functional understanding of Israel's election? Harink's critical study of Gen 12 and Isa 40-55 revealed to him, in contrast to Wright, that Abraham's role was as mediator to the nations, which was the purpose of his election, not the other way around. For Harink, Abraham does not operate as a "means and goal." According to van Driel: "Harink says only

---

31. Martyn, "Apocalyptic Gospel," 255.
32. See Martyn, *Galatians*.
33. van Driel, "Climax of the Covenant," 14.
34. van Driel, "Climax of the Covenant," 15.
35. van Driel, "Climax of the Covenant," 20.

this: "The apocalypse of Jesus Christ is the recapitulation and sustaining of God's electing of historical Israel."[36] Harink does not continue to explain this enigmatic statement. What is van Driel's proposal for a solution to his perceived problem with Wright, Martyn, and even Harink?

Edwin van Driel offered the proposal called "supralapsarian." He defined this term as "an understanding of the incarnation as not simply a response to human sin, but as motivated by considerations that go deeper than the need to deal with the sin problem."[37] Taking his cue from the two similar letters, Ephesians and Colossians, van Driel argued that these two letters in their teachings (whether Paul or not) offered three truths: First, Christ is "the firstborn of creation" and thus is not contingent on sin. In other words, Israel does not have to "fail" before Christ comes to redeem the world. Second, Christ's incarnation is a mystery (Eph 3:5, Col 1:26) hidden but now revealed so that all things are gathered up into Christ (Eph 1:9). This is apocalyptic language. Thus, "apocalyptic" and "salvific history" are compatible. Third, a new humanity is created from the division of Jews and gentiles (Eph 2:13–22), forming a new temple in which God dwells. Van Driel declared that this new humanity is not "a response to sin but the goal of creation."[38] Basically, van Driel tried to weave together the "apocalyptic event" and the "salvific history" and give them a whole different purpose than either Wright or Martyn—i.e., the "supralapsarian" (goal of creation) solution.

What do I make of this? Perhaps I have dug a hole and cannot climb out! However, I see a problem with van Driel's criticism of both Wright and Martyn. Neither is completely wrong in his analyses of the texts he considers. Van Driel too easily dismisses the "sin problem" and even the so-called purpose of God's call and vocation of Israel. I will end with Wright's own statement about van Driel's work:

> If I have understood Paul, he would have said that the one who was from all eternity "equal with God," the "image of the invisible God, the firstborn of all creation," would have appeared anyway "when the time had fully come," not then to redeem, but to rule gloriously over the completed creation. However, granted the sin of humankind and the consequent corruption and decay of creation, the creator God called Abraham and his family so that through them the problem could be dealt with, *so that he*

---

36. van Driel, "Climax of the Covenant," 21.
37. van Driel, "Climax of the Covenant," 23.
38. van Driel, "Climax of the Covenant," 24.

might himself deal with the problem by coming as Abraham's seed, coming in person as Israel's representative Messiah. And Paul's point throughout [Romans] chapters 9–11 is that this divine redeeming action, for which Israel's election was the necessary means, both in the original choice and in the outworking, down to the remnant, casts its light around it, so that the history of the redemption-bearing people is also redemptive even though it is the Messiah, not Israel, in whose flesh "sin is condemned" (8.3).[39]

Needless to say, I see no reason to deny any of the insights of the men above, including van Driel, though I disagree with van Driel dismissing the "sin problem." Perhaps none of us explain ourselves clearly and often enough. I see no problem with recognizing sin as a major reason for Abraham's calling nor for blessing the nations by eventually incorporating the nations into Israel by means of the Messiah. Even the apocalyptic nature of Jesus' incarnation, death, and resurrection, with the promise of a Second Coming, is legitimate.[40] In another context, I have stated clearly that Paul does not separate his concept of "justification by faith" (Rom 1–4) with "participation in Christ" (Rom 5–8), as some have done. It is good to sit back and look at the big picture. Sometimes what we accuse others of doing, we do ourselves. I am more in line with Wright's arguments than with Martyn's or even van Driel's critique.

7. The New Testament Use of Old Testament Language

It is obvious to any student of the Bible that the New Testament is constantly appealing to the Hebrew Bible (Old Testament) for support of its theological ideas. If I could live my life over again, I would spend more time studying the Septuagint (LXX) and its vocabulary that certainly influenced the authors of the New Testament. Most of the quotations in the New Testament come from some form of the Septuagint, the Greek translation of the Hebrew text. Granted, there probably were several versions of the Greek text as well as Aramaic targums. As complex as the

---

39. Wright, *Paul and the Faithfulness of God*, 2:1210-11.

40. Wright disagrees with Martyn's apocalyptic approach to Paul (in Galatians). See Wright, *History and Eschatology*, 134. Wright explained in that same context: "If, however, you say that 'apocalyptic' must mean 'vertical revelation from above with no horizontal connection', you rule out not only all the Jewish 'apocalyptic' texts which give the term such historical anchorage as it claims to possess. You rule out, also, the interpretative frameworks evoked by Jesus, Paul, the evangelists, and, not least, the book of Revelation itself, the ultimate 'apocalypse'" (*History and Eschatology*, 151).

study of the Septuagint can be, it is important to note that the Hebrew text is "behind" every idea in the Greek text. Therefore, it is imperative that when one studies a Greek word, especially in a quote from the Old Testament, we attempt to understand the Hebrew word behind the Greek word or words used in translation. This is especially true when we look at Romans and how Paul utilized the Septuagint. As Geoffrey Turner expressed it: "Part of the problem is that translations of the New Testament have not paid attention to the possible influence on Paul of the language of the Septuagint or the content of the Psalms."[41]

One of the most important words is δικαιοσύνη, dikaiosunē, "righteousness." Many have undertaken a study of this word in the Bible, and while there are differences of opinion about its use and meaning, there can be no doubt in my mind that the Hebrew word צְדָקָה, tsedaqah, is the word behind the Greek.[42] When one looks at this word in the Psalms and Isaiah, it is clearly God's righteousness we are talking about. The psalmist cried out: "For your name's sake, O LORD, preserve my life! In your righteousness bring my soul out of trouble!" (Ps 143:11).

"Righteousness" is associated with deliverance in the psalmist's case. At the beginning of the psalm other ideas are related to "righteousness": "In your faithfulness answer me, in your righteousness! Enter not into judgment with your servant, for no one living is righteous before you" (Ps 143:1c-2). The psalm parallels "faithfulness" with "righteousness" and acknowledges that no one is "righteous" before God. So, the psalmist (David?) appealed to God's mercy and grace by appealing to his faithfulness and righteousness to save or deliver him from his enemies. Clearly this is how the apostle Paul understood the passage as he alluded to Ps 143:2 at Rom 3:20. Isaiah often paralleled "righteousness" with "salvation/deliverance."

The following are two examples: "I bring near my righteousness; it is not far off, and my salvation will not delay" (Isa 46:13a) and "My righteousness draws near, my salvation has gone out . . . but my salvation will be forever, and my righteousness will never be dismayed" (Isa 51:5a, 6c). God's righteousness is a righteousness that seeks to save his people and his world. That is precisely what we find in Rom 3:21—the manifestation of God's righteousness to save all people through the faithfulness of

---

41. Turner, "Righteousness of God," 294.

42. Note that the Hebrew word for "righteousness" (*tsedaqah*) is paralleled by several other words, the most important being "justice" (*mishpat*). See B. Johnson's article on "*tsadaq*" in *TDOT* 243–64.

Conclusion

Jesus the Messiah, including the salvation of the cosmos (Rom 8:19–23). Turner concluded his study of Psalms and Isaiah in Romans: "I suggest that Paul used Psalms for his understanding of righteousness through faithfulness and that he used Isaiah for a scriptural justification for God's inclusion of the gentiles into the promises first delivered to Israel."[43]

Another very important word is אֱמוּנָה (*'emûnā*ʰ), which means "faithfulness, fidelity." I provided an excursus in chapter 2 to argue strongly for the messianic use of Hab 2:4b: "but the righteous shall live by his faith." The "his" could refer either to God's faithfulness or the righteous one's faithfulness. We discovered that the Septuagint translator misread the *waw* for a *yod*, and translated it μου, "my," in Greek. Somehow it was transposed to "the righteous (one)" to convey "my righteous one" (see Heb 10:38). Paul either left the μου out or used a different text without the μου. Whatever the case, we argued that Paul used it as a messianic text to say: "The righteous (One = Jesus) shall live [resurrection] by faithfulness [to the Father's will]." If *pistis* is understood in this way, then every use of *pistis* in Paul's letters at least should be reevaluated, especially the phrase *ek pisteōs*, which we considered a "catchphrase" for Jesus' faithfulness.

Tangential to these two words is the consistency of translation or lack of it in English translations. One example is Rev 19:11 where the "Divine Warrior" (Jesus) comes on a white horse (the *Parousia*) and he is called "Faithful and True." I have no problem with the word "Faithful" to describe Jesus at his Second Coming. However, the very same phrase is found in Rev 21:5 and 22:6 and is translated differently: "these words are trustworthy and true." Why not translate the Rev 19:11 passage the same way: "Trustworthy and True"? Beale's comment is appropriate here: "Christ has promised to judge the wicked in order to vindicate his name and his followers, and he will be 'faithful and true' in fulfilling this promise. This is confirmed by the use of the same phrase, though in the plural, in 21:5 and 22:6. There πιστοὶ καὶ ἀληθινοί refers not merely to the Apocalypse's promises as 'valid and trustworthy' but more precisely to the sure fulfillment of the prophecies of the new creation (cf. 21:5b with 21:1–5a) and of the new Jerusalem (cf. 22:6 with 21:9—22:5)."[44] I would opt for "trustworthy and true" in all three passages.

The two words of "righteousness" and "faith/faithfulness" illustrate the need for scholars to take seriously the Old Testament use of words

---

43. Turner, "Righteousness of God," 301.

44. Beale, *Revelation*, 950. Beale indicated that John is alluding to this Greek phrase found only in 3 Macc 2:11, referring to God.

and their parallels and how that understanding feeds into the New Testament—used very similarly. Many years ago, while I was in graduate school, the University of Chicago was proposing a new translation of the Bible that would do just that, take seriously how the original text used literary devices and words to communicate its message. Can an English version reflect such usage? The project never received the funds necessary to get the job done. I was excited about the project but disappointed it never got off the ground. It is still needed. I contend that the study of the *pistis Christou* phrases in Paul's traditional letters and the *pistis* word group throughout the New Testament encourages us that we still need institutions and financiers that could finance such a project.

8. Bible Translations, Commentaries, and Language Tools

Not until there are English versions of the Bible that place the translation of the subjective genitive in the text before the reader, rather than simply as a footnote (see NRSV), will the public come to understand the text in that light. As far as I know, only the NET Bible and the CEB (Common English Bible) do so. Single author translations (Wright and Stern) are not often read or used, even though they may translate with the subjective genitive understanding as these two do.

Also, Greek grammars and dictionaries should give more space and discussion to this possible interpretation. Wallace's *Greek Grammar Beyond the Basics* is an exception to the rule. Commentaries, too, ought to be more consistent in this matter. As we have noted earlier, major commentaries on Romans use the traditional objective genitive interpretation, while many commentaries on Galatians use the subjective genitive. This is not consistent and is confusing to the uninitiated student. Most of the Hebrew and Greek tools used by students of the original texts are old editions and do not reflect present-day scholarship on the subjective/objective genitive debate. Most of these tools need serious revisions.

9. No "Cheap Faith"!

Those who hold tenaciously to the formula "justification by faith" need not fear the subjective genitive interpretation, for clearly God is seeking the "obedience of faith," however we understand that phrase, from each one of us.[45] The human response to the gospel can only be "by faith." I must add that my approach would emphasize that "faith" must be understood as "faithfulness" in the concept of a "long obedience." Indeed, when we confess "Jesus is Lord," we are expressing our allegiance to a King, one who rules the universe. That is no small commitment. Bonhoeffer knew this during the Nazi reign in Germany with his *The Cost of Discipleship* and "cheap grace."[46] Bonhoeffer defined "cheap grace" in the following way: "Cheap grace is the preaching of forgiveness without requiring repentance, baptism without church discipline, Communion without confession, absolution without personal confession. Cheap grace is grace without discipleship, grace without the cross, grace without Jesus Christ, living and incarnate."[47] And he paid for that costly discipleship with his life just before the war ended. Indeed, Bonhoeffer understood this commitment when he wrote: "When Christ calls a man, he bids him come and die."[48] It is a *martyr* faith—the willingness to die for the faith.

Modern day scholars are more and more understanding that biblical faith must be robust and obedient. They understand that Paul's phrase "the obedience of faith" (Rom 1:5; 16:26) probably means "a faith that obeys." Michael Bird has attempted to reconcile scholars on both ends of the spectrum: from the "justification by faith" (Reformation theology) to "participation in Christ" (New Perspective), bringing the two ideas together. I have said before that Rom 1–4 (justification by faith) should not be separated from Rom 5–8 (participation in Christ). Bird wrote:

> Thus, works are christocentricized by Paul as Jesus Christ is both the object of faith and, via the Spirit, the author of faithfulness. Works as christologically conceived, pneumatically empowered, and divinely endowed are necessary for salvation in so far as they reveal the character of authentic faith expressed in the form of obedience, love, faithfulness, righteousness and holiness.[49]

I would say there is no "cheap faith." In John's Gospel we learned that this was precisely what Jesus encountered on many occasions when those who exhibited faith, in the end had no faith at all. As Seglenieks recounted concerning his study of the Gospel of John: "In four key episodes, we

---

45. See Wright, *History and Eschatology*, 140.
46. See Bonhoeffer, *Cost of Discipleship*, 43–56.
47. Bonhoeffer, *Cost of Discipleship*, 44–45.
48. Bonhoeffer, *Cost of Discipleship*, 89.
49. Bird, *Saving Righteousness of God*, 178.

are presented with the believers whom Jesus does not trust (2:23–25), the disciples who no longer follow (6:60–66), those who apparently believe yet call Jesus demon-possessed (8:30–48), and the 'branches' who are in Jesus, but cast out (15:1–6)."[50] Jesus is always looking for genuine faith—a faithfulness to the end. To quote Bonhoeffer again: "For faith is only real when there is obedience, never without it, and faith only becomes faith in the act of obedience."[51]

The New Testament, as we have seen, confirms this truth:

- James 2:17: "So also faith by itself, if it does not have works, is dead."
- 1 Peter 1:7: "So that the tested genuineness of your faith—more precious than gold that perishes though it is tested by fire—may be found to result in praise and glory and honor at the revelation of Jesus Christ."
- 2 Peter 1:5–7: "For this very reason, make every effort to supplement your faith with virtue, and virtue with knowledge, and knowledge with self-control, and self-control with steadfastness, and steadfastness with godliness, and godliness with brotherly affection, and brotherly affection with love."
- Hebrews 12:2: "Looking away to Jesus, the trailblazer and completer of faithfulness, who in spite of the joy set before him, endured the cross, having despised the shame, and is seated at the right hand of the throne of God" (my translation).
- Romans 3:25a: "Whom God presented as a sacrifice of atonement through [Jesus'] faithfulness by [at the cost of] his blood" (my translation).
- Galatians 2:20: "I live, but yet not I, indeed Messiah lives in me. But what I live in flesh, I live by the faithfulness of the Son of God who loved me and gave up himself on behalf of me" (my translation).
- 1 John 3:10: "By this it is evident who are the children of God, and who are the children of the devil: whoever does not practice righteousness is not of God, nor is the one who does not love his brother."
- Jude 3b: "I found it necessary to write appealing to you to contend for the faith that was once for all delivered to the saints."

---

50. Seglenieks, "Untrustworthy Believers," 56.
51. Bonhoeffer, *Cost of Discipleship*, 64.

- Revelation 11:7–8: "And when they have finished their testimony, the beast that rises from the bottomless pit will make war on them and conquer them and kill them, and their dead bodies will lie in the street of the great city that symbolically is called Sodom and Egypt, where their Lord was crucified."

There is no "cheap faith." Revelation, the last book of the New Testament, insisted that the church must be a "martyr church." The idea is expressed at the center of the apocalyptic book of prophesy: "And they have conquered him by the blood of the Lamb and by the word of their testimony, for they loved not their lives even unto death" (Rev 12:11). Do Christians live by this commitment today? Hardly. But there are encouraging signs.

There are scholars who try to recapture such an attitude. Matthew Bates published a recent book entitled *Salvation by Allegiance Alone*. Bates has been appropriately criticized for his use of "allegiance" for "faith," but his overall idea is correct: Christians who confess Jesus to be their Lord make a commitment to the King of the universe. Allegiance to the King is what counts. I suggest the more biblical term to use is "faithfulness." Also, Gorman says the same thing with his use of a new vocabulary within his books: *Cruciformity*, *Apostle of the Crucified Lord*, and *Inhabiting the Cruciform God*. Whatever vocabulary we use, it is all referring to God's faithfulness, Jesus' faithfulness, and our responding faithfulness—all motivated by love! *See the epigraph.*

10. The Expansive Nature of "the Faithfulness of Jesus the Messiah"

When we began this journey with a study of Romans and Galatians, it was clear that "the faithfulness of Jesus" was a faithfulness to the Father's will by going to a cross and becoming God's means of atoning for the world's sins (see Rom 3:21–26). This fact was highlighted in Rom 5:19: "For as by the one man's disobedience the many were made sinners, so by the *one man's obedience* the many will be made righteous" (my emphasis). All who respond to this faithfulness will become faithful themselves, thus an "obedient faith." God is just and he justifies those who live "out of Jesus' faithfulness" (Rom 3:26). I think this is what Paul meant when he wrote in Gal 2:20b: "And the life I now live in the flesh I live by the faithfulness of the Son of God, who loved me and gave himself for me" (my change of the ESV to a subjective genitive interpretation). Paul concluded: "I do not nullify the grace of God, for if righteousness were through the law, then Christ died for no purpose" (Gal 2:21). To make the point even stronger, Paul wrote in hymn-like fashion (if it is Paul's original wording): "And being found in human form, he humbled himself by becoming obedient to the point of death, even death on a cross" (Phil 2:8). In other words, righteousness came through the death of Jesus on the cross. For Paul's *pistis Christou* phrases, this is the primary meaning.

However, we were reminded by Shuji Ota that "the faithfulness of the Son of God" was also *toward humanity*.[52] I agreed with this statement, for in several places where we translated the *pistis Christou* phrases as subjective genitives there was also expressed the purpose of that faithfulness—"for all who believe" (see Rom 3:22; Gal 2:16; 3:22). Jesus' faithfulness was not only directed toward the Father's will but also toward humanity. This thought is clearly established in the most well-known passage of Scripture—John 3:16: "For in this manner God loved the world so that he gave the only-begotten Son in order that all who believe in him may not perish but have eternal life" (my translation).

In the Gospels we found the human response to "the faithfulness of Jesus" expanded even more, particularly in John's Gospel. Marianne Thompson summarized her findings in John's Gospel in six statements that I will recount in brief form:

1. Faith entails discernment, both about the nature of Jesus' work and about the kind of God to whom faith is directed.

2. Faith has a corporate or communal dimension. . . . If faith denotes the response of the people of God, love denotes their response to each other.

3. Faith entails a commitment to life in the midst of death, to love in the midst of hate, to truth in the midst of error, to God in the midst of the world.

4. Faith is essentially gratitude, gratitude to God for grace, mercy, healing, wholeness; gratitude for life itself.

5. Because God is the source and destiny of life, faith is faithfulness in trusting God, for God was before all human life and always lives . . . , for it [life] comes through the Logos who was in the beginning with God, and has life from the Father himself. To such a God corresponds a faith which perseveres.

---

52. Ota, "Holistic *Pistis* and Abraham's Faith," 3.

6. Faith is faith in God, mediated through the person of Jesus ... "In him was life."[53]

The book of Hebrews expanded the concept of "the faithfulness of Jesus the Messiah" beyond all other New Testament books. Jesus came to earth as a real human being, sharing in our "flesh and blood" (Heb 2:14). This reality allowed Jesus to become "a merciful and faithful high priest in the service of God" (Heb 2:17). Not only that, but as high priest, he continues to function as one who helps believers "who are being tempted" (Heb 2:18). Jesus' priesthood is "after the order of Melchizedek" (Heb 5:6, 10). His sinless life (Heb 4:15; 7:26) was offered as a sacrifice for the sins of humanity (Heb 9:26, 28; 10:12). As a consequence, we can "draw near with a true heart in full assurance of faith, with our hearts sprinkled clean from an evil conscience and our bodies washed with pure water . . . for he who promised is faithful" (Heb 10:22, 23b). Thus, just as many under the old covenant exhibited faithfulness to God in spite of dire circumstances, even death (Heb 11:32–38), so now we are exhorted to look to Jesus who trailblazed the path of faithfulness to its completion (Heb 12:2). We must suffer with him if need be (Heb 12:3–11). Hence, believers continually have a high priest who intercedes on their behalf. Jesus' faithfulness continues to the present for all who believe.

The book of Revelation emphasized not only a "slain Lamb" (Rev 5:6) who is Lord over history, but also one who returns in victory at his *Parousia* (Second Coming), called "Faithful [Trustworthy] and True," with a name on his robe and thigh: "King of kings and Lord of lords" (Rev 19:11, 16).

Jesus' faithfulness extends from his birth, life and ministry, death, burial, resurrection, and exaltation to God's right hand as high priest to his ultimate return and establishment of "the new heavens and new earth." The resurrection will reveal the faithful Messiah. Paul wrote: "Christ the firstfruits, then at his coming those who belong to Christ. Then comes the end, when he delivers the kingdom to God the Father after destroying every rule and authority and power. . . . When all things are subjected to him, then the Son himself will also be subjected to him who put all things in subjection under him, that God may be all in all" (1 Cor 15:23–24, 28).

---

53. Thompson, "Signs and Faith," 107–8.

A Final Appeal

The major theme of the New Testament is "the faithfulness of Jesus the Messiah." It is the gospel emphasis. All the Gospels present Jesus' life in a very limited time frame: his birth (Mark doesn't, John only theologically), as a twelve-year-old in Jerusalem (only Luke 2:41–52), and his ministry (Synoptics, no time frame; John, three years). All the Gospels present the last week of Jesus' ministry in detail—from his triumphal entry to his crucifixion and resurrection (Mark 11–16; Matt 21–28; Luke 19–24; and John 12–21). This tells me that the Gospel writers pointed toward that important week where Jesus fulfilled all prophecies about himself from the Hebrew Scriptures concerning his messianic mission: his death and resurrection (see Mark 8:31; 9:31; and 10:33–34). It was all concerned about the faithfulness of Jesus.

The book of Acts was a continuation of "all that Jesus began to do and teach" through the Holy Spirit who would come upon the disciples on the Day of Pentecost (Acts 1–2). In the middle of persecution of the new Jewish messianic community, the "glorified" Jesus appeared to Saul and commissioned him to preach also to gentiles (Acts 9). From that point on, Paul never quit preaching the faithful Jesus as Son of God and Messiah and all his letters reflected it.

The book of Hebrews was clearly about Jesus' faithfulness as a Son over God's house (Heb 3:2). He blazed the trail of faithfulness (Heb 12:1–2) and became our "merciful and faithful high priest" (Heb 2:17). First Peter 1:2, in a trinitarian formula, opens with what has been almost always mistranslated. Jesus is described as "toward *obedience* and sprinkling of the blood of Jesus the Messiah" (my translation and emphasis). Peter describes Jesus' obedience and faithfulness in some detail at 1 Pet 2:21–25 and encourages all believers to "follow in his steps" (2:21b). Second Peter 1:4 encourages us to "become partakers of the divine nature." John emphasizes that Jesus is "faithful and just to forgive our sins," if we confess our sins on a continual basis (1 John 1:9).

Finally, the book of Revelation was clearly about the faithfulness of Jesus as the "slain Lamb" who is worthy to open the seals and reveal what is to come (Rev 5:9–12). In apocalyptic terms Jesus is described at his Second Coming as "faithful (trustworthy) and true" (Rev 19:11). From beginning to end, the New Testament proclaimed from many different angles that Jesus is the faithful Messiah who continues to be the light that enlightens our way as we enter the "New Jerusalem" (Rev 21:23).

A journal article was published several years ago (2012), while still relevant to this discussion. It covered many of the same texts I have used throughout this book about the *pistis Christou* phrases, yet the article is opposite my position![54] Sincere and honest scholars can certainly disagree as evidenced throughout the years of this debate. Hopefully we can humbly agree to disagree on such matters and yet hold to "the faithfulness of Jesus the Messiah." God is faithful and Jesus is faithful. Will he find us faithful?

---

54. Eurell, "Faith."

Glossary

alpha privative—an alpha (Greek letter, α) placed on the front of a word to negate its meaning. Example: *apistis*, meaning "unbelief."

anthropological—having to do with human beings in all their physical, cultural, social, and spiritual relationships.

apocalypse/apocalyptic—a prophetic revelation; a divine invasion in human history in a cataclysmic event such as the coming of Christ and his Second Coming, the end of the world events.

Arminian—a term derived from the doctrines of Jacobus Arminius who stressed human free will as opposed to Calvinistic predestination.

beatific vision—in reference to Jesus, having a constant vision of God, thus living by sight, not by faith, usually a Catholic position.

bifid—description of a Bible book that is overtly divided into two equal halves. Example: in the OT, Daniel 1–6 and 7–12; Isaiah 1–39 and 40–66 (some divide 1–33 and 34–66). In the NT, Eph 1–3 and 4–6; Revelation 1–11 and 12–22.

Calvinist—a term derived from the doctrines of Calvin concerning the predestination of the elect to salvation.

catch-phrase—a phrase that is meant to catch the attention of the reader in terms of an original meaning. It becomes "shorthand" as a result for a broader meaning. Example: *Ek pisteōs*, meaning "from/out of Jesus' faithfulness."

chiasm/chiastic—a rhetorical literary device creating two or more parallel ideas or phrases having an inversion in the middle, thus in the form of the Greek letter *chi* (χ). Example: A-B-B1-A1 or A-B-C-B1-A1.

christological—having to do with Jesus the Christ (Messiah) exclusively.

diatribe/diatribal—a form of argumentation using dialogue and question and answer (from the Socratic philosophical schools). The apostle Paul used a form of this method in his letters. Examples: 1 Cor 6:12–20; 15:29–41; and Gal 3:1–9, 19–22. Diatribe is used heavily in Romans.

dictum—a statement or saying of fact, opinion, or principle of one's judgment.

efficacy—power to produce intended results.

epexegetical—an additional explanation by use of a word or phrase. Often in the New Testament the conjunction *kai* ("and") introduces such a phrase, meaning "that is."

eschatology—having to do with the last days: Second Coming of Christ, Judgment Day, heaven, and hell. Some would include a millennial reign of Christ in the last days. Others think we are living in the last days now and the millennial reign is the church age.

excursus—a lengthy discussion of some point in a literary work, a digression but related point.

exhortation—in New Testament letters a plea and urging earnestly for moral behavior based on the teachings of Jesus and the apostles. Example: Romans 12:1.

exposition—the explaining of facts, ideas, and arguments in support of a proposition.

firstfruit—the first produce of the season; in the Bible the firstfruit of anything—man, beast, or soil—belonged to God as Creator of everything. Thus, the firstfruit was holy. Christ, in his resurrection, is a firstfruit for all who will be resurrected at his Second Coming.

gnostic Christ—a view of Christ that denies his humanity as real. He only "seemed" (docetic) to be human. Docetism is another form of Gnosticism which taught that Jesus only "seemed" to be human. They taught that all matter is evil, created by an evil god, and only spirit is good.

Granville Sharp rule—a Greek grammar rule which says that when two nouns or an equivalent of the same case (only nouns that are personal, singular, and non-proper) are connected by *kai* ("and") and the article precedes only the first, the latter noun always refers to the same person as the first. Examples: Heb 3:1—"*the* apostle *and* high priest of our confession." Also, see Eph 6:21; Heb 12:2; and Rev 1:9.

gnōsis—the Greek word for "knowledge." This word was applied to a heretical sect called "Gnostics" because they declared man's problem was not sin but lack of knowledge. With the right knowledge one could attain to God.

imputed righteousness—a teaching that states on the basis of faith God declares the sinner to be righteous in a legal transaction (imputed). It is a gift and faith is the means of obtaining the gift.

inclusion/*inclusio*—in ancient literary documents authors often used words, phrases, or even ideas to begin and close a section of text to indicate what moderns would call a paragraph or section of text. However, this device could be used for a brief sentence as well as many. Examples: Rom 5:1–5 with 8:20–25 ("hope") and Heb 4:12–13 (*logos*).

intercalation—a Markan literary technique and characteristic where the gospel story wraps a story within a story to give a fuller message. Example: Mark 5:21–43 (the healing of an older woman in the midst of the healing of Jairus' daughter).

messianic/messianically—referring to anything connected to the Jewish Messiah (Anointed One), Jesus of Nazareth.

motif—an idea, feature, or subject that runs through a piece of literature. Examples: "coats" and "weeping" in Joseph's story (Gen 37–50) and "drawing near to God" in the book of Hebrews.

nominalization—a noun derived from an adjective rather than a verb. Example: "righteousness" (*dikaiosune* derived from *dikaios*).

objective genitive—a Greek grammatical form (genitive) which becomes the object of the verbal action of the noun before it. Example: Rom 3:22—"Faith in Jesus Christ," i.e., believing in Jesus Christ.

parody—the imitation of some other figure, sometimes in grotesque ways. Example: The Trinity (Father, Son, Spirit) is parodied in Revelation by the red dragon and two beasts.

Parousia—a Greek word referring to the Second Coming of Christ, his "Presence" or "Appearance."

perfect tense—in Greek this grammatical term means completed action with results continuing to the present.

pericope—a passage, usually short, from a written text.

pistis—the Greek word for "faith," "faithfulness," or "trust," "trustworthiness." Other meanings depend on context. Example: 2 Tim 4:7, "pledge."

probatio—a Latin word to express the exposition and arguments following a proposition.

propitiation—signifies the removal of God's wrath against sinful men by means of a sacrifice. Jesus was the perfect sacrifice that atoned for the sins of the world. The motivation for this sacrifice was God's love for the world (John 3:16). Many consider this a "pagan" idea and prefer the term "expiation" where the removal of sin is emphasized, not the removal of God's personal wrath.

propositio—a Latin word to express the proposition for an entire passage or text. Example: Gal 2:15–21.

pseudonymity—a writing under a fictitious name.

recapitulation—a literary device that restates the same idea in slightly different ways. Example: the seven seals, seven trumpets, and seven bowls in Revelation. Revelation 12–14 is also part of the recapitulation except that it does not use the symbolism of the number seven. Intensification is also communicated by increased percentages of destruction.

"strong" in faith—Christians in Rome who considered all foods and days alike, nothing was unclean in terms of their freedom in Christ. The apostle Paul considered himself in this category.

Septuagint—the Greek translation of the Hebrew Scriptures, symbolized by the number LXX, supposedly seventy-two Jewish scholars did the translation in Alexandria, Egypt (c. 250 BC).

subjective genitive—a Greek grammatical form (genitive) which becomes the subject of the verbal action of the noun before it. Example: Rom 3:22—"the faith[fulness] of Jesus Christ," i.e., Jesus Christ's faith (believing) or faithfulness.

Suetonius—a Roman biographer and historian who recounted the "Lives of the Caesars" in a lively gossipy way. He was born at the end of the Julian-Claudian Dynasty c. AD 69 and lived to c. AD 140. His full name was Gaius Suetonius Tranquillus.

supersessionism—a theological conclusion that the church has superseded Israel as the true people of God. Often, appeal is made to Paul's statement in Gal 6:16: "the Israel of God."

supralapsarian—"an understanding of the incarnation as not simply a response to human sin, but as motivated by considerations that go deeper than the need to deal with the sin problem."[1] The word comes from *supra*, "before," and *lapsus*, "fall." This position is against the infralapsarian Christology of Wright and Martyn, meaning the incarnation is contingent upon sin. *Infra* means "after."

theodicy—having to do with the justice of God in an evil world or seeking to explain how the existence of evil in the world can be reconciled with the justice and goodness of God.

theosis—Gorman's term for justification. He defined this term himself by writing: "For Paul holiness is redefined as participation in and conformity to the cruciform character of the triune God, Father, Son, and Spirit. Holiness is not a supplement to justification but the actualization of justification, and may be more appropriately termed theosis."[2] He also called it "theoformity."

"weak" in faith—Christians in Rome whose consciences did not allow them to eat certain meats, thus they ate only vegetables to perhaps avoid unclean food. They also elevated certain days above others, probably the sabbath day and/or some of the Jewish festival days.

"works of the law"—the deeds expected of the Jews under the law, obeying the commandments in general. In some contexts, it could mean the deeds that marked the Jews from their gentile neighbors, such as circumcision, diet, and sabbath-keeping.

---

1. Van Driel, "Climax of the Covenant vs Apocalyptic Invasion," 22.
2. Gorman, *Inhabiting the Cruciform God*, 2.

Bibliography

Achtemeier, Paul J. "Romans 3:1–8: Structure and Argument." *Anglican Theological Review* 11 (1990) 77–87.
Agnew, Francis H. "1 Peter 1:2—An Alternative Translation." *Catholic Biblical Quarterly* 45 (1983) 68–73.
Allan, J. A. "The 'in Christ' Formula in the Pastoral Epistles." *New Testament Studies* 10 (1963) 115–21.
Aune, David E., ed. *Rereading Paul Together: Protestant and Catholic Perspectives on Justification.* Grand Rapids: Baker, 2006.
Baird, William. "Abraham in the New Testament: Tradition and the New Identity." *Interpretation* 42.4 (1988) 367–79.
Bandstra, A. J. "Christ and Our Salvation in Galatians." *Calvin Theological Journal* 2 (1967) 57–60.
Barnes, J. Matthew. "Philippians 3.2–11 and the New Perspective on Paul." PhD diss., Fuller Theological Seminary, Center for Advanced Theological Study, ProQuest Dissertation Publication, 2017.
Barnett, Paul. *The Second Epistle to the Corinthians.* The New International Commentary on the New Testament. Grand Rapids: Eerdmans, 1997.
Barr, James. *The Semantics of Biblical Language.* London: Oxford University Press, 1961.
Barth, Karl. *The Epistle to the Romans.* Translated by Edwyn C. Hoskyns. New York: Oxford University Press, 1933.
Barth, Markus. *Ephesians 1–3.* The Anchor Bible 34. New York: Doubleday, 1974.
———. *Ephesians 4–6.* The Anchor Bible 34A. New York: Doubleday, 1974.
———. "The Faith of the Messiah." *Heydrop Journal* 10 (1969) 363–70.
———. "Justification from Text to Sermon on Galatians 2:11–21." *Interpretation* 22.2 (1968) 147–57.
———. *Justification: Pauline Texts Interpreted in the Light of the Old and New Testaments.* Translated by A. M. Woodruff, III. Grand Rapids: Eerdmans, 1971.
———. "The Kerygma of Galatians." *Interpretation* 21.2 (1967) 131–46.
———. Review of *Galatians in Greek*, by J. Bligh. *Catholic Biblical Quarterly* 30 (1968) 76–79.
Bartsch, Hans-Werner. "The Concept of Faith in Paul's Letter to the Romans." *Biblical Research* 13 (1968) 41–53.
Bassler, Jouette M. "Divine Impartiality in Paul's Letter to the Romans." *Novum Testamentum* 26 (1984) 43–58.
———. *Divine Impartiality: Paul and a Theological Axiom.* SBL Dissertation Series 59. Edited by William Baird. Atlanta: Scholars, 1982.

Bauckham, Richard. *God Crucified: Monotheism and Christology in the New Testament.* Grand Rapids: Eerdmans, 1999.

———. *The Theology of the Book of Revelation.* Cambridge: Cambridge University Press, 1993.

Beale, Gregory K. *The Book of Revelation.* The New International Greek Testament Commentary. Grand Rapids: Eerdmans, 1999.

Beasley-Murray, George R. *John.* Word Biblical Commentary 36. Waco: Word, 1987.

Beker, J. C. "The Faithfulness of God and the Priority of Israel in Paul's Letter to the Romans." *Harvard Theological Review* 79 (1986) 10–16.

Bird, Michael. "Incorporated Righteousness: A Response to Recent Evangelical Discussion Concerning the Imputation of Christ's Righteousness in Justification." *Journal of Evangelical Theological Society* 47.2 (2004) 253–75.

———. "Justification as Forensic Declaration and Covenant Membership: A *Via Media* between Reformed and Revisionist Readings of Paul." *Tyndale Bulletin* 57.1 (2006) 109–30.

———. *The Saving Righteousness of God: Studies on Paul, Justification, and the New Perspective.* Biblical Monographs. Eugene, OR: Wipf & Stock, 2007.

Bird, Michael F., and Michael R. Whitenton. "The Faithfulness of Jesus Christ in Hippolytus's *De Christo et Antichristo*: Overlooked Patristic Evidence in the Πίστις Χριστοῦ Debate." *New Testament Studies* 55 (2009) 552–62.

Bird, Michael F., and Preston M. Sprinkle, eds. *The Faith of Jesus Christ: Exegetical, Biblical, and Theological Studies.* Milton Keynes, UK: Paternoster, 2009.

Blackman, Cyril. "Romans 3.26b: A Question of Translation." *Journal of Biblical Literature* 87.2 (1968) 203–4.

Blaising, Craig A. "Gethsemane: A Prayer of Faith." *Journal of Evangelical Theological Society* 22.4 (1979) 333–43.

Bligh, John. "Did Jesus Live by Faith?" *Heydrop Journal* 9 (1968) 414–19.

———. *Galatians: A Discussion of St. Paul's Epistle.* London: St. Paul, 1969.

———. *Galatians in Greek.* Detroit: University of Detroit Press, 1966.

Blomberg, Craig L. *The Historical Reliability of John's Gospel: Issues and Commentary.* Downers Grove: InterVarsity, 2001.

Bock, Darrel L. *A Theology of Luke and Acts: God's Promised Program, Realized for All Nations.* Biblical Theology of the New Testament, gen. ed. Andreas J. Köstenberger. Grand Rapids: Zondervan, 2012.

Bockmuehl, Markus. *The Epistle to the Philippians.* Black's New Testament Commentary. Peabody: Hendrickson, 1998.

Boers, Hendrikus. *The Justification of the Gentiles: Paul's Letters to the Galatians and Romans.* Peabody: Hendrickson, 1994.

———. "Polysemy in Paul's use of Christological Expressions." In *The Future of Christology,* edited by A. Malherbe and W. Meeks, 91–108. Philadelphia: Fortress, 1993.

Bolt, Peter G. "The Faith of Jesus Christ in the Synoptic Gospels and Acts." In *The Faith of Jesus Christ: Exegetical, Biblical, and Theological Studies,* edited by Michael F. Bird and Preston M. Sprinkle, 209–22. Milton Keynes, UK: Paternoster, 2009.

Bonhoeffer, Dietrich, *The Cost of Discipleship.* New York: Simon & Schuster, 1959. (First published 1937, copyright 1959 by SCM.)

Braaten, Carl E, and Robert W. Jenson, eds. *Union with Christ: The New Finnish Interpretation of Luther.* Grand Rapids: Eerdmans, 1998.

Broneer, Oscar. "The Apostle Paul and the Isthmian Games." In *The Biblical Archaeologist Reader*, 2, edited by David Noel Freedman and Edward F. Campbell, Jr., 393–420. Cambridge: Cambridge University Press, 1964.

Brownlee, William H. "Messianic Motifs of Qumran and the New Testament." *New Testament Studies* 3 (1956–57) 195–210.

———. "The Placarded Revelation of Habakkuk." *Journal of Biblical Literature* 82.3 (1963) 319–25.

Buber, Martin. *Two Types of Faith*. Translated by N. P. Goldhawk. London: Routledge & Kegan Paul, 1951.

Burk, Denny. "The Righteousness of God (*Dikaiosunē Theou*) and Verbal Genitives: A Grammatical Clarification." *Journal for the Study of the New Testament* 34.4 (2012) 346–60.

Butterworth, Robert. "Bishop Robinson and Christology." *Religious Studies* 11.1 (1975) 73–85.

Byrne, Brendan. "Christ's Pre-existence in Pauline Soteriology." *Theological Studies* 58.2 (1997) 308–30.

———. "Interpreting Romans Theologically in a Post-'New Perspective' Perspective." *Harvard Theological Review* 94.3 (2001) 227–41.

———. "Living Out the Righteousness of God: The Contribution of Rom 6:1—8:13 to an Understanding of Paul's Ethical Presuppositions." *Catholic Biblical Quarterly* 43 (1981) 557–81.

———. *Reckoning with Romans*. Wilmington: Michael Glazier, 1986.

———. *Romans*. Sacra Pagina 6. Collegeville: Liturgical, 1996.

Byrskog, S. "Epistolography, Rhetoric and Letter Prescript: Romans 1.1–7 as a Test Case." *Journal for the Study of the New Testament* 65 (1997) 27–46.

Cairns, D. S. "The Faith of Jesus." In *The Faith That Rebels: A Re-examination of The Miracles of Jesus*, 200–223. New York: Richard R. Smith, Inc., 1930.

Calhoun, Robert Matthew. "John Chrysostom on ΕΚ ΠΙΣΤΕΩΣ ΕΙΣ ΠΙΣΤΙΝ in Rom. 1:17: A Reply to Charles L. Quarles." *Novum Testamentum* 48 (2006) 131–46.

Campbell, Douglas A. "2 Corinthians 4:13: Evidence in Paul That Christ Believes." *Journal of Biblical Literature* 128.2 (2009) 337–56.

———. "The Atonement in Paul." *The Anvil* 11 (1994) 237–50.

———. "An Attempt to be Understood: A Response to the Concerns of Matlock and Macaskill with *The Deliverance of God*." *Journal for the Study of the New Testament* 34 (2011) 162–208.

———. "The Crisis of Faith in Modern New Testament Scholarship." In *Religious Studies—Essays in Honour of Albert C. Moore*, edited by M. Andrew et al., 163–74. Dunedin: University of Otago, 1991.

———. *The Deliverance of God: An Apocalyptic Rereading of Justification in Paul*. Grand Rapids: Eerdmans, 2009.

———. "Determining the Gospel through Rhetorical Analysis in Paul's Letter to the Roman Christians." In *Gospel in Paul: Studies on Corinthians, Galatians and Romans for Richard N. Longenecker*, edited by G. P. Richardson and L. Ann Jervis, 327–49. Sheffield: JSOT, 1994.

———. "The ΔΙΑΘΗΚΗ from Durham: Prof. Dunn's *The Theology of Paul the Apostle*." *Journal for the Study of the New Testament* 72 (1998) 91–111.

———. "An Evangelical Paul: A Response to Francis Watson's *Paul and the Hermeneutics of Faith*." *Journal for the Study of the New Testament* 28.3 (2006) 337–51.

———. "The Faithfulness of Jesus Christ in Romans 3:22." In *The Faith of Jesus Christ: Exegetical, Biblical, and Theological Studies*, edited by Michael F. Bird and Preston M. Sprinkle, 57–71. Milton Keynes, UK: Paternoster, 2009.

———. "False Presuppositions in the ΠΙΣΤΙΣ ΧΡΙΣΤΟΥ Debate: A Response to Brian Dodd." *Journal of Biblical Literature* 116 (1997) 713–19.

———. "Is Tom Right? An Extended Review of N. T. Wright's Justification: God's Plan and Paul's Vision." *Scottish Journal of Theology* 65.3 (2012) 323–45.

———. "The Meaning of ΠΙΣΤΙΣ and ΝΟΜΟΣ in Paul: A Linguistic and Structural Perspective." *Journal of Biblical Literature* 111.1 (1992) 91–103.

———. "Participation and Faith in Paul." In *"In Christ" in Paul: Exploration in Paul's Theology of Union and Participation*, edited by Michael J. Thate et al., 37–60. Wissenschaftliche Untersuchungen zum Neuen Testament 2.384; Tübingen: Mohr Siebeck, 2014.

———. *The Quest for Paul's Gospel: A Suggested Strategy*. London/New York: T. & T. Clark, 2005.

———. *The Rhetoric of Righteousness in Romans 3:21–26*. Journal for the Study of the New Testament, Supplement Series 65. Sheffield: Sheffield Academic, JSOT, 1992.

———. "Rom. 1:17—A *Crux Interpretum* for the ΠΙΣΤΙΣ ΧΡΙΣΤΟΥ Debate." *Journal of Biblical Literature* 113.2 (1994) 265–85.

———. "The Story of Jesus in Romans and Galatians." In *Narrative Dynamics in Paul: A Critical Assessment*, edited by B. W. Longenecker, 97–124. Louisville: Westminster John Knox, 2002.

Campbell, William S. "Romans iii as a Key to the Structure and Thought of the Letter." *Novum Testamentum* 23.1 (1981) 22–40.

———. "Salvation for Jews and Gentiles: Krister Stendahl and Paul's Letter to the Romans." *Studia Biblica* 3 (1978) 65–72.

Caneday, Ardel B. "The Faithfulness of Jesus Christ as a Theme in Paul's Theology in Galatians." In *The Faith of Jesus Christ: Exegetical, Biblical, and Theological Studies*, edited by Michael F. Bird and Preston M. Sprinkle, 185–205. Milton Keynes, UK: Paternoster, 2009.

———. "Galatians 3:22ff.: A *Crux Interpretum* for ΠΙΣΤΙΣ ΧΡΙΣΤΟΥ in Paul's Thought." Conference paper, Evangelical Theological Society, Philadelphia (Nov 16–18, 1995).

———. "'Redeemed from the Curse of the Law': The Use of Deut. 21:22–23 in Gal. 3:13." *Trinity Journal* 10 (1989) 185–209.

———. "'They Exchanged the Glory of God for the Likeness of an Image': Idolatrous Adam and Israel as Representatives in Paul's Letter to the Romans." *Southern Baptist Journal of Theology* 11 (2007) 34–44.

Carlson, Richard Paul. "The Role of Baptism in Paul's Thought." *Interpretation* 47.3 (1993) 255–66.

Carson, D. A. *The Gospel according to John*. Grand Rapids: Eerdmans, 1991.

———. "Reflections on Salvation and Justification in the New Testament." *Journal of the Evangelical Theological Society* 40 (1997) 581–608.

Carson, D. A., et al., eds. *Justification and Variegated Nomism*. Vol. 1: "The Complexities of Second Temple Judaism." Grand Rapids: Baker Academic, 2001.

———, eds. *Justification and Variegated Nomism*. Vol. 2: "The Paradoxes of Paul." Grand Rapids: Baker Academic, 2004.

Cavallin, Hans C. C. "'The Righteous Shall Live by Faith': A Decisive Argument for the Traditional Interpretation." *Studia Theologica* 32 (1978) 33–43.

Chester, Andrew, and Ralph P. Martin. *The Theology of the Letters of James, Peter, and Jude*. New Testament Theology. Cambridge: Cambridge University Press, 1994.

Choi, Hung-Sik. "Πίστις in Galatians 5:5–6: Neglected Evidence for the Faithfulness of Christ." *Journal of Biblical Literature* 124 (2005) 467–90.

Chung, Yun Lak. "Redundancy as a Means of Clarification: In the Case of ΠΙΣΤΙΣ ΧΡΙΣΤΟΥ in Galatians." SBL International Meeting, Dublin (July 21–24, 1996).

Cockerill, Gareth Lee. *The Epistle to the Hebrews*. The New International Commentary on the New Testament. Grand Rapids: Eerdmans, 2012.

———. "Structure and Interpretation in Hebrews 8:1—10:18: A Symphony in Three Movements." *Bulletin of Biblical Review* 11 (2001) 179–201.

Cook, Michael L. "The Call to Faith of the Historical Jesus: Questions for the Christian Understanding of Faith." *Theological Studies* 39 (1978) 679–700.

Corsani, B. "ΕΚ ΠΙΣΤΕΩΣ in the Letters of Paul." In *The New Testament Age: Essays in Honor of Bo Reicke*, edited by W. C. Weinrich, 1:87–93. Macon: Mercer University Press, 1984.

Cosgrove, Charles H. "Arguing like a Mere Human Being: Galatians 3.15–18 in Rhetorical Perspective." *New Testament Studies* 34 (1988) 536–49.

———. *The Cross and the Spirit: A Study in the Argument and Theology of Galatians*. Macon: Mercer University Press, 1988.

———. "Justification in Paul: A Linguistic and Theological Reflection." *Journal of Biblical Literature* 106.4 (1987) 653–70.

Cousar, Charles B. *The Letters of Paul*. Nashville: Abingdon, 1996.

———. *A Theology of the Cross: The Death of Jesus in the Pauline Letters*. Minneapolis: Fortress, 1990.

Cranfield, C. E. B. *The Epistle to the Romans*. ICC new ed., vol. 1. Edinburgh: T. & T. Clark, 1975.

———. "On the Πίστις χριστοῦ Question." In *On Romans and Other New Testament Essays*. Edinburgh: T. & T. Clark (1998) 81–97.

Cranford, Michael. "Abraham in Romans 4: The Father of All Who Believe." *New Testament Studies* 41 (1995) 71–88.

———. "The Possibility of Perfect Obedience: Paul and an Implied Premise in Galatians 3:10 and 5:3." *Novum Testamentum* 36 (1994) 242–58.

Crowe, Brandon D. *The Last Adam: A Theology of the Obedient Life of Jesus in the Gospels*. Grand Rapids: Baker Academic, 2017.

Cummins, S. A. "Divine Life and Corporate Christology: God, Messiah Jesus, and the Covenant Community in Paul." In *The Messiah in the Old and New Testaments*, edited by S. E. Porter, 190–209. Grand Rapids: Eerdmans, 2007.

Das, A. Andrew. "Another Look at ἐὰν μὴ in Galatians 2:16." *Journal of Biblical Literature* 119.3 (2000) 529–39.

———. *Paul and the Jews*. Library of Pauline Studies. Peabody: Hendrickson, 2003.

———. *Paul, the Law, and the Covenant*. Peabody: Hendrickson, 2001.

Davids, Peter H. *A Theology of James, Peter, and Jude*. Biblical Theology of the New Testament. Grand Rapids: Zondervan, 2014.

Davies, Glenn N. *Faith and Obedience in Romans: A Study in Romans 1–4*. Journal for the Study of the New Testament, Supplement Series 39. Sheffield: JSOT, 1990.

Davis, Christopher A. *Revelation*. The College Press NIV Commentary. Joplin: College Press, 2000.

de Boer, Martinus C. *Galatians: A Commentary*. New Testament Library, Louisville: Westminster John Knox, 2011.

———. "N. T. Wright's Great Story and Its Relationship to Paul's Gospel." *Journal for the Study of Paul and His Letters* 4.1 (2014) 49–57.

———. "Paul's Use and Interpretation of a Justification Tradition in Galatians 2.15–21." *Journal for the Study of the New Testament* 28.2 (2005) 189–216.

Deer, Donald S. "Whose Faith/Loyalty in Revelation 2.13 and 14.12?" *Bible Translator* 38.3 (1987) 328–30.

DeSilva, David A. "On the Sidelines of the Πίστις Χριστοῦ Debate: The View from Revelation." In *The Faith of Jesus Christ: Exegetical, Biblical, and Theological Studies*, edited by Michael F. Bird and Preston M. Sprinkle, 259–74. Milton Keynes, UK: Paternoster, 2009.

———. *Perseverance in Gratitude: A Socio-Rhetorical Commentary on the Epistle "to the Hebrews."* Grand Rapids: Eerdmans, 2000.

Despotis, Athanasios. *Participation, Justification, and Conversion: Eastern Orthodox Interpretation of Paul and the Debate between "Old and New Perspectives on Paul."* Tübingen: Mohr Siebeck, 2017.

Dillon, R. J. "The Spirit as Taskmaster and Troublemaker in Romans 8." *Catholic Biblical Quarterly* 60.4 (1998) 682–702.

Dockery, David S. "The Use of Hab. 2:4 in Rom. 1:17: Some Hermeneutical and Theological Considerations." *Westminster Theological Journal* 22.2 (1987) 24–36.

Dodd, Brian. "Rom. 1:17—A *Crux Interpretum* for the ΠΙΣΤΙΣ ΧΡΙΣΤΟΥ Debate?" *Journal of Biblical Literature* 114 (1995) 470–73.

Dodd, C. H. *According to the Scriptures: The Sub-Structure of New Testament Theology*. New York: Charles Scribner's Sons, 1953.

Donaldson, T. L. "The 'Curse of the Law' and the Inclusion of the Gentiles: Galatians 3.13–14." *New Testament Studies* 32 (1986) 94–112.

Downing, F. Gerald. "Ambiguity, Ancient Semantics, and Faith." *New Testament Studies* 56 (2010) 139–62.

Downs, David J. "Faith(fulness) in Christ Jesus in 2 Timothy 3:15." *Journal of Biblical Literature* 131.1 (2012) 143–60.

Dunn, James D. G. "ΕΚ ΠΙΣΤΕΩΣ: A Key to the Meaning of *PISTIS CHRISTOU*." In *The Word Leaps the Gap: Essays on Scripture and Theology in Honor of Richard B. Hays*, edited by J. R. Wagner et al., 351–66. Grand Rapids: Eerdmans, 2008.

———. *The Epistles to the Colossians and to Philemon*. The New International Greek Testament Commentary. Grand Rapids: Eerdmans, 1996.

———. "The Justice of God: A Renewed Perspective on Justification." *Journal of Theological Studies* 43 (1992) 1–22.

———. "The New Perspective on Paul." *Bulletin of the John Rylands Library* 65 (1983) 95–122.

———. "Once More, ΠΙΣΤΙΣ ΧΡΙΣΤΟΥ." In *Pauline Theology*, edited by David M. Hay and E. Elizabeth Johnson, 4:61–81. SBL Symposium Series. Atlanta: Scholars, 1997. Also appears as "Appendix 1" in Richard B. Hays, *The Faith of Jesus Christ* (2002) 249–71.

———. *Romans 1–8*. Word Biblical Commentary 38A. Dallas: Word, 1988.

———. *Romans 9–16*. Word Biblical Commentary 38B. Dallas: Word, 1988.

———. *The Theology of Paul the Apostle*. Edinburgh: T. & T. Clark, 1998.

———. "Works of the Law and the Curse of the Law (Galatians 3:10–14)." *New Testament Studies* 31 (1985) 523–42.

———. "Yet Once More—'The Works of the Law': A Response." *Journal for the Study of the New Testament* 46 (1992) 99–117.

Dunnill, John. "Saved by Whose Faith? The Function of *pistis Christou* in Pauline Theology." *Colloquium* 30.1 (1998) 3–25.

Dunson, Ben C. "Faith in Romans: The Salvation of the Individual or Life in Community?" *Journal for the Study for the New Testament* 34.1 (2011) 19–46.

Easter, Matthew C. "The *Pistis Christou* Debate: Main Arguments and Responses in Summary." *Currents in Biblical Research* 9.1 (2010) 33–47.

Eastman, Susan. "Imitating Christ Imitating Us: Paul's Educational Project in Philippians." In *The Word Leaps the Gap: Essays on Scripture and Theology in Honor of Richard B. Hays*, edited by J. Ross Wagner et al., 427–50. Grand Rapids: Eerdmans, 2008.

———. "Israel and the Mercy of God: A Rereading of Galatians 6:16 and Romans 9–11." *New Testament Studies* 56.3 (2010) 367–95.

Eller, Vernard. *The Most Revealing Book of the Bible: Making Sense out of Revelation*. Grand Rapids: Eerdmans, 1974.

Elliott, John H. *A Home for the Homeless: A Sociological Exegesis of 1 Peter, Its Situation and Strategy*. Philadelphia: Fortress, 1981.

Enns, Peter. *The Sin of Certainty: Why God Desires Our Trust More Than Our "Correct" Beliefs*. New York: HarperCollins, 2016.

Eurell, John-Christian. "Faith: An Activity of Christ or of the Believer? A Contribution to the ΠΙΣΤΙΣ ΧΡΙΣΤΟΥ Debate." *Swedish Exegetical Annual* 77 (2012) 139–68.

Fesko, J. V. "N. T. Wright on Imputation." *The Reformed Theological Review* 66.1 (2007) 2–22.

Fitzmyer, Joseph A. *Romans: A New Translation with Introduction and Commentary*. The Anchor Bible 33. New York: Doubleday, 1993.

Foster, Paul. "The First Contribution to the Πίστις Χριστοῦ Debate: A Study of Ephesians 3.12." *Journal for the Study for the New Testament* 85 (2002) 75–96.

———. "Πίστις Χριστοῦ Terminology in Philippians and Ephesians." In *The Faith of Jesus Christ: Exegetical, Biblical, and Theological Studies*, edited by Michael F. Bird and Preston M. Sprinkle, 91–109. Milton Keynes, UK: Paternoster, 2009.

France, R. T. "Faith." In *Dictionary of Jesus and the Gospels*, edited by Joel B. Green et al., 223–26. Downers Grove: InterVarsity, 2013.

———. *The Gospel according to Matthew: An Introduction and Commentary*. Leicester: InterVarsity, 1985.

Fredriksen, Paula. "Paul's Letter to the Romans, the Ten Commandments, and Pagan 'Justification by Faith.'" *Journal of Biblical Literature* 133.4 (2014) 801–8.

Fretheim, Terence Erling. "Theological Reflections on the Wrath of God in the Old Testament." *Horizons in Biblical Theology* 24.2 (2002) 1–26.

Fudge, Edward W. *Our Man in Heaven: An Exposition of the Epistle to the Hebrews*. Grand Rapids: Baker, 1974.

Furnish, Victor P. "'He Gave Himself [Was Given] Up . . .': Paul's Use of a Christological Assertion." In *The Future of Christology: Essays in honor of Leander E. Keck*, edited by A. J. Malherbe and W. A. Meeks, 109–21. Minneapolis: Augsburg Fortress, 1993.

Gager, John G. *Reinventing Paul*. Oxford: Oxford University Press, 2000.

Gamble, Harry, Jr. *The Textual History of the Letter to the Romans: A Study in Textual and Literary Criticism*. Grand Rapids: Eerdmans, 1977.

Garlington, Don B. *Faith, Obedience, and Perseverance: Aspects of Paul's Letter to the Romans*. Wissenschaftliche Untersuchungen zum Neuer Testament 2.79. Tübingen: Mohr Siebeck, 1994.

———. "'The Obedience of Faith': A Pauline Phrase in Historical Context. Wissenschaftliche Untersuchungen zum Neuer Testament 2.38; Tübingen: Mohr Siebeck, 1991.

———. "The Obedience of Faith in the Letter to the Romans, Part I: The Meaning of ὑπακοὴ πίστεως (Rom 1:5; 16:26)." *Westminster Theological Journal* 52 (1990) 201–24.

———. "'Partisan ἐκ' and the Question of Justification in Galatians." *Journal of Biblical Literature* 127.3 (2008) 567–89.

———. "Role Reversal and Paul's Use of Scripture in Galatians 3:10–13." *Journal for the Study of the New Testament* 65 (1997) 85–121.

Gaston, Lloyd. *Paul and The Torah*. Vancouver: University of British Columbia Press, 1987.

Gaventa, Beverly Roberts. "The Character of God's Faithfulness: A Response to N. T. Wright." *Journal for the Study of Paul and His Letters* 4.1 (2014) 71–79.

———. "Galatians 1 and 2: Autobiography as Paradigm." *Novum Testamentum* 28.4 (1986) 309–26.

———. "The Singularity of the Gospel: A Reading of Galatians." In *Society of Biblical Literature 1988 Seminar Papers*, edited by David J. Lull, 27:17–26. Atlanta: Scholars Press, 1988.

Gombis, Timothy G. "Ephesians 2 as a Narrative of Divine Warfare." *Journal for the Study of the New Testament* 26.4 (2004) 403–18.

Gorman, Michael J. *Apostle of the Crucified Lord: A Theological Introduction to Paul and His Letters*. Grand Rapids: Eerdmans, 2004.

———. *Cruciformity: Paul's Narrative Spirituality of the Cross*. Grand Rapids: Eerdmans, 2001.

———. *Inhabiting the Cruciform God: Kenosis, Justification, and Theosis in Paul's Narrative Soteriology*. Grand Rapids: Eerdmans, 2009.

———. "Wright about Much, but Questions about Justification: A Review of N. T. Wright, 'Paul and the Faithfulness of God.'" *Journal for the Study of Paul and His Letters*. 4.1 (2014) 27–36.

Gosnell, Peter W. "Law in Romans: Regulation and Instruction." *Novum Testamentum* 51 (2009) 252–71.

Goudge, H. L. *The Second Epistle to the Corinthians*. London: Methuen, 1927.

Grayston, K. "'Not ashamed of the Gospel': Romans 1, 16a and the Structure of the Epistle." In *Studia Evangelica II*, ed. F. L. Cross, 569–73. Berlin: Akademie-Verlag, 1964.

Grieb, A. Katherine. "The Righteousness of God in Romans." In *Reading Paul's Letter to the Romans*, edited by Jerry L. Sumney, 65–78. Atlanta: Society of Biblical Literature, 2012.

Grundmann, W. "The Teacher of Righteousness of Qumran and the Question of Justification by Faith in the Theology of the Apostle Paul." In *Paul and Qumran: Studies in New Testament Exegesis*, edited by J. Murphy-O'Conner, 108. Chicago: Priory Press, 1968.

Guthrie, George H. "Hebrews." In *Commentary on the New Testament Use of the Old Testament*, edited by G. K. Beale and D. A. Carson, 919–95. Grand Rapids: Baker Academic, 2007.

———. *The Structure of Hebrews: A Text-Linguistic Analysis*. Grand Rapids: Baker, 1998.

Hagner, Donald A. "Paul and Judaism: Testing the New Perspective." In *Revisiting Paul's Doctrine of Justification: A Challenge to the New Perspective*, edited by P. Stuhlmacher, 75–105. Downers Grove: InterVarsity, 2001.

Hamm, Dennis. "Acts 3:12–26: Peter's Speech and the Healing of the Man Born Lame." *Perspective in Religious Studies* 11.3 (1984) 199–217.

———. "Faith in the Epistle to the Hebrews: The Jesus Factor" *Catholic Biblical Quarterly* 52 (1990) 270–91.

Han, K. *Pauline Soteriology in Galatians with Special Reference to* πίστις Ἰησοῦ Χριστοῦ. PhD. diss., University of Birmingham. Ann Arbor: ProQuest Dissertation Publishing, 2007.

Hansen, G. Walter. *Abraham in Galatians: Epistolary and Rhetorical Contexts*. JSNTS 29. Sheffield: JSOT, 1989.

Hanson, Anthony T. *The Paradox of the Cross in the Thought of St Paul*. Journal for the Study of the Old Testament Supplement Series 17. Sheffield: JSOT, 1987.

———. *Studies in Paul's Technique and Theology*. London: SPCK, 1974.

———. *The Wrath of the Lamb*. London: SPCK, 1957.

Harink, Douglas. "J. L. Martyn and Apocalyptic Discontinuity: The Trinitarian, Christological Ground of Galatians in Galatians 4:1–11." *Journal for the Study of Paul and His Letters* 7.1–2 (2017) 101–11.

———. *Paul among the Postliberals: Pauline Theology Beyond Christendom and Modernity*. Grand Rapids: Brazos, 2003.

Harrington, Chad. "Justification by the Faithfulness of Jesus Christ." *The Asbury Journal* 65.2 (2010) 7–25.

Harrisville, Roy A, III. "Before ΠΙΣΤΙΣ ΧΡΙΣΤΟΥ: The Objective Genitive as Good Greek." *Novum Testamentum* 48 (2006) 353–58.

———. "Πίστις Χριστοῦ and the New Perspective on Paul." *Logia* 19.2 (2010) 19–28.

———. "ΠΙΣΤΙΣ ΧΡΙΣΤΟΥ: Witness of the Fathers." *Novum Testamentum* 36 (1994) 233–41.

Hartin, Patrick J. *James*. Sacra Pagina Series 14. Collegeville: Liturgical, 2009.

Haussleiter, Johannes. "Der Glaube Jesu Christi und der christliche Glaube: ein Beitrag zur Erklarung des Romerbriefes." *Neue kirchliche Zeitschrift* 2 (1891) 109–45.

———. "Was versteht Paulus unter christlichen Glauben." *Theologische Abhundlungen Hermann Cremer dargebracht*. Gütersloh: Bertelsmann (1895) 159–81.

Hay, David M. "Paul's Understanding of Faith as Participation." In *Paul and His Theology*, edited by Stanley E. Porter, 45–76. Leiden: Brill, 2006.

———. "*Pistis* as 'Ground for Faith' in Hellenized Judaism and Paul." *Journal of Biblical Literature* 108.3 (1989) 461–76.

Hay, David M., and E. Elizabeth Johnson, eds. *Pauline Theology*. Vol. 3: "Romans." Minneapolis: Fortress, 1995.

———, eds. *Pauline Theology*. Vol. 3: "Looking Back, Pressing On." Atlanta: Scholars, 1997.

Hays, Richard B. "Apocalyptic Hermeneutics: Habakkuk Proclaims 'The Righteous One.'" In *The Conversion of the Imagination: Paul as Interpreter of Israel's Scripture*, 119–42. Grand Rapids: Eerdmans, 2005.

———. "Christ Prays the Psalms: Israel's Psalter as Matrix of Early Christology." In *The Conversion of the Imagination: Paul as Interpreter of Israel's Scripture*, 101–18. Grand Rapids: Eerdmans, 2005.

———. "Christ Prays the Psalms: Paul's Use of an Early Christian Exegetical Convention." In *The Future of Christology: Essays in Honor of Leander E. Keck*, edited by Abraham J. Malherbe and Wayne A. Meeks, 122–36. Minneapolis: Fortress, 1993.

———. "Christology and Ethics in Galatians: The Law of Christ." *Catholic Biblical Quarterly* 49 (1987) 268–90.

———. "Crucified with Christ: A Synthesis of the Theology of 1 & 2 Thessalonians, Philemon, Philippians, and Galatians." In *Pauline Theology*, edited by Jouette M. Bassler, 1:227–46. Minneapolis: Fortress, 1991.

———. *Echoes of Scripture in the Letters of Paul*. New Haven: Yale University Press, 1989.

———. *First Corinthians*. Interpretation. Louisville: Knox, 1997.

———. *The Faith of Jesus Christ*. SBL Dissertation Series 56. Chico: Scholars, 1983.

———. *The Faith of Jesus Christ: The Narrative Substructure of Galatians 3:1—4:11*. 2nd ed. Grand Rapids: Eerdmans, 2002.

———. "'Have We Found Abraham to Be Our Forefather according to the Flesh?' A Reconsideration of Rom 4:1." *Novum Testamentum* 27.1 (1985) 76–98.

———. "Jesus' Faith and Ours: A Re-reading of Galatians 3." *Theological Student Fellowship Bulletin* (Sept.–Oct. 1983) 2–6.

———. "JUSTIFICATION." In *ABD* 3:1129–33. New York: Doubleday, 1992.

———. "ΠΙΣΤΙΣ and Pauline Christology: What Is at Stake?" In *Pauline Theology*, edited by David M. Hay and E. Elizabeth Johnson, 4:35–60. Atlanta: Scholars, 1997.

———. "Psalm 143 and the Logic of Romans 3." *Journal of Biblical Literature* 99.1 (1980) 107–15.

———. "'The Righteous One' as Eschatological Deliverer: A Case Study in Paul's Apocalyptic Hermeneutics." In *Apocalyptic and the New Testament: Essays in Honour of J. Louis Martyn*, edited by J. Marcus and M. Soards, 191–215. Sheffield: JSOT, 1988.

Hebert, Gabriel. "'Faithfulness' and 'Faith.'" *The Reformed Theological Review* 14 (1955) 33–40. Reprinted in *Theology* 58 (1955) 373–79.

Heilig, Christoph, et al. *God and the Faithfulness of Paul*. Tübingen: Mohr Siebeck, 2016.

Heliso, Desta. *Pistis and the Righteous One: A Study of Romans 1:17 against the Background of Scripture and Second Temple Literature*. Wissenschaftliche Untersuchungen zum Neuen Testament 2.235; Tübingen: Mohr Siebeck, 2007.

Hewitt, J. Thomas. "Ancient Messiah Discourse and Paul's Expression ἄχρις οὗ ἔλθῃ τὸ σπέρμα in Galatians 3.19." *New Testament Studies* 65 (2019) 398–411.

Hoehner, Harold W. *Ephesians: An Exegetical Commentary*. Grand Rapids: Baker Academic, 2002.

Holmes, Christopher T. "'Utterly Incapacitated': The Neglected Meaning of ΠΑΡΕΣΙΣ in Romans 3:25." *Novum Testamentum* 55 (2013) 349–66.

Hooker, Morna D. "Another Look at Πίστις Χριστοῦ." *Scottish Journal of Theology* 69.1 (2016) 46–62.

———. "Interchange and Atonement." *Bulletin of the John Rylands Library* 60 (1978) 462–81.

———. "On Becoming the Righteousness of God: Another Look at 2 Cor 5:21." *Novum Testamentum* 50 (2008) 358–75.

———. "ΠΙΣΤΙΣ ΧΡΙΣΤΟΥ." *New Testament Studies* 35 (1989) 321–42.

Hoppin, Ruth. *Priscilla's Letter: Finding the Author of the Epistle to the Hebrews.* San Francisco: Christian Universities Press, 1997.

Howard, George. "Christ the End of the Law: The Meaning of Rom 10:4ff." *Journal of Biblical Literature* 88 (1969) 331–37.

———. "FAITH OF CHRIST." In *ABD* 2:758–60. New York: Doubleday, 1992.

———. "The 'Faith of Christ.'" *Expository Times* 85 (1974) 121–25.

———. "Justification by Faith." In *Paul: Crisis in Galatia*, 46–97. Society for NT Studies Monograph Series 35. Cambridge University Press, 1979.

———. "Notes and Observations on the 'Faith of Christ.'" *Harvard Theological Review* 60 (1967) 459–65.

———. *Paul: Crisis in Galatia.* 2nd ed. Society for NT Studies Monograph Series 35. Cambridge: Cambridge University Press, 1990.

———. "Phil. 2:6–11 and the Human Christ." *Catholic Biblical Quarterly* 40 (1978) 368–87.

———. "Romans 3:21–31 and the Inclusion of the Gentiles." *Harvard Theological Review* 63 (1970) 223–33.

Hultgren, Arland J. "The PISTIS CHRISTOU FORMULATION IN PAUL." *Novum Testamentum* 22.3 (1980) 248–63.

Hunn, Debbie. "Debating the Faithfulness of Jesus Christ in Twentieth-Century Scholarship." In *The Faith of Jesus Christ: Exegetical, Biblical, and Theological Studies*, edited by Michael F. Bird and Preston M. Sprinkle, 15–31. Milton Keynes, UK: Paternoster, 2009.

———. "Ἐὰν μή in Galatians 2:16: A Look at Greek Literature." *Novum Testamentum* 49 (2007) 281–90.

———. "Galatians 3:6–9: Abraham's Fatherhood and Paul's Conclusions." *Catholic Biblical Quarterly* 78.3 (2016) 500–514.

———. "Galatians 3:13–14: MERE ASSERTION?" *The Westminster Theological Journal* 80.1 (2018) 141–57.

———. "*Pistis Christou* in Galatians 2:16: Clarification from 3:1–6." *Tyndale Bulletin* 57 (2006) 23–33.

———. "PISTIS CHRISTOU IN GALATIANS: The Connection to Habakkuk 2:4." *Tyndale Bulletin* 63.1 (2012) 75–91.

Husbands, Mark A., and Daniel J. Treier, eds. *Justification: What's at Stake in the Current Debates.* Downers Grove: InterVarsity, 2004.

Imes, Carmen Joy. *Bearing God's Name: Why Sinai Still Matters.* Downers Grove: InterVarsity, 2019.

Irons, Charles Lee. "The Object of the Law Is Realized in Christ: Romans 10:4 and Paul's Justification Teaching." *Journal for the Study of Paul and His Letters* 6.1 (2016) 33–54.

Janzen, J. Gerald. "Coleridge and *Pistis Christou*." *Expository Times* 107 (1996) 265–68.

———. "Eschatological Symbol and Existence in Habakkuk." *Catholic Biblical Quarterly* 44 (1982) 394–414.

———. "Habakkuk 2:2–4 in the Light of Recent Philological Advances." *Harvard Theological Review* 73 (1980) 53–78.

Jaspers, Karl. *The Great Philosophers.* Edited by Hannah Arendt, trans. Ralph Manheim. New York: Harcourt, Brace and World, 1962.

Jepsen, Alfred. "אָמֵן." In *TDOT* 1:292–323.

Jerrard, Raymond Edmund. "An Investigation into the Significance and Possible Implications of the Phrase 'The Faith of Jesus.'" MA thesis, Andrews University School of Graduate Studies, June 1984.

Jervis, L. Ann. "'The Commandment Which Is for Life' (Romans 7:10): Sin's Use of the Obedience of Faith." *Journal for the Study of the New Testament* 27 (2004) 193–216.

Jipp, J. W. "Rereading the Story of Abraham, Isaac, and 'Us' in Romans 4." *Journal for the Study of the New Testament* 32.2 (2009) 217–42.

Johnson, B. "צֶדֶק." In *TDOT* 12:243–64.

Johnson, Luke Timothy. *The Acts of the Apostles*. Sacra Pagina Series 5. Collegeville: Liturgical, 1992.

———. "Human and Divine: Did Jesus Have Faith?" *Commonweal* 135 (2008) 10–16.

———. *Reading Romans: A Literary and Theological Commentary*. Macon: Smyth & Helwys, 2001. Previously published at New York: Crossroad, 1997.

———. "Rom 3:21–26 and the Faith of Jesus." *Catholic Biblical Quarterly* 44 (1982) 77–90.

Johnson, Robert Clyde. *The Meaning of Christ*. Philadelphia: Westminster, 1958.

Just, Arthur A., Jr. "Christ and the Law in the Life of the Church at Galatia." In *The Law in Holy Scripture: Essays from the Concordia Theological Seminary Symposium on Exegetical Theology*, edited by Charles A. Gieschen, 173–87. St. Louis: Concordia Academic, 2004.

———. "The Faith of Christ: A Lutheran Appropriation of Richard Hays's Proposal." *Concordia Theological Quarterly* 70 (2006) 3–15.

Käsemann, Ernst. *Commentary on Romans*. Translated and edited by Geoffrey W. Bromily. Grand Rapids: Eerdmans, 1980.

———. "'The Righteousness of God' in Paul." In *New Testament Questions of Today*, translated by W. J. Montague, 168–82. Philadelphia: Fortress, 1969.

Keck, Leander. "Jesus in Romans." *Journal of Biblical Literature* 108.3 (1989) 443–60.

Keener, C. S. "John, Gospel of." In *Dictionary of Jesus and the Gospels*, edited by Joel B. Green et al., 419–36. 2nd ed. Downers Grove: InterVarsity, 2013.

Kerr, A. R. *The Temple of Jesus' Body*. Journal for the Study of the New Testament 220. Sheffield: Sheffield Academic, 2002.

Kettler, Christian D. *The God Who Believes: Faith, Doubt, and the Vicarious Humanity of Christ*. Eugene, OR: Cascade, 2005.

Khobnya, Svetlana. *The Father Who Redeems and the Son Who Obeys: Consideration of Paul's Teaching in Romans*. Eugene, OR: Pickwick, 2013.

Kim, Sungwon (Moses). "N. T. Wright's Theological Perspective and Methodology—An Evangelical Analysis and Evaluation." *The Asbury Journal* 71.2 (2016) 138–55.

Kingsbury, Jack Dean. "The Title 'Son of David' in Matthew's Gospel." *Journal of Biblical Literature* 95.4 (1976) 591–602.

Kirk, J. R. Daniel. "Reconsidering *Dikaiōma* in Romans 5:16." *Journal of Biblical Literature* 126.4 (2007) 787–92.

———. "The Sufficiency of the Cross (I): The Crucifixion as Jesus' Act of Obedience." *Scottish Bulletin of Evangelical Theology* 24.1 (2006) 36–64.

———. "The Sufficiency of the Cross (II): The Law, the Cross, and Justification." *Scottish Bulletin of Evangelical Theology* 24.2 (2006) 133–54.

———. *Unlocking Romans: Resurrection and the Justification of God*. Grand Rapids: Eerdmans, 2008.

Kittel, Gerhard. "Πίστις Ἰησοῦ Χριστοῦ bei Paulus." *Theologische Studien und Kritiken* 79 (1906) 419–36.

Knight, George W. III. *The Faithful Sayings in the Pastoral Letters*. Grand Rapids: Baker, 1979.

———. *The Pastoral Epistles: The New International Greek Testament Commentary*. Grand Rapids: Eerdmans, 1992.

Koehler, Ludwig, and Walter Baumgartner. *The Hebrew and Aramaic Lexicon of the Old Testament*. 5 vols. New York: E. J. Brill, 1994.

Konstan, David. "Trusting in Jesus." *Journal for the Study of the New Testament* 40.3 (2018) 247–54.

Koperski, Veronica. "The Meaning of *Pistis Christou* in Philippians 3:9." *Louvain Studies* 18 (1993) 198–216.

Köstenberger, Andreas J. *Encountering John: The Gospel in Historical, Literary, and Theological Perspective*. Grand Rapids: Baker, 1999.

Kruse, Colin G. *Paul, the Law, and Justification*. Peabody: Hendrickson, 1996.

Kugler, Chris. "ΠΙΣΤΙΣ ΧΡΙΣΤΟΥ: The Current State of Play and the Key Arguments." *Currents in Biblical Research* 14.2 (2016) 244–55.

Lambrecht, Jan. "Paul's Reasoning in Galatians 2:11–21." In *Paul and the Mosaic Law*, edited by James D. G. Dunn, 53–74. Wissenschaftliche Untersuchungen zum Neuen Testament 89. Tübingen: J. C. B. Mohr (Paul Siebeck), 1996.

Lambrecht, Jan, and Richard W. Thompson. *Justification by Faith: The Implications of Romans 3:27–31*. Wilmington: Michael Glazier, 1989.

Lane, William L. *Hebrews 1–8*. Word Biblical Commentary 47A. Dallas: Word, 1991.

———. *Hebrews 9–13*. Word Biblical Commentary 47B. Dallas: Word, 1991.

Lange, Johann P., and F. F. Fay. *The Epistle of Paul to the Romans*. Translated by J. F. Hurst et al., 2nd ed. New York: Charles Scribner's Sons, 1869.

Laws, Sophie. "The Blood-Stained Horseman: Revelation 19.11–13." *Studia Biblica* 3 (1978) 245–48.

Lee, Sank Mok. "Christ's Πίστις vs. Caesar's *Fides*: Πίστις Χριστοῦ in Galatians and the Roman Imperial Cult." *The Expository Times* 130.6 (2018) 243–55.

Leenhardt, F. J. *The Epistle to the Romans*. London: Lutterworth, 1961.

Leslie, A. "Christ's Faithfulness and Our Salvation." In *Donald Robinson—Selected Works—Appreciation*, edited by P. G. Bolt and M. D. Thompson, 73–81. Camperdown, NSW: Australian Church Record/Moore College, 2008.

Licona, Michael R. *The Resurrection of Jesus: A New Historiographical Approach*. Downers Grove: InterVarsity, 2010.

Lindars, Barnabas. *New Testament Apologetics: The Doctrinal Significance of the Old Testament Quotations*. London: SCM, 1961.

———. "The Rhetorical Structure of Hebrews." *New Testament Studies* 35 (1989) 382–406.

———. *The Theology of the Letter to the Hebrews*. New Testament Theology. Cambridge: Cambridge University Press, 1991.

Lindsay, Dennis R. *Josephus and Faith: Πίστις and Πιστεύειν as Faith Terminology in the Writings of Flavius Josephus and in the NT*. Leiden and New York: E. J. Brill, 1993.

———. "The Roots and Development of the πιστ- Word Group as Faith Terminology." *Journal for the Study of the New Testament* 49 (1993) 103–18.

Linebaugh, Jonathan A. "The Christo-Centrism of Faith in Christ: Martin Luther's Reading of Galatians 2.16, 19–20." *New Testament Studies* 59.4 (2013) 535–44.

Ljungman, H. *Pistis: A Study of Its Presuppositions and Its Meaning in Pauline Use*. Lund: C. W. K. Gleerup (1964) 9–108.

Longenecker, Bruce W. "Defining the Faithful Character of the Covenant Community: Galatians 2.15–21 and Beyond." In *Paul and the Mosaic Law*, edited by James D. G. Dunn, 75–97. Grand Rapids: Eerdmans, 1994.

———. *Eschatology and the Covenant: A Comparison of 4 Ezra and Romans 1–11*. JSNTS 57. Sheffield: JSOT, 1991.

———. "The Faith of Abraham Theme in Paul, James, and Hebrews: A Study in the Circumstantial Nature of New Testament Teaching." *Journal of the Evangelical Theological Society* 20 (1977) 203–12.

———. *The Triumph of Abraham's God: The Transformation of Identity in Galatians*. Nashville: Abingdon, 1998.

Longenecker, Richard N. "Chapter IX: Major Interpretive Approaches Prominent Today." In *Introducing Romans: Critical Issues in Paul's Most Famous Letter*, 290–349. Grand Rapids: Eerdmans, 2011.

———. *The Christology of Early Jewish Christianity*. London: SCM, 1970.

———. *The Epistle to the Romans: A Commentary on the Greek Text*. The New International Greek Testament Commentary. Grand Rapids: Eerdmans, 2016.

———. "The Foundational Conviction of New Testament Christology: The Obedience/Faithfulness/Sonship of Christ." In *Jesus of Nazareth: Lord and Christ: Essays on the Historical Jesus and New Testament Christology*, edited by Joel B. Green and Max Turner, 473–88. Grand Rapids: Eerdmans, 1999.

———. *Galatians*. Word Biblical Commentary 41. Dallas: Word, 1990.

———. "The Obedience of Christ in the Theology of the Early Church." In *Reconciliation and Hope: New Testament Essays on Atonement and Eschatology Presented to L. L. Morris on His 60th Birthday*, edited by Robert Banks, 142–52. Grand Rapids: Eerdmans, 1974.

———. *Paul, Apostle of Liberty*. New York: Harper & Row, 1964.

———. "ΠΙΣΤΙΣ in Romans 3.25: Neglected Evidence for the 'Faithfulness of Christ.'" *New Testament Studies* 39 (1993) 478–80.

Lowe, Bruce A. "James 2:1 in the Πίστις Χριστοῦ Debate: Irrelevant or Indispensable?" In *The Faith of Jesus Christ: Exegetical, Biblical, and Theological Studies*, edited by Michael F. Bird and Preston M. Sprinkle, 239–57. Milton Keynes, UK: Paternoster, 2009.

Lührmann, Dieter. "FAITH (NEW TESTAMENT)." In *ABD* 2:749–58. New York: Doubleday, 1992.

Lyall, Frances. "Roman Law in the Writings of Paul-Adoption." *Journal of Biblical Literature* 88 (1969) 458–66.

———. *Slaves, Citizens, Sons: Legal Metaphors in the Epistles*. Grand Rapids: Zondervan, 1984.

Macchia, Frank D. "Justification through New Creation: The Holy Spirit and the Doctrine by Which the Church Stands or Falls." *Theology Today* 58.2 (2001) 202–17.

Mackey, James P. "The Faith of the Historical Jesus." *Horizons* 3.2 (1976) 155–74.

Malevez, L. "Le Christ et la foi." *La nouvelle revue théologique* 78 (1966) 1009–43.

Mangina, Joseph L. *Revelation*. Brazos Theological Commentary on the Bible. Grand Rapids: Brazos, 2010.

Mannermaa, Tuomo. *Christ Present in Faith: Luther's View of Justification*. Minneapolis: Fortress, 2005.

Manson, Thomas W. "The Argument from Prophecy." *Journal of Theological Studies* 46 (1945) 129–36.

———. "The Problem of the Epistle to the Hebrews." *Bulletin of the John Rylands Library* 32.2 (1949) 171–93.

———. "Romans." In *Peake's Commentary on the Bible*, edited by M. Black and H. H. Rowley, 940–53. 2nd ed. London: Nelson, 1962.

Marcus, Joel. "'Under the Law': The Background of a Pauline Expression." *Catholic Biblical Quarterly* 63 (2001) 72–83.

Marohl, Matthew J. *Faithfulness and the Purpose of Hebrews: A Social Identity Approach.* Eugene, OR: Pickwick, 2008.

Marshall, I. Howard. *The Epistles of John*. The New International Commentary on the New Testament. Grand Rapids: Eerdmans, 1978.

Martin, Ira J. *The Faith of Jesus*. 3rd ed. New York: Exposition, 1956.

Martyn, J. Louis. "The Apocalyptic Gospel in Galatians." *Interpretation* 54.3 (2000) 246–66.

———. "Covenant, Christ, and Church in Galatians." In *The Future of Christology: Essays in Honor of Leander E. Keck*, edited by Abraham J. Malherbe and Wayne A. Meeks, 137–51. Minneapolis: Fortress, 1993.

———. "Events in Galatia: Modified Covenantal Nomism Versus God's Invasion of the Cosmos in the Singular Gospel: A Response to J. D. G. Dunn and B. R. Gaventa." In *Pauline Theology*, edited by J. M. Bassler, 1:160–79. Minneapolis: Augsburg Fortress, 1991.

———. *Galatians: A New Translation with Introduction and Commentary*. Anchor Bible 33A. New York: Doubleday, 1997.

———. *Theological Issues in the Letters of Paul*. Nashville: Abingdon, 1997.

Matera, Frank J. *Galatians*. Sacra Pagina 9. Collegeville: Liturgical, 1992.

———. "Galatians in Perspective: Cutting a New Path through Old Territory." *Interpretation* 54.3 (2000) 233–45.

———. *God's Saving Grace: A Pauline Theology*. Grand Rapids: Eerdmans, 2012.

———. *Romans*. Grand Rapids: Baker Academic, 2010.

Matlock, R. Barry. "Detheologizing the ΠΙΣΤΙΣ ΧΡΙΣΤΟΥ Debate: Cautionary Remarks from a Lexical Semantic Perspective." *Novum Testamentum* 42 (2000) 1–23.

———. "'Even the Demons Believe': Paul and πίστις Χριστοῦ." *Catholic Biblical Quarterly* 64 (2002) 300–318.

———. "*Pistis* in Galatians 3:26: Neglected Evidence for 'Faith in Christ'?" *New Testament Studies* 49 (2003) 433–39.

———. "The Rhetoric of πίστις in Paul: Galatians 2.16, 3.22, Romans 3.22, and Philippians 3.9." *Journal for the Study of the New Testament* 30.2 (2007) 173–203.

———. "Zeal for Paul but Not According to Knowledge: Douglas Campbell's War on 'Justification Theory.'" *Journal for the Study of the New Testament* 34.2 (2011) 115–49.

Mattill, Andrew J., Jr. "Translation of Words with the Stem Δικ- in Romans." *Andrews University Seminary Studies* 9.2 (1971) 89–98.

McCaffrey, James. *The House with Many Rooms: The Temple Theme of Jn. 14, 2–3*. Analecta Biblica 114. Roma: Editrice Pontificio Instituto Biblico, 1988.

McCormack, Bruce. "Can We Still Speak of 'Justification by Faith'? An In-House Debate with Apocalyptic Readings of Paul." In *Galatians and Christian Theology: Justification, the Gospel, and Ethics in Paul's Letter*, edited by Mark A. Elliott, Scott J. Hafemann, N. T. Wright, et al., 159–84. Grand Rapids: Baker Academic, 2014.

———, ed. *Justification in Perspective: Historical Developments and Contemporary Challenges*. Grand Rapids: Baker, 2006.

McKnight, Scot. *Reading Romans Backwards: A Gospel of Peace in the Midst of Empire*. Waco: Baylor University Press, 2019.

Meyer, Ben F. "The Pre-Pauline Formula in Rom. 3.25–26a." *New Testament Studies* 29.2 (1983) 198–208.

Michaels, J. Ramsey. *1 Peter*. Word Biblical Commentary 49. Waco: Word, 1988.

Michel, O. πίστις. In *NIDNTT* 1:593–605. Grand Rapids: Zondervan, 1975.

Mininger, Marcus A. *Uncovering the Theme of Revelation in Romans 1:16—3:26: Discovering a New Approach to Paul's Argument*. Tübingen: Mohr Siebeck, 2017.

Moberly, R. W. L. *The Bible, Theology, and Faith: A Study of Abraham and Jesus*. Cambridge: Cambridge University Press, 2000.

Moo, Douglas J. "Israel and Paul in Romans 7.7–12." *New Testament Studies* 32 (1986) 122–35.

———. "'Law,' 'Works of the Law,' and Legalism in Paul." *Westminster Theological Journal* 45 (1983) 73–100.

Moody, R. M. "The Habakkuk Quotation in Romans 1:17." *The Expository Times* 92 (1980–81) 205–8.

Morgan, Teresa. *Roman Faith and Christian Faith: Pistis and Fides in the Early Roman Empire and Early Churches*. New York: Oxford, 2017.

Morris, Leon. *The Epistle to the Romans*. Grand Rapids: Eerdmans (1988) 174–76.

———. "The Meaning of ἱλαστήριον in Romans 3:25." *New Testament Studies* 2 (1955) 33–43.

———. "The Use of ἱλάσκεσθαι etc. in Biblical Greek." *The Expository Times* 62 (1950–51) 227–33.

Mosher, Steve. *God's Power, Jesus' Faith, and World Mission: A Study in Romans*. Scottsdale: Herald (1996) 87–127.

Moule, C. F. D. "The Biblical Conception of Faith." *Expository Times* 68 (1957) 157, 222.

Moulton, W. F., and A. S. Geden, eds. *A Concordance to the Greek Testament*. 4th ed. Edinburgh: T. & T. Clark, 1963.

Moxnes, Halvor. "Honour and Righteousness in Romans." *Journal for the Study of the New Testament* 32 (1988) 61–77.

Murphy-O'Conner, Jerome. "Christological Anthropology in Phil., II, 6–11." *Revue Biblique* 83 (1976) 25–50.

———. "Faith and Resurrection in 2 Cor 4:13–14." *Revue Biblique* 95 (1988) 543–50.

Myers, Benjamin. "From Faithfulness to Faith in the Theology of Karl Barth." In *The Faith of Jesus Christ: Exegetical, Biblical, and Theological Studies*, edited by Michael F. Bird and Preston M. Sprinkle, 291–308. Milton Keynes, UK: Paternoster, 2009.

Nielsen, Rodney Edward. "The Translation of ΠΙΣΤΕΩΣ ΙΗΣΟΥ ΧΡΙΣΤΟΥ In Romans 3:22." MA thesis, Lincoln Christian Seminary, April 29, 1981.

Novenson, M. V. *Christ among the Messiahs: Christ Language in Paul and Messiah Language in Ancient Judaism*. Oxford: Oxford University Press, 2012.

Oakes, Peter. "*Pistis* as Relational Way of Life in Galatians." *Journal for the Study of the New Testament* 40.3 (2018) 1–25.

O'Brien, Peter T. *Commentary on Philippians*. New International Greek Testament Commentary. Grand Rapids: Eerdmans, 1991.

O'Collins, Gerald, and Daniel Kendall. "The Faith of Jesus." *Theological Studies* 53 (1992) 403–23.

O'Rourke, J. J. "Πίστις in Romans." *Catholic Biblical Quarterly* 35 (1973) 188–94.
Ota, Shuji. "Absolute Use of ΠΙΣΤΙΣ and ΠΙΣΤΙΣ ΧΡΙΣΤΟΥ in Paul." *Annual of the Japanese Biblical Institute* 23 (1997) 64–82.
———. "The Holistic *Pistis* and Abraham's Faith (Galatians 3)." *Hitotsubashi Journal of Arts and Sciences* 57 (2016) 1–12.
———. "*Pistis* in Acts as Background of Paul's Faith Terminology." *Hitotsubashi Journal of Arts and Sciences* 56 (2015) 1–12.
———. "ΠΙΣΤΙΣ ΧΡΙΣΤΟΥ: CHRIST'S FAITHFULNESS TO WHOM?" *Hitotsubashi Journal of Arts and Sciences* 55 (2014) 15–26.
Owen, Paul L. "The 'Works of the Law' in Romans and Galatians: A New Defense of the Subjective Genitive." *Journal Biblical Literature* 126.3 (2007) 553–77.
Parke-Taylor, G. H. "A Note on εἰς ὑπακοὴν πίστεως in Romans 1:5 and 16:26." *The Expository Times* 55 (1943–44) 305–6.
Peckham, Brian. "The Vision of Habakkuk." *Catholic Biblical Quarterly* 48 (1986) 617–36.
Perry, Edmund. "The Meaning of 'emuna in the Old Testament." *Journal of Bible and Religion* 21 (1953) 252–56.
Peterson, Eugene H. *Reversed Thunder: The Revelation of John and the Praying Imagination*. San Francisco: HarperCollins, 1988.
Peterson, G. W. "Δικαιωθῆναι διὰ τῆς ἐκ χριστοῦ πίστεως: Notes on a Neglected Greek Construction." *New Testament Studies* 56 (2009) 163–68.
Piper, John. "The Demonstration of the Righteousness of God in Romans 3:25, 26." *Journal for the Study of the New Testament* 7 (1980) 2–32.
———. *The Future of Justification: A Response to N. T. Wright*. Wheaton: Crossway, 2007.
———. *The Justification of God: An Exegetical and Theological Study of Romans 9:1–23*. Grand Rapids: Baker, 1983.
Plevnik, Joseph. "The Understanding of God as the Basis of Pauline Theology." *Catholic Biblical Quarterly* 65.4 (2003) 554–67.
Polhill, John B. "Outline of Acts." In *The ESV Study Bible*, 2077–79. Wheaton: Crossway Bibles, 2008.
Pollard, Jesse Paul. "The 'Faith of Christ' in Current Discussion." *Concordia* 23 (1997) 213–28.
———. "The Problem of the Faith of Christ." University Microfilms International. PhD diss., Baylor University, 1982.
Pollard, T. E. *Fullness of Humanity: Christ's Humanness and Ours*. Sheffield: Almond Press, 1982.
Porter, Stanley E. "The Argument of Romans 5: Can a Rhetorical Question Make a Difference?" *Journal of Biblical Literature* 110.4 (1991) 655–77.
Porter, Stanley E., and Andrew W. Pitts, "Πίστις with a Preposition and Genitive Modifier: Lexical, Semantic, and Syntactic Considerations in the πίστις Χριστοῦ Discussion." In *The Faith of Jesus Christ: Exegetical, Biblical, and Theological Studies*, edited by Michael F. Bird and Preston M. Sprinkle, 33–53. Milton Keynes, UK: Paternoster, 2009.
Price, James L. "God's Righteousness Shall Prevail." *Interpretation* 28 (1974) 259–80.
Prothro, James B. "An Unhelpful Label: Reading the 'Lutheran' Reading of Paul." *Journal for the Study of the New Testament* 39.2 (2016) 119–40.
Pryor, John W. "Paul's Use of Iesous—A Clue for the Translation of Romans 3:26?" *Colloquium* 16.1 (1983) 31–45.

Quarles, Charles L. "From Faith to Faith: A Fresh Examination of the Prepositional Series in Romans 1:17." *Novum Testamentum* 45.1 (2003) 1–21.

Reasoner, Mark. *Romans in Full Circle: A History of Interpretation*. Louisville: Westminster John Knox, 2005.

Rhee, Victor (Sung Yul). "Christology in Hebrews 1:5–14: The Three Stages of Christ's Existence." *Journal of the Evangelical Theological Society* 59.4 (2016) 717–29.

———. "The Role of Chiasm for Understanding Christology in Hebrews 1:1–14." *Journal of Biblical Literature* 131.2 (2012) 341–62.

Riches, Aaron. *Ecce Homo: On the Divine Unity of Christ*. Grand Rapids: Eerdmans, 2016.

Robbins, John W. "The Ground of Justification." *The Trinity Review* 161 (1998) 1–3.

Robinson, D. W. B. "'Faith of Jesus Christ'—a New Testament Debate." *The Reformed Theological Review* 29.3 (1970) 71–81. Reprinted in *Verdict* 2.4 (1979) 15–21.

Robinson, John A. T. *Wrestling with Romans*. Philadelphia: Westminster, 1979.

Rodríguez, Rafael. *If You Call Yourself a Jew: Reappraising Paul's Letter to the Romans*. Eugene, OR: Wipf & Stock, 2014.

Rodríguez, Rafael, and Matthew Thiessen, eds. *The So-Called Jew in Paul's Letter to the Romans*. Minneapolis: Fortress, 2016.

Rogers, Oliver E. *The Faith of Christ: The Relationship of Christ's Faith, Our Faith, and Salvation*. Mustang, OK: Tate, 2008.

Salier, Willis H. "The Obedient Son: The 'Faithfulness' of Christ in the Fourth Gospel," In *The Faith of Jesus Christ: Exegetical, Biblical, and Theological Studies*, edited by Michael F. Bird and Preston M. Sprinkle, 239–57. Milton Keynes, UK: Paternoster, 2009.

Sanders, J. A. "Habakkuk in Qumran, Paul, and the Old Testament." *Journal of Religion* 39 (1959) 232–44.

Schellenberg, Ryan S. "οἱ πιστεύοντες: An Early Christ-Group Self-Designation and Paul's Rhetoric of Faith." *New Testament Studies* 65 (2018) 33–42.

Schenck, Kenneth. "2 Corinthians and the Πίστις Χριστοῦ Debate." *Catholic Biblical Quarterly* 70 (2008) 524–37.

Schliesser, Benjamin. "'Abraham Did Not "Doubt" in Unbelief' (Rom. 4:20): Faith, Doubt, and Dispute in Paul's Letter to the Romans." *Journal of Theological Studies* 63.2 (2012) 492–522.

———. *Abraham's Faith in Romans 4: Paul's Concept of Faith in Light of the History of Reception of Genesis 15:6*. Wissenschaftliche Untersuchungen zum Neuen Testament 2.224. Tübingen: Mohr Siebeck, 2007.

———. "'Christ-Faith' as an Eschatological Event (Galatians 3.23–26): A 'Third View' on Πίστις Χριστοῦ." *Journal for the Study of the New Testament* 38.3 (2016) 277–300.

———. "'EXEGETICAL AMNESIA' AND ΠΙΣΤΙΣ ΧΡΙΣΤΟΥ: THE 'FAITH OF CHRIST' IN NINETEENTH-CENTURY PAULINE SCHOLARSHIP." *Journal of Theological Studies* 66.1 (2015) 61–89.

Scott, James M. "A New Approach to Habakkuk II 4–5A." *Vetus Testamentum* 35.3 (1985) 330–40.

Scroggs, Robin. "Rom. 6.7 'ὁ γὰρ ἀποθανὼν δεδικαίωται ἀπὸ τῆς ἁμαρτίας.'" *New Testament Studies* 10.1 (1963) 104–8.

Seglenieks, Christopher. "Untrustworthy Believers: The Rhetorical Strategy of the Johannine Language of Commitment and Belief." *Novum Testamentum* 61 (2019) 55–69.

Seifrid, Mark A. *Christ, Our Righteousness: Paul's Theology of Justification*. Downers Grove: InterVarsity, 2000.

———. *Justification by Faith: The Origin and Development of a Central Pauline Theme*. Novum Testamentum 68. Leiden: Brill, 1992.

———. "The Near Word of Christ and the Distant Vision of N. T. Wright." *Journal of the Evangelical Theological Society* 54.2 (2011) 279–97.

Selwyn, Edward Gordon. *The First Epistle of St. Peter*. London: Macmillan, 1946, 1969.

Shaw, David A. "Apocalyptic and Covenant: Perspectives on Paul or Antinomies at War?" *Journal for the Study of the New Testament* 36.2 (2013) 155–71.

Sierksma-Agteres, Susan J. M. "Imitation in Faith: Enacting Paul's Ambiguous *Pistis Christou* Formulations on a Greco-Roman Stage." *International Journal of Philosophy and Theology* 77.3 (2016) 119–53.

Simpson, A. B. *The Christ Life*. Harrisburg: Christian Publications, 1980.

Smith, D. Moody. "Ο ΔΕ ΔΙΚΑΙΟΣ ΕΚ ΠΙΣΤΕΩΣ ΖΗΣΕΤΑΙ." In *Studies in the History and Text of the New Testament in Honor of Kenneth Willis Clark*, edited by Boyd L. Daniels and M. Jack Suggs, 13–25. Salt Lake City: University of Utah, 1967.

Smolik, Josef. "Christ: The Foundation of Faith for Our Salvation." *Communio viatorum* 31 (1988) 47–55.

Snodgrass, Klyne R. "Justification by Grace—to the Doers: An Analysis of the Place of Romans 2 in the Theology of Paul." *New Testament Studies* 32 (1986) 72–93.

———. "Spheres of Influence: A Possible Solution to the Problem of Paul and the Law." *Journal for the Study of the New Testament* 32 (1988) 93–113.

Sprinkle, Preston. "'Two's Company, Three's a Crowd?': Another Option for the '*PISTIS CHRISTOU*' Debate." Conference paper, Far West Region of the Evangelical Theological Society, Sun Valley, CA, May 2, 2003.

Stanley, Christopher D. "'Under a Curse': A Fresh Reading of Galatians 3.10–14." *New Testament Studies* 36 (1990) 481–511.

Staples, Jason A. "What Do the Gentiles Have to Do with 'All Israel'? A Fresh Look at Romans 11:25–27." *Journal of Biblical Literature* 130.2 (2011) 371–90.

Starling, David I. "Covenants and Courtrooms, Imputation and Imitation: Righteousness and Justification in 'Paul and the Faithfulness of God.'" *Journal for the Study of Paul and His Letters* 4.1 (2014) 37–48.

Stegman, Thomas D. "Ἐπίστευσα, διὸ ἐλάλησα (2 Corinthians 4:13): Paul's Christological Reading of Psalm 115:1a LXX." *Catholic Biblical Quarterly* 69 (2007) 725–45.

———. "Paul's Use of *Dikaio*-Terminology: Moving Beyond N. T. Wright's Forensic Interpretation." *Theological Studies* 72.3 (2011) 496–524.

Stern, David. *The Jewish New Testament*. Clarksville, MD: Jewish New Testament Publications, 1989.

Still, Todd D. "*Christos* as *Pistos*: The Faith(fulness) of Jesus in the Epistle to the Hebrews." *Catholic Biblical Quarterly* 69 (2007) 746–55.

Stott, John R. W. *The Cross of Christ*. Leicester: InterVarsity, 1986.

Stowers, Stanley K. "'ΕΚ ΠΙΣΤΕΩΣ AND ΔΙΑ ΤΗΣ ΠΙΣΤΕΩΣ' in Romans 3:30." *Journal of Biblical Literature* 108.4 (1989) 665–74.

———. "God's Merciful Justice in Christ's Faithfulness (3:21–31)." In *A Rereading of Romans: Justice, Jews, and Gentiles*, 194–226. New Haven: Yale University Press, 1994.

———. "No One Seeks for God: An Exegetical and Theological Study of Romans 1:18—3:20." *Journal of Biblical Literature* 119.2 (2000) 370–73.

———. "What Is 'Pauline Participation in Christ.'" In *Redefining First-Century Jewish and Christian Identities: Essays in Honor of Ed Parish Sanders*, edited by F. E. Udoh, 352–71. Notre Dame: Notre Dame University Press, 2008.

Stubbs, David L. "The Shape of Soteriology and the *Pistis Christou* Debate." *Scottish Journal of Theology* 61.2 (2008) 137–57.

Suetonius. *Suetonius II*. Translated by J. C. Rolfe. Loeb Classical Library 38. Cambridge: Harvard University Press, 1979.

Sumney, Jerry L., ed. *Reading Paul's Letter to the Romans*. Atlanta: Society of Biblical Literature, 2012.

Talbert, Charles H. *The Epistle to the Romans*. Macon: Smyth & Helwys, 2002.

Tannehill, Robert C. "Participation in Christ: A Central Theme in Pauline Soteriology." In *The Shape of the Gospel: New Testament Essays*, 223–37. Eugene, OR: Cascade, 2007.

Taylor, Greer M. "The Function of ΠΙΣΤΙΣ ΧΡΙΣΤΟΥ in Galatians." *Journal of Biblical Literature* 85 (1966) 58–76.

Taylor, John W. "From Faith to Faith: Romans 1:17 in the Light of Greek Idiom." *New Testament Studies* 50 (2004) 337–48.

Thatcher, Tom, ed. *What We Have Heard from the Beginning: The Past, Present, and Future of Johannine Studies*. Waco: Baylor University Press, 2007.

Thielman, Frank. "God's Righteousness as God's Fairness in Romans 1:17: An Ancient Perspective on a Significant Phrase." *Journal of the Evangelical Theological Society* 54.1 (2011) 35–48.

Thiselton, Anthony C. *The First Epistle to the Corinthians*. The New International Greek Testament Commentary. Grand Rapids: Eerdmans, 2000.

Thompson, Marianne Meye. *The Incarnate Word: Perspectives on Jesus in the Fourth Gospel*. Peabody: Hendrickson, 1988.

———. "Signs and Faith in the Fourth Gospel." *Bulletin for Biblical Research* 1 (1991) 89–108.

Thornton, T. C. G. "Propitiation or Expiation?" *Expository Times* 80 (1968–69) 53–55.

Thurston, B. B., and J. M. Ryan. *Philippians and Philemon*. Sacra Pagina 10. Collegeville: Liturgical, 2005.

Timmins, Will N. "A Faith Unlike Abraham's: Matthew Bates on Salvation by Allegiance Alone." *Journal of the Evangelical Theological Society* 61.3 (2018) 595–615.

Tobin, Thomas H. *Paul's Rhetoric in Its Contexts*. Peabody: Hendrickson, 2004.

Tonstad, Sigve. "Πίστις Χριστοῦ: Reading Paul in a New Paradigm." *Andrews University Seminary Studies* 40 (2002) 37–59.

———. *Saving God's Reputation: The Theological Function of Pistis Iesou in the Cosmic Narratives of Revelation*. New York: T. & T. Clark, 2006.

Torrance, Thomas F. "The Biblical Conception of 'Faith.'" *Expository Times* 69 (1958) 221–22.

———. "One Aspect of the Biblical Conception of Faith." *Expository Times* 68 (1957) 111–14, 221–22.

Tripp, Jeffrey. "Jesus's Special Knowledge in the Gospel of John." *Novum Testamentum* 61 (2019) 269–88.

Turner, Geoffrey. "The Righteousness of God in Psalms and Romans." *Scottish Journal of Theology* 63.3 (2010) 285–301.

Turner, Nigel. *Syntax*. A Grammar of New Testament Greek 3. Edited by J. H. Moulton. Edinburgh: T. & T. Clark, 1963.

Ulrichs, Karl Friedrich. *Christusglaube: Studien zum Syntagma pistis Christou und zum paulinischen Verständnis von Glaube und Rechtfertigung.* Wissenschaftliche Untersuchungen zum Neuen Testament 2.227. Tübingen: Mohr Siebeck, 2007.

Valloton, Pierre. *Le Christ et la Foi.* Geneva: Labor et Fides, 1960.

Vanderkam, James C. "Righteous One, Messiah, Chosen One, and Son of Man in 1 Enoch 37–71." In *The Messiah: Developments in Earliest Judaism and Christianity*, edited by James H. Charlesworth, 169–91. Minneapolis: Fortress, 1992.

van Daalen, D. H. "'Faith' according to Paul." *Expository Times* 87 (1975) 83–85.

van Driel, Edwin C. "Climax of the Covenant vs. Apocalyptic Invasion: A Theological Analysis of a Contemporary Debate in Pauline Exegesis." *International Journal of Systematic Theology* 17.1 (2015) 6–25.

van Henten, J. W. "The Tradition-Historical Background of Romans 3.25: A Search for Pagan and Jewish Parallels." In *From Jesus to John: Essays on Jesus and New Testament Christology in Honour of Marinus de Jonge*, edited by M. C. DeBoer, 101–28. Sheffield: JSOT, 1993.

van Nes, Jermo. "'Faith(fulness) of the Son of God'? Galatians 2:20b Reconsidered." *Novum Testamentum* 55 (2013) 127–39.

von Balthasar, H. U. "Fides Christi." *Sponsa Verbi* 2 (1967) 45–79.

von Wahlde, Urban C. "Faith and Works in Jn VI 28–29: Exegesis or Eisegesis?" *Novum Testamentum* 22.4 (1980) 304–15.

Wagner, J. Ross, et al. *The Word Leaps the Gap: Essays on Scripture and Theology in Honor of Richard B. Hays.* Grand Rapids: Eerdmans, 2008.

Wallace, Daniel B. *Greek Grammar Beyond the Basics: An Exegetical Syntax of the New Testament.* Grand Rapids: Zondervan, 1996.

Wallis, Ian G. *The Faith of Jesus Christ in Early Christian Traditions.* Society for New Testament Studies, Monograph Series 84. Cambridge: University Press, 1995.

Wallis, Wilber B. "The Translation of Romans 1:17—A Basic Motif in Paulinism." *Journal for the Evangelical Theological Society* 16 (1973) 17–23.

Walton, John H. *The Lost World of Genesis One: Ancient Cosmology and the Origins Debate.* Downers Grove: InterVarsity, 2009.

Wanamaker, Charles A. *Commentary on 1 and 2 Thessalonians.* New International Greek Testament Commentary. Grand Rapids: Eerdmans, 1990.

Wardlaw, Terry. "A Reappraisal of 'From Faith to Faith' (Romans 1:17)." *European Journal of Theology* 12.2 (2012) 107–19.

Watson, Francis. *Paul and the Hermeneutics of Faith.* London; New York: T. & T. Clark, 2004.

———. "Paul the Reader: An Authorial Apologia." *Journal for the Study of the New Testament* 28.3 (2006) 363–73.

Wedderburn, A. J. M. "Some Observations on Paul's Use of the Phrases 'in Christ' and 'with Christ.'" *Journal for the Study of the New Testament* 25 (1985) 83–97.

Whitsett, C. G. "Son of God, Seed of David: Paul's Messianic Exegesis in Romans 1:3–4." *Journal of Biblical Literature* 119 (2000) 661–81.

Wilder, Terry L., et al. *Faithful to the End: An Introduction to Hebrews through Revelation.* Nashville: Broadman & Holman Academic, 2007.

Williams, Sam K. "Again *Pistis Christou.*" *Catholic Biblical Quarterly* 49 (1987) 431–47.

———. "The Hearing of Faith: ΑΚΟΗ ΠΙΣΤΕΩΣ In Galatians 3." *New Testament Studies* 35 (1989) 82–93.

———. *Jesus' Death as Saving Event: The Background and Origin of a Concept.* HDR 2. Missoula: Scholars, 1975.

———. "Justification and the Spirit in Galatians." *Journal for the Study of the New Testament* 29 (1987) 91–100.

———. "'Promise' in Galatians: A Reading of Paul's Reading of Scripture." *Journal of Biblical Literature* 107.4 (1988) 709–20.

———. "The 'Righteousness of God' in Romans." *Journal of Biblical Literature* 99.2 (1980) 241–90.

Witherington, Ben, III. "The Influence of Galatians on Hebrews." *New Testament Studies* 36 (1991) 146–52.

———. *Paul's Letter to the Philippians: A Socio-Rhetorical Commentary.* Grand Rapids: Eerdmans, 2011.

Witherington, Ben, III, with Darlene Hyatt. *Paul's Letter to the Romans: A Socio-Rhetorical Commentary.* Grand Rapids: Eerdmans, 2004.

Wood, Shane J. "Simplifying the Number of the Beast (Rev 13:18): An Interpretation of 666 and 616." In *Dragons, John, and Every Grain of Sand; Essays on the Book of Revelation in Honor of Dr. Robert Lowery*, edited by Shane J. Wood, 131–40. Joplin: College Press, 2011.

Wright, N. T. *The Climax of the Covenant: Christ and the Law in Pauline Theology.* Minneapolis: Fortress, 1991.

———. *Colossians and Philemon.* Tyndale New Testament Commentaries. Downers Grove: InterVarsity, 1986.

———. *The Day the Revolution Began: Reconsidering the Meaning of Jesus's Crucifixion.* New York: HarperCollins, 2016.

———. *History and Eschatology: Jesus and the Promise of Natural Theology.* The 2018 Gifford Lectures. Waco: Baylor University Press, 2019.

———. *Jesus and the Victory of God.* Christian Origins and the Question of God 2. Minneapolis: Fortress, 1996.

———. "Justification by (Covenantal) Faith to the (Covenantal) Doers: Romans 2 Within the Argument of the Letter." In *Doing Theology for the Church: Essays in Honor of Klyne Snodgrass*, edited by R. A. Eklund and J. E. Phelan, 95–108. Eugene, OR: Wipf & Stock, 2014.

———. *Justification: God's Plan and Paul's Vision.* Downers Grove: InterVarsity, 2009.

———. *The Kingdom New Testament: A Contemporary Translation.* New York: HarperCollins, 2011.

———. "The Letter to the Galatians: Exegesis and Theology." In *Between Two Horizons: Spanning New Testament Studies and Systematic Theology*, edited by Joel B. Green and Max Turner, 205–36. Grand Rapids: Eerdmans, 2000.

———. "The Letter to the Romans: Introduction, Commentary, and Reflections." In *The New Interpreter's Bible*, edited by Leander E. Keck et al., 10:395–770. Nashville: Abingdon, 2002.

———. "Messiahship in Galatians?" In his *Pauline Perspectives: Essays on Paul, 1978–2013*, 510–46. London: SPCK, 2013.

———. "New Exodus, New Inheritance: The Narrative Structure of Romans 3–8." In *Romans and the People of God: Essays in Honor of Gordon D. Fee on the Occasion of His 65th Birthday*, edited by S. K. Soderlund and N. T. Wright, 26–35. Grand Rapids: Eerdmans, 1999.

———. *The New Testament and the People of God.* Christian Origins and the Question of God 1. Minneapolis: Fortress, 1992.

———. *Paul and the Faithfulness of God*. 2 vols. Christian Origins and the Question of God 4.1–2. Minneapolis: Fortress, 2013.

———. "Paul and the Patriarch: The Role of Abraham in Romans 4." *Journal for the Study of the New Testament* 35.3 (2013) 207–41.

———. *Paul for Everyone: Galatians and Thessalonians*. Louisville: Westminster John Knox, 2004.

———. *Pauline Perspectives: Essays on Paul, 1978–2013*. Minneapolis: Fortress, 2013.

———. *Paul: In Fresh Perspective*. Minneapolis: Fortress, 2005.

———. *The Resurrection of the Son of God*. Christian Origins and the Question of God 3. Minneapolis: Fortress, 2003.

———. "Romans and the Theology of Paul." In *Pauline Theology*, edited by David M. Hay and E. Elizabeth Johnson, 3:30–67. Minneapolis: Fortress, 1995. Originally published in *SBL Seminar Papers 1991*, edited by David J. Lull. Atlanta: Scholars, 1991.

———. "The Shape of Justification." *Bible Review* 17.2 (2001) 8, 50.

———. *Simply Christian: Why Christianity Makes Sense*. San Francisco: HarperOne, 2006.

———. *Simply Jesus: A New Vision of Who He Was, What He Did, and Why He Matters*. New York: HarperCollins, 2011.

———. *Surprised by Hope: Rethinking Heaven, the Resurrection, and the Mission of the Church*. New York: HarperCollins, 2008.

———. *What Saint Paul Really Said: Was Paul of Tarsus the Real Founder of Christianity?* Grand Rapids: Eerdmans, 1997.

———. *Who Was Jesus?* Grand Rapids: Eerdmans, 1992.

Wright, N. T., and Michael F. Bird. *The New Testament in Its World: An Introduction to the History, Literature, and Theology of the First Christians*. Grand Rapids: Zondervan, 2019.

Yeung, Maureen W. *Faith in Jesus and Paul: A Comparison with Special Reference to "Faith That Can Remove Mountains" and "Your Faith Has Healed/Saved You."* Wissenschaftliche Untersuchungen zum Neuen Testament 2.147. Tübingen: Mohr-Siebeck, 2002.

Young, Stephen L. "Paul's Ethnic Discourse on 'Faith': Christ's Faithfulness and Gentile Access to the Judean God in Romans 3:21—5:1." *Harvard Theological Review* 108.1 (2015).

———. "Romans 1.1–5 and Paul's Christological Use of Hab. 2.4 in Rom. 1.17: An Underutilized Consideration in the Debate." *Journal for the Study of the New Testament* 34.3 (2012) 277–85.

Zemek, George J., Jr. "Interpretive Challenges Relating to Habakkuk 2:4b." *Grace Theological Journal* 1.1 (1980) 43–69.

Zetterholm, Magnus. *Approaches to Paul: A Student's Guide to Recent Scholarship*. Minneapolis: Fortress, 2009.

Ziesler, J. "Justification by Faith in the Light of the 'New Perspective' on Paul." *Theology* 94 (1991) 188–94.

———. *The Meaning of Righteousness in Paul: A Linguistic and Theological Enquiry*. Studiorum Novi Testamenti Societas Monograph Series 20. Cambridge: Cambridge University Press, 1972.

———. *Paul's Letter to the Romans*. Trinity Press International New Testament Commentary. Philadelphia: Trinity, 1989.

---. "Salvation Proclaimed IX: Romans 3:21–26." *The Expository Times* 93 (1981–82) 356–59.

Zoccali, Christopher. "'And So All Israel Will Be Saved': Competing Interpretations of Romans 11.26 in Pauline Scholarship." *Journal for the Study of the New Testament* 30 (2008) 289–318.

---. "What's the Problem with the Law? Jews, Gentiles, and Covenant Identity in Galatians 3:10–12." *Neotestamentica* 49.2 (2015) 377–415.

Zorn, Walter D. "The 'Faith of Jesus' and Our Salvation (Part One)." *Integrity* 17.6 (1986) 99–103.

---. "The 'Faith of Jesus' and Our Salvation (Part Two)." *Integrity* 18.1 (1987) 3–6.

---. "The Messianic Use of Habakkuk 2:4a [sic] in Romans." *Stone-Campbell Journal* 1.2 (1998) 213–30.

---. "*Segullah*: A Word of Worth." In *Deuteronomy: The Prophets and the Life of the Church; A Festschrift in honor of Dr. Gary Hall*, edited by Jason T. LeCureux et al., 36–54. Preston, Australia: Mosaic, 2013.

www.ingramcontent.com/pod-product-compliance
Lightning Source LLC
Chambersburg PA
CBHW071230230426
43668CB00011B/1370